Public Finance
and
Private Wealth

Sir Stephen Fox aged about forty-three, by Lely. National Portrait Gallery, London.

PUBLIC FINANCE
AND
PRIVATE WEALTH

The Career of Sir
Stephen Fox, 1627–1716

CHRISTOPHER CLAY

Clarendon Press · Oxford
1978

Oxford University Press, Walton Street, Oxford OX2 6DP

OXFORD LONDON GLASGOW
NEW YORK TORONTO MELBOURNE WELLINGTON
IBADAN NAIROBI DAR ES SALAAM LUSAKA CAPE TOWN
KUALA LUMPUR SINGAPORE JAKARTA HONG KONG TOKYO
DELHI BOMBAY CALCUTTA MADRAS KARACHI

© *Christopher Clay 1978*

British Library Cataloguing in Publication Data

Clay, Christopher
  Public finance and private wealth.
  1. Fox, *Sir*, Stephen   2. Capitalists and financiers—England—Biography
  I. Title
  332'.092'4   HC254.5   78-40071

ISBN 0-19-822467-2

Printed in Great Britain by
Butler & Tanner Ltd., Frome and London

to

RACHEL CLAY

Who, at Horseblock Hollow Cottage,
first aroused my interest in history

Preface and Acknowledgements

THIS BOOK is not, strictly speaking, a biography, for it does not trace the development of Sir Stephen Fox's character, nor does it tell the reader much about his thoughts, nor, save in very general terms, about his private life. This is because the necessary evidence for such a treatment does not exist, or at any rate has not come to light. Many of his business and official papers have survived, and the records of the branches of government with which he was involved provide further evidence of what he did in his public capacities, but he kept no diary and relatively few letters written by him seem to have been preserved. This dearth of personal material is partly filled by the large number of autobiographical fragments he composed at various times, but these pose problems of interpretation. They probably provide a factually accurate account of his earlier years, but those which deal with the period after about 1680 are mainly concerned with real or imagined grievances, are demonstrably unreliable in parts, and are as revealing in ways which their author did not intend as in those he did. It has therefore been necessary to concentrate on what Fox did, rather than on what he said, thought, or wrote, and since he was primarily a financier, most of what follows concerns how he accumulated a fortune and what he did with it. Fox was also a courtier, although I have not dealt with this aspect of his career in so much detail, and in his later years a government minister, although not, as we shall see, to any great extent a politician.

It is probably because Fox remained, as far as he could, outside the political hurly-burly of the later seventeenth century, that he has attracted so little attention from historians. Only twice, in 1679 when he received a savaging from the House of Commons, and in 1696–7 when he was acting First Lord of the Treasury, can he be said to have stood in the spotlight of national affairs. During the rest of his long public career, which began before the Civil War and ended in the reign of Queen Anne, he stood in the shadows. But in his time he was no insubstantial figure. Not only was he on close, if not invariably friendly, terms with virtually every leading statesman from Clarendon to Godolphin, but it was he who in the 1660s developed a financial system which enabled the Restoration government to keep in being an army which it could not really afford; who for much of the 1670s was the main financial prop of the government as a whole; and who in the 1680s and 1690s was the longest serving and most experienced of the financial advisers of the Crown. Contemporaries mostly regarded him with respect, some with a mingling of awe, others with affection, and a few (especially when he was growing old) with irritation, but all would have been surprised at the historical obscurity into which he has sunk. In most modern works on the period he merits little more than a footnote or a passing reference, and apart from an anonymous and inaccurate sketch of his life published shortly after he died, the only significant accounts of him have been those in the *Dictionary of National Biography,* in the early pages of Lord Ilchester's book on Henry Fox, Lord Holland, and in Dean's work on Chelsea Hospital. As a result of this neglect he has long borne the stigma, probably first firmly attached to him by Walton in his *History of the British Standing Army,* of having amassed a fortune as a corrupt office holder who, as Paymaster, exploited the wretched soldiery to his own inordinate profit. This, I think, is an exceedingly misleading libel upon a man whose standards of probity were notably higher than those of most others of his generation.

As for myself, I had never heard of Sir Stephen Fox until a very short while before I began the first of a series of rather disjointed periods of research upon which this work is based, and it was pure chance that I ever did hear of him, for I was not at that time working in the field of late seventeenth-century finance at all. Moreover, having come across a stray reference to him in some nineteenth-century title deeds which had aroused a mild curiosity, it was chance again that led me to the Dorset County Record Office where many of Fox's papers are to be found, for I went there on another errand (alas still undischarged nine years later) from which Sir Stephen diverted me. It was also chance that the March day in 1968 on which, on impulse, I drove down from Bristol to Dorchester was so gloriously fine, for it was the bewitching beauty of the Dorset countryside that afternoon which made me determine to abandon temporarily my then current research for the sake of being able to spend the summer working in those marvellous surroundings. In the end as much or more work had to be done in Bloomsbury, Chancery Lane, and the Bristol University Library, but nevertheless my first debt of gratitude is of course to my cousin

Malcolm Cockburn, whose open-ended promise of hospitality, made on the evening of that first visit to Dorchester, was so generously fulfilled in the years that followed. I must also thank the late Earl of Ilchester, who deposited his family archives in record offices where they could be made available for historical research; and Margaret Holmes, the Dorset County Archivist, who allowed me so much freedom to explore the uncharted depths of the Ilchester collection, and her successive assistants who fetched so many heavy boxes and volumes for me. I also owe a very great deal to the staff of the Manuscripts Reading Room at the British Library and of the Public Record Office; and to Williams and Glyn's Bank, Mr. Sandelson of the Wiltshire Archaeological Society, Mr. Sibthorpe of the Wardenry at Farley, the Marquess of Northampton, and the Librarian of Christ Church, Oxford, for allowing me to see documents belonging to them or in their care. Thanks are also due to Lady Theresa Agnew and the late Lord Galway for showing me Fox family portraits at Melbury House, and to John Edwards who tried to find Sir Stephen's missing ledgers by searching the old muniment room at Melbury. Professor F. J. Fisher read part of the manuscript for me, and his penetrating comments saved me from several errors in my analysis of Fox's financial methods, although he failed to convince me that Sir Stephen was a rogue after all! My colleagues Richard Morris and Bernard Alford helped me to calculate the rate of return on annuities; Professor Basil Yamey corresponded with me on seventeenth-century accounting methods; and John Cannon did something to make good my ignorance of parliamentary history. I am also indebted to Dr. Henry Roseveare for permission to quote from his unpublished Ph.D. thesis. My wife Diana did some of the research on the *Calendar of Treasury Books* which I would never have had the patience for, and then typed most of the manuscript with immaculate care until the arrival of a second child finally, as Fox might have put it, 'disabled her from meddling any further therein'. Lastly I must also thank my own university for financial assistance which paid for most of the considerable travelling expenses I incurred whilst working away from Bristol, and con-tributed towards the cost of the typing which my wife was unable to undertake.   C. C.

Bristol,
February 1977

Contents

CONTENTS

List of Tables

Abbreviations

Add. MSS.	Additional Manuscripts
B.I.H.R.	*Bulletin of the Institute of Historical Research*
B.L.	British Library
C.S.P.D.	*Calendar of State Papers. Domestic Series*
C.T.B.	*Calendar of Treasury Books*
D.N.B.	*Dictionary of National Biography*
Ec.H.R.	*Economic History Review*
Eng. Hist. Rev.	*English Historical Review*
Evelyn	*The Diary of John Evelyn* (ed. E. S. De Beer, 6 vols., Oxford, 1955)
Gloucs. R.O.	Gloucestershire County Record Office
H.C.	House of Commons
H.M.C.	Historical Manuscripts Commission
Ilchester	Ilchester Collection (D. 124), Dorset County Record Office
Mich.	Michaelmas
N.S.	New Series
Pepys	*The Diary of Samuel Pepys* (ed. R. Latham and W. Matthews, 10 vols., London, 1970 continuing)
P.R.O.	Public Record Office
T.R.H.S.	*Transactions of the Royal Historical Society*
Wilts. Arch. Soc.	Wiltshire Archaeological and Natural History Society
Wilts. R.O.	Wiltshire County Record Office

NOTE ON DATES

The calendar year has been taken as beginning on 1 January, but dates are otherwise given in the old style.

NOTE ON QUOTATIONS

The original spelling has been retained, but punctuation and the use of capitals has been modernized. This policy has been adopted because most of the passages quoted are from Sir Stephen Fox's own writings, in which capitals and small letters are almost impossible to distinguish, and punctuation of any sort is largely lacking.

NOTE ON DOCUMENTARY REFERENCES

Sir Stephen Fox's surviving papers are divided between the Ilchester Collection in the Dorset Record Office, and the Holland House Collection in the British Library. The latter have been bound up into volumes, but their arrangement is still (in 1977) provisional, and I have therefore given not only folio references but also a brief description of the document cited. The former are still almost entirely unsorted, and although detailed cataloguing has recently begun it has not gone far enough at the time of writing to provide a basis upon which references could be given. In order to enable the reader to identify documents from the Ilchester Collection I have therefore used group classifications derived from the Dorset County Record Office's highly abbreviated summary list, together with the box number, and a description of the item to which reference is being made. Documents from other collections have been described by their call number wherever possible.

CHAPTER I

A Wonderful Child of Providence

SIR STEPHEN FOX was a remarkable man, there is no doubt about that. He was remarkable because he rose to immense wealth and great prominence in public affairs from genuinely humble origins, and because at a time when he had become a byword for riches he remained so likeable a person that he retained not only good, but golden, opinions from almost everyone who knew him. Fox once described himself as 'a wonderful child of providence', by which he meant that fortune had given him more worldly success than he could possibly have dreamed of when he stood on the threshold of his career. It was certainly extremely rare for anyone in the seventeenth century to climb almost the entire social ladder from bottom to top, to be born in almost complete obscurity yet to die rich and famous. Families quite often achieved such a transformation of their status in the course of two or three generations, especially where son followed father in the practice of law or in business, and where care was taken for the son in each generation to marry a wealthy bride. But for a man to achieve so much in the course of a single lifetime required an extraordinary combination of first-rate ability and good luck. Stephen Fox was one of those rare individuals blessed by both. He began as a page-boy unable to afford a new suit of clothes, and he rose almost as high in society as it was possible to get. He never became a peer, although he was probably offered a title which he refused, but he did become the contemporary equivalent to a millionaire. He was also in large measure responsible for managing the nation's finances over a period of more than twenty years, and eventually, albeit briefly, occupied the position of First Lord of the Treasury, an office whose importance was already becoming so great that its holder was far on the way to being the first among the King's ministers.

About Fox's parents, and the home in which they brought him up, only a little information can be gleaned, almost all of it from his own autobiographical writings.[1] When Stephen was born in 1627

[1] This and the following paragraphs on Fox's family background and early life are mainly based on two autobiographical narratives compiled by him many

they were living at Farley, a very small village about five miles east of Salisbury, in a dwelling which he describes at least once as a cottage. Nowhere does Stephen mention that his father, William Fox, followed any particular trade or profession.[1] He may have been a working farmer, although it seems more likely that he did not work for a living, in which case he probably maintained his family from the rent of a piece of land. All the indications are that William Fox was on the lowest fringe of that blurred borderline between gentleman and peasant: not working with his own hands, related to those who were indisputably gentle, but yet not entitled to a coat of arms and living in near-poverty. He clearly had pretensions to respectability, but equally clearly was not at all well off, a fact that the size of his family may have been chiefly responsible for. Stephen was the seventh child in a family of ten, most of whom survived into adulthood.

Stephen later recorded that his parents stood out because of their 'orderly and pious living'. This may have been only an expression of filial respect, but elsewhere he writes more specifically that 'tho' they had but little to support them yet they bred up their children so well that they were distinguished from all their neighbours'. This second comment was echoed by Canon Eyre when, nearly ninety years later, he preached the sermon at Sir Stephen's funeral. Speaking of the parents, he referred to 'the great care that they were observ'd to take in well educating and disposing of their children, [which] was remarkable in their circumstances, which at that time were not great'.[2] Eyre is not likely to have known anything of the early part of Sir Stephen's life save what had come directly or indirectly from the subject of his sermon, so we may conclude that Sir Stephen himself appreciated that his parents had paid unusual attention to the education of their children, and that he realized that this education had been important to him. In educating at least two of their boys the Fox parents received a good deal of help from Mrs. Fox's uncle, Richard Rawkins, a man

---

years later: B.L., MS. 51324, commencing f. 30; and Ilchester: Family (box 237): small volume with green cover. Quotations are from one or other of these sources unless otherwise indicated. Fox left many other fragments of what may have been intended to be a complete account of his official career and some of these, too, have been drawn on in this chapter.

[1] I have not succeeded in tracing any will left by William Fox.

[2] R. Eyre, *A Sermon preach'd at the Funeral of . . . Sir Stephen Fox* (London, 1716), p. 6.

of some substance with a house in the cathedral close at Salisbury. He had seen their eldest son, John, through school, and when Stephen was six years old he too went to stay with great-uncle Richard and attended the choir school which was also in the close. Stephen remained at this school until he was thirteen. How broad was the education that it provided is an open question, but he subsequently recalled that by the end of his time there he had 'advanced to make lattin verse upon a theame', and that he was the 'top boy of the dancing scoole'. These scraps of information suggest a curriculum intended to fit pupils for the life of a gentleman, but Salisbury was a busy commercial town and many of the pupils at the school must have been the sons of local merchants and manufacturers, who would have expected a practical element in the teaching. Certainly Stephen's later success as a financial administrator suggests that he probably also learnt some arithmetic and how to keep accounts.[1]

Family funds clearly did not run to any further education, whether at a university or one of the Inns of Court, and so when Stephen's usefulness in the cathedral choir began to come to an end he had to start making his own way in the world. He left the school soon after his thirteenth birthday in the spring of 1640, and almost at once left home to seek his fortune. Some sort of opportunity seemed to be offered by the modest success of his elder brother John in starting a career in the royal service. John owed this success partly to his own abilities as a musician, but much more to the patronage of an influential friend of great-uncle Richard Rawkins. The latter had recommended him to Dr. Edmund Mason, Dean of Salisbury, who was for a few years before his death in 1635 tutor to the young Prince of Wales, and it was apparently through this contact that John found his way to Court.[2] By 1640 he was employed in the chapel of the Prince's household in the dual capacity of Closet Keeper and Organist, receiving £18. 5s. 0d. board wages for each post and a further £5 ordinary wages for the former. The closet was the private part of the chapel, reserved for the members of the royal family themselves, and John's first duty was clearly to attend there and keep it clean and tidy, although he

---

[1] D. H. Robertson, *Sarum Close* (London, 1938), provides a history of the school, but the author has nothing to say about the curriculum at this period, which was, incidentally, a bad one in its history.

[2] W. H. Jones, *Fasti Ecclesiae Sarisberiensis* (Salisbury, 1879), p. 322.

was probably also responsible for laundering the surplices used in the chapel at large. The modest remuneration he received for his duties suggests their relatively menial nature and low status, for his board wages were no higher than those allowed to the porter at the back stairs.[1] Nevertheless, where there had been an opening for one Fox there might be room for another, and so in May 1640 Stephen travelled up from Wiltshire to join his brother with the Court at Richmond. Certainly his arrival there to help John with his official duties would have caused no surprise with the latter's superiors, for the royal Household at this period usually included a good many people who were not officially on the pay-roll. Most royal servants had servants and helpers of their own, who were in effect unauthorized deputies and who might discharge all or most of their master's duties. Several attempts had been made during the 1630s to keep this practice in check, and one of the measures adopted was a quarterly census of everyone at Court in order to exclude those servants of servants who had no right to be there. However, all but the very lowest members of the household were in practice permitted to have their helpers, provided that they were 'comelie and seemlie persons well apparelled and meete to attend in the Prince his house'.[2] Stephen apparently passed this test and so began a career in royal service that eventually ended in the reign of Queen Anne.

Surviving an attack of smallpox, he remained with his brother at Court for the next two years or so, a sort of juvenile hanger-on with no post of his own. However, his presence was more than tolerated for, according to his own account, he was frequently allowed to play with the royal children, the eldest of whom was only a few years younger than he. Then, when the Prince and his brother James left London to go north with the King in March 1642 and John Fox went with them, Stephen took over his duties as Closet Keeper in the chapel which was maintained at St. James's for the younger princes and princesses. This seems to have been an unofficial or at least a temporary arrangement, and in the circumstances of 1642, sooner or later Stephen would probably have had to go home to Farley if he had not found someone to employ

---

[1] B.L., Harleian MS. 7623: also Stowe MS. 562, which explains the significance of the chapel closet.
[2] G. E. Aylmer, *The King's Servants* (London, 1961), pp. 127–8; B.L., Harleian MS. 7623, f. 16.

him. But in the event this was not necessary and he spent the next few years as a page-boy being passed from one royalist peer to another.[1] His first employer was Lady Stafford, who was taking the King's crown to Oxford and wanted someone to attend her. It was she who gave Stephen the first new suit, of black cloth, which he had had since leaving Wiltshire two years and more before: John's pay as Closet Keeper had not been able to stretch to extravagances of that sort for a younger brother. Lady Stafford then passed Stephen on to the Countess of Sunderland, who was looking for a page for her husband, but when the Earl saw him he decided that he was not sufficiently big and strong to accompany him on a military campaign. So Stephen did not see any action in 1643, and instead remained with the Countess, first in London, and then at Penshurst where he was in September when the news came through that the Earl had been killed at the first battle of Newbury. After this Stephen had a period in the service of the bereaved Countess's father, the Earl of Leicester, who in 1641 had been appointed by Parliament as Lord-Lieutenant of Ireland against the wishes of the King, but heeded the latter's order that he should not leave England. At this stage he was still at Oxford whither Charles had summoned him, uncertain whether he would ever be able to take up his post. Early in 1644 he was at last obliged by the King to resign it, and was replaced by the Marquess of Ormonde. So Stephen did not go to Ireland and was again transferred to a new master, his fourth in two years. His employer this time was Leicester's brother-in-law, Henry Lord Percy, one of the less reliable of Charles's supporters but a protégé of the Queen, owing to whose influence he had been appointed General of the Ordnance. Percy was with the King's own army in 1644 and Stephen went with him, so that he was present at the royalist victory over Waller at Cropredy Bridge, and at the surrender of the Earl of Essex's army at Lostwithiel in September.

In Cornwall Stephen met up again with his brother John, who was still in the service of the Prince of Wales. However, this family reunion turned out to be short-lived. Lord Percy had fallen into

[1] The following outline of Fox's movements during the Civil War and its aftermath is also based on the two narratives mentioned in note 1, p. 1. They are interpreted in the light of the sequence of events described in S. R. Gardiner, *History of the Great Civil War, 1642–1649* (4 vols., London, 1893). See also another short autobiographical fragment in Ilchester: Family (box 237): two sheets enclosed in small volume with green cover.

bad odour with the King because of his involvement in Wilmot's intrigues to oblige Charles to make peace, and had resigned his command. The following spring, after a brief period when the King had actually placed him under arrest for holding correspondence with the enemy, he set off for France to join the Queen at Saint Germain.[1] Stephen seems to have accompanied him, and so presumably shared the experience of capture by Waller and Cromwell at Andover, although he does not mention this in his brief autobiographical account of these years. It was not long before others followed them abroad, for the shattering defeat of the main royalist army at Naseby in June 1645 and the fall of Bristol three months later made it clear to all that, militarily speaking, the King's cause was hopeless. By the time that the Prince of Wales arrived in the summer of 1646, Fox, now aged nineteen, had been raised by his master to the position of Gentleman of the Horses. Percy was Master of the Horse to the Prince so that this was an important and responsible position, for its holder had to handle all the expenses of such stables as the exiled Court could afford to maintain, and to assume responsibility for all the journeys that it might undertake. In the normal course of events Fox would probably not have received such rapid promotion, but in the abnormal circumstances of exile and adversity the choice of candidates for such a post was naturally much reduced. For the next few years he remained abroad with the Court in this capacity. He certainly did not have much to go home for: he was not yet married so there was no family of his own to call him back, and as the younger son of a father of very modest means there would be no family estate to support him. Service under an exiled prince was not financially very rewarding, for the Court was always desperately short of money, and Fox later recorded that in September 1649 his total wealth was £85, all of which he had lent to his brother John, who had also come over to France, to send home to his wife and children. However, Stephen took advantage of his stay abroad to learn several foreign languages. How many he came to speak does not emerge, but Clarendon comments on his linguistic accomplishments, and in time they certainly increased his usefulness to his master.[2]

The Prince of Wales remained with the Queen in France for

---

[1] *D.N.B.*, under 'Percy, Henry, Lord Percy of Alnwick.'

[2] Earl of Clarendon, *History of the Rebellion* (ed. W. D. Macray, 6 vols., Oxford, 1888), v. 337–8.

nearly two years, throughout the period of negotiations and intrigues which finally produced the risings in England and the Scottish invasion of the north known as the Second Civil War.[1] Not until June 1648, when part of the Parliamentary fleet in the Downs mutinied and sailed for Holland, did Charles and most of the exiled Court move to Helvoetsluys to meet the mutineers. Fox went with them, and they were all still in Holland when the King was executed in January 1649. However, the murder of Dorislaus, the envoy of the new republic, by royalist exiles, made further continuation of Prince Charles's residence at The Hague an embarrassment to the States-General. So it was decided that he should join the Marquess of Ormonde in Ireland, and in June 1649 he moved to Antwerp in the Spanish Netherlands, thence to Brussels, and so to France. Fox was in attendance on this move and organized the practical details of it. As the royal party entered Spanish territory, however, he suffered a very unpleasant accident which he described graphically many years later.

I rideing in my post just behind the King's coach, in the giveing a joyfull volley [somebody] shot me wth a musket and filld my face full of powder, wch had disfigured me for ever but Mr. Pile, the King's chirugeon, took that care of me that he pict out almost every corne of powder, wch made it a tedious painefull cure and the King's residence at Brussells the longer, for untill I was fitt for it the King did not remove from Brussells.[2]

Once well again, Fox rode ahead to Paris and took back an 'equipage' of five coaches and sixty-five horses to the frontier to convey the whole party to St. Germain.

After a brief stay in France, Charles and his followers, including both the Fox brothers, moved to Jersey where they spent the winter. Cromwell's victories in Ireland made it pointless for them to continue the voyage there, and so in February 1650 Charles returned to Holland to resume negotiations with the Scots. His plight was now more forlorn than ever, and so he agreed to the terms on which they offered him their aid, although even nine months before he had rejected them as too severe, and in June sailed to Scotland. This time Stephen Fox did not accompany the royal party, but stayed behind in charge of the horses and equipage

---

[1] The narrative of the Prince's movements is based on that in E. Scott, *The King in Exile* (London, 1905).
[2] B.L., Add. MS. 51324, autobiographical narrative commencing f. 30.

at The Hague. The intention was to have these sent over to Scotland as well in due course, but before anything had been done the whole position of the royalists in the United Provinces was undermined by the death of the Prince of Orange in November. This meant an abrupt change of political climate in Holland: power passed to the States party, who were determined that the House of Orange should be excluded from power for the future. They refused to elect William II's infant son as Stadtholder, and had no sympathy with the plight of his Stuart relatives and their followers. The *émigrés* were thus deprived of official support and it was found necessary to sell the horses to pay the expenses of those who had remained behind.[1] This left Fox without a job, and instead of following the King to Scotland he decided to run the risk of arrest (for this was before the Act of Oblivion) by returning to England in order to visit his family at Farley.

When he got there in June 1651 he found his father ill, and his sister-in-law, John's wife, and her children in great distress, for John had been away for years and they had received nothing from him since the arrival of the £85 that Stephen had lent him two years before. However, he also found that his sister-in-law had a friend staying, Elizabeth Whittle, whose company was sufficiently agreeable for him to propose to her. She accepted him, and they got married in December 1651.[2] Meanwhile in September John had arrived, a fugitive from the battle of Worcester. He had been with the King in Scotland and during his invasion of England right up to the end, but had luckily escaped both death and capture at the rout of Charles's army. So the reunited family spent the whole winter in their father's cottage 'as chearfully together and as religeuously as if wee had bin rich, for my sister did manage a little as well as ever any good houswife did'. However, both brothers had to decide how to maintain themselves now that their careers in the royal service seemed to have been utterly wrecked. They were considering whether or not to go into farming together when Stephen, who had by now established a reputation for himself as a reliable and efficient servant, received an offer of employment from the Earl of Devonshire. The latter, to use Fox's own words, 'sent his Governor, the famous Mr. Hobbs, to enliste mee to be

---

[1] Ilchester: Family (box 237): two sheets enclosed in small volume with green cover.

[2] See a further short autobiographical fragment in B.L., Add. MS. 51324, f. 105.

Keeper of his Privy Purse, wch was indeed to be receivor of all his mony that came from his great estate into his house'.

Fox accepted Devonshire's offer, and although he does not say where his new post took him it was probably up to the Earl's seat of Chatsworth. Had he remained with the Earl he would doubtless have ended his days as the chief steward of his estates, or of those of some other great magnate. This would have been a worthy achievement for someone of his relatively lowly origins, and the opportunity was much too good a one to be thrown lightly aside. All the same, when less than a year later the call came once more to give his services to the exiled King, Fox resigned his appointment and left for France, taking his new wife with him. It would be interesting to know for certain whether he made this decision out of loyalty to his sovereign and former master, or out of a shrewd appreciation that a restoration of the monarchy sooner or later was highly probable, and that when it happened loyal servants would be well rewarded. The precise date of his return to France does not appear, but it must have been some time in the early part of 1653, a time when the fortunes of the exiled Court were at their very lowest ebb. Charles had returned to France after the battle of Worcester absolutely destitute, and though the French government had granted him a pension it was rarely and irregularly paid. Other sources of income were no more reliable, and the financial position of the exiles was desperate. It was reported in the English press that the King was reduced to eating in a tavern because he could not maintain a proper household of his own; and Sir Edward Hyde could barely afford pens, ink, and postage for his letters. Starvation sometimes seemed a real possibility, and in June 1653 Hyde commented: 'I do not know that any man is yet dead for want of bread, which really I wonder at.' The mutual jealousies and hostilities that divided the royalists in France, indeed divided the royal family itself, made the situation even worse.[1] If Fox knew even part of the truth about what he would find when he got to France, then surely loyalty must have been the main factor in his decision.

Charles remained in France until July 1654, and during that time Fox fulfilled much the same function as before, being in charge of the horses and stables. Long before this, however, both Charles himself and most of his advisers had been anxious to move

[1] For the condition of Charles II and his followers in France, see Scott, *The King in Exile*, chapter xviii, esp. pp. 429–38.

elsewhere. Charles wanted to go since it was clear that he had far outstayed his welcome at the French Court, and because as long as he was there he was so greatly dependent on his mother, whose jealousies and ambitions were a prime cause of the dissensions amongst his followers. His advisers, too, wanted him out of France: they could see him deteriorating before their eyes, and as long as he stayed they feared for his religious integrity. But to leave France was easier urged than accomplished: it required money to pay off debts incurred in Paris, and to pay the expenses of the journey, and sufficient money was not to be had. Another problem was where Charles might find a haven to go to, for none seemed to offer. Holland would not have him, and his own sister Mary, widow of William II of Orange, had been forbidden to receive him on Dutch territory; Spain was hostile; and the Emperor and the German princes were preoccupied and indifferent, despite the promise of financial aid they had made the year before. As the year 1654 drew on, the need to leave France became increasingly acute, for Mazarin was moving towards an alliance with Cromwell and it would clearly be only a matter of time before Charles would suffer the humiliation of expulsion. Certainly Mazarin now found his royal guest a very embarrassing one, and in his eagerness to be rid of him, he was willing to furnish him with funds. An agreement was quickly made, and in early July 1654 Charles and his train left Paris for Flanders, *en route* for the Spa where he was to meet his sister Mary, who was to take the waters there. The low ebb of the exiles' fortunes was demonstrated to the world by the fact that their King had to travel on horseback because his coach horses were needed to pull a cart containing clothes and bedding.[1]

Up to this time the finances of the exiled Court seem to have been completely hand-to-mouth and without system, as was inevitable when the King had no assured income. No regular salaries could be paid to members of the royal entourage, and no scheme of expenditure could be drawn up and adhered to. However, Mazarin's sudden fit of generosity meant that there was now enough money in hand to support the whole Court for a year, and that a regular, if modest, income seemed to be assured for at least the immediate future, so that it was possible for some sort of order to be introduced into the financial situation.[2] The first step was to

[1] *The King in Exile*, chapters xviii–xix, *passim*.
[2] E. Scott, *The Travels of the King* (London, 1907), p. 4.

appoint a reliable man who could be depended upon to administer the King's meagre resources both honestly and efficiently, a man who could make a little go a long way, and who could say 'no' firmly and often. The appointment was clearly an important, but not a prestigious one. It required a domestic servant rather than a courtier, for the duties were those of a sort of house steward and needed a good deal of practical experience. This experience was certainly possessed by Stephen Fox, for he had managed the horses and stables for several years, but he was not the first name that sprang to the mind of those close to the King. According to Edward Nicholas, one Clements was being canvassed for the post months before Fox was thought of as a possible, but once his name had been mentioned Sir Edward Hyde, himself a native of Wiltshire, seems to have pressed for him and carried the day.[1] When he set down his great *History of the Rebellion* the latter described Fox at this time as 'a young man bred under the severe discipline of the Lord Percy ... and very well qualified with languages and all other parts of clerkship, honesty, and discretion, that were necessary for the discharge of such a trust'.[2]

Fox could be well satisfied that his long apprenticeship as page-boy, Gentleman of the Horses, and finally Clerk of the Stables, had at last borne fruit in the form of a highly responsible position, but he presumably did not know of an understanding arrived at between Hyde and those who had opposed his candidature. The appointment had, in fact, been made subject to an assurance, conveyed by Hyde from the King, that it was to be 'without title or promise for the future'. This assurance was made because of the implications that this, like every other Court appointment, would have if and when the King was restored. The post being filled might be a relatively lowly one for the time being, but nevertheless it was that of the chief executive official of the royal Household, and once the King was back in Whitehall it could be assumed that his Household would be re-established on the old basis. The full royal Household with its responsibility for spending many tens of thousands of pounds yearly, its elaborate administrative hierarchy, and its ruling Board of Green Cloth, contained several extremely lucrative posts, and the man who had been the chief

[1] G. F. Warner, *The Nicholas Papers*, ii (Camden Society, 1892), pp. 101–2; Anon., *Memoirs of the Life of Sir Stephen Fox Kt.* (London, 1717), pp. 9–11.
[2] Clarendon, *History of the Rebellion*, loc. cit.

(indeed the sole) Household official during the exile might have a strong claim, amounting virtually to a right, to one of them. There were apparently those who were content that Fox should carry out the difficult task that had been assigned to him, but not that their own claims on the higher Household offices by virtue of seniority should be adversely affected by the promotion of a former page-boy. Nicholas wrote to Lord Hatton that 'as wee do not grudge him the present execution out of our modesty who would not press upon the king att this time, soe wee expect not that he shall be a barr or delay to us heereafter, since wee were next after His Matyes' and his blessed father's servants formerly actually in those places and continuing honest . . .'[1] As a result of these negotiations, Fox was apparently only appointed Clerk of the Kitchen, although he was fulfilling a function that might have entitled him to the important post of Cofferer of the Household. However, his duties were so much wider than those traditionally associated with the former office that the title was clearly inappropriate, and it was doubtless for this reason that he became known as the King's *maître d'hôtel*.[2] This more adequately described Fox's position, but it was not an office known to the hierarchy of the royal Household, and consequently would not give its holder any awkward claim to preferment after the King had recovered his throne.

Fox's appointment was made shortly before the royal party left Paris, and soon afterwards Hyde drew up the scheme of economy that he was to administer. The French government pension, which Mazarin had promised to continue after Charles's departure from France, amounted to the equivalent of about £6,000 sterling a year, and the 'establishment' was strictly within this limit, so that any additional income, for instance contributions from the English royalists or the German princes, could be used to meet emergencies or to help the royalists in Scotland. The allowances of Charles's six principal advisers, including Hyde himself, Ormonde, Culpeper, and Nicholas, were fixed at 150 guilders a month; seven courtiers of the second rank were each to receive eighty guilders if they provided their own food, but only half as much if they eat at the King's table; followers of the third rank, who included Fox, were to receive forty guilders; whilst fourteen menial servants, including

---

[1] Warner, *The Nicholas Papers*, loc. cit.
[2] Ilchester: Family (box 237), doc. cit. See also *Calendar of the Clarendon State Papers*, iii (ed. W. D. Macray, Oxford, 1876), p. 118.

a coachman and a postilion, received sums varying from thirty-five to fifteen guilders. No allowances at all were to be paid to anyone not actually in attendance on the King. Other sums were set aside for a variety of purposes, notably 2,000 guilders for the King's personal expenses, but as long as he remained his sister's guest this amount was to be saved for some future contingency.[1] Hyde also laid down the general principles that Fox was to follow: that the establishment he had drawn up should never be exceeded, even if Charles's finances temporarily seemed to warrant it, and that whenever the King left a town all debts must be scrupulously honoured. The latter course of action was essential if any sort of credit was to be preserved, for, as Hyde told Charles when he was about to move his entourage from Cologne to Bruges in 1656, 'your parting fairly in that place will be the best harbinger to prepare your welcome in the next'.[2] Fox himself tells us that the King never left a place but all his debts for living expenses were paid, and it is true that they were, sooner or later. But sometimes it was later rather than sooner, and immediately before the return to England in 1660 Fox was still paying off sums which the King had owed since 1651.[3]

At first Fox did not find the problems of making ends meet for the exiled Court too difficult. Charles did not spend as long at the Spa as he had intended and, because of a smallpox scare there, he and his sister moved to Aachen at the end of August. However, not until early November did Mary return home to Holland, and until then she bore a large part of his expenses. After she had gone the King went to Cologne to spend the winter of 1654–5. At Cologne the citizens proved extremely generous and provided him with a house, fuel, food, and drink, without charge, and this generosity meant that for yet a further period financial embarrassment was held at bay.[4] But as it turned out, these months between the departure from Paris and the spring of 1655 were only an interlude of relative security from worry. By the middle of 1655 things were once again as bad as they had ever been, and right until the very eve of the Restoration a virtually continuous series of financial

[1] Scott, *The King in Exile*, p. 430, and *The Travels of the King*, pp. 4–5; B.L., Stowe MS. 677, f. 80.

[2] Scott, *The Travels of the King*, p. 201.

[3] Ilchester: Family (box 237): autobiography in small volume with green cover; ibid.: Official, Sir S. Fox, Royal Service (box 267): account book of exile and Secret Service payments, April and May 1660.

[4] Scott, *The Travels of the King*, pp. 7–22.

crises beset the exiled Court. The King relied on several sources of income: at first the pension from the French government, and then after the treaty with Spain one from the Spanish government instead; contributions from some of the German princes and the English royalists; and gifts from Mary of Orange. But all these were more or less uncertain, and the supposedly regular pensions were usually in arrears. The income that Fox had to administer was frequently less than had been hoped or even feared, and inadequate to meet foreseeable needs, whilst the charges on it were always liable to unexpected increase from the need to send someone on a diplomatic mission, or from the arrival of yet more needy adherents to swell the royal train. Consequently, money was always in short supply, and frequently it was desperately so.

In fact, Fox personally seems to have borne the main brunt of the day-to-day practical problems caused by Charles's shortage of money. When the King left Cologne his continuing presence there was used to reassure those members of the royal entourage who remained behind that they were not being abandoned, and that they would eventually receive their arrears of salary. Similarly, the local authorities were also assured that Fox, as *maître d'hôtel*, would not leave the city until everything that was owed had been paid, an assurance that seems to have kept him there for several months. Nor was this the only occasion when he stayed behind to settle debts which could not be honoured immediately, for in October 1657 it was decided that he would have to remain in Brussels in order that the King might leave it. It was Fox who had to deal with the local tradesmen, to try to obtain credit from them, and to fend off importunate requests for payment for what had already been provided. Often it was very hard. In April 1656, for instance, whilst he was still at Cologne, he told Hyde that he could not get another week's credit for the Duke of Gloucester's table. On another occasion, when he was at Bruges in November 1657, he found additional difficulties in obtaining credit because the townspeople thought that Charles was risking his life by his presence near the scene of the fighting around Dunkirk. In the following spring he was again desperate, and wrote to Nicholas from Antwerp: '. . . unless we can have a speedy supply [of money], we must break with all mankind; and if we get the money, it must go to paying bills charged from Bruges to enable us to remove thence.' And again, 'We are in the greatest want that ever I saw this Court, nor have I any hope of our arrears . . . I am at the end of my credit, and the day is come for large payments which have been staved off all this while.'[1]

Sometimes Fox was himself able to think of ways in which the financial pressure might be alleviated, at least temporarily: for instance, he effected a considerable saving by procuring an ecclesiastical licence for the King to employ his own butcher during Lent of 1658. Often, however, he could only urge further economies and retrenchment on his superiors, as in the previous September when he had been obliged to suggest to Hyde that the King should be content with just one course at mealtimes. But there is no doubt that his main contribution during these years was the great efficiency and scrupulous honesty with which he administered Charles's finances. 'Mr Fox knows to a stiver what money you can depend upon,' the Marquess of Ormonde told the King in July 1658, and the neatly kept account books which still survive bear witness to the care with which he discharged his responsibilities. As a result he earned the trust, respect, and even friendship, not only of Ormonde, but of Hyde, and of Charles himself. Hyde's testimonial to Fox in his *History* was that 'his great industry, modesty, and prudence did very much contribute to the bringing the family, which for so many years had been under no government, into very good order; by which his Majesty, in the pinching straits of his condition, enjoyed very much ease from the time he left Paris.'[2] Pecuniary reward was naturally out of the question as long as they remained abroad, but Charles showed his appreciation of Fox's loyalty by making him a grant of arms in October 1658, and almost immediately afterwards adding to them an 'augmentation of honour' derived from the royal arms in the form of a golden *fleur de lys* on azure. The preamble to the original grant stated that the reason for it was that Fox,

having been advanced unto ye trust and charge of Clerke of His Majesty's Kitchen, ta4keing likewise care of and ordering the expences of the

[1] B.L., Egerton MS. 2542, f. 233; *Clarendon State Papers*, iii. 109, 118, 380; Scott, *Travels of the King*, pp. 201-4, 319, 353; D. Nicholas, *Mr. Secretary Nicholas* (London, 1955), pp. 287-8.

[2] Scott, *Travels of the King*, pp. 316-17, 352; *C.S.PD.*, 1658-9, p. 104; *Clarendon State Papers*, iii. 357; Ilchester: Official, Sir S. Fox, Charles II's Household (box 268): three account books covering expenses of the exiled court, 1654-9; B.L., Add. MS. 51318: similar account book 1654-5; Clarendon, *History of the Rebellion*, loc. cit.

Household in His Majesty's journeys and residence in these parts, hath in the execution thereof behaved himself with extraordinary diligence, fidelity, prudence and ability, to the great advantage and satisfaction of his Majesty and his service.

The King again showed how much he valued Fox as a servant when he agreed to stand as godfather to his second son, also named Charles, who was born at Brussels in December 1659.[1]

Nevertheless, useful though Fox was found to be in the managing of financial and household matters, it does not seem that he was ever employed outside these spheres. The anonymous biographer who published an account of Fox's career soon after his death claimed that, during the months immediately preceding the Restoration, he was sent on a series of secret political missions to Monk and Speaker Lenthall.[2] However, no other references to the alleged missions have materialized, and Fox himself makes no mention of them in any of his autobiographical writings. Nor does it seem at all probable that they ever took place. There was nothing in Fox's training or experience to fit him for such highly sensitive political undertakings, and there is no evidence that he was ever in any way concerned with political matters during the exile. Hyde's voluminous correspondence contains fairly numerous references to him during the years after 1654, but never once does he appear in any guise other than that of the man responsible for receiving money or making payments.[3]

By the end of May 1660 the years of anxiety and poverty-stricken exile were finally over. The King had crossed the Channel in the warship *Naseby*, hastily renamed the *Royal Charles* for the occasion; had landed at Dover; had embraced General Monk as 'father'; and finally on the 29th had entered London to be greeted with such acclaim that it prompted him to observe that 'he doubted it had been his own fault that he had been absent so long, for he saw no one that did not protest he had ever wished for his return'.[4] Fox had been one of the party on the *Royal Charles*, where Samuel

---

[1] B.L., Add. MS. 15856, ff. 89v–90; Stowe MS. 677, f. 78; Ilchester: Official, Sir S. Fox, Royal Service (box 267): account book of exile and Secret payments, at end.

[2] *Memoirs of Sir Stephen Fox*, pp. 21–2.

[3] *Clarendon State Papers*, especially iii and iv (ed. F. J. Routledge, Oxford, 1932).

[4] D. Ogg, *England in the Reign of Charles II* (2 vols., Oxford, 1956 edn.), i. 33–4; Scott, *The Travels of the King*, pp. 474–8.

Pepys had encountered him, finding him 'a very fine gentleman'.[1] A fine gentleman perhaps, but one whose future prospects were clouded with uncertainty. He had no home or property of his own to come back to, and he had been able to accumulate little or nothing whilst abroad. His administration of the finances of the exiled Court seems to have been entirely honest. No one ever seems to have levelled any charge of malpractice against him, though with such relatively small sums passing through his hands the opportunities for this would have been very limited. Even an anonymous character assassin who was prepared to tell the world that Fox, once 'a serving man', had permitted his wife to be 'common' when they were abroad, did not accuse him of any dishonesty during that time.[2] For later periods in his life we can cite the opinion of contemporary observers as to Fox's rectitude and integrity,[3] and although for the years before 1660 we have to take his own word for it, there seems no reason to doubt it. He tells us,

I did so little consider my owne interest that I cam into England wth the King who I had faithfully served for the space of fourteen years wthout any recompence but 72 pistolls per ann established, nor did I ever deduct a penny as fees or any profitt in payments, wch the King observing gave me that testemony that . . . no man ever accusd mee to His Matie of my stoping any thing from them. . . . And it was observed that those that served the Queen Mother in the offices that I served the King cam over rich when I had not any of my owne portion left to begin the world . . .[4]

It was not quite literally true that Fox had no 'portion' to begin his career in post-Restoration England, for the accounts he kept after his return show that he had in fact accumulated a small capital of a few hundred pounds. Some of this he had invested in a lavish set of Flemish tapestry hangings, which he subsequently sold to the Duke of Richmond for £270, and the rest he had lent out, and these loans were only partly counter-balanced by the debts he owed to others.[5] He may have acquired most of this money in the relatively

[1] *The Diary of Samuel Pepys* (ed. R. Latham and W. Matthews, 10 vols., London, 1970 continuing), i. 157.

[2] Library of the Wiltshire Archaeological Society, Devizes: Hungerford Family Collections, Personal History, iii. 59a.

[3] See below, p. 313.

[4] Ilchester: Family (box 237): autobiography in small volume with green cover.

[5] Ilchester: Official, Sir S. Fox, Army: day-book for 1660–4, for instance under Sept. 1660, 4 Feb. 1660/1, 29 Apr. 1661, 10 Aug. 1661, 28 Feb. 1662/3.

affluent last few weeks of exile, but almost certainly some of it had been built up by moneylending, by making advances to other courtiers on the security of the wages they were due to receive from his hands, a service for which in the circumstances he would have been able to charge a very high rate of interest. Nevertheless he had little enough to fall back on, and his future livelihood, and his ability to maintain his wife and the three children so far born to them, depended totally on the continued favour of his master, the King. He had shown himself to be a discreet and reliable servant, particularly in money matters, but his promotion had been entirely due to the unique circumstances of the exile. Once Charles was back in Whitehall and surrounded by throngs of courtiers, old and new, all pressing their claims to positions in the Household and to the royal bounty in general, there was a fair possibility that a man like Fox would be shunted aside, his usefulness over, and that he would never regain a position which was comparable in responsibility and importance to that which he had held abroad. Thus perhaps Fox mused, as the royal cavalcade made its way through Kent towards the capital and his last few days as the King's sole financial official passed away. He recorded the events of this time in his account book entries: 5,000 guilders distributed amongst the sailors of the *Royal Charles*, 'as a gratuity for His Maties passage'; £73. 15s. 0d. for the hire of horses and carts to transport the King's servants and luggage from Dover to London; £9 given to the drummers who proclaimed the King's entry to the town at Canterbury and at Rochester.[1] Charles had regained his kingdom, but for Fox the outlook was less certain.

[1] Ilchester: Royal Service (box 267): account book, May 1660, doc. cit.

CHAPTER II

Clerk of the Green Cloth and Paymaster of the Guards

IN 1660 Stephen Fox's hopes and expectations were clearly focused on the King's Household, and throughout his long public life in post-Restoration England he continued to have a great deal to do with it. A look at this institution, which was re-established by Charles II in an almost identical form to that which had existed before the Civil War, is thus necessary to an understanding of how and why Fox's career developed as it did.

The royal Household in the seventeenth century was an extremely elaborate organization consisting of many hundred officials and more lowly servants, whose function was to provide the Court with supplies of food, drink, fuel, lighting, furnishings, clothing, and the like, and with a variety of services including transport and entertainment. It was split into two main sections each with its own administrative structure: the Chamber, under the Lord Chamberlain, which was broadly speaking responsible for ceremonial and entertainment, and the Household below Stairs, under the Lord Steward, which dealt with the supply of necessaries.[1] The latter, it should be said, was more usually referred to simply as 'the House' or (confusingly) 'the Household', and since it was with the Household in this more limited sense that Fox was almost exclusively concerned, what follows will be principally concerned with that. Within it there were a large number of sub-departments, each with a specialized function and its own internal hierarchy, most important of which was the Counting House which provided general financial control and supervision. Next in seniority came the Kitchen, the Spicery, and the Stables, of which the latter enjoyed a much greater degree of autonomy than all the others, and below these three a series of others such as the Acatery (responsible for purchasing meat), the Bakehouse, the Buttery, the Pastry, the

---

[1] For a general account of the royal Household see Aylmer, *The King's Servants*, pp. 26–32, 472–5.

Poultry, the Pantry, Scullery, Woodyard, and the Porters. The senior official in most sub-departments was either a clerk or a sergeant, and subordinate to them were, in order of seniority, a number of yeomen, grooms, and pages, and in some there were also specialist or menial functionaries such as cooks, scourers, turn-broaches, or door-keepers. Internal promotion was generally by seniority, so that when a post became vacant all those remaining moved up one rung and a new entrant was admitted at the lowest grade. Such appointments formed part of the patronage of the higher officials in the Household, who also had the right to fill certain more important vacancies by nomination, but where clerkships especially were involved they would have to choose their candidate from amongst those properly qualified by experience.

The organization of the Counting House was quite different, as befitted its supervisory and accounting functions. The three senior members, collectively known as 'the Whitestaves', were the Lord Steward, The Treasurer, and the Comptroller, posts which were honorific and highly lucrative, and consequently tended to go to members of the nobility or leading courtiers. Then there was the Master of the Household who was responsible for discipline and order, and the Cofferer who was in practice the most important financial official to whom money was issued from the Exchequer to meet the needs of the whole Household and who, in turn, issued it to meet the expenses incurred by the various sub-departments. The other important members of the Counting House were two Clerks of the Green Cloth and two Clerks Comptroller. They were responsible for ensuring that all routine expenditure on wages and supplies was in accordance with the establishment of the sub-department in question; for examining and approving non-routine expenditure such as might be incurred at Court balls, masques, or receptions; for authorizing the Cofferer to issue the appropriate sums of money; and for keeping an account of any debts which the sub-departments might accumulate. Together the Treasurer, Comptroller, and Cofferer, with the four Clerks, formed the Board of Green Cloth (a term which referred to the table at which they sat), which was collectively responsible for the financial administration and good government of the Household.

On the Board there was promotion by seniority up to and including the post of Cofferer, so that a Clerk Comptroller could expect (if he survived) one day to rise to a Clerkship of the Green

Cloth, and perhaps even to the Cofferership itself. The junior Clerk Comptroller, however, was not recruited from within the Counting House, even though there were various subordinates of lower rank, yeomen and grooms, who in other sub-departments could have expected further promotion. When a Clerk Comptrollership became vacant the post was filled by the elevation of either the senior of the two Clerks of the Kitchen, or the Clerk of the Spicery, or the Avenor (who held a post in the Stables comparable to a clerkship), these three taking turns one after the other. The clerks of the other sub-departments were not in line for promotion direct to the Board of Green Cloth, but it was from their ranks that the vacancies left at the Kitchen, Spicery, or Stables were filled, so that some of them might eventually get within striking distance of the Board. In normal times these rules of succession within the Household were fairly strictly adhered to, but if they were broken and some outsider brought straight in to a senior position it caused a great deal of resentment because all the way down the line men were deprived of an expected promotion. On the other hand, the rules were not so strictly followed that men were promoted irrespective of their ability to perform their duties effectively, and those who were notoriously incapable, aged or infirm would probably be passed over.[1]

The great question for Fox in the early days of the Restoration was where, as the elaborate structure of the Household was gradually reconstituted, would he be fitted in? He seems to have hoped that he would be made Cofferer and to have believed that the King intended this, and indeed it is very possible that Charles had promised it.[2] According to Clarendon, when a return appeared to be imminent the King had determined to reward those who had remained with him abroad by granting them appropriate offices, and had not only made many promises but in some cases had even issued the necessary warrants. Once home, however, 'most of those predeterminations, and many other resolutions of that kind, vanished and expired in the jollity of the return, and new inclina-

---

[1] B.L., Harleian MS. 5010, ff. 45–8; Ilchester: Family (box 235, bundle 1, part 1): 'A paper concerning the succession of the officers below stairs'. See also various Household 'establishments' amongst Fox's papers, Ilchester: Official, Sir S. Fox, Charles II's Household (boxes 269 and 270).

[2] Ilchester: Family (box 237): autobiography in small volume with green cover, and narrative on two sheets enclosed in it.

tions and affections seemed to be more seasonable'.[1] Certainly Fox must have been very optimistic if he believed that the King would actually be able to carry out his promise, and that he was really a serious candidate for such a post. The Coffererership was a very senior and very profitable office, which before the Civil War had been worth over £2,000 a year to its holder, and which by the 1680s Fox himself reckoned as worth £4,000 yearly.[2] There were thus bound to be other and much more influential contestants for the place.

Fox considered that he had, in effect, been acting as Cofferer since 1654 for he had been the sole accounting official amongst the King's household servants. However, we have seen that the leading members of the royal entourage regarded him only as the Clerk of the Kitchen, and this was how his position during the exile was still officially described after it was all over.[3] The Clerk of the Kitchen was by no means an unimportant person, for he was head of one of the key sub-departments of the Household and in line for promotion to the Board of Green Cloth, but he could not expect immediate elevation to a senior position on the Board. What in fact happened was that a rival claimant for the Coffererership, William Ashburnham, brother of the more famous royalist Jack Ashburnham, was able to produce a warrant from Charles I, issued at Oxford in 1645, making him a reversionary grant of it after the death of the then holder. Ashburnham's warrant carried the day, and Fox got the best promotion he could really expect, which was on to the Board of Green Cloth as Second Clerk Comptroller. A warrant for his appointment was issued little more than a fortnight after the King reached London, and on 25 June he was sworn in. He might be the most junior member of the Board, but given the rule of promotion by seniority, the fact that he was still only thirty-three, and that several of those above him were old servants from the previous reign, he could expect to climb a considerable way up the ladder in due course. In fact his promotion began almost at once, for the death of two members of the Board within a few months led to his appointment as Chief Clerk Comptroller in

[1] *The Life of Edward Earl of Clarendon* (2 vols., Oxford, 1857), i. 311.

[2] Aylmer, *The King's Servants*, pp. 205, 221. B.L., Add. MS. 51324, f. 54[v]: document headed 'Losses sustained by Sr Ste Fox . . .'

[3] For instance in the warrant granting Fox's petition for land in East Meon, 23 Nov. 1660. See Ilchester volume cited in the next note in section entitled 'Transactions concerning East Meane'.

August, and then as Second Clerk of the Green Cloth in January 1661.[1] It was, however, to be another ten years before he got any higher than that.

As Clerk Comptroller or Clerk of the Green Cloth, Fox received only the small salary of £44. 6s. 8d. yearly, but the substantial allowances and perquisites which went with these offices probably brought their total value up to well over £600 a year.[2] Doubtless he could have made more than he did had he been prepared to accept the semi-official gratuities which were so often offered to men in important positions at that time, but we can be fairly certain that he was not so prepared. His attitude to such sources of income is suggested by what he told John Fox, the nephew whom he employed as a deputy in the early months of the Restoration: that he must not take any fee or reward for what he paid out 'because 'twas below a gentleman'.[3] Stephen could perhaps afford to take this attitude better than many others because, in addition to his office, he had also secured from the King, towards the end of 1660, a grant of land which was specifically stated to be a reward for his fidelity and 'his prudent care in managing the expenses of our family during our tedious continuance abroad'. The property in question consisted of a small group of farms in East Meon, Hampshire, which was leasehold of the Dean and Chapter of Winchester, and having passed into the hands of the regicide Francis Allen had consequently become forfeit to the Crown. Fox first obtained a reversionary lease to the property from the Church of Winchester, but this cost him only £310 since the leases already granted still had two and three lives to run respectively, and he was able to recoup the cost by the immediate sale of part of what he had acquired. He then petitioned for a grant of the Crown's title to the existing leases, which was duly granted, and eventually found himself in possession of property whose clear annual value was £196. 16s. 8d. over and above the rent he had to pay to the

---

[1] B.L., Add. MS. 51324, f. 61: statement of Sir Stephen's grievances without date, heading, or endorsement; Ilchester: Official, Sir S. Fox, Royal Service (box 267): volume mainly containing copies of royal warrants relating to Fox's official career.

[2] The volume just cited contains some accounts of Fox's receipts from his clerkships. He was receiving a similar amount as First Clerk of the Green Cloth in the 1680s, see below, pp. 113, 197. Also P.R.O., L.S. 13/31 etc. The largest single item in his total remuneration was 'board-wages', that is cash payments in lieu of diet.

[3] B.L., Add. MS. 51324, f. 10ᵛ: narrative of the life of John Fox junior.

Dean and Chapter. The value of the grant, according to the King's Surveyor-General, was £1,965.[1]

An important Household office and a small country estate: these represented Fox's immediate reward for his services in the years of exile. Possibly also the appointment of his brother John as Clerk of the Acatery, and of John's wife Elizabeth as Laundress to the Duke of Gloucester, should be regarded as part of that reward, for although John had been abroad with Charles in the early days of the exile he had not gone back after the battle of Worcester, and it is unlikely that he would have obtained such a relatively senior post unless Stephen had been there to remind the King of his existence.[2] As for Stephen himself, he had spent the whole of his life hitherto in relative poverty, and now suddenly he was in possession of considerable material wealth, more indeed than perhaps he had ever hoped for when he joined the royal service in so lowly a capacity twenty years before. He was able to spend some money enlarging and improving the modest lodgings he had been assigned within the Palace of Whitehall, to make them into a comfortable home for his wife and three young children; and to commence living in some style. He paid £80 in order to acquire a small house adjoining his rooms, and by March 1661 had spent nearly £240 on improvements to it. Yet even before this work was completed Pepys, who had known Elizabeth Fox before her marriage and was invited to dine towards the end of November 1660, recorded that he was served a 'most princely dinner'.[3]

Meanwhile Stephen discovered that the duties of his official post

[1] *C.S.P.D.*, 1660–1, p. 337, and 1661–2, p. 131. *C.T.B.* i (1660–7), pp. 88, 109, 288. Also Ilchester (box 267), doc. cit., section entitled 'Transactions concerninge East Meane'; and ibid.: Official, Sir S. Fox, Army: day-book for 1660–4, under 22 Aug., 7 and 16 Oct. 1661.

[2] *C.S.P.D.*, 1670, p. 717, 1672–3, p. 620. The fact that the King issued the warrant for John Fox's appointment from Breda, i.e. before the Restoration, strongly suggests that Stephen's influence (probably through Hyde and Ormonde) secured the post for him: see B.L., Egerton MS. 2542, f. 347. John Fox subsequently succeeded to the Spicery, a Clerkship senior to that of the Acatery. His only son (another John) was employed by Stephen immediately after the Restoration, although this did not prove to be a success. John himself combined his post-Restoration career in the Household with that of regimental agent to the Foot Guards, and later in life he managed the estate in the West Country which Stephen began to build up after 1672. He died in 1691. See below, pp. 154, 197, 200.

[3] Ilchester: Estate, London (box 161): documents relating to Fox's Whitehall lodgings; ibid.: Official, Sir S. Fox, Army: day-book for 1660–4, under 30 Mar. 1661; B.L., Add. MS. 51319, f. 11: certificate from the Gentlemen-Ushers, 29 Jan. 1660; *Pepys*, i. 299.

were not the only ones he was expected to perform. The King found it useful to continue to make use of his services as a confidential financial agent who could be trusted with custody of considerable sums of money and relied on to pay it out as directed, promptly, and without all the formality and delay that were unavoidable if the Exchequer with all its elaborate procedures was involved. This aspect of the royal finances was referred to in the seventeenth century as 'Secret Service', although very little of what was disbursed was of a genuinely secret nature and the phrase had totally different connotations to those which it has subsequently come to bear. Secret Service was essentially an administrative convenience. It provided a mechanism for making payments, frequently though not invariably of small amounts, which did not conveniently fall within traditional departmental responsibilities. It also enabled the government to make these payments with the minimum of formality and the maximum of flexibility, and without overloading the always heavily worked Exchequer.[1] In the immediate aftermath of the Restoration there were debts of gratitude to be paid ranging from a gift of £4,000 to the Earl of Sandwich and £1,000 to Major-General Massey, down to an allowance of £20 a year to one Charles Conor 'an old servt of Coll. Blaggs . . . being in a sick & weake condition . . . to keepe him alive'. In addition, a few very small sums were paid out to persons who had provided the government with intelligence reports. But once times had returned to normal most of what Fox disbursed went as salaries, gifts, or pensions, to those whom the King wished to reward for services of a perfectly straightforward nature. The Lord Chancellor, the Lord Treasurer, the Chancellor of the Exchequer, and some of the ambassadors abroad were, for instance, regularly paid by Fox out of Secret Service funds. Other expenses discharged in this way were essentially the private concerns of the King: £200 for 'a jewel given to a dumb Polander'; £4,570. 1s. 8d. for an elaborate set of gold toilet plate for the new Queen Catharine; £1,177. 10s. 5d. for over 7,500 lime trees imported from Holland for the royal gardens at Whitehall and Hampton Court.

Altogether nearly £45,000 passed through Fox's hands between the Restoration and the end of 1660, but thereafter the rate of his

---

[1] J. Walker, 'The Secret Service under Charles II and James II', *Transactions of the Royal Historical Society*, 1932, p. 214; *C.T.B.* ix (1689–92), p. xl, quoting a speech in Parliament by Mr. Guy on 20 March 1689.

disbursements on this account was considerably reduced and averaged no more than about £24,000 a year over the period 1661 to 1675. He did not receive any regular salary for this responsibility, but at least twice (in 1665 and again in 1675) the King made him a substantial lump sum payment of over £2,000 on each occasion by way of reward and to cover certain expenses.[1] In addition, he seems to have been allowed to deduct six pence in the pound, 2½ per cent, from certain of the payments he made, as Pepys found in November 1660 when he went to collect Lord Sandwich's £4,000.[2] Pepys describes this as 'the fee of the office', and doubtless it was partly to pay Fox's clerks and the fees which all recipients of money at the Exchequer had to pay to the officials there, but there was at least something over for himself. It is difficult to ascertain on how many of his payments Fox took these fees, but in April 1661 he recorded an accumulated profit of £277. 11s. 4d. from them, and in August one of £136. 16s. 6d. 'by fee of 6d. per pound in payment of 24 severall sumes' since the former date.[3] He was thus getting a useful addition to his income, but making no great fortune at the expense of those for whom the money was intended. Moreover, it is worth noting that such fees were perfectly respectable and official, and that most pensions and salaries were subject to them in the seventeenth century. They are not to be confused with the irregular gratuities which might be offered to men in Fox's position, or demanded by them, for instance for making payment to one man sooner than to another: these, we have seen, he had almost certainly foresworn. Many of the payments he was directed to make from Secret Service money involved the remittance of money abroad, and in 1660 and 1661 Fox found that he had quite a considerable amount of foreign business, which made it possible for him to undertake similar transactions for others, charging them an appropriate commission for his services. From the first, therefore, he combined the financial business he transacted for the Crown with private financial activity on his own account, even though at first it was only on a very small scale.[4]

Early in 1661 Fox found himself with a new assignment which

[1] Ilchester: Official, Sir S. Fox, Royal Service (box 267): various accounts of Secret Service disbursements covering 1660–74.   [2] *Pepys*, i. 293.
[3] Ilchester: Official, Sir S. Fox, Army: day-book for 1660–4, under 30 Apr. and 26 Aug. 1661.
[4] Ilchester: Official, Sir S. Fox, Army: day-book for 1660–4.

involved handling even larger sums of money than those he had received and paid out on account of Secret Service, for quite unexpectedly he was appointed Paymaster of the King's Guards. This was the event which was to determine the whole course of his career in Restoration England, and it was unexpected because the decision to retain a body of guards in the royal service was taken very suddenly and represented a reversal of government policy. In the first seven or eight months of Charles II's rule one of the most pressing tasks that faced ministers was the disbanding of the army which had dominated politics since the Civil War. Even though regimental commands had been transferred to men loyal to the King and unreliable officers had been purged, Charles could never really feel secure as long as any part of the force which had obeyed the commands of Cromwell for so long remained in being. Thus as money became available the regiments were paid off one by one, and by the beginning of the new year 1661 only General Monk's regiment of foot and a single troop of horse remained. Then the very day before the last units were due to be likewise disbanded occurred the disturbance known as Venner's Rising.[1]

This, it must be admitted, did not amount to much. A small group of Sectaries, apparently no more than thirty strong, attempted an armed insurrection in the City of London. They scattered the trainbands which went against them and spread a great deal of alarm and confusion, but were easily overwhelmed by Monk's experienced troops. However, a nervous Council, which at this time was constantly receiving reports of real or imagined plots, was badly shaken, and felt that if the soldiers had not been available they would have been faced with an awkward situation. They decided that it was not safe for the government to be left without any military force at all, and promptly suspended the disbanding of what remained and advised the King to supplement them by raising more. A month later there was a formal ceremony on Tower Hill at which Monk's men, the last of the New Model Army, laid down their arms and then immediately re-enlisted in the royal service.[2] When the new army had been properly organized it consisted of three troops of horse-guards, together 500 men besides

---

[1] J. W. Fortescue, *A History of the British Army* (13 vols., London, 1910–30), i. 291–2.

[2] *C.S.P.D.*, 1660–1, pp. 470–1; *Life of Clarendon*, i. 404–6; D. Mackinnon, *Origin and Services of the Coldstream Guards* (2 vols., London, 1833), i. 98–102

officers; a regiment of horse of 500 men; and two regiments of foot-guards of 1,200 men and 1,000 men respectively. The total strength, including commissioned and non-commissioned officers, was 3,557.[1] When it is remembered that the New Model at the time of the Restoration numbered about 65,000 men, it may easily be accepted that this miniature establishment did not represent a very formidable military force. Nor indeed was it even referred to as 'the army' at all in the 1660s or for a long time afterwards, but rather as 'the Guards', as though to emphasize the difference in function between it and the force which had just been disbanded. It provided a reasonably substantial garrison for London and Westminster, and a mobile force which could be dispatched to any part of the kingdom, large enough to deter any attempted *coup d'état* or to nip in the bud any local outbreak of rebellion, but not so large as to threaten the liberties of the people, whatever critics of the regime subsequently purported to believe. Moreover, the maintenance of such a force clearly was essential. The country had just passed through two decades of political upheaval which contemporaries had no reason to be sure had necessarily come to an end with the King's return, and there were numerous religious extremists, discontented Cromwellian officers, and other republican sympathizers, who could be expected to plot trouble. It is sometimes argued that because Venner and his companions were obviously unbalanced fanatics who could not conceivably have been a serious threat to the government, his rising can only have been a pretext which the royal advisers eagerly seized on to justify the maintenance of an armed force. Such an argument is based on a misunderstanding of the historical situation. In the early 1660s ministers had every reason to fear plots and insurrection, and it is only hindsight which enables us to dismiss these fears as unfounded. True, Venner's rising, taken in isolation, was an inadequate reason for keeping even such a diminutive standing army, but the rising did not occur in isolation, and so it served to persuade the government that *not* to have some troops available was to take too great a risk.

As soon as it had been decided to keep a force of guards, arrangements had to be made for paying them, and this made it necessary

---

[1] P.R.O., S.P. 29/29, item 47. In addition to the Guards there were also at this time troops at Dunkirk, besides the home garrisons. For the latter see below, pp. 43–4.

to appoint an official who would be responsible for the task. Since the post was an entirely new one there was no one who had any prior claim to it, and since the need for it had arisen so suddenly, and it had to be filled quickly, there was no opportunity for a host of seekers-after-office to press their cases on their respective patrons, and their patrons to press their respective clients on the King. Thus Charles, almost certainly making a genuinely personal decision, was able to appoint Fox, whom he knew to be a thoroughly reliable financial servant, and whose disappointment over the Cofferership had (according to Fox) troubled his conscience.[1] He acted very promptly, for the royal warrant making the appointment was dated 19 January, less than a fortnight after the Venner episode. There is no doubt that Fox owed his post to the good impression he had made during the exile, because the warrant is quite explicit. It recites that the appointment of a person of experience and integrity would much conduce to the good of the new regiments, and that 'out of ye experience wee have in this kind (as well in other services of other natures) whilest wee were abroad wee have made choice of our servt Stephen Fox and doe hereby constitute him Paymaster of all ye Guards wee now raise'. A few days later Lord Treasurer Southampton wrote to the King on the subject of the new Paymaster's salary: 'I have regard to ye good service Mr Fox hath done you abroad as well as to this present service when I thinke fitt to allow Mr Fox foure hundred pounds by ye yeare . . .'[2]

Fox's appointment as Paymaster took effect on 26 January 1661, and to start with his function was a limited and relatively simple one. Money was issued to him at the Exchequer, and what he received he paid out to the Guards as the establishment laid down, making no deductions from their pay save for two pence in the pound to meet the cost of the fees he himself had to pay to the Exchequer officials. However, it was not long before he began to find that, because of delays in the issue of money to him, he was unable to pay to the regiments under his care the money which was owed to them until some considerable time after it had fallen due.[3] From the very beginning Charles II's government was beset

---

[1] Ilchester: Family (box 237): autobiography in small volume with green cover.

[2] Copies of the relevant documents will be found in Ilchester: Official, Sir S. Fox, Royal Service: volume containing copies of royal warrants.

[3] Ilchester: Family (box 237): autobiography in small volume with green cover.

by financial difficulties, and in April 1661 even the preparations for the Coronation were threatened by lack of money.[1] The main cause of these difficulties was that the actual yield of the revenue fell considerably short of the £1,200,000 a year which Parliament had undertaken to provide, and which was the amount required to meet the Crown's normal expenditure, but the position was considerably aggravated by the decision to maintain military forces. The Guards cost nearly £123,000 a year,[2] but no extra revenue was forthcoming to match this since Parliament had not been consulted about them, and indeed regarded their very existence in peacetime as a grievance. Increasingly the government was forced to meet its obligations by anticipating the future yield of taxes, since ready money was simply not available. The principal method by which this was done was the issue of tallies.[3] Government creditors or officials who had to make payments on the government's behalf received, in the form of a notched and inscribed piece of wood, what was in effect a claim to be paid a stated sum out of the Exchequer in general or a particular branch of the revenue. When the Exchequer or the revenue receiver in question eventually had the necessary cash in hand the holder of the tally would receive payment. The delays experienced by tally holders in getting their money varied, according to the state of the branch of the revenue on which their tally had been struck, according to their own importance as creditors and the priority consequently assigned to them, and even according to their own importunity. However, as the revenue became further and further anticipated, and more and more of these tallies were issued, the delays tended to get longer.

In this situation the holders of tallies who needed money immediately had two choices. They could either attempt to sell, necessarily at a considerable discount, to someone who did have ready cash and was prepared to wait until the tallies matured when he would collect their full value and thus realize a profit; or, alternatively, they could use their tallies as security for a loan, the principal of which would be discharged when the tallies were paid off, and on which they or the Exchequer would pay interest in the meanwhile. Both these courses were frequently adopted by the

[1] C.T.B. i (1660–7), p. 234.   [2] P.R.O., S.P. 29/29, item 47.
[3] S. B. Baxter, The Development of the Treasury 1660–1702 (London, 1957), pp. 134–5; C. D. Chandaman, The English Public Revenue 1660–1688 (Oxford, 1975), Appendix I, pp. 285–95.

chief financial officials of government spending departments, such as the Treasurer of the Navy, the Cofferer of the Household, and the Treasurer of the Chamber, who had an almost constant need to get their revenue assignments discounted, or to negotiate loans, so as to be able to carry on the work of the departments for which they were responsible.[1] Fox was soon obliged to act in a similar fashion, and during the course of 1661 and 1662 he succeeded in raising a series of increasingly large sums on the Crown's behalf: borrowing from goldsmith bankers by pledging his tallies and applying the proceeds to the discharge of his official responsibilities.[2] The scale of his activities in this respect began modestly, but expanded rapidly. In the early summer of 1661 he advanced £1,928. 17s. 4d. towards the cost of the new uniforms which the King had given to his Guards as a present but which he could not afford to pay for in cash.[3] Then in October he advanced a further £5,000; in March 1662 he succeeded in raising £25,000 for the purpose of disbanding the remnants of the Cromwellian forces in Scotland; and finally, between May and July 1662, he found £28,247. 19s. 0d. which represented the entire amount due to the Guards for the preceding three months.[4] Such loans did not bring any financial gain to the officials who arranged them, but at the same time Fox had also begun to undertake some independent financial activity in connection with his Paymastership. On the basis of a private agreement with the various commanders he raised what money he could on his own account, again drawing on the bankers, and perhaps also on the unexpended balances of Secret Service money he held, and used it to make part-payment of what was owing to the forces before he received their pay from the Exchequer. In return he received interest from the commanders until his advances were reimbursed by the Crown. This meant that the officers were having to pay interest on money which rightfully belonged to their units, but for which otherwise they would

---

[1] In addition, wealthy officials might lend the money their departments needed from their own resources, in which case, of course, they would claim the interest for themselves. See R. Ashton, 'The Disbursing Official under the Early Stuarts', *Bulletin of the Institute of Historical Research*, 1957.

[2] For a detailed consideration of Fox's sources of finance at this time, see below, pp. 57–63.

[3] P.R.O., E. 403/2593, ff. 7–7ᵛ.

[4] P.R.O., A.O. 1/48/9; S.P. 29/88, item 6; Ilchester: Official, Sir S. Fox, Army (box 273): summary account of money advanced and received for the forces.

have had to wait. The first entries in Fox's accounts which reveal these transactions are dated 1 May 1661, and by June he was making such advances to all the constituent elements of the little army, and he continued to do so for more than a year.[1] Nevertheless, the Guards remained two months or more in arrears, and both Monk and his officers and the Lord Treasurer became increasingly concerned. The grounds for this concern were not merely that the officers naturally wanted their own pay when it fell due, or even that they wanted to see justice done to their men, but in large part because recent history had shown how dangerous an unpaid army could become to its nominal masters. Yet by the summer of 1662 it was clear to all that Charles II's finances were so strained that the pay due to the Guards would inevitably fall further and further into arrears unless something was done.

The remedy that Monk and Southampton looked to in order to ensure that the new army would be properly paid was one frequently resorted to in the seventeenth century, both in the collection of revenue and in the provision of services nowadays considered the function of civil service departments. They decided to turn the business over to a private contractor. Fox had already established good contacts among the bankers, and so they asked him to find an individual or a syndicate who would agree, on terms which would ensure them a reasonable profit, to lend to the Crown as much money as might be necessary to keep the pay of the Guards up to date, irrespective of delays in their reimbursement. According to Fox, he tried, and the officers of the Guards also tried, to persuade first the bankers and then the farmers of the Excise to undertake the task, but neither of them were prepared to do so. Doubtless, they considered that it was an unnecessarily risky venture in view of the fact that they could already do extremely well by lending to the government in a more normal way. An 'Undertaking' could involve them in a virtually unlimited liability to advance ever larger sums for ever longer periods, whereas by lending to individual officials on the security of their tallies they could more easily limit the amount of their loans to what was convenient, and fairly quickly liquidate their involvement simply

---

[1] Ilchester: Official, Sir S. Fox, Army: day-book for 1660–4. Most of the entries relating to the transactions in question specifically refer to the payments made for the advance of money before Fox had received it as being 'per accord' i.e. on the basis of prior agreement.

by ceasing to advance more. An Undertaking would necessarily be much more difficult to escape from.

The established financiers, then, would not become directly involved, but they were prepared to increase the scale of their advances to Fox. Thus when it was suggested to him that he might therefore attempt the Undertaking himself, despite the fact that this would involve him in a financial operation which completely dwarfed what he had been conducting hitherto, he agreed albeit 'with feare and trembling'. He describes in some detail what happened:

At last being commanded by the King, encouraged by my Lord High Treasurer Southampton, & every day prest by the Duke of Albermarle, the Generall, I told His Grace that I would use my utmost endeavor, whereupon hee sent the chieffe officers to make a proposition to mee, wch brought to my lodging seventeene officers wth Coll. Russell, Chieffe Commander by being Coll. of His Maties first Regiment of Foot Guards, who said they were glad to be sent from the Generall wth a proposall for the undertaking of a steddy constant paying the forces commanded by them, & having considered it at a meeting of officers they resolved to give 12d. out of every 20s. to ye undertaker besides the Exchequer fees of 2d. per £ that they hitherto had paid. Whereupon I told the sd Coll. & the rest of ye officers that if I could not doe it for a shilling in the pound, including the sd fees, I would not consent a greater deduction should be made from the establishment. To wch Coll. Russell & the rest of ye officers said they were likely to be infinitely beholding. And Sr Robert Byron the Lt Coll & Sr John Skelton the Major, staying at dinner wth mee wondered at my accepting of doing it at so reasonable a rate, when in their consultation [they had] resolved to give mee 18d. in the pound rather than bee refused in a paymt so absolutely necessary for the service. . . .[1]

The details of this account cannot, it seems, be verified from any other source, but the general tenor of it is confirmed by a letter from the King to the Lords of the Treasury written in October 1667. In this the Commissioners were told that the agreement between Fox and the officers had been arrived at 'upon the earnest request of many of the said officers to the Lord Generall to dispose the said Paymr to undertake the same with the allowance of a reasonable deduction out of their pay for interest of what money

---

[1] Ilchester: Family, Sir Stephen Fox (box 237): autobiography in small volume with green cover.

should be paid or advanced to them before the said Paymaster received the money appointed for their pay.'[1]

Under the agreement of August 1662 Fox was to advance to the Guards a proportion of their pay every week in order to provide them with subsistence money, and was then to pay over the remainder at the end of every 'muster', the six or eight week periods into which the army year was divided for accounting purposes. In return he took a shilling in the pound (5 per cent) of all the money passing through his hands, of which two-thirds (eight pence in the pound or $3\frac{1}{3}$ per cent) was to cover interest on the money he would have to borrow, and the remaining one-third (four pence in the pound or $1\frac{2}{3}$ per cent) to cover Exchequer fees and his own expenses.[2] Corresponding to the agreement with the officers there was also, although Fox's account makes no reference to it, some kind of understanding or agreement with the Treasury. The undertaking could only be viable if both the Paymaster and those on whom he would be relying for loans had an assurance that, whatever delays there might be in repaying him the full amount of his advances, there would be a constant flow of cash into his hands. Thus in October 1662 we find Lord Treasurer Southampton informing the Customs farmers that the King had promised General Monk that £25,000 should be paid to Fox for the Guards; that 'at present my Lord Generall calls hard for ye same and his Matie expects it to be hastened'; and that accordingly they were to furnish Fox with such money as he should require against the tallies shortly to be struck on them. In the early months of 1663 Fox was receiving £1,000 a week from the Customs, whilst in the following autumn and winter his account with the goldsmith banker Edward Backwell was being credited with £5,000 a month from the London Excise farmers.[3] Indeed, throughout the whole period of Fox's Paymastership, there seem to have been a series of agreements with the Treasury for regular payments of cash, a new one being negotiated every few months as his own requirements and the circumstances of the royal Treasury altered.[4]

In so far as Fox did actually receive his regular weekly or

---

[1] P.R.O., S.P. 44/26, pp. 13–13ᵛ.   [2] B.L., Add. MS. 28082, f. 101.

[3] Ilchester: Official, Sir S. Fox, Royal Service (box 267): volume containing copies of royal warrants, sections relating to payment of the Guards etc.; ibid.: Official, Sir S. Fox, Army (box 273): summary account of money advanced and received for the forces; Williams and Glyn's Bank: Backwell's Ledger I, f. 541.

[4] For example see C.T.B. ii (1667–8), pp. 234, 236. Also below, pp. 92–3.

monthly instalments—and at certain periods they too fell into arrears—the amounts he needed to raise to carry on his Undertaking were considerably less than the full amount due to the Guards. However, he received his shilling in the pound on their whole pay, and it was the difference between what the agreement with the officers allowed him for interest, and what he actually had to pay out, together with what was allowed for his 'expenses', which provided him with the possibility of profit. Nevertheless, according to Fox, it was not only the officers who were surprised that he was prepared to accept the Undertaking on the terms which he had been offered. He tells us that, 'when Sr Stephen Fox upon the Lord Generall's mocōn and proposall went about to attempt this service, the persons with whom . . . [he] advised wondered hee would attempt a matter of soe greate trouble & danger for soe little proffitt . . .'[1] And in the event, those who doubted whether it was worth doing for only a shilling in the pound were proved right.

There is relatively little evidence of the rate of interest at which Fox borrowed the money which he advanced to the Guards, but he must have paid the going rate which, for government borrowers in the 1660s, was frequently 8 per cent, and sometimes 10 per cent or even more.[2] Now, since Fox's poundage only provided him with $3\frac{1}{3}$ per cent interest, he could only afford, if interest on his borrowings stood as high as 10 per cent, to allow the loans he contracted to remain outstanding for four months before the interest he would have to pay out would amount to more than was being allowed to him. If he was paying 8 per cent then the period could be extended somewhat, but clearly the longer were the delays in the payment of the tallies which reimbursed his advances, the more he had to pay out in interest, and at any given rate of interest there would come a point when the terms on which he was paying the forces would become less favourable than the agreement of August 1662 had intended to provide.

At about the time the Undertaking began, Fox's tallies were being paid after eight to ten weeks,[3] but as the government's financial problems were intensified rather than eased with the

---

[1] B.L., Add. MS. 51319, f. 24: statement of Fox's case in his dispute with Lord Gerard. Fox was not, in fact, knighted until 1665.

[2] For such evidence as does survive, see below, pp. 61–2.

[3] Ilchester: Family (box 237): autobiography in small volume with green cover.

passage of time, the interval between their issue and their redemption continued to grow. This did not immediately threaten the viability of the August agreement. The government regarded the provision of funds for the forces as a high priority, as is illustrated by the Lord Treasurer's remark to the farmers of the Customs in October 1662 that 'there is noe service more important and none more seasonable at this present [time] than that His Maties Guards be supplyed'. Accordingly, during much of 1663, a considerable proportion of the Paymaster's advances were repaid in cash at the Exchequer and with reasonable promptitude, either out of the money received by the government for the sale of Dunkirk to the French, or some other source of ready money. For the remainder, Fox received tallies on the Customs and Excise which, at this stage, were still being paid after delays of no longer than three to four months.[1] But the delays continued to lengthen, and on some sources of revenue were already considerably longer than this. At some stage during 1663, Fox was issued with a number of tallies on the Hearth Tax which were not due to be paid for so long that the bankers would not accept them as security for loans on any terms. The Treasury was thus forced to recall them, and instead to issue him with less remote tallies on the Excise.[2]

But by this stage even the delays on the Excise had lengthened past the point which Fox found acceptable, and since the Excise had become the principal source of funds for the Guards, a revision of the terms of the Undertaking became essential. Fox recounted how this was done in the following terms.

Which branch of the King's revenue [i.e. the Excise] soone grew to be soe far anticipated that the Paymaster could not find his acctt by the said agreement [i.e. for a deduction of a shilling in the pound], which the then Lord Treasurer & my Lord Generall finding, and with all the greate ease that the steddy payment of the Guards for some time past had given their Lordps they thought fitt to encourage the Paymaster's proceedings by allowing interest at 6 per cent & 2 per cent reward, to begin at the end of two months after the money was due to the forces, by which accomodacon the Guards were constantly paid, and the King paid noe more interest than 8 per cent for XIV months, the rest being made good by the deduction from the soldiers which came to $3\frac{1}{3}$ per cent more. Soe the Paymaster had in all for interest and advance of

---

[1] Ilchester . . . volume containing copies of royal warrants, doc. cit., section relating to payment of the Guards etc.; B.L., Add. MS. 28082, f. 11.

[2] *C.T.B.* i (1660–7), pp. 580, 593.

money $11\frac{1}{3}$ per cent for 14 months, which method continued till the Stopp of the Excheqrr ...[1]

This arrangement was probably arrived at towards the end of 1663, although Fox's interest accounts show that it was backdated to August 1662.[2] The effect of it was not to make the terms of the Undertaking any more favourable to the Paymaster than had originally been agreed, but to ensure that, however long it might be before his tallies were honoured, they would not be any less favourable to him. It needs to be explained that, technically, the pay of the forces did not become due to them until the end of each muster, and it was at that point that tallies were struck for the appropriate amount and delivered to the Paymaster. Thus in August 1662, when his tallies were being paid in eight or ten weeks, he had been able to count on receiving reimbursement of his advances about two months 'after the money was due to the forces', and on that basis had accepted a deduction of $3\frac{1}{3}$ per cent to cover his interest charges. Under the new agreement, Fox still received no more than this percentage of his turnover (which was of course a once-and-for-all lump-sum payment) for the first two months after the close of each muster. It was only thereafter that his advances qualified for a continuing rate of interest at 8 per cent which would be paid as long as they remained outstanding: that is, until such time as his assignments were redeemed. Moreover, the extra 8 per cent was only allowed on money actually advanced and still outstanding after two months: it was not, like the poundage, allowed on the whole of his turnover. It would thus be wholly absorbed by the interest which Fox himself had to pay on loans which, as he indicated in the passage quoted above, sometimes remained outstanding for a further fourteen months, and at certain periods for even longer.

These revised arrangements proved to be sufficiently satisfactory, both to the Treasury and to the Paymaster, to remain the basis on which Fox carried on his Undertaking for the next nine years, and they enabled him to survive the strains imposed by a foreign war as well as a succession of credit crises. From the government's point of view, the terms were satisfactory because the interest it

---

[1] B.L., Add. MS. 28082, f. 101. After the Stop of the Exchequer in January 1672, the delays in the payment of assignments on the revenue were so much reduced that the need for the extra interest ceased.

[2] P.R.O., E. 403/2610, ff. 66ᵛ et seq.

paid on the Paymaster's loans was lower than the going rate, since part of what the latter received was paid by the soldiers. From Fox's point of view they were satisfactory because they gave him a substantial margin of profit. 'He gains soundly', commented Pepys approvingly when, a few years later, Fox explained to him how he operated.[1]

We shall return to Fox's gains in later chapters, but our study of the origins of his Undertaking should have made their nature and their justification apparent. It has usually been assumed that he grew rich by exploiting the soldiers, by taking a shilling in the pound of their already meagre pay in return for doing nothing more than letting them have their money on time. Passing over the fact that for anyone employed by the government to receive payment 'on time' was quite something in Restoration England, this judgement is neither accurate nor fair. Fox made a fortune as a risk-taking financier and, as he observed later, if the Lord Treasurer had not allowed him extra interest as his tallies became increasingly remote, 'the Pay-master by his Undertaking had soone afterwards beene undone'.[2] He raised money for which he had to pledge his own credit as collateral security along with his tallies, and then re-lent to the government to enable it to pay its forces: that he combined this function with that of actually dispensing the money he had lent was a historical accident arising from the fact that no one else had been prepared to accept the Undertaking. The two functions were essentially separate, and it was the former, not the latter, from which Fox made by far the largest part of his profits.[3] It was not he who was taking advantage of the soldiers by deducting poundage from their wages but the government which was doing so, using this means to shift on to them the burden of paying, at first all, and then, under the revised arrangement, a still substantial proportion of Fox's interest charges. Of course, the government's financial difficulties in the 1660s were such that it could not afford prompt payment for the Guards in any other way, a fact which the officers clearly realized when they embraced the idea of a private undertaking so readily. A further reason why they did so was that under the agreement with Fox, they and their men were not simply to get their pay when it was due (at the end of each muster), but were actually to get a considerable part of it

before it was due in the form of the weekly or fortnightly instalments for subsistence. To that extent they *were* getting something
for that part of their poundage which represented interest charges,
and something which was sufficiently unusual in the seventeenth
century to be worth paying for. As for the part of the poundage
which represented the Paymaster's Exchequer fees and expenses,
at that time virtually all recipients of government money took it for
granted that some such deduction would be made. The soldiers
had paid two pence in the pound towards fees even before Fox
took over the Undertaking, and Fox himself paid something on the
various salaries and pensions which he gradually accumulated as
time went by. For instance, in the 1670s he only received £975
per annum out of a royal pension which was nominally £1,000
per annum, a deduction of 2½ per cent for fees, which was a considerably higher rate than that paid by the Guards.[1] During Fox's
tenure of the Pay Office the poundage was therefore a perfectly
reasonable deduction from the pay of the forces, and historians of
the British Army who have so roundly condemned it have done so
without properly understanding its significance. Its continuance
in the eighteenth and even the nineteenth centuries, long after the
Paymastership had ceased to be an Undertaking and when the
money for army pay was issued directly to the Paymaster by the
Treasury was, however, quite another matter.

[1] Ilchester: Official, Sir S. Fox, Army: ledger for 1672–9, f. 5. This pension,
incidentally, was paid to Fox not for his own use but for distribution to such
persons as the King should direct.

CHAPTER III

The Great Undertaking:
I. The Guards and Garrisons

WHEN FOX agreed to become 'Undertaker' for the pay of the Guards he ceased to be merely a government official and became a financier in his own right. His position was therefore different in an important respect from that of other contemporary departmental treasurers, who were also issued with government paper of rather uncertain worth which they had to convert into the funds they needed to keep their departments operating. They normally appear either to have sold their tallies outright, after which they had nothing further to do with them and no interest to pay, or, if they did use them as security for borrowing themselves, to have played the part of negotiators on the government's behalf rather than to have been borrowers on their own account as Fox was.[1] At any rate this seems to be the reason why none of the others accumulated a fortune out of their offices, even when, like Cofferer Ashburnham, they were responsible for the expenditure of sums comparable to those Fox was concerned with, and for a much longer period. As for Fox himself, though he was acting as an independent financier, he was not at first an independent source of loans for the Crown: he had no substantial resources of his own, and he was wholly reliant on the willingness of the bankers to make him advances. However, the revised terms of the Undertaking provided him with a considerable margin of profit out of which he quickly accumulated capital. For a long time, virtually everything he made was ploughed back into the Undertaking, so that his dependence on borrowed money soon began to decrease. As a larger and larger proportion of what he advanced to the forces was his own money on which he did not have to pay out any interest, so the rate at

---

[1] Fox was not, however, unique in combining the functions of departmental paymaster and independant financier if the whole seventeenth century is considered. He had a number of predecessors at least as far back as the 1620s: see below, p. 109.

which he grew richer accelerated. By the beginning of the 1670s he had already become one of the wealthiest of the 'moneyed men' of the day, although down to that time almost everything he was worth was tied up in government paper and he still had few tangible assets.

Fox was, of course, not the only man to make a fortune out of lending to the government in the later seventeenth century, and indeed the reign of Charles II was a period which offered particularly lucrative possibilities to financiers. Professor Coleman has pointed out, in his study of the East India Company director Sir John Banks, that the desperate financial straits to which the Crown was reduced in the Restoration period, and its constant need to borrow, put a great premium on liquidity, so that anyone who had large amounts of ready cash to lend could expect an extremely high rate of profit.[1] Fox's career suggests a rather different point, for he succeeded in accumulating much greater wealth than Banks although he started with less. In fact he started with virtually nothing, save the good opinion of the King and one or two of his ministers, and although this secured him his office it did not provide him with any capital with which to commence his operations in high finance. Sir Stephen's success provides a spectacular example of the rewards available to those who seized the opportunity to act as financial middlemen, as intermediaries between the government and those who possessed liquid funds, or, like the bankers, were able to mobilize them. Such people, in effect, grew rich by taking a commission for arranging loans which were provided by others. The revenue farmers, who provided large advances to the Crown against the security of the future yield of taxes which they would themselves be collecting, were also intermediaries of this type, for it is clear that they too borrowed much of their advance money; so were loan brokers such as John Knight and Bartholomew Burton in the 1690s. The need for financial middlemen existed because the government's own financial machinery was so extremely rudimentary in relation to its rapidly increasing need to borrow. There existed no institutions through which the government could raise money direct from the public, and the Crown's lack of creditworthiness in the eyes of the average investor made it very difficult to remedy the deficiency. An attempt to do so was made by Sir George Downing in the later 1660s when interest-bearing

[1] D. C. Coleman, *Sir John Banks* (Oxford, 1963), esp. Ch. II.

Treasury Orders, assignable by endorsement, were offered to anyone who would lend money; but they did not attract a great volume of funds and the experiment was effectively destroyed by the Stop of the Exchequer of January 1672.[1] The Crown was thus obliged to continue to rely almost exclusively on the bankers and other professional dealers in money, but even so, the practical problems of negotiating an endless succession of short-term loans from a wide circle of monied men were beyond its administrative capacity. The Treasury itself could, and did, arrange loans from a few of the greatest lenders, such as the Corporation of the City of London, the East India Company, and the most prominent goldsmith bankers, but for dealing with the rest unavoidably it relied on the services of intermediaries. Bankers and moneyed men, moreover, often preferred to lend to individual intermediaries rather than direct to the government. One of the most important reasons for this was that if the Crown defaulted on its debts, the lender had no remedy against it, since a subject could not sue his sovereign for debt or anything else, and in the last resort, the Crown's bond was thus worth nothing.[2] Unless they were able to insist on the deposit of jewels or bullion, lenders to the Crown itself could never receive a real security for their loans until the practice of funding developed, that is charging payments of interest and repayments of principal onto specific sources of tax revenue under the authority of a parliamentary statute. Funding, however, was not adopted as a general practice until after 1688, although it was used in a number of isolated instances before that date, and until it was it tended to be safer to lend to individuals. A private person who defaulted could be taken before the courts, the bonds he had given could be put in suit against him, and there was at least a chance that the money might be recovered from his private estate and that of his co-guarantors. Further, bankers probably found that tallies issued to a man with political influence within the government were liable to be paid sooner than those issued directly to themselves, which might be given a very low priority when it came to deciding the order of redemption.[3] Lending to an intermediary whose financial

---

[1] For the Order system see references cited in note 1, p. 48.

[2] R. Ashton, *The Crown and the Money Market 1603–1640* (Oxford, 1960), pp. 9–10.

[3] Another purpose which the introduction of the Order system in the later 1660s was intended to serve was to remove the fear in the minds of potential lenders that their prospects of repayment would be jeopardized by their lack of

services were highly valued by the Crown was thus the best way to ensure that loans did not remain outstanding for dangerously long periods.

As Fox became more firmly established as a financier, so the scale of his operations grew. In the early days of the Undertaking the pay of the forces for which he was responsible amounted to about £133,000 a year, but it did not long remain at this level.[1] Increases derived partly from permanent additions to the establishment of the Guards, partly from an extension of his responsibilities to include the pay of the garrison troops, and partly from short-lived but substantial expansions of the armed forces in times of war. The first major addition to the Guards came very soon after the agreement with the officers had been concluded, for when Dunkirk was sold to the French late in 1662 the troops which had been stationed there were formed into a new regiment, under the command of Lord Wentworth, and their pay added some £24,000 a year to Fox's concerns. However, after about a year the component companies of this new unit were dispersed amongst the various garrison towns and castles, and therefore came to be paid in the same way as most of the other garrison troops, that is, not by Fox but directly by the Exchequer through their respective governors or commanders.[2] Another substantial addition was made to the strength of the Guards during the Second Dutch War. Early in the hostilities two new regiments, which came to be known as the Lord Admiral's and the Holland regiments, were raised in order to provide soldiers to serve with the fleet.[3] For this reason their pay came to them from the Treasurer of the Navy, but from May 1667 Fox took over from him, and though after the war they too were mostly sent to garrison duties, by that time Sir Stephen had become Paymaster of the Garrisons as well, and so they remained within his sphere. It should be explained that there were more than thirty garrisons, mostly coastal or island fortresses. Most of them had fairly small establishments, but there were a few large ones at important places like Berwick, Hull, Portsmouth, and Plymouth.

---

political influence. Orders were all numbered and repayment in strict numerical sequence was guaranteed. See references cited in note 1, p. 48.

[1] £123,000 odd for the Guards and £10,250 for the garrison of Portsmouth. See below, p. 44.

[2] B.L., Add. MS. 28082, f. 41.

[3] Fortescue, *History of the British Army*, i. 295–7; P.R.O., A.O. 1/48/12.

They were manned by infantry companies specifically raised for this duty, independent of any regimental organization, and not normally available for service elsewhere, or, in the case of the smaller forts, simply by a few gunners. The garrison forces in the latter part of 1663 consisted of 697 officers and artillerymen and 4,181 men, whose total pay was some £75,000 a year, which may be compared to the 374 officers and 3,200 men of the Guards regiments (excluding Lord Wentworth's), whose pay came to £123,000 a year.[1] From the beginning, the largest garrison, Portsmouth, whose pay amounted to about £10,250 a year, had been included in the Undertaking, but it was not until the Second Dutch War that Fox assumed responsibility for paying any of the other important ones.[2] Possibly the motive for changing the arrangements at this time was to improve the reliability of key strongholds by ensuring that their pay, which had hitherto often been seriously in arrears, should be issued to them promptly. At any rate, Fox took over payments of the garrison in the Scilly islands from June 1664; Berwick from August 1665; Jersey from October 1665; Guernsey from November 1665; and the Isle of Wight from August 1666. Finally, from Michaelmas 1667 he became Paymaster for virtually all the remaining garrisons, except the Cinque Ports which remained outside his ken for a few years more.[3] One good reason for this final step was that by the later 1660s the distinction between the Guards on the one hand and the garrisons on the other, which was very clear when Fox was first appointed, was becoming increasingly blurred, as the old-style garrison forces were repeatedly reduced in numbers and replaced by detachments from regiments on the Guards' establishment. The combined payroll of the land forces paid by Sir Stephen was £188,581 per annum in September 1668 when they consisted of 7,650 officers and men, but piecemeal additions over the following few years raised the numbers to 8,946 by the beginning of 1672. By that time, Fox's responsibilities had reached the level of £223,000 per annum.[4]

The exigencies of wartime naturally led the government to make

---

[1] B.L., Add. MS. 28082, f. 41.

[2] Fox was appointed Receiver and Paymaster of the garrison at Portsmouth, with a salary of £100 a year, in February 1662. *C.S.P.D.*, 1661–2, p. 279; P.R.O., A.O. 1/309/1214.

[3] P.R.O., A.O. 1/48/12, 14, and E. 351/366; B.L., Add. MSS. 28077, f. 110, 28082, ff. 55–6.

[4] B.L., Add. MS. 28082, ff. 43–4, 63.

sharply increased demands of the Paymaster, as extra troops had to be raised, sometimes at very short notice. We have seen that the two new regiments called into being at the beginning of the Second Dutch War were not at first paid by Sir Stephen, and the only other increase in the land forces before the middle of 1666 was an expansion in the size of some of the existing units. However, the entry of France into the war at the beginning of that year raised the possibility that an invasion might be attempted, and this led the government to levy eighteen troops of horse and to maintain them throughout the late summer and early autumn at a cost of some £18,324. France's involvement also meant the return of a regiment of Scottish soldiers, under Lord Douglas, which had been serving the French Crown. This unit was added to the establishment in June 1666 and remained in existence until the end of the war, by which time they had received pay totalling £23,991. Moreover, 1667 saw another and more serious invasion scare. The success of the Dutch attack on the fleet at Chatham in June produced something of a panic: a new army of no less than thirty-seven troops of horse and twelve regiments of foot was hastily raised, and further additions made to the Horse Guards and some of the existing foot regiments. In fact peace was signed at the end of July, and two months later all these extra forces had already been disbanded, but even so they had cost £45,527. Altogether, the expansion in the size of the army during the war had involved an increase in Fox's concerns of well over £130,000, almost all of which accrued in the fifteen months between June 1666 and September 1667.[1]

The Third Dutch War of 1672–4 produced a considerably more prolonged, and consequently much more expensive, increase in the land forces since on this occasion the purpose was not to deter invasion but actually to undertake offensive operations on the Continent. In March 1672 a regiment of dragoons and a new regiment of foot were raised, in July another regiment of foot, and at the beginning of 1673 eight more regiments whose strength was substantially increased later in the year. Together with additions to existing units this brought the establishment to a temporary peak of £471,731. 3s. 1d. per annum by the summer of 1673, and, although there were some reductions in the autumn, most of these

[1] B.L., Add. MS. 51319, f. 17: minutes of Privy Council meeting, 22 June 1666; P.R.O., A.O. 1/48/11, 12; C.S.P.D., 1665–6, pp. 475–6, 489, 490, 1667, pp. 178–83.

troops remained in pay until March 1674. In fact, Fox's Undertaking did not increase to quite this degree because he was not
required to pay the forces sent abroad. The projected invasion of
Zeeland never took place, but nearly 3,500 officers and men of
various regiments did go to France in 1673 and so were removed
from Sir Stephen's care.[1] Even so, Sir Stephen's financial requirement rose from some £39,850 per muster in the latter part of 1671
to £59,650 in the first half of 1673,[2] and Table I, which provides
a summary of his military payments, shows clearly that these were
the years when the flow of money through his hands to the army
reached its highest level. In the middle of the 1670s, after the war
was over for England and the Guards and garrisons had been returned to a peacetime footing, the establishment was once again
at or even slightly below what it had been at the beginning of the
decade, that is between £200,000 and £210,000 per annum.[3]

The growing scale of Fox's financial dealings with the government was not wholly accounted for by the periodic additions to
his responsibilities as Paymaster, and well before the end of the
1660s he was also making advances to the Crown for purposes
other than the forces, particularly towards the expenses of the
Household and Secret Service, both of which he was involved in
as a spending official. The main source of information about these
non-military advances is a volume in which Sir Stephen kept a
record of the Treasury Orders he received between the end of
1667 and the end of 1671.[4] Some reference has already been made
to the introduction of these Orders in the later 1660s. They represented an important innovation in government finance as, under
the influence of Sir George Downing, the Treasury moved from
the rather haphazard anticipation of the future yield of the revenue
by means of tallies which had hitherto prevailed, to a more systematic method of raising short-term credit. Unlike tallies, which
were presented for payment to the receiver of the branch of the
revenue on which they were charged, Orders received payment at
the Exchequer itself, and an even more important difference was

[1] B.L., Add. MS. 28082, ff. 45, 47, 57, 65; P.R.O., W.O. 24/3, and A.O. 1/49/20, 21, 22.

[2] Ilchester: Official, Sir S. Fox, Army (box 273): interest account for money advanced to the forces, 1671–4.

[3] B.L., Add. MS. 28082, ff. 87, 99; P.R.O., A.O. 1/50/23.

[4] Ilchester: Official, Sir S. Fox, Customs and Excise (box 271): volume entitled 'Account of Orders Received from the Excheqr . . .'

TABLE I

The Undertaking of the Army: Money paid to the Forces by Sir Stephen Fox, 1662–1675

(£. s. d.)

	Guards	Wartime forces	Portsmouth	Other garrisons	Arrears to forces not thitherto paid by Fox
1662–3	224,099 7. 3.			—	4,377 18. 8.
1663–4				—	17,488 16. 6.
1664–5	367,360 10. 11¾.	20,132 9. 6.	58,270 2. 4.		
1665–6				46,984 14. 0.	
1666–7	235,096 0. 9½.		66,680 15. 0.		
1667–8	117,237 7. 4½.				
1668–9		188,985 2. 11.			
1669–70		192,266 13. 1.			
1670–1		208,213 7. 10.			
1671–2		259,511 14. 8½.			
1672–3		379,105 10. 9.			
1673–4 (1½ yrs)		350,386 19. 7¼.			
1675		207,837 5. 4.			2,606 14. 2.
TOTAL					2,946,641 10. 9¼.

Sources: P.R.O., A.O. 1/48/9–16, 49/17–22, 50/23, 309/1214; E.351/64, 353, 364, 366.

that they were numbered and payment in strict numerical sequence was guaranteed. The holders of Orders thus had a fairly good idea of when they would get their money, and did not have to fear that official interference, or the more urgent claims of a rival creditor, would lead to any postponement. Orders given to those who actually lent money into the Exchequer bore interest at 6 per cent, which was paid at six-monthly intervals, but those issued to departmental treasurers, which they were expected to turn into cash by assigning to bankers or otherwise, did not carry interest.[1] The moneyed men who made advances against the security of departmental Orders of course received interest, and at a higher rate, but they obtained it by a different procedure which involved the submission of a carefully calculated interest account and its scrutiny by the King's auditor. When the account was eventually allowed by the Treasury, additional Orders would be issued to cover the amount owing, and these in turn would accumulate interest until they were paid. In many cases these claims for interest came directly from the bankers, but Fox and certain other departmental treasurers who raised loans in their own names and then re-lent to the government, normally settled the bankers' demands themselves, so that the interest accounts presented to the Treasury came from them, not from those who had supplied them with funds.[2]

The new system of short-term borrowing by means of Orders was applied to one source of revenue after another from 1665 onwards, and the book in which Sir Stephen noted the details of those which passed through his hands provides an almost, but probably not quite, complete summary of his financial dealings with the government during the four years with which it deals.[3] It records that between December 1667 and December 1671 he received Orders worth £1,200,448, mostly charged on the Excise

[1] The best accounts of the Order system will be found in Chandaman, *English Public Revenue*, Appendix I, pp. 295–300; and H. G. Roseveare, 'The Advancement of the King's Credit, 1660–1673' (Univ. of Cambridge, Ph.D. thesis 1962), pp. 49–53. See also Roseveare's *The Treasury* (London, 1969), pp. 61–2.

[2] Some of Fox's interest accounts were transcribed in full into the volumes in which authorizations for the issue of money from the Exchequer were entered, see for instance P.R.O., E. 403/2572, ff. 86–9ᵛ, 2575, ff. 1–44, 2995, ff. 12–25.

[3] Orders of Loan to the value of £1,750 in 1670–1 and £3,692 in 1671–2 are certainly omitted from Fox's account of the Treasury Orders he received: P.R.O., E. 403/2575, ff. 1–3. These have been included in the Tables and all subsequent discussions take them into account, but it is highly likely that there are other minor omissions which it has not been possible to make good.

and the receipts from the sale of the Crown's fee farm rents, with smaller amounts on the Customs and various other funds. However, £72,810 of these Orders were on account of interest accrued on earlier lending, and so must be omitted in order to arrive at a figure of £1,137,638 which Fox received to cover new lendings in the years in question. Of this amount, as Table II shows, £841,146, or almost three-quarters (73·9 per cent), represents advances to the forces, and the remaining £286,492 (26·1 per cent), loans for other purposes. A small fraction of the latter were indeed not strictly speaking loans to the government at all. £33,450 worth of Orders came to Sir Stephen by the assignment of the various persons to whom they had originally been issued, and were accepted by him as security for private advances. Much the most important of these were made to the Duke of Monmouth, whose financial affairs were at this time being managed by Sir Stephen at the King's request, and the Duke assigned £31,200 in Orders between 1668 and 1670, thereby turning Charles's paper largesse into ready cash. Fox was also beginning to lend substantial sums to private borrowers on other types of security by this time, but it is not until after 1672 that a clear picture of this aspect of his finances emerges.

The year in which Fox's non-military loans to the government reached their highest level was 1668–9, when the Orders he accepted against such advances soared from only £14,500 in 1667–8 to no less than £120,300. This enormous increase was wholly accounted for by a vast expansion in the scale of Sir Stephen's dealings with the Cofferer of the Household, from which he received £115,000 worth of Orders. £5,000 of these related to a transaction left over from before Michaelmas 1668, but all the rest were Fox's security for advancing £100,000, paid over in numerous small instalments, which was enough to cover all or almost all the expenditure of the Cofferer's department for an entire year. Fox did not make any comparable loans to the Cofferer in the years immediately following, nor was the big loan of 1668–9 renewed or extended, and in later years he reverted to his earlier status of occasional supplier of credit. Why he should have assumed responsibility for meeting virtually the entire financial needs of the Household for one year, but for one year only, is a little mystifying, but the probable explanation is that Cofferer Ashburnham unexpectedly found himself unable to raise funds on his Orders in his usual way. It emerges that he had not been keeping his accounts with

TABLE II

Treasury Orders received by Sir Stephen Fox, 1667–1671

Orders[1] (£. s. d.) issued on account of:	1667–8[2]	1668–9	1669–70	1670–1	1671–2[3]	TOTALS	
Guards and Garrisons	208,757	177,999	207,303	181,638	65,449	841,146	841,146
Cofferer of the Household	8,500	115,000	—	—	8,000	131,500	
Secret Service	6,000	5,000	—	10,000	—	21,000	
Other government departments	—	300	150	—	—	450	
London Excise Farmers	—	—	26,218	14,000	—	40,218	286,492
Orders of Loan	—	—	18,286	30,296	11,292	59,874	
Duke of Monmouth	7,000	1,800	22,400	—	—	31,200	
Other private persons	2,250	—	—	—	—	2,250	
Interest due to Fox	12,810	14,500	25,500	20,000	—	72,810	72,810
	245,317	314,599	299,857	255,934	84,741	1,200,448	1,200,448

[1] All sums given to the nearest pound.
[2] The years run from Michaelmas to Michaelmas, save for 1671–2.
[3] Up to the Stop of the Exchequer only.
Sources: Ilchester: Official, Sir S. Fox, Customs and Excise (box 271): 'Account of Orders Received from the Excheqr . . .'. P.R.O., E. 403/2575, ff. 1–3. See also n. 3 on p. 48.

sufficient care, and in particular had failed to take dated receipts for the money he had paid out, so that when he presented them to the auditor for his approval the latter refused to pass them. This must certainly have precipitated a crisis in the financing of the Household, for if there was any possibility that Ashburnham might have to pay part of the expenses of his department out of his own pocket, or even that he would not be reimbursed the full interest on money he had borrowed, either of which would probably have ruined him, it must certainly have destroyed his credit with the bankers, and so have prevented him from raising any more money in his own name. Eventually, the Treasury Lords satisfied themselves that no money had gone astray, and that all payments had been made at the times Ashburnham asserted they had, and, presumably on their recommendation, the Privy Council agreed that his accounts should be allowed 'notwithstanding the defects of vouchers by reason the said Cofferer had not kept his books and legiers in a more exact and punctuall manner'. However, a delay of several months had been involved, and the continued functioning of the Household would have been in jeopardy, if Ashburnham had not been able to fall back on the now soundly established financial contacts and skills of his colleague on the Board of Green Cloth. Of course, most of the money Fox lent was not his own, any more than was most of what he advanced to the forces, and it had to be borrowed in the same way. Nor was there any question of 'poundage' on the money, but Sir Stephen ensured a margin of profit for himself, over and above the interest he had to pay out, by taking the Cofferer's Orders at a 10 per cent discount, which increased the nominal 10 per cent interest he received to over 11 per cent in real terms.[1]

In 1668–9 Fox had demonstrated that his ability to raise funds on the money market was sufficiently good to enable him to supply the Household as well as the forces, but for the next few years Ashburnham was once more able to manage on his own, and the total of Sir Stephen's non-military advances returned to a much lower level, though still well above that of 1667–8. Thus in 1669–70 and 1670–1 he accepted £44,454 and £51,946 worth of Orders by way of security, and it is unlikely that he was allowed a discount on any of them. A large proportion of these were assigned to him by the farmers of the London Excise, though unfortunately the

[1] P.R.O., E. 403/2610, ff. 177ᵛ–178ᵛ, 2611, ff. 11ᵛ–12, 1612, ff. 130 et seq.

circumstances in which he was lending them money are hidden from us. It is, however, possible that the sums involved represent payments which the farmers had, at the government's behest, agreed to make to Sir Stephen, but which in the event they had been unable to afford when they fell due, and that in effect Sir Stephen in his private capacity was lending money to himself in his public capacity.[1] Such a complexity, it may be said, would be very characteristic of the involved nature of government finance at this period. If this assumption were correct then the loans to the farmers (£26,218 in 1669–70 and £14,000 in 1670–1) should properly be added to the total of Fox's military advances. Some of the other Orders he received on account of his non-military loans were, as Table II shows, not departmental ones like those given him by the Excise farmers, by the Cofferer, or to cover his advances on account of Secret Service, but were Orders of Loan which represent his securities for cash actually paid into the Exchequer. The sums lent in this way, nearly £60,000 in only two and a quarter years, were substantial in absolute terms, although amounting to only a very small fraction of his total advances. After the end of 1671 Sir Stephen's book of Treasury Orders received no longer provides any guide to the extent of his non-military loans, and for a year or two it is difficult to discover what fresh ones he made. However, during 1673 he again began to assume a major responsibility for advancing the money required for the Household and, from late in 1674, he was financing both the Household and the Chamber in full, besides making substantial contributions to the needs of other departments and aspects of government expenditure. We shall look at the circumstances in which this final expansion in the scope of his financial concerns took place in more detail later on. Here it is enough to note that the annual budget of the Household was some £90,000 a year in the mid-1670s and that of the Chamber some £30,000 a year.[2] The advances they required thus meant that, despite the reduction in the size of the army at the end of the Third Dutch War, the financial demands on Sir Stephen remained at a very high level right down to the moment of his sudden and unexpected dismissal as Paymaster at the beginning of 1676.[3] His ledger shows that the sum total of payments he was having to make

---

[1] Some support for this interpretation is to be found in P.R.O., E. 403/2575, f. 33, where interest on the £14,000 loan of 1670 is calculated.
[2] See below, p. 100.   [3] See below, pp. 104–6.

increased from an average of £31,511 a month during the last eight months of 1672, to £46,562 a month during 1673, and then remained at this level throughout 1674 and 1675, when they averaged £44,581 and £45,491 respectively. During each of the three years 1673, 1674, and 1675, Fox's payments on all accounts, including his non-government business, well exceeded half a million pounds sterling![1] This was an enormous turnover for a single financier, for the whole of government's annual expenditure in peacetime was never more than £1½ m. in the 1670s.[2]

However, the total amount of Fox's advances to the Crown outstanding at any one time was not only determined by the size of the departmental expenditure he was financing: it also depended on the length of time which elapsed before he was reimbursed. Indeed, the latter was no less important than the former, for if the government's repayments became less prompt then the outstanding total of his loans would inevitably grow larger even without any new responsibilities, whilst, contrarily, a more rapid turnover would enable him to finance a larger part of government expenditure without a corresponding increase in the total amount lent. The intervals between the issue of revenue assignments and their final redemption seem to have been particularly long during and immediately after the Second Dutch War, and again on the eve of the Stop of the Exchequer in January 1672, but to have been considerably shorter in the period after the Stop, although there were always considerable differences in the extent of the delays between one source of revenue and another, since some were very much more heavily anticipated than others and some extraordinary sources were hardly anticipated at all. It should also be noted that Fox's assignments were almost always paid to him in instalments over a period of several weeks, or even several months, so that he received part repayment of his advances within a shorter period than the final redemption dates of his tallies and Orders would suggest. Nevertheless, a comparison of these at different periods illustrates the way in which the duration of his loans to the government varied from time to time. His interest account for advances made to the Guards between September 1664 and September 1666 shows that his tallies were rarely repaid in full in less than a year

---

[1] Ilchester: Official, Sir S. Fox, Army: ledger for 1672-9, cash account commencing f. 95.
[2] Chandaman, *English Public Revenue*, pp. 354-5, 358-9.

at that time, and sometimes not for eighteen months or more. The quickest repayment recorded in this account was 288 days on tallies on the London Excise for £33,964. 15s. 0d., which were struck on 20 August 1666, and of which the last instalment was received on 4 June 1667. By contrast the slowest was one year and 279 days on tallies on the Country Excise, struck on 23 February 1665 but not fully redeemed until 1 December 1666.[1] In fact, the periods during which the advances remained outstanding were even longer than these delays suggest. Tallies were not struck until anything from two weeks to three months after the end of the muster to which they related, and a considerable proportion of Fox's payments in each muster consisted of 'subsistence money', which had to be made weekly during the two-month period. It was therefore sometimes nearly two years before his loans were completely reimbursed. On the other hand, many of the extra payments which he was put to at this time on account of forces specially raised for the Dutch War seem to have been reimbursed to him very much more quickly, which was possible because the money was paid to him partly out of the loans made by others on the credit of the parliamentary taxes voted to meet the costs of the war, and partly out of other sources of ready cash such as the receipts from the sale of naval prizes.[2] This meant that, despite the length of time which the loans on account of the regular part of the Undertaking remained unpaid, Fox was nevertheless able to support a temporary expansion in its scope without having to raise an impossibly large volume of new funds at very short notice, and at a time when credit was extremely tight.

The delays before Fox received full payment of the assignments made to him at the end of 1667 and during 1668 were, in general, considerably shorter than those revealed by the interest account for money advanced in 1664–6. However, by the latter part of 1669, and throughout 1670, they were once again almost as great, and he was often having to wait up to eighteen months before he received back the last of the money. On the other hand, the Treasury Orders in use at this time were issued more promptly than tallies had been, so that the whole period from actual advance to

[1] P.R.O., E. 403/2572, ff. 86–9ᵛ; Ilchester: Official, Sir S. Fox, Army: interest account for 1664–6.
[2] Ilchester: Official, Sir S. Fox, Army: account book relating to payment of troops during the Second Dutch War.

final repayment was still usually rather shorter. But delays in the redemption of Orders were steadily increasing, and some of those which had been issued to Sir Stephen towards the end of March 1670 were still unpaid more than twenty-one months later in January 1672. After the Stop of the Exchequer the revenue was no longer so heavily burdened with interest on old debts, and so could be applied to the rapid discharge of new ones. The assignments on the thitherto grossly over-anticipated Country Excise which Fox received during 1672 were almost all paid during the course of the same year, though a few of them were not redeemed until after the middle of 1673.[1] For the remaining years of his Paymastership, Sir Stephen's accounts do not enable us to measure the extent of the delays he experienced in getting money from the Exchequer, but although they certainly tended to increase once again in the mid 1670s, they were never again as prolonged as they had been earlier on.

It is much easier to trace the gradual expansion of Fox's role as a financial intermediary between the Crown and the money market than it is to ascertain the total sum which he was lending at any one time, let alone to trace in detail the fluctuations in the size of the government's debt to him. Whether Sir Stephen ever kept any formal accounts which brought together all his outstanding advances to the Crown, and provided a general statement of his financial position in respect of government lending, is very doubtful; but if he did they have not survived, and in their absence any precise reconstruction is impossible. What have survived are a series of very detailed calculations of the interest due to him on his military and part of his non-military lending, and these, together with his account of the Treasury Orders he received between 1667 and 1671, do provide a basis for estimating the approximate amount owed to him over a considerable part of his Paymastership.[2] The interpretation of the figures yielded by these two sources poses considerable problems, and the estimates given in Table III are certainly subject to a margin of error, but it is reasonably safe to say that if anything they are too low rather than too high, and that except in the case of the totals for January 1674 the extent of the error is unlikely to be more than £10,000 or £20,000 at most, which is a small percentage of the sums involved.

[1] Ilchester: 'Account of Orders Received from the Excheqr . . .', doc. cit.
[2] These sources are listed at the foot of Table III on p. 56.

Taking the estimates as they stand, we find that they do bear out Fox's own statement that his Undertaking 'could not well be managed' with less than £200,000 or even £300,000,[1] for his outstanding military advances alone had approached the former figure before the end of the 1660s and the latter figure by the time

TABLE III

Estimates of the Government's Debt to Sir Stephen Fox,
1666–1676

(£. s. d.)

	Military loans	Other loans	Interest unpaid	Total
Sept. 1666	167,200	?	?	?
Jan. 1669	188,000	27,500	14,500	230,000
Jan. 1670	224,100	121,900	14,500	360,500
Jan. 1671	284,600	82,500	25,500	392,600
Jan. 1672	281,500	61,300	20,000	362,800
Jan. 1673	262,300	46,500	Interest included in loan totals	308,800
Jan. 1674	225,800	22,300*		248,100*
Jan. 1675	321,400	?		?
Jan. 1676		? 445,000		? 445,000

* These figures are certainly incomplete.

Sources: Ilchester: Official, Sir S. Fox, Army (box 273): interest accounts for military advances for 1665–6 and 1671–5; ibid.: Official, Sir S. Fox, Customs and Excise (box 271): volume containing 'Account of Orders Received from the Excheqr . . .'; P.R.O., E. 403/2510, ff. 102–4, 2572, ff. 86–9ᵛ, 2575, f. 1 et seq.; S.P. 29/302, item 53, 29/335, items 24–6.

of the Stop of the Exchequer. The total sum owed to him by the government was increasing rapidly in these years, partly because the intervals between the issue and redemption of Orders was getting longer, and partly because of the massive financial support he had provided for the Household in 1668–9, until by the beginning of 1671 it was approaching £400,000. A year later, at the time of the Stop of the Exchequer, it had fallen somewhat to £362,800, mainly because his £100,000 loan to the Cofferer had been finally paid off. After the Stop, the much more rapid repayment of

[1] B.L., Add. MS. 51324, f. 40ᵛ: document headed 'A short acctt of ye birth, liffe, and alliances of Sr Stephen Fox . . .'

revenue assignments led to a further and much heavier drop in the sum outstanding to about £273,600 by July 1672, but thereafter it began to rise once again. The increase in the figure for military loans alone to £321,400 by the beginning of 1675 reflects the expansion of the land forces in the Third Dutch War and the reappearance of delays at the Exchequer. During 1675 the Crown's military debt to Sir Stephen may not have increased by much, but the non-military debt grew enormously as he took on the financing of both the Household and the Chamber, and when he was dismissed as Paymaster at the beginning of 1676 the sum owed to him was almost certainly greater than ever before. Two months later, in March 1676, £250,580 was still outstanding on account of advances made since September 1674, and in the meanwhile several tens of thousands had been paid to him. To this must be added what was owing from before September 1674, most of which had originally been advanced before the Stop, seemingly about £125,000; and interest not included in either of the above sums amounted to something further. All in all, Sir Stephen's claim that he was 'out' £445,000 at the height of his involvement in government finance does not seem to have involved much, if any, exaggeration.[1]

Fox had assumed the Undertaking for the pay of the Guards because none of the established financiers had been willing to do so, but he could not have even attempted it unless he had had assurances of support from some of them. In the beginning his own resources were negligible and his dependence on the bankers almost total. With the passage of time this dependence became less complete, but throughout his career as Paymaster the good relationships he had established with them remained the key factor in his ability to raise large sums for the government. He quickly proved to be an exemplary borrower. He added his own security which, even at the beginning when he was not a rich man, was worth something because of the flow of money through his hands from the poundage, and became progressively more valuable as he grew in wealth. He also paid the interest on his loans himself, and paid it promptly, whilst on other loans the government's creditors had to spend long

---

[1] Ibid. Elsewhere Fox states that he was in debt 'above £400,000' at the time of his dismissal. B.L., Add. MS. 51324, f. 54: document headed 'Losses sustained by Sr Ste Fox . . .'

hours soliciting at the Treasury.[1] In addition, there can be little doubt that he cultivated good relations with the bankers on a personal level, that his well-bred courtesy and his charm, the 'fair demeanour' to which many contemporaries bear witness, was a further reason why they were so constantly ready to help him.[2] Nevertheless, over and above these good relations and Fox's own punctiliousness about matters of business, there was another factor which goes far to explain his success in mobilizing funds. This was that Fox was more likely than most other departmental treasurers, or others seeking loans on behalf of the Crown, to get his tallies paid at an early date, partly because behind him stood the Lord General, George Monk, Duke of Albemarle, who was enormously influential in the King's counsels, and partly because the dangers of an unpaid army were such that the Treasury necessarily had to give the revenue assignments issued to him a high priority. In other words, by lending money to Fox, the bankers were able to ensure a more rapid turnover of funds than could be had from most other government borrowers. That Fox's tallies were regarded by them as first-class securities is borne out by the fact he apparently never needed to allow his creditors a discount on them, although most of his fellow treasurers were often obliged to do so.

The first banker with whom Fox established contact after the Restoration was Francis Meynall, who was apparently as willing to deal with Charles II's courtiers as he had been to provide financial services for the republican governments of the 1650s. It was with Meynall that Fox directed should be deposited the large sums of cash allocated to him for Secret Service in the autumn of 1660, and through him that he subsequently made payments out of the money, giving the intended recipients an 'assignment' on the banker (in effect a cheque), and leaving them to make their own arrangements to collect what was due to them. In short, from the first Fox kept a current account with Meynall, thereby greatly reducing his need to store and handle money in a physical sense, which was not only risky but, where large sums were involved, a laborious and time-consuming process. When he took over responsibility for paying the Guards at the beginning of 1661 he was

[1] Ilchester: Family (box 237): autobiography in small volume with green cover.
[2] *Pepys*, i. 286, 299; *Diary of John Evelyn* (ed. E. S. De Beer, 6 vols., Oxford, 1955), iv. 217–19; A. Grey, *Debates in the House of Commons 1667–1694* (10 vols., London, 1763), vii. 318.

still making much use of Meynall, and he continued to do so throughout the first half of that year, employing him to make military payments on his behalf as formerly he had made Secret Service ones. However, he gradually came to have less and less to do with him, and more and more to do with a group of other bankers, Edward Backwell, Sir Thomas Vyner, and John Colville. During 1661 and 1662 these three successively became involved in the business of paying out money to the forces, and what is more important, they were soon not only making payments out of cash deposited with them, but doing so in advance of receiving cash. In other words they were lending Fox the money he was using to pay the Guards.[1]

There is much that remains obscure about the details of Fox's dealings with the bankers at this stage, but the general outline of their relationship is clear enough.[2] For several years Alderman Backwell played much the largest role in Fox's affairs, which was perhaps not surprising for he had been deeply involved in the financing of the large English garrison at Dunkirk since its capture by Cromwell in 1657, so that it was a natural development of his existing business that he should take a large share in providing the funds for the forces at home.[3] Fortunately his ledgers have survived, and although the entries in them are not always sufficiently explicit for the nature of the transactions to which they refer to be apparent, the amounts passing through Fox's account indicate the scale of their dealings. These were at their height in the years 1663 to 1665, as Table IV shows. In the two years down to Lady Day 1665 Backwell's payments to Fox or at his order must, when the missing three months are taken into account, have considerably exceeded £200,000. His total advances were not quite so large since the account sometimes stood in credit, but certainly most of these payments must have represented loans. Since the total pay

---

[1] Ilchester: Official, Sir S. Fox, Army: day-book for 1660–4.

[2] The main sources of information are Sir Stephen's day-books, in which he recorded all his receipts and payments in summary form, and the ledgers of the banker Backwell. The day-books cover the years 1660–4, 1666–70, 1670–2, and 1672–9 (reference as in the previous note), but the ledgers to which they refer have all been lost save for that covering the last of these periods. Backwell's ledgers are the property of Williams and Glyn's Bank and are kept at 67 Lombard Street, London. The series run from 1663 (ledger I) to 1671 (ledger T), but ledgers K and N are missing: each volume is indexed.

[3] R. D. Richards, *The Early History of Banking in England* (London, 1929), pp. 32–3.

TABLE IV

Stephen Fox's Account with Edward Backwell, 1663–1666

(£. s. d.)

	Credit	Debit	Allowed to Backwell Interest	Expenses
Lady Day 1663 to 31 Dec. 1663	} 9 months 66,663 13. 1.*	73,328 11. 9.	1,775 9. 3.	520 0. 0.
1 Jan. 1664 to Lady Day 1664	} 3 months	Ledger missing	Ledger missing	
Lady Day 1664 to Mich. 1664	} 6 months 63,628 3. 10.*	63,459 13. 3.	7,580 12. 2.	—
Mich. 1664 to Lady Day 1665	} 6 months 71,603 6. 8.	56,530 17. 10.	—	—
Lady Day 1665 to Mich. 1665	} 6 months	Ledger missing	Ledger missing	
Mich. 1665 to Midsummer 1666	} 9 months 3,550 0. 0.	13,329 12. 0.	1,310 8. 0.	—

* Excluding credit balances brought forward from the previous account.
Source: Williams and Glyn's Bank archives: Backwell's ledgers I, L, M, and O.

of the troops for which Fox was responsible came to some £300,000 during the same period,[1] and he was not making any other large advances at this early stage of his career, it becomes clear that Backwell was by far his most important source of finance. Most of the payments that Backwell made on his behalf were either to army officers and regimental agents, to his assistant Richard Kent, or to other financiers with whom he had dealings. As mentioned, most, though not all, of these payments represented expenditure of the advances which the banker had agreed to make, and the credit side

[1] P.R.O., A.O. 1/48/10, 11.

of the account records how they were repaid. Thus between Lady Day and Michaelmas 1664 £63,628. 3s. 10d. was credited to Fox's account in the form of ten tallies on the farmers of the London Excise struck on various dates between 23 March and 22 August for a total of £50,485. 13s. 4d., two tallies on the farmers of the Customs for £6,160. 8s. 0d., three tallies on the Commissioners of the Country Excise for £6,182. 2s. 6d., and £1,050 from various persons in cash.[1] All these tallies had been issued to Fox to cover the payment of the forces over the preceding few musters, and he had assigned them to Backwell to provide him with security. No money would be forthcoming from those on whom the tallies had been struck for many months to come, but when payment was finally made the advances thus secured would automatically be liquidated. Until that time Backwell would charge Fox interest for what he had lent. The amounts of interest which accumulated on Backwell's advances were very considerable, as Table IV shows, but unfortunately neither the ledgers nor Fox's day-books give much indication of how the figures were arrived at. There are, however, a few instances in which the rate of interest which Fox paid is explicitly stated or can be inferred from the details given. At the end of 1663 interest on money Backwell had advanced earlier in the year was calculated at only 6 per cent, and amounted to some £1,775, but the real rate allowed him was considerably higher, for on top of this Fox paid £500 by way of 'voluntary aditionall consideration'. Nine months later, in September 1664, the calculation was based on interest at '6 and 4' according to Backwell's ledger, that is 10 per cent.[2] Six per cent was the maximum rate allowed by law, but throughout much of Charles II's reign it was impossible for the government to attract the funds it needed at that rate and an additional 2 or 4 per cent 'reward' or 'gratuity' had to be allowed to major lenders. In the early 1660s, when tallies were being paid within a matter of a few months, 8 per cent was still usually adequate, but by 1665 delays in payment could be as long as two years and 10 per cent had established itself as the standard rate for government borrowers.[3] Fox was no exception to this rule and in the late 1660s and early 1670s was still

[1] Backwell's ledger L, ff. 178, 414, 465, 538, 598.
[2] Ilchester: Official, Sir S. Fox, Army: day-book for 1660–4, under 29 Dec. 1663 and 30 Sept. 1664; Backwell's ledger L, f. 598.
[3] Roseveare, 'Advancement of the King's Credit', pp. 11, 38–9.

paying 10 per cent, or occasionally 9 per cent, to the bankers and other financiers who were then lending him money. However, if the date on which repayment could be expected was particularly remote or uncertain, or the borrower's need was particularly pressing, higher rates still might have to be offered to induce lenders to part with their funds. Thus, probably for a combination of these reasons, Fox is found to be paying Colville as much as 12 per cent on a series of loans beginning with £6,000 advanced towards the end of 1662, and concluding with £10,000 which was finally repaid in February 1664.[1]

During the early part of 1665 Backwell ceased to be Fox's principal financial support, probably because he was also deeply involved in providing money for the fleet, and the expansion of naval expenditure in the early stages of the Dutch War must have stretched his resources to the point where he was unable to continue supplying the army as well.[2] He continued to make occasional advances to Sir Stephen, but no longer on a scale commensurate with the latter's needs, and Fox was obliged to find an alternative source of credit. Neither Sir Thomas Vyner, his nephew and successor Sir Robert, nor Colville, was able, or at any rate willing, to fill the gap, and so Sir Stephen was obliged to look beyond the small coterie of bankers with whom he had hitherto almost exclusively dealt. Thus 1665 marked an important stage in Fox's own development as a financier, for it saw him becoming less dependent on just two or three major lenders and beginning to draw his funds from a very much wider circle of contacts, not all of whom were from Lombard Street. This was a sign of improvement in his own status as a borrower, and at the same time it was an increased source of strength, since it made it less likely that he could be brought down by the sudden failure of a single associate. Laurence Debusty and Jeremiah Snow, both bankers of the second rank who were fast rising to prominence, were among the most important of those Fox turned to at this time, and, from the end

---

[1] Ilchester: Official, Sir S. Fox, Army: day-book for 1660–4, under 19 Dec. 1662, 30 June 1663, 16 Apr. 1664. The 12 per cent interest was charged on a series of 'accommodation loans', one of many referred to in 1662 and 1663. These were short-term advances, often only for two months or so, apparently unsecured by any deposit of tallies, and probably always attracting a higher rate of interest than Fox's other loans, although in no other case does it emerge what he paid on them.

[2] D. K. Clark, 'Edward Backwell as Royal Agent', *Ec.H.R.*, 1938.

of 1666, they were joined by yet another goldsmith, John Lindsey. A fourth source of new loans were the farmers of the London Excise, who were lending him a regular £4,500 a month during much of 1666, and a fifth was John Ball, Cashier of the Excise.[1] Ball may have been lending money personally, but it is more likely that he was doing so on behalf of the Excise Commissioners. The Commissioners themselves were a group of financiers appointed by the Crown to exercise administrative and judicial control over the collection of the Excise duties, and to whom the farmers paid over their quarterly instalments of rent. It may well have been out of the balances of Excise money which they held in their hands for a time before they paid it into the Exchequer that the Commissioners, or their Cashier, were able to lend money to Fox.

Fox was also, more frequently than before, raising money on an occasional basis from bankers and financiers other than those whom he used regularly; and, in addition, he was beginning to borrow independently of the professional dealers in money. He had himself begun to accept deposits from private investors as early as winter 1661–2, but it was several years before the sums involved were of much significance in relation to his total financial needs. By the middle of 1666, however, he was holding £20,000 or more of such money, including £5,000 belonging to the Countess of Chesterfield, £4,500 of the Duke of Albermarle's, £2,000 of Lord Crofts's, and several other sums of £1,000 or more.[2] He had in fact come to act to some extent as a banker himself, accepting loans from one set of clients and re-lending their money, not only to the Crown but to other private clients as well, although this last aspect of his business was not yet very extensively developed. The knowledge that he was already becoming a man of some means, together with the regular flow of cash through his hands which the Undertaking necessarily involved, endowed him with sufficient credit for people, particularly those with whom he came in contact in Court circles, to entrust him with their spare money. Thus gradually Fox began to tap a source of funds which was not only independent of the goldsmith bankers and the City financiers, but was available at a considerably lower rate of interest. The bankers had to pay 5 or 6 per cent to their own depositors, and therefore

<hr />

[1] Ilchester: Official, Sir S. Fox, Army: day-book for 1664–6.

[2] Ibid.: day-books for 1664–6 and 1667–70, under 7 Apr., 11 July, 31 Dec. 1666, and *passim*.

TABLE V

Sir Stephen Fox's 'Deliveries' of Treasury Orders,[1] 1667–1671

(£. s. d.)

	1667–8	1668–9	1669–70	1670–1	1671	TOTALS	Percentages
John Lindsey	55,000	72,500	27,727	62,000	—	217,227	
Jeremiah Snow	38,756	67,829	63,131	20,000	10,000	199,716	
John Colville	25,700	61,200	—	—	—	86,900	
Sir Thomas Player	—	—	64,710	290	—	65,000	727,896 87·7
John Ball	26,275	21,196	10,106	—	—	57,577	
John Portman	6,265	30,727	19,499	—	—	56,491	
Lawrence Debusty	10,000	11,064	23,921	—	—	44,985	
John Hervey	—	—	7,315	8,653	—	15,968	
Robert Welstead	—	—	10,034	5,000	—	15,034	53,823 6·5
Messrs. Finch and Fortescue	3,590	2,205	3,826	3,200	—	12,821	
Farmers of the London Excise	5,000	5,000	—	—	—	10,000	

Duke of Albermarle	3,772	3,836	—	—	—	7,608	
Joseph Hornby	—	—	5,000	—	—	5,000	
Richard Kent	5,000	—	—	—	—	5,000	
Isaac Meynall	—	—	4,978	—	—	4,978	
Sir George Downing	—	—	3,920	—	—	3,920	
Thomas Crompton	1,083	1,083	—	1,621	—	3,787	
Capt. Thomas Morley	—	1,883	1,773	—	—	3,656	
Lord Culpepper	—	1,057	1,255	—	—	2,312	
William Ashburnham	—	2,205	—	—	—	2,205	48,024 5·8
Capt. Hartgill Barron	—	—	1,082	1,000	—	2,082	
Dr. Clarke	—	500	1,106	—	—	1,606	
Col. Somerset Fox	—	—	—	1,125	—	1,125	
Sir Samuel Tuke	—	—	—	1,100	—	1,100	
Mrs. Mary Darnell	524	—	546	—	—	1,070	
Richard Morley	—	—	945	—	—	945	
James Hamilton	—	—	696	—	—	696	
Sir John James	—	—	601	—	—	601	
Mr. Halsey	—	—	333	—	—	333	
Orders not assigned	180,965	282,285	252,504	103,989	10,000	829,743	
	64,352	32,314	47,353	151,945	74,741	370,705	
TOTALS	245,317	314,599	299,857	255,934	84,741	1,200,448	

¹ All sums given to the nearest £.
Source: Ilchester: Official, Sir S. Fox, Customs and Excise (box 271): 'Account of Orders received from the Excheqr . . .' See also note 3 on p. 48.

could not accept less than 8 or 10 per cent from Fox or any other government borrower. Now Sir Stephen was borrowing direct from the public at the same rate as they did.[1]

For most of the 1660s only one of the many types of account Sir Stephen must have kept has survived, that is his journals or day-books. These provide a general impression of how he obtained access to the money he re-lent to the Crown, but they are in a format which would make it an excessively laborious, and perhaps impossible, task to construct a detailed analysis of his sources of credit. However, from the end of 1667 the day-books can be supplemented by the separate account in which he kept a record of the Treasury Orders he received.[2] Here, unencumbered by the thousands of entries recording out-payments and the posting of items back and forth from one account to another, which render the day-books so difficult to use, there is a straightforward list of the securities assigned to him, a note of the value of each, and of what became of them. Those persons to whom Fox 'delivered' Orders are, of course, those from whom he was borrowing, and the analysis of these 'deliveries' to be found in Table V reveals not only the identity of his principal creditors in the later 1660s and early 1670s, but also something more about their relative importance and the extent of their loans than can easily be got from the day-books.[3] Over the four years from December 1667 to December 1671 Fox delivered Orders worth nearly £830,000, which, when allowance is made for the fact that they had to provide security for the interest as well as the principal of the advances, must represent the borrowing of about £750,000. It is true that if Sir Stephen was obliged to part with his Orders at a discount, as was Cofferer Ashburnham in 1668-9,[4] then the principal sum would be correspondingly less, but there is no evidence that he ever found this necessary. What also emerges from Table V is both the extent and the limits of Fox's success in broadening the basis of his financial support since the days when he had relied almost completely on Backwell, Vyner, and Colville. By the end of 1667 he had lost not only the first of

---

[1] For a fuller discussion of this aspect of Fox's affairs see below, pp. 71, 83-91.

[2] Ilchester . . . 'Account of Orders Received . . .'

[3] The term 'delivered' is the one normally used throughout Fox's 'Account of Orders Received . . .', his day-books, and his surviving ledger. It is clearly intended to imply that the securities had been 'pawned' to cover a debt rather than sold or assigned outright.

[4] See above, p. 51.

this trio, but the second as well, yet even so enjoyed the assistance of no less than seven major lenders, each of whom accepted over £40,000 worth of Orders during the period. On the other hand, two of them, Lindsey and Snow, were far more important than all the others, taking £217,227 and £199,716 worth of Orders respectively, although until his death in 1669 Colville, who took £86,900 in the space of less than two years, was not far behind them. Next came Sir Thomas Player, Chamberlain of the City of London, whose £65,000 of Orders represented a single loan of £60,000 made by the City in 1670. The City Corporation, however, was not one of Fox's regular sources of supply. The loan was negotiated not by Fox but by the Treasury, apparently in order to provide the Paymaster with his regular instalments of ready money during part of that year: it was thus a transaction in a somewhat different category from the others under discussion.[1] The next of the large lenders was John Ball, the Excise Cashier; the sixth was John Portman, a relatively minor goldsmith banker with whom Fox had only just begun to deal; and the last was Laurence Debusty who, like Ball, had already been supplying him for two or three years before the earliest date to which the Table refers. The totals of the Orders accepted by these three were £57,577, £56,491, and £44,985 respectively.

In addition to the seven major lenders there were a larger number of individuals to whom Fox delivered Orders, either on an occasional basis or on a much smaller scale, sometimes to the value of only a few thousand or even a few hundred pounds at a time. However, such people provided a very small percentage of the money he raised by this method, and it will be seen that the eighteen persons who accepted less than £10,000 worth of Orders during the whole period accounted for only 5·8 per cent of Fox's deliveries, and the four others who received more than £10,000 but less than £20,000 only took up a further 6½ per cent. Several of these small or occasional lenders, however, were also bankers and professional financiers and men of much greater wealth and standing than the scale of their advances to Fox might suggest, and his dealings with them did provide him with something of a second line of defence should any of his principal suppliers of money fail him. There were at least four more goldsmith bankers among them: Messrs. Welstead, Hornby, Isaac Meynall, and Crompton. The first two

[1] *C.T.B.* iii (1669–72), pp. 463, 470, 471–2, 475, 729.

of these were probably fairly small operators as bankers went, and
the last is a shadowy figure, but Isaac Meynall, who had inherited
the business of Fox's original financial backer, Francis Meynall,
was very deeply involved in other aspects of government finance.
Indeed, at the time of the Stop of the Exchequer he was, after
Vyner and Backwell, the third largest of the state's creditors.[1]
Francis Finch was an Excise Commissioner with a finger in a
number of financial pies, although his partner Fortescue remains
obscure, and both John Hervey and Sir John James were certainly
financiers although not goldsmiths. Hervey was the Queen's
Receiver-General and lent money to the government on a number
of other occasions, and James was another of the Excise Commissioners and a man with whom Fox was later to have considerably
more to do.[2] Finally in this catalogue of financiers amongst the
small lenders, we must include the farmers of the London Excise.
Altogether these people received £68,189 of Fox's Orders, and
when this is added to the £727,896 received by the seven major
lenders it appears that 95·9 per cent of the total went to professional
financiers of one sort or another. Of course, the bankers and financiers who took these Orders did not necessarily keep all of them until they matured, and to the extent that it suited their business they
assigned them to colleagues in Lombard Street some of whom did
not otherwise have any dealings with Sir Stephen. Unfortunately,
such secondary transactions were not normally recorded by Fox
in the accounts which have come down to us and details of them
rarely come to light. However, an example is provided by certain
Orders on the Country Excise which Fox had delivered to Mr.
Ball in March 1670, and which at the time of the Stop of the
Exchequer were in the hands of George Snell, one of the less important of the bankers who dealt in government paper, and who
does not himself appear anywhere in Fox's Treasury Order
account.[3] Of the small fraction of Fox's Orders which went outside
the financial community, £5,000 was assigned to Fox's own
assistant Richard Kent. It is uncertain whether Kent was acting

[1] The value of Orders in the hands of the various goldsmith bankers at the
time of the Stop is clearly set out by H. G. Roseveare, 'Advancement of the
King's Credit', Appendix V. Crompton did not hold any orders in 1672, but he
is referred to as a goldsmith in C.T.B. ii (1667–8), p. 413.

[2] C.T.B. i (1660–7), p. 75, iii (1669–72), p. 191, and iv (1672–5), pp. 175, 579.
For Sir John James see also below, pp. 94–8, 101–8.

[3] P.R.O., E. 403/2576, ff. 66–9.

for his employer, so that this sum should really be added to the total of Orders kept by Sir Stephen unassigned, or whether (which is equally possible) Kent was already beginning to accumulate capital and develop contacts of his own, and really did advance the money himself. Most of the thirteen remaining recipients, who included the Duke of Albemarle, Lord Culpepper, Sir George Downing, and Cofferer Ashburnham, were from either Court or army circles. As we shall see later, by the 1670s courtiers and

TABLE VI

Holders of Sir Stephen Fox's Treasury Orders, January 1672

Name of holder	Value of unpaid Orders at the time of the Stop of the Exchequer (£. s. d.)
John Lindsey	44,000
Jeremiah Snow	38,260
Lawrence Debusty	10,000
John Portman	11,530
John Ball	7,103
Robert Welstead	5,000
Messrs. Finch and Fortescue	3,729
John Hervey	1,497
Sir Samuel Tuke	1,100
Capt. Hartgill Barron	1,000
Thomas Crompton	579
TOTAL	123,798

Source: Ilchester: Official, Sir S. Fox, Customs and Excise (box 271): volume containing 'Account of Orders Received from the Excheqr . . .'

officers were investing their savings by depositing them in Fox's hands on a considerably larger scale than this, but such people did not usually receive revenue assignments as security, and it is not clear why this group did.[1]

The extent of Fox's indebtedness on account of Orders delivered to creditors tended to fluctuate a great deal from month to month, since a high proportion of his deliveries were made in large parcels at relatively infrequent intervals, and the ultimate redemption of the Orders at the Exchequer followed a similar pattern. Throughout most of the four years 1668–71 it was somewhere between

[1] See below, pp. 83–91.

£150,000 and £300,000 at any one time, but by the end of this period it was tending to decline and when the Stop of the Exchequer was declared at the beginning of 1672 it was only £123,798 (see Table VI). Since we have seen that the outstanding total of Fox's advances to the government remained at a much higher level than this it might appear that his dependence on the bankers was already rapidly diminishing. Certainly, it was less than total by this stage for Sir Stephen had accumulated a substantial fortune of his own, but the sudden fall in the proportion of his Orders which he assigned away, from 84·2 per cent of those issued to him in the year 1669–70 to only just over 40 per cent of those issued in 1670–1, was probably due as much to the growing reluctance of the financial community to accept any more. By the latter part of 1671 Orders on the Country Excise which had been issued at the very beginning of the previous year were only just coming up for payment, and several other sources of revenue in which the bankers were concerned, although Fox was not, were probably almost as far anticipated. A very large amount of their capital was thus tied up in government paper, and the prospect was that redemption dates would grow progressively more distant. A general refusal by the bankers to grant the Crown further credit eventually precipitated the Stop of the Exchequer at the turn of 1671 and 1672, but Fox seems to have run into difficulties considerably sooner, for three of his major sources of funds in the later 1660s, Portman, Debusty, and the Cashier of the Excise Mr. Ball, did not take any more Orders after May 1670. A number of new names appear in Fox's book of Treasury Orders in the latter part of 1670, notably the bankers Welstead, Hornby, and Meynall, and that of the financier Hervey, but none of them accepted deliveries on the scale of their predecessors, and it looks as though he may have been finding it difficult fully to replace the suppliers he had lost. It is also probably significant that at the time of the Stop he had apparently succeeded in making no delivers of Orders on the Country Excise for several months, although as recently as the beginning of December 1671 he had got rid of £45,000 worth on the less seriously anticipated London Excise to John Lindsey.

During the later 1660s the value of the Orders which Fox kept in his own hands until they matured provides some guide to the extent to which he was meeting the financial demands made on him out of his own accumulated profits. He retained £64,352 of the Orders which were issued to him during 1667–8, and on top of this received back a further £12,442 from his creditors before they had been paid by the Exchequer, either because he had given them more than proved necessary to cover their interest accounts, or because he had paid off part of the principal which the Orders secured. Since Fox's private banking business was still in its infancy, most of this must represent reinvestment of what he had made out of his Undertaking down to the close of the Second Dutch War, and the amount he was able to put up in the following two years was inevitably smaller, because of the time-lag before his 1667–8 Orders fell due for payment, and because of delays in settling his claims for interest. Of the Orders issued in 1668–9 and 1669–70 he kept only £32,314 and £42,353 respectively, and he received back only a further £2,135 of the former year's deliveries and £18,395 of the latter's. However, in 1670–1 the value of the Orders which Fox kept soared to £151,845, and before the Stop of the Exchequer he received back a further £23,198. It is not quite clear how many he was holding at the time of the Stop because his account book omits some important details in the last few months with which it deals, but it must have been in the region of £210,000.[1] Four months later, at the end of April 1672, after the process of redeeming Orders held by departmental treasurers had already begun, he had £160,849 of them.[2] Even if the first of these figures is an overestimate, it is clear that by the early 1670s Fox was carrying an enormous volume of Orders, and rich though he had become there is no doubt that it would have been beyond his means to do so alone. He was only able to shoulder so large a burden because of the expansion of his own banking activities, which were making an increasingly important contribution to his financial resources by this stage. Thus, when he opened a new ledger on 30 April 1672 he owed some £48,000 to eighty clients, over and above his debt to the professional financiers, and it may well have been more before the financial crisis of the previous January, although because he was also making some private loans the net addition to his operating capital was not so large.[3] An exact calculation of his wealth at this stage of his career is not possible,

---

[1] The whole of the foregoing discussions of Fox's Orders is derived from Ilchester . . . 'Account of Orders Received'.

[2] Ilchester: Official, Sir S. Fox, Army: ledger for 1672–9, f. 80.

[3] Ibid., *passim*. See also below, pp. 163–4.

but the value of the Orders he held unassigned in April 1672, compared to the value of the deposits he held, and making allowance for other assets and liabilities, suggests that he must then have been worth at least £120,000, and possibly somewhat more. He was ploughing back into his Undertaking virtually everything he made from it, and as we shall see in later chapters, he neither maintained an extravagant life-style, nor, down to 1672, made any major investments in any other direction.[1] His fortune was thus almost wholly tied up in government lending, but just for this reason was growing very rapidly. The more Fox could contribute towards the Undertaking from his own resources the faster those resources would increase, since it meant that his outgoing interest payments were progressively reduced, and he was able to retain for himself the whole profit from an ever larger proportion of his advances. It will be remembered from the previous chapter that part of the interest on what he lent derived from the shilling in the pound he deducted from all payments he made to the Guards and the garrisons. This he received automatically, since the tallies and Orders issued to him for the forces covered not only what he had actually paid to them but the deduction as well, and until they matured interest accrued on both elements. The other part of the interest Fox received, the 8 per cent commencing two months after the end of each muster, had to be claimed from the Treasury, and in practice there were considerable delays before his interest accounts were approved and arrangements made to pay them. However, at least from the end of 1668, and probably earlier, at the end of every six months unpaid interest was added to the principal of what the government owed him, and thenceforward itself gathered interest at 8 per cent until the Orders issued to cover it were eventually redeemed at the Exchequer.[2] Fox's interest money thus accumulated at what was in effect a compound rate and provided him with an ever increasing capital of his own to lend, steadily reducing his once total dependence on borrowed money.

It has now been made clear that Sir Stephen Fox provided Charles II's government with loans on a very large scale, and it seems that throughout his Paymastership he was able to meet all the calls made on him for money. He later recalled proudly that once begun the Undertaking was

[1] See below, chapters VIII and X. [2] P.R.O., E. 403/2995, ff. 19–25.

... Carryed on to the great sattisfaction of the King who never after was troubled with complaints, & the Generall & all the officers [who] were abundantly sattisfyed to see it performed. Notwithstanding an expencive war ensued with Holland, [neither] a raging plague & a devouring fire in London, nor the business at Chatham, gave any interruption to the punctuall paymt of the forces tht remaind at Whitehall, or those that remaind wth the King, nor in those new raisd forces wch the war occationd to bee raisd, but all was so carryd on that the King and High Treasurer and the Generall, upon enquiry, thought it a seasonable & good service. ... Even when those forces occationally levied for the war were to be disbanded they were never retarded a day for want of money to disband them [for] my credit was at all times sufficient to raise the mony upon remote funds, so that no forces were kept a day longer than the service did require their continuance, so that it became a proverb that I never wanted mony for disbanding . . .[1]

In fact, all this was not achieved as easily as Fox seems to be implying, for there were periodic crises when he found raising funds extremely difficult, and on several occasions he came very near to being unable to honour his commitment to keep the pay of the troops from falling behind. The summer and early autumn of 1667 was one period of particularly acute crisis. After two and a half years of war the economic life of the country was suffering from the effects of unusually heavy taxation, the dislocation of trade, and the destruction of the capital city in the Great Fire of 1666. The government had already borrowed enormous sums, thereby forcing the rate of interest up, and the revenue was so far anticipated that delays in the payment of tallies were greater than ever. Credit was very difficult to obtain, especially after the Dutch attack on the Medway had precipitated a run on the London bankers.[2] Sir Robert Vyner, who had hitherto been one of his principal suppliers of money, ceased to be willing, or perhaps able, to help him, and yet Fox had to secure unprecedentedly large sums. During the year that followed his financial needs remained at a higher level than they had been before the war, yet the credit situation, at least for government borrowers, remained tight.

[1] Ilchester: Family (box 237): autobiography in small volume with green cover.
[2] W. R. Scott, *The Constitution and Finance of the English* . . . *Joint Stock Companies to 1720* (3 vols., Cambridge, 1912), i. 279; Chandaman, *English Public Revenue*, pp. 212–13; A. Browning, 'The Stop of the Exchequer', *History*, 1930, p. 333 n. 5.

Three times between August 1667 and August 1668 Fox told the Treasury that he was nearing the end of his credit and that he could not go on paying the forces for much longer, and on a number of other occasions he was obliged to ask them to bring pressure to bear on possible lenders on his behalf.[1] Another anxious period seems to have been the summer of 1670 when, as we have seen, several more of the bankers who had hitherto supported Sir Stephen apparently cut off their flow of loans. Yet another was in the weeks before the Stop of the Exchequer.[2]

Nevertheless, somehow each successive crisis was overcome, and there is no doubt that the land forces were much better paid than was the navy during these years. No evidence has been found to contradict Fox's claim that, thanks to his advances, it was possible for the government to pay off the troops raised in the emergencies of 1666 and 1667 as soon as the need for them had passed. Equally, it seems to be the case, as Fox repeatedly implied elsewhere in his writings,[3] that the pay of the forces for which he was responsible was never in arrears at any time during his Paymastership.[4] The seamen of the fleet, on the other hand, were sometimes kept waiting eighteen months or more for their wages, were obliged to accept 'tickets' instead of the cash the authorities were unable to provide, and generally treated so badly in matters of pay that they were driven to virtual mutiny in an attempt to get their due. The naval budget was much larger than that of the land forces, but it is only when the appalling consequences of chaotic naval finances are recalled, and these included the disaster at Chatham as well as the terrible hardships imposed on the men, that the value of Fox's services can be fully appreciated.[5]

---

[1] C.T.B. ii (1667–8), pp. 58, 139–40, 259, 268, 272, 273, 278, 413; B.L., Add. MS. 28078, f. 12.

[2] See above, p. 70.

[3] For instance, B.L., Add. MS. 51324, f. 57: document headed 'Recollections relating to My Self . . .'

[4] This is not to say that the officers necessarily paid their men as promptly as they themselves received the money: see below, p. 151.

[5] Ogg, Charles II, i. 260–2.

CHAPTER IV

The Great Undertaking
2. The Army, the Household, and the Excise

F OX'S RELATIVE importance as an independent source of loans for the government was increasing rapidly in the early 1670s, but it received an unexpected boost from the event which rocked the financial world at the beginning of 1672, the Stop of the Exchequer. The Stop was in effect a declaration of bankruptcy by the government, precipitated by the imminence of war with Holland. The revenue had become so far anticipated by the over-issue of Treasury Orders that the only way in which sufficient funds could be made available for the fighting services was by suspending the process of their redemption. The debt represented by the Orders was not repudiated, but all further repayments of principal were postponed for twelve months and the declaration to this effect was accompanied by a promise that creditors would receive 6 per cent interest on what was owed to them. Maybe the government really did hope that at the end of a year it would be able to start paying off the Orders again, but the great cost of the war made this impossible and the Stop had to be continued for a second year, and then indefinitely. However, there were some exceptions to the general ban on the payment of outstanding Orders. It did not extend to the Orders secured on taxes recently granted by Parliament for a limited period, nor to certain other extraordinary sources of revenue, but it *did* cover the three main props of the ordinary revenue, the Customs, the Excise, and the Hearth Tax. On the other hand, even Orders charged on a fund which had been stopped were exempt if they had been issued to departmental treasurers for the purposes of their departments and remained in their possession unassigned, a provision which was necessary if they were to continue their operations and thus ensure the maintenance of the services their departments gave. Finally, the government provided itself with some freedom of manœuvre by exempting any Orders which it might specifically command to be paid.[1]

The Stop did not, then, affect the whole of the government's debt, but it extended to about £1,170,000 of it, and it had a shattering effect on the bankers who held the Orders, the clients whose deposits had provided the bankers with the money they had lent, and on the financial life of the country in general. The bankers were unable to honour the deposits they had accepted, so that their business was ruined and their credit badly damaged. In fact most of them survived somehow and even the worst affected were able to remain afloat for a number of years, Sir Robert Vyner, the largest of the government's creditors, until 1684, and Edward Backwell, the second largest, until 1682, but naturally the government could no longer look to them for serious financial help.[2] From the point of view of Lombard Street perhaps the most significant result of the Stop was that it meant the eclipse of the leading figures of the first generation of post-Restoration financiers, and opened the way for successors who arose to fill the vacuum thus left. As we shall see, one of the most important of those successors was Sir Stephen Fox. At first sight it may seem that Fox was as vulnerable to a government suspension or repudiation as any banker, for he had not only lent to the Crown virtually the whole of the personal wealth which he had accumulated in more than nine years of the Undertaking, but he had also lent large sums which he had borrowed from others. Yet in fact Fox's position was different from that of other major creditors of the government in two vital respects. Firstly, he was at once a creditor *and* a departmental treasurer. Most of the money he had lent personally had not been on the security of Orders assigned to him by someone else, as was the bankers' case, but on Orders issued directly to himself as Paymaster for the pay of the Guards and the garrisons, which he had retained unassigned in his own hands, and which were therefore not subject to the Stop. It is true that Fox also held other categories of Orders which were stopped: £20,000 which had been issued to him for interest on his past advances, and some £23,726 worth which had originally been issued to him, which he

---

[1] *C.T.B.* iii (1669–72), p. 1172; *C.S.P.D.*, 1671–2, p. 87–8. See also Chandaman, *English Public Revenue*, pp. 224–8; Roseveare, 'Advancement of the King's Credit', pp. 195–7; and A. Browning, 'The Stop of the Exchequer', *History*, 1930.

[2] C. Wilson, *England's Apprenticeship 1603–1763* (London, 1965), p. 215.

had delivered to various persons, and which they had subsequently re-delivered to him.[1] Now if the government had refused to pay any of Fox's stopped Orders it would have done him grave damage, and by undermining his credit might very well have made it impossible for him to continue the Undertaking. But the collapse of the Undertaking would have faced the government with the impossible task of finding a new Undertaker at the very moment it had destroyed its own credit with moneyed men, and obviously the eve of a foreign war, for which the expansion of the land forces had already begun, was not the time to throw the arrangements for paying the army into disarray. In other words, Fox had become too useful to be sacrificed, and this was the second respect in which his position differed from others who had lent large sums to the Crown. Thus although he had to wait considerably longer for payment of some of his Orders than he would otherwise have done, virtually all of them had been honoured by the end of September 1674. Thereafter only £2,500 worth of interest Orders and twelve re-delivered Orders worth some £1,953 remained outstanding, and Fox was still trying to get them paid in the middle of 1678.[2] When, or indeed whether, he eventually succeeded is not clear, but these do seem to have been the only losses he suffered on account of the Stop, and though they caused him irritation they were not great enough even to be seriously inconvenient.

The government not only kept faith with Fox, it also enabled him to keep faith with those who had provided him with loans. At the beginning of 1672 his creditors held £123,798 worth of Orders which he had delivered to them by way of security, and since they were Orders on the Excise all of them were affected by the Stop. However, Fox had also given his creditors his own personal bond as collateral security for all or most of what he had borrowed.[3] As long as the Orders were duly paid the creditors had no claim against him for the principal of their loans, but now that it had been announced that the Orders would not be paid Sir Stephen became liable to repay the whole amount himself. This then was another threat of ruin, but Fox managed to avert it by persuading the government to resume responsibility for the Orders he had pledged. No details emerge of when or how he prevailed on the Treasury to

---

[1] Ilchester . . . 'Account of Orders Received . . .'
[2] B.L., Add. MS. 28078, f. 296.
[3] Ilchester: Family (box 237): autobiography in small volume with green cover.

honour these Orders, but doubtless he used the argument that if they did not he would not be able to continue the Undertaking, since his ability to raise any further credit would be undermined, and eventually his bonds would be put in suit against him.[1] Anyway, Fox's account of the Treasury Orders issued to him seems to show that in 1673 and 1674 the government itself redeemed some of the stopped Orders in the hands of his creditors, and in his ledger it is possible to detect a series of transactions in which he lent it the money to liquidate most of the remainder. Fox repaid to the creditors the money which they had lent him, and which should have been reimbursed to them by the Exchequer when the Orders matured; they re-delivered the Orders to him; he then exchanged them at the Exchequer for tallies on the Excise, or some other good source of revenue, and in due course received payment on the tallies by way of reimbursement. Some of these transactions did not take place until 1677, but by that time Fox's creditors seem to have been repaid all, or virtually all, that was owing to them.[2] Meanwhile, Fox had continued to pay interest on the loans out of his own resources, although it is clear that, in the immediate aftermath of the Stop when payment of his own interest Orders was delayed and fresh credit very hard to obtain, doing so imposed considerable strain upon him. Much of the interest which fell due in 1672 he did not pay until the following year, but between May 1672 and the end of 1674 he paid out at least £14,778 in interest to the holders of stopped Orders. The Crown itself did not even begin to pay interest to the bankers caught by the Stop until June 1674.[3]

Fox thus survived the Stop not only with his capital largely intact, but, what was no less important, with his credit undamaged,

[1] Fox may also have tried to argue that since he had not technically assigned away his Orders, but only pledged them as security, they were still legally his property and ought not therefore to be affected by the Stop.

[2] Ilchester . . . 'Account of Orders Received'; and ibid.: Official, Sir S. Fox, Army: ledger for 1672–9, ff. 80, 200, 227, 250. In these sources it is possible to identify positively the repayment of virtually all the money lent to Fox on the security of 'delivered' Orders which was still outstanding in January 1672. The few sums whose repayment cannot be traced may either have escaped identification or have been repaid later.

[3] Ilchester: Official, Sir S. Fox, Army: ledger for 1672–9, f. 101 etc. An entry in the Treasury minutes for 24 February 1677 suggests that eventually the interest that Fox paid to his creditors on account of stopped Orders was reimbursed to him. *C.T.B.* v (1676–9), p. 429. See also G. O. Nichols, 'English Government Borrowing, 1660–1688, *Journal of British Studies*, 1971, p. 101.

and he was one of the few financiers who was really intimately and deeply involved in lending to the government to do so. Sir John Banks was another man involved in government finance who escaped virtually unscathed, but Banks's advances to the Crown were on an altogether smaller scale.[1] It was thus an exaggeration, but a pardonable one, when Fox wrote that the effect of the Stop was to 'breake all credit except mine who being security in conjunction with the funds & likewise oblidged to pay interest, wch wth great difficulty I performed, made all the Credit in the King's affairs center in mee'.[2] It was in these circumstances that Fox was able to extend the scope of his activities into new fields, first to financing part of the expenditure of the royal Household, then to financing the whole of it, and finally to supporting several other spending departments as well.

Before we look in detail at this extension of Sir Stephen's financial commitments, we must consider how he was able to mobilize the resources necessary to meet them. The first point is that he was now very wealthy in his own right, and although it is impossible to say exactly how much of his own money he lent to the government at any one time, there can be no doubt that he was very much less reliant on borrowing in order to re-lend than he had been in the years before 1670. Indeed, in the months immediately following the Stop he hardly took up any loans at all: the ledger which begins at the end of April 1672 records no borrowings from the banking community until almost the end of that year, nor any substantial deposits by anyone else, although there was a trickle of smallish ones.[3] This doubtless reflects the general blow to the confidence of investors which the events of January had administered, but Fox was able to get by because of the new situation at the Exchequer which was one of the other results of the Stop. The purpose of the suspension of payments on outstanding Orders had been to free the royal income to meet the costs of the impending war with the Dutch, and indeed the government was now able to meet its financial obligations to Fox, as Paymaster of the Forces, reasonably promptly for the first time since the Restoration. Later in the decade delays built up once again, but during 1672 at least Fox was receiving money at the Exchequer very soon

---

[1] Coleman, *Sir John Banks*, chapter iv.
[2] Ilchester: Family (box 237): autobiography in small volume with green cover.   [3] Ilchester: . . . ledger for 1672–9.

after Orders or tallies had been issued to him. The loans that he made to the forces thus remained outstanding for a very much shorter time than they had done previously, consequently reducing the capital required to support the Undertaking at any given level of establishment. Thus the considerable expansion in the size of the forces on account of the war did not require from Fox correspondingly increased advances, and he was able to survive without raising substantial additional funds until conditions in the money market improved.

Fox began to borrow again on a substantial scale in 1673. At first he was dealing only with a single creditor, or rather group of creditors, the Commissioners of Country Excise, who, like Fox himself, had successfully survived the Stop. By March he had borrowed £24,000 from them,[1] and was probably already looking round for fresh sources of credit. This was necessary since only one of his regular suppliers from before the Stop, Debusty, was apparently able to resume lending on the same scale as before, although the City Corporation was still prepared to make occasional advances. Of the other large creditors of the previous period, Colville was dead, Snow only made a few moderate-sized loans in the years after 1672, Lindsey made a cash deposit of some £1,560 in early 1673 but nothing more, and Portman made no further loans at all. Amongst the creditors of middle rank, the London Excise Farmers and Hervey were still able to be of help, but Welstead, and Finch and Fortescue did not lend anything more.[2] Fox thus had to build new contacts in the financial world, and to look to them for the largest part of his requirements. In this he was very successful, and between 1673 and 1676, when he lost the Paymastership, he was dealing with a much wider circle of lenders than in earlier years, although he continued to obtain a high proportion of what he needed from a relatively restricted group of large-scale creditors, most of whom were bankers or professional financiers of some sort. Throughout 1674 and 1675, when his operations reached their highest level, he was probably holding about £240,000 of borrowed funds, sometimes rather more and sometimes rather less. If we define major lenders as those whose loans amounted to £10,000 or more in aggregate between the Stop and 1676, we find that such people provided some £140,000 of this money. A list of them is

---

[1] Ilchester: . . . ledger for 1672–9, f. 142.
[2] Ibid., ff. 18, 23, 38, 41, 42, 49, 89, 91, 158, 192.

given in Table VII, and there it will be seen that by far the most important single source of funds to Sir Stephen during this time was the banker Charles Duncombe, a former employee of Alderman Backwell who was still in the early stages of developing an

TABLE VII

Sir Stephen Fox's Principal Creditors, 1673–1676

Lender	Description	Total of loans	Max. loan at any one time
Charles Duncombe	Banker	£166,300	£50,000
Lawrence Debusty	Banker	45,300	20,000
Richard Kent	Banker	40,000	25,000
Thomas Kirwood	Banker	28,000	15,000
Farmers of the General Excise		27,000	27,000
Commissioners of the Country Excise		24,000	24,000
Sir Thomas Player	Chamberlain of London Corporation	20,000	20,000
Charles Toll	Financier	15,000	15,000
Farmers of the London Excise		14,000	14,000
Jeremiah Snow	Banker	14,000	9,000
John Hervey	Courtier/Financier	13,800	9,800
Earl of Suffolk	Courtier	12,982	5,000
Lord Crofts	Courtier	10,267	5,500
Alderman James Ward	Merchant	10,000	10,000
Roger Whitley	Courtier, M.P.	10,000	10,000
Henry Guy	Courtier/Financier	10,000	10,000

This list includes all those whose loans exceeded £10,000 in aggregate in the years 1673–6. It excludes debts which remained outstanding on account of the Stop of the Exchequer.

Source: Ilchester: Official, Sir S. Fox, Army: ledger for 1672–9.

independent business which was ultimately to bring him enormous wealth.[1] The closeness of his financial relationship with Fox in the mid-1670s must have owed a good deal to the fact that he had recently, probably in 1672, gone into partnership with Sir Stephen's

[1] J. B. Martin, *The 'Grasshopper' in Lombard Street* (London, 1892), pp. 28, 30–6; E. Hughes, *Studies in Administration and Finance 1558–1825* (Manchester, 1934), pp. 164–6.

assistant Richard Kent, a partnership in which it seems likely that Duncombe furnished most of the capital and Kent provided the contacts in government circles and the knowledge of government methods. One may indeed wonder whether Fox had not deliberately launched Kent into the banking world as part of his search for new sources of credit in the post-Stop era, but in any event Kent's new partner and his former master soon became very important to each other. Duncombe provided Fox with a large slice of the funds he needed during the years when he was in effect Paymaster of the Household as well as Paymaster of the Forces, and there can be little doubt that at this stage Duncombe's ability to attract deposits from the public was helped by the fact that he was known to be re-lending them to the one great government borrower whose creditworthiness had, if anything, improved as a result of the Stop. Duncombe began by advancing £20,000 in the late summer of 1673, all apparently secured on Fox's Orders on the Eighteen Months Tax. Half of this had been repaid to him by Christmas, and the other half on the first of May following, by which time Duncombe had lent another £35,300. By the end of June 1674 he had advanced £24,000 more, and during the rest of that year and most of 1675 the total of Duncombe's loans to Fox outstanding at any one time probably never fell below £50,000. In the latter months of 1675 they stood at £39,000, and during 1676 were gradually reduced until Fox closed the account in September with balances of £166,300 on either side.[1] Richard Kent does not seem to have been involved in these advances, for there is a separate account of the money lent by him, beginning with a loan of £20,000 on tallies in November 1674, which was increased to £25,000 the following spring. Despite various repayments by Fox, fresh advances seem to have kept a loan of this size outstanding until the autumn of 1676 and only thereafter was it paid off in a series of unequal instalments.[2] However, as we shall see, Fox and Kent had other dealings of a rather different nature which overshadowed these loans in importance.[3]

Other lenders whose advances were on a comparable scale to Kent's included the two bankers, Debusty and Kirwood. The former had been caught in January 1672 with some Orders which had been assigned to him by Fox, but he seems to have been other-

---

[1] Ilchester: . . . ledger for 1672–9, f. 177.
[2] Ibid., f. 266.   [3] See below, pp. 98–104.

wise uninvolved in the Stop and was thus still able to furnish money on a substantial scale; the latter had certainly been established as a banker before 1672, but had apparently not been directly involved in government lending at that time.[1] Then there were two separate groups of those participating in the collection and management of the Excise, both of whom made a single large loan on the security of tallies: £27,000 in the case of the General Farmers and £24,000 in the case of the Country Commissioners.[2] Next there was a single loan of £20,000 made in the name of Sir Thomas Player, but this was clearly provided by the Corporation of the City of London.[3] The remaining eight names in the Table, all of whose loans were less than £20,000 in aggregate, also included at least five who were professional financiers: the Farmers of the London Excise; the banker Jeremiah Snow, who had been very badly hit by the Stop but who was still in business, although apparently on a reduced scale; and Charles Toll, Alderman Ward, and John Hervey. Toll was the Cofferer's man of business, but like Duncombe and Kent he was on the way to becoming an important financier in his own right. As for Ward, he was first and foremost a merchant, but his subsequent appointment as a Customs Commissioner suggests that he had other more strictly financial irons in the fire and so it may be proper to consider him amongst the professional dealers in money. Hervey we have already met because he had lent money to Fox before 1672: he was at once a financier and a courtier, as was Sir Stephen himself. Henry Guy, the future Secretary to the Treasury and at this time a Groom of the Bed Chamber, probably also ought to be placed in this half-way category, for he was also involved in Excise farming and other forms of tax collection.[4] The Earl of Suffolk and Lord Crofts, both Gentlemen of the King's Bed Chamber, and Roger Whitley, the King's Harbinger, who was M.P. for Flint, were, on the other hand, courtiers, but could not possibly be regarded as financiers, although they were also substantial landowners.[5]

[1] Ilchester: . . . ledger for 1672–9, ff. 18, 155. For Debusty's holdings of Fox's Orders at the time of the Stop, see Table VI on p. 69.

[2] Ilchester: . . . ledger for 1672–9, ff. 142, 162.

[3] Ibid., f. 41, account in the name of Sir Thomas Player.

[4] Ibid., ff. 89, 91, 158, 185, 192, 247, 272. For Snow's involvement in the Stop, see Roseveare, 'Advancement of the King's Credit', Appendix V. For Ward, see J. R. Woodhead, *The Rulers of London* (London, 1965), p. 170.

[5] Ilchester: . . . ledger for 1672–9, ff. 77, 79, 181, 323, 328.

It is more difficult to estimate at all precisely the size of the contribution the smaller depositors made to Fox's resources. However, there is no doubt that by 1674 and 1675 he was accepting medium-sized and small deposits from many more people than he had been doing in the early part of 1672, and that their importance to him had increased correspondingly. When Fox began his new ledger on 30 April 1672 there were seventeen private accounts with credit balances of less than £10,000 but more than £1,000; fifteen with balances of between £1,000 and £500; and forty-eight with balances of less than £500.[1] Between then and 1676 when Fox began to run down his financial operations, besides additional deposits from established clients, a further forty-three individuals made deposits of more than £1,000 but less than £10,000, twenty-three more deposited more than £500 but less than £1,000, and seventy-nine deposited less than £500.[2] Of these three categories of depositor it was the first which contributed by far the largest total sum, and at no stage was the third group, whose deposits were sometimes in only two figures and occasionally in only one, of much importance. On the other hand, not all the small depositors were necessarily of small means, and a few were men of great wealth who probably had more extensive, regular dealings with other financiers. So we find amongst those whose credit balances with Fox never exceeded £500 such people as the Earl of Shaftesbury, the Earl of Devonshire, Lord St. John, and Sir Edward Carteret.[3] Nevertheless, most of them were obscure figures, who must necessarily remain no more than names, and it is difficult to generalize about their economic and social background. Most of those whose deposits were between £1,000 and £10,000 in aggregate over the period 1672–6 can, however, be identified, and their occupations are summarized in Table VIII. It seems that, whereas the lenders of more than £10,000 were mostly financiers with a smattering of courtiers, this latter group were mostly courtiers

[1] Ilchester: . . . ledger for 1672–9, *passim*. Those whose advances were secured on stopped Treasury Orders have been excluded from this count.

[2] Ibid. Owing to the difficulties of interpreting some accounts these numbers must be regarded as approximate only. I have used the term 'deposit' in the text to describe money held by Fox to the credit of a client, irrespective of whether it was paid to him in cash or came into his hands by some other means (e.g. a salary payment for which he was responsible). It should be noted that the ledger never makes use of the word.

[3] Ibid. Folio references will be given only for the larger depositors and where details of the deposits are given in the text.

with only a few financiers among them. They included, it is true, three goldsmith bankers: Lindsey, whose deposit of £1,560 in 1673 has already been mentioned, and Messrs. Reeves and Herriott, who deposited £5,000 each for a few months in 1673 and 1675–6 respectively.[1] At least two of those classified in the Table as revenue officials were certainly also financiers on their own account: Richard Mountney, Cashier of the Customs, and Patrick Trant, a Customs official who was also agent for the farmers of the 4½ per cent duty on Barbados sugar, and it is possible that some or all of the other three were also. But there seem to have been no other

TABLE VIII

Background of those whose Deposits with Sir Stephen Fox were between £1,000 and £9,999 in aggregate, 1672–1676

Court and government office	30
Court connections	10
Military officers	6
Revenue collection and management	5
Churchmen	4
Bankers	3
Lawyers	1
Merchants	1
Unknown	7
	67

Source: Ilchester: Official, Sir S. Fox,
Army: ledger for 1672–9.

professional dealers in money amongst the sixty-seven depositors now under consideration.

By contrast, nearly half of them actually held some kind of post at Court, in the administration, or in the revenue, and the next largest group too were closely connected with the Court through receipt of a pension, possession of lodgings within the Palace of Whitehall, or by virtue of being the wife or widow of a courtier. The courtiers and officials included several leading figures in the government, notably Sir Thomas Osborne, Treasurer of the Navy and subsequently (as Viscount Latimer and then Earl of Danby) Lord Treasurer, who left £2,000 with Fox for several months in 1673, and other sums for brief periods in 1674. There was also

[1] Ibid., ff. 24, 158.

Sir John Duncombe, Chancellor of the Exchequer, whose credit balance with Fox in the early part of 1675 was £3,000; and Sir Joseph Williamson, Secretary of State, who deposited some £8,677 in the thirteen months after September 1674.[1] Among the others in this category were four important Exchequer officials: Sir Robert Long, Auditor of the Receipt; Sir Richard Mason, his deputy; Charles Twitty, who also had a post in the Receipt; and Thomas Hall, who was an attorney in the Exchequer and First Secretary in the King's Remembrancer's Office. There was also a long list of men with senior positions in the King's Household. From the Household below Stairs there was Lord Newport, Treasurer of the Household, who deposited a total of £7,460 in 1674–6; William Ashburnham, the Cofferer, who lent £7,000 in May 1675; and at a more junior level, Petley Garnham, a Groom of the Counting House, whose deposits between March 1674 and March 1676 came to £3,030. 15s. 0d.[2] From the Chamber there was the Earl of St. Albans, who was Lord Chamberlain; Marmaduke Darcy, Surveyor of the Great Wardrobe; Francis Rogers, Keeper of the King's Wardrobe; Tobias Rustatt, Yeoman of the Robes; Baptist May, Keeper of the Privy Purse; and two Grooms of the Bed Chamber, Thomas Wyndham and the young Sidney Godolphin. Then there was Sir Allen Apsley, Master and Surveyor of the King's Hawks, who was also a financial agent for the Duke of York; Lord Hawley, a Gentleman of the Bed Chamber to the Duke; Sir Richard Bellings, Principal Secretary to Queen Katharine; Sir Thomas Bond, a former Comptroller of the Queen Mother's Household; Sir Henry Wood, her Treasurer and Receiver-General; and so on . . . , down to Laurence de Puys, Keeper of the Mall. Many of these office-holders were, of course, also Members of Parliament.[3] Those with Court connections, but who did not themselves hold office, were a largely female group, which included the widows of two peers and Sir Stephen's own wife to whom he paid interest on a deposit of £1,000 which was later increased to £1,600.[4]

---

[1] Ilchester: . . . ledger for 1672–9, ff. 76, 159, 236, 251.

[2] Ibid., ff. 114, 158, 165, 280, 315, 337.

[3] Of those mentioned above the following were Members of Parliament at the time: Duncombe, Williamson, Long, Ashburnham, Darcy, May, Wyndham, Godolphin, Apsley, Hawley, and Wood. The offices held by the depositors have mostly been ascertained from *C.T.B.*

[4] Ilchester: . . . ledger for 1672–9, ff. 39–41.

The six military men in the Table were all senior officers and some, if perhaps not all, could also be regarded as belonging to Court circles. This was particularly true, for instance, of Sir Edward Brett, a troop captain in the Regiment of Horse, and of Colonel Somerset Fox, a retired soldier who was an M.P. and received a regular pension from the King. On the other hand, those tough old fighting men, Sir Thomas Morgan and Sir Robert Holmes, now Governors of Pendennis Castle and the Isle of Wight respectively, were not in any sense courtiers. The four ecclesiastics do not call for any particular mention, though it may be noted that they included the Bishop of Lincoln, the Dean of Durham, and Father Patrick, a priest who formed part of the entourage of Charles II's Catholic Queen. The solitary lawyer was Sir Job Charlton, Sergeant at Law, Chief Justice of Chester, and briefly Speaker of the House of Commons in 1673, who must have known Sir Stephen as a fellow M.P. The only merchant, John Kent, was fairly certainly Richard Kent's elder brother, through whom he was well acquainted with Stephen Fox.[1] There is no doubt then that the people from whom Fox was attracting substantial deposits were overwhelmingly from those Court, government, and military circles to which Sir Stephen himself belonged, and in which he was a familiar figure. This in turn suggests that personal contact was the principal means whereby he attracted funds. As for the depositors of smaller sums, when anything can be learnt about them, they also appear to be mainly from Court circles with a smattering of army officers amongst them. Those whose deposits were in aggregate less than £1,000 but more than £500 included, for instance, Sir William Boreman, Fox's colleague as Clerk of the Green Cloth; another Groom of the King's Bed Chamber; a Groom of the Queen's Privy Chamber; the Comptroller of the Works; the Keeper of the King's library; the secretary to Secretary of State Coventry; the Adjutant-General of the Army; and the Governor of the Scilly islands.[2] But even some quite lowly functionaries of the royal Household contributed to Fox's financial requirements, men like Henry Cocksedge, a Groom of the Buttery, or Walter

---

[1] Biographical details mainly from *D.N.B.* and *C.T.B.* See also Ilchester: . . . ledger for 1672–9, f. 58; R. Boucher, 'Kent of Boscombe', *Wiltshire Notes and Queries*, vii (1912), pp. 228–35. For information about Father Patrick I am indebted to Dr. John Miller.

[2] They were Henry Seymour, Charles Le Gard, Hugh May, Thomas Ross, John Cooke, Mr. Romfass, and Col. Anthony Buller, respectively.

Mackaloo, a Bread-Bearer, who had £100 deposited with him from before April 1672.

If we turn to the terms on which Fox was able to obtain funds we find that bankers and professional financiers usually lent on the security of tallies and Orders, of which the former had, after the Stop, again become the main instrument of short-term credit used by the government. They probably always had his bond as additional security, and occasionally lent just on bond, whereas non-professionals almost invariably lent on bond alone or some-times on the less formal 'note', which was simply an I.O.U. scribbled on a sheet of paper. The duration of loans made against revenue assignments was of course limited by the fact that tallies and Orders would (after the Stop) come up for payment in a matter of a few months. As for deposits made on bond, a period of formal notice was sometimes required before the money could be with-drawn. On 20 March 1674, for instance, Sir Thomas Bond lent £1,000 'payable at six months', whereas in the following year a deposit of £1,000 by the Earl of Suffolk and another of £5,000 by James Herriott were both repayable 'within one month after demand'.[1] In most cases, however, neither the ledger nor the bonds themselves specify whether any notice of withdrawal was required. Judging by the few references to be found in the former,[2] most loans of this type were probably repayable on demand, but where large sums were involved there may have been a gentleman's agree-ment that some notice should be given. Repayment on demand also seems to be implied in a large number of bonds which lay down the dates on which the first interest payments were to be made, and then promise repayment of the principal thereafter 'without fraud or further delay'.[3] In December 1675 the Earl of Devonshire lent £400 which, it was noted in the ledger, was to be repaid the follow-ing February, as it duly was,[4] and probably there were other de-posits entrusted to Fox for a fixed period in the same fashion. A very few left their money with him as long-term loans. Thus Sir Henry Wood had lent £6,000 some time before April 1672 and did not withdraw it until March 1678; Robert Earnly left his loan of £800 outstanding over the same period; and £650 which Petley

---

[1] Ilchester: .... ledger for 1672–9, f. 91; Ilchester: Family (box 237, bundle 5): original bonds of the Earl of Suffolk and James Herriott.

[2] Ilchester: ... ledger for 1672–9, ff. 147, 173, 251, 340.

[3] Ilchester: Family (box 237, bundles 5 and 6): original bonds.

[4] Ilchester: ... ledger for 1672–9, f. 112.

Garnham deposited in 1675 remained in Fox's keeping until 1711![1]
Such cases were not unique, but they were unusual. Most of those
who lent money to Fox in the 1670s withdrew it again, often in
several instalments, within two or three years, and many of them
did so within a matter of months or even weeks. Henry Guy lent
£10,000 on bond on 23 June 1675, received £4,000 of it back only
two days later, and the rest at the rate of £2,000 a week over the
three weeks following. Sir Job Charlton deposited £1,000 on 26
May 1673 and withdrew it again on 30 June of the same year, and
the £1,000 paid in by Patrick Trant on 19 July 1673 'on noate to
pay att demand' was taken out again by him on 1 October.[2] Of the
sixty-six individuals who made single deposits in the years 1672–6,
twenty-six left their money with Sir Stephen for less than a year.
Fox provided, therefore, a short-term resting place for funds,
enabling those who had some accumulated capital, or some surplus
of income over expenditure, which they wished to retain in a liquid
form, to earn interest until they needed to draw on it.

The entries in Fox's ledger which record interest payments
never state the rate involved, but where it can be inferred it was
invariably 6 per cent in the case of lenders who were not professional financiers, and all the original bonds which survive amongst
his papers from the 1670s specify the same rate, save in one isolated
instance from early 1676 when Henry Seymour was ready to accept
4 per cent on a deposit of £900. Fox indeed continued to pay full
legal interest on the money lent to him by non-professionals until
1684, but in that year he reduced his norm to 5 per cent and seems
to have had no difficulty in obtaining the money he wanted in the
years that followed.[3] However, there is every reason to think that
professional financiers and bankers, lending on the security of
revenue assignments, always received a higher rate of interest than
ordinary lenders, although this cannot be definitely established one
way or the other, either from the ledger or from the corresponding
day-books. In all probability such lenders required at least 10 per
cent in the 1670s, and indeed in January 1676 Richard Kent, in
whose name Fox was then making most of his advances to the
government, claimed that he was having to pay that rate on the

---

[1] Ibid., ff. 29, 41; Ilchester: Family (box 237, bundle 6): bond of Petley
Garnham.
[2] Ilchester: . . . ledger for 1672–9, ff. 105, 173, 272.
[3] Ilchester: Family (box 237, bundles 5 and 6): original bonds.

greater part of what he had lent.[1] On the other hand, a hostile critic of Fox's financial activities, Lord Keeper North, claimed that Sir Stephen made 'greater advantage than any officer in England', because men were prepared to entrust him with their cash interest-free.[2] A close examination of his ledger, however, shows that although some men did so, North greatly exaggerated the significance of this.[3] Fox sometimes received money on someone else's behalf, at the Exchequer or elsewhere, and held it to that person's credit for a few weeks, without allowing any interest, until it was withdrawn. Similarly, recipients of payments which he was responsible for making himself might leave the money in his hands for a while until they had a need for it. Sir Herbert Price, for instance, left £318. 16s. 0d. with Fox from 25 July 1673, when it was credited to him on account of a pension which Sir Stephen was paying on the Cofferer's behalf, until 30 September, and he does not seem to have been either paid or credited with any interest. Sometimes, it seems, people deposited funds with Fox specifically in order that he might make a series of payments for them, and their accounts might stand in credit for a while until all the money had been paid out again. Finally, Sir Stephen handled a number of what were, in effect, current accounts, through which large sums passed fairly quickly. Some of these, like the Duke of Monmouth's, were usually overdrawn, but others, like the Earl of Plymouth's, were usually in credit and yet apparently did not receive any interest. How much money Fox may have held interest-free at any one time it is impossible to say, but it was not a great deal in relation to the sums on which he did pay interest.[4]

In the years after 1672 Fox raised the bulk of his financial requirement from bankers, professional financiers, and those involved in the revenue, but he had an important supplementary

[1] B.L., Add. MS. 28078, f. 286.

[2] Sir John Dalrymple, *Memoirs of Great Britain and Ireland* (3 vols., London, 1790 edn.), Appendix to Part I, Book I, p. 145.

[3] In Fox's ledger depositors' accounts frequently contain no reference at all to interest, since if the amounts falling due were actually paid over in cash they would be recorded in the 'interest account'. Only if they were credited and added to the principal of a deposit do they appear in the depositor's account. However, if no mention of interest is found in either place it probably means that none was allowed, although occasionally interest was paid in cash to a person other than the creditor himself, for instance to his agent or steward. In such cases the sum paid would be entered in an account in the name of the actual recipient.

[4] Ilchester: . . . ledger for 1672–9, ff. 10, 86, 133, 335.

source of credit in his ability to attract short-term deposits from Court, official, and army circles. He seems to have obtained little or nothing from landowners unconnected with the Court or government, and not much from either the mercantile or the legal communities, both of whom were amongst the wealthiest groups in society. It may therefore be observed that if all the pensions, sinecures, and honorific Court offices formed a heavy drag on Charles II's revenue, the recipients of these royal favours did (through Sir Stephen Fox) make some contribution towards furnishing the government with the credit it so desperately needed. Part of Fox's business in the 1670s thus came to consist of advancing money to the King at interest to enable him to pay those entitled to Secret Service pensions, Household salaries, and the like; accepting back part of the same money as deposits on which he paid interest, but at a lower rate; and then re-lending it to the King at the higher rate of interest to meet the next instalment of the same pensions and salaries. Such were the opportunities for gain which were offered to the well-placed financier because of the government's inability to meet one year's expenditure out of one year's revenue.

We can now return to tracing the process whereby Fox extended the scope of his involvement in government finance in the years after 1672. The first step was his assumption of responsibility for advancing money to meet the needs of the royal Household, or rather that part of it technically known as the Household below Stairs, in which as First Clerk of the Green Cloth he was already an important figure. The chief financial official of the Household, the Cofferer, was still William Ashburnham, and hitherto, like other departmental treasures, he had raised ready money by assigning his tallies and Orders to the bankers. Now the bankers could help him no more and he turned, as he had done once before in a moment of crisis in 1668-9,[1] to his wealthy colleague. Fox began in April 1673 by paying the wages, salaries, and pensions, of a group of thirty or more important Household officials, including himself, which were already more than six months in arrears. At that time he could not do more because the additional forces raised for the Third Dutch War were still in being, and advancing the necessary money for their pay must have been stretching his

---

[1] See above, pp. 49, 51.

resources severely. However, by the following March, the extra regiments had been disbanded, and Fox could consider extending his commitments in other directions. From September 1674 the scale of his advances for the Household greatly increased, and his ledger begins to record a succession of payments of several thousands of pounds at a time to Charles Toll, who received the money on the Cofferer's behalf. From this time until the end of 1676 Fox was financing virtually the entire Household, for the sums recorded

TABLE IX

Sir Stephen Fox's payments for the King's Household, 1673–1676

$(\pounds. s. d.)$

	Paid by Fox on the Cofferer's account		Exchequer issues for the Cofferer
Jan. to Dec. 1673	23,124 12. 5.	Midsummer and Mich. 1673	135,200 0. 0.
Jan. to Dec. 1674	64,482 12. 7.	Easter and Mich. 1674	87,241 12. 6.
Jan. to Dec. 1675	112,904 12. 11.	Easter and Mich. 1675	107,461 1. 8.
Jan. to Dec. 1676	80,519 1. 0.	Easter and Mich. 1676	81,655 7. 10.

in his ledger as having been paid out on the Cofferer's account come very close to the total of Exchequer issues for this purpose.[1]

No detailed record seems to have survived of the negotiations which must have preceded Fox's assumption of this new responsibility, but the general terms on which he accepted it are clear enough, and there is an undated memorandum by the Cofferer amongst Danby's papers which spells them out in part.[2] Fox was to advance as much money as was necessary to make all payments as they fell due, and in return he received tallies on the Excise, a

[1] Ilchester: . . . ledger for 1672–9, account in the name of William Ashburnham, f. 94 etc.; B.L., Add. MS. 28078, ff. 315–16. The figures for the Exchequer issues derive from a document drawn up at the time for Lord Treasurer Danby. They differ slightly from those given by Chandaman, *English Public Revenue*, pp. 355, 358.

[2] B.L., Add. MS. 28078, f. 243.

proportion of which were paid every month to provide him with a regular flow of cash, and the remainder when the royal finances permitted. Fox did not receive poundage on Household payments, and so was allowed interest at 8 per cent on his advances for the whole period until they were repaid. The quid pro quo he obtained for this extension of his financial support was that the interest due to him on former lending should be made a priority assignment on the revenue, whereupon he promised to re-lend the whole amount when it came due for payment.

Most of Fox's advances as Paymaster of the Forces were made against the future yield of the Excise, and it was likewise the Excise which was used to support the Household. Fox was thus much concerned with this tax and the administration of the proceeds, for it was tallies on the Excise which provided the basis of his credit, and the status of these tallies, and their attractiveness to potential lenders, could be considerably altered by any changes in its management. In fact Sir Stephen's next step forward in the field of government finance was to gain control of those aspects of the management of the Excise which impinged on his own operations, but before we can understand the circumstances in which he was able to do this we must look more closely at the Excise itself and those concerned with it in the early 1670s. The Excise was a sales tax on certain alcoholic drinks, tea, and coffee, which throughout the period with which we are now concerned was farmed, that is to say leased by the Crown at an annual rent to various syndicates of moneyed men, who then undertook its collection themselves and derived their profit from the difference between their rent and the actual yield of the duties. From the government's point of view, farming had various advantages over direct collection, and at one time or another it was also applied to several other taxes including the Customs and the Hearth Tax. For a start, it relieved the state of the need to provide the machinery for actual tax gathering, and further it stabilized the yield of taxes which were inclined to fluctuate with changing economic conditions, or were uncertain for any other reason. Besides, for a government like that of Charles II which was perennially short of cash and for ever needing to anticipate its income, the farmers were a useful source of loans, and a standard feature of every farming contract was that they should provide a large advance which was subsequently repaid out of their rent. From the point of view of the farmers, the system seems to have been enormously profitable, and those of the Excise in particular appear to have made huge sums. One of their great advantages under the earlier contracts was that although their rent had only to be paid by quarterly or monthly instalments, the Excise money was coming in to them all the time, thus providing them with a large amount of ready money constantly at hand which they could, for instance, lend out at interest and pocket the proceeds.[1]

Late in 1673, when a new farm of the whole Excise was being negotiated by Lord Treasurer Danby, the syndicate that was to take it found it necessary to raise a loan in order to meet his requirement of an advance of £245,000.[2] As an inducement to would-be lenders, they offered, in return for the sum they required, to pay their daily receipts of Excise money, the so-called 'running cash', direct to them, which was a highly attractive proposition to any banker, since public knowledge that there was a continual flow of money on this scale into his coffers would greatly extend and strengthen his credit. The opportunity was seized on by a group of three of the Excise Commissioners, Sir John James, Major Robert Huntingdon, and Captain Richard Kingdon. The Commissioners were a body of government appointees responsible for supervising the conduct of the farmers, but these three were financiers in their own right and, in addition to being Commissioners, were also the Receivers-General of the Excise to whom the farmers paid their rents, a position which gave them security for the advances they were expected to make to the government. It may therefore be assumed that they were acting in their own interests quite as much or more than in those of the Crown, although naturally they defended their action in terms of the advantage which they were able to secure for the latter. At any rate, rather than see the running cash go to a goldsmith banker they stepped in, provided the farmers with the £50,000 they required, and secured it for themselves.[3] As they put it, they 'thought it their prudence

---

[1] For the Excise revenue at this period see E. Hughes, *Studies*, p. 143 et seq.; Chandaman, *English Public Revenue*, chapter ii.

[2] B.L., Add. MS. 28078, ff. 191–2, 195–7.

[3] The question subsequently arose whether the Commissioners had, by means of this loan, taken a share in the farm, which because of their position they should not have done. This misdemeanour does not, however, seem to have been the reason for their subsequent dismissal in favour of Sir Stephen. *C.T.B.* iv (1672–5), pp. 239–41; also see below, pp. 96–9.

to interpose, and become the medium by which the dayly cash might be paid directly into ye [Excise] office, and thereby the credit of the office [be] greatly advanced'. Having done so, they resisted repeated approaches from certain unnamed bankers

... who since the loane of that mony have once and againe offered to supply the mony borrowed upon that account, if the Commrs would consent and suffer the dayly cash to become theirs, which they refused, because by so doing that creditt which was like to become the King's, by the current of the said dayly cash, would then go from the King and become usefull only to the bankers.[1]

Sir John James and his partners were thus in a position to raise large loans on the credit of the running cash, which they could re-lend to the Crown to their own profit. As Kingdon put it, they were now in possession of a credit that would enable them, 'whatsoever emergency of estate or occasion shall fall out ... they may order almost any reasonable summ of money at any time in any part of England for the King's service'.[2] As far as the Crown was concerned there was advantage in the fact that, by virtue of their position as Receivers-General through whose hands the entire Excise revenue passed, the James syndicate would be prepared to lend on more favourable terms than would any goldsmith banker. Lord Treasurer Danby thus acted promptly to ensure that the agreement between the farmers and the three Commissioners became a permanent feature of the management of the Excise, by inserting a clause into the lease which was under negotiation, which bound the farmers to pay over the running cash daily during the whole period of the new farm.[3] There is no question, however, that the original initiative for this important step had come from James, Huntingdon, and Kingdon, and not from Danby himself.

Fox's comment when he heard of the three Commissioners' *coup* was, allegedly, that 'they had sowen very well'.[4] The Commissioners themselves took this to be a complimentary reference to the advantage they had gained for the King, but it may equally well have been an ironic one to the good turn they had done themselves at the expense of his own arrangements for raising money on his Excise tallies. Exactly what these arrangements were is obscure, but they seem to have depended on the farmers, on whom the tallies were struck, retaining the running cash in their own hands,

[1] B.L., Add. MS. 28078, ff. 468–9.
[2] Ibid., f. 438.   [3] Ibid., ff. 191–2.   [4] Ibid., ff. 468–9.

unpledged in any other way. Thus within a few weeks Fox is found complaining to the Lord Treasurer that, because of the change in the custody of the running cash, the Commissioners (in their capacity as Receivers-General) 'did not furnish him with a credit as formerly for carrying on the King's business', and that he could no longer take up any money on the credit of his tallies on the 'present receipt' of the Excise. He had other complaints about the way in which the Commissioners had failed to pay certain of his tallies as he had expected, and whether his accusations were justified is perhaps less important than the evidence the dispute provides of the 'ill correspondency' that was beginning to grow up between financiers whose co-operation was essential to the smooth running of the government's affairs.[1] Again in April 1674 the Treasury minutes record a repeat of the complaint that, because of the advance against the running cash, 'Sir Stephen Fox could not be supplyed as formerly was done'.[2] Indeed, as the year 1674 advanced, there developed something of a struggle between Fox on the one hand, and the James syndicate on the other, with Lord Treasurer Danby holding the ring and out to reap from it what advantage he could for the Crown. The issue at stake was whether the three Commissioners could retain the important position in government finance which control of the running cash had given them, and extend it at Fox's expense, or whether Fox would be able to withstand the challenge and further enlarge his sphere of operations by wresting the running cash from them.

In the middle of August 1674 we find Sir Stephen, in a paper presented to the Lord Treasurer, again expressing his dissatisfaction with the Excise as a source of credit since the new arrangements had come into operation.[3] He also alleged that he could not carry on the payment of the forces and the Household unless the Excise Commissioners (again in their capacity as Receivers-General) could provide him with large sums of ready money. It had always been an essential feature of the Undertaking that Fox should receive regular payments of so much per week or per month in cash, originally out of the Exchequer, later from other sources. At some stage the Commissioners had become responsibile for advancing this money (as a loan to the King, not to Fox) and Sir Stephen was now demanding that they should let him have more

---

[1] *C.T.B.* iv (1672–5), p. 217; B.L., Add. MS. 28078, ff. 468–9.
[2] *C.T.B.* iv (1672–5), p. 240.   [3] B.L., Add. MS. 28078, f. 167.

up to the point where the accumulated total of their advances was £120,000, which, he suggested, should carry interest at only 7 per cent. He also urged that the running cash should be applied to the payment of his tallies immediately it was received. This last proposal would presumably have had the effect of transferring the credit of the running cash back from the three Commissioners to the tallies, thereby making them, and through them Fox himself, as creditworthy as they and he had formerly been. The tone of the lengthy and detailed reply which James and his allies submitted to Danby makes it clear that battle had now been joined in earnest. Having asserted that the credit of the Excise was perfectly good, they went on to question whether Fox really needed so large an advance and suggested an audit of his accounts to find out. Their paper leaves the impression that Fox's tactics were to try to drive them out by demanding an enormous loan at an unrealistically low rate of interest, whilst simultaneously depriving them of one of their main sources of credit. At any rate this is how they interpreted his proposals, although it is hard to be sure whether they were justified in doing so. It is equally possible that they did not have the resources to meet the demands that Fox's commitments necessarily involved, and were trying to conceal the fact by claiming that he was deliberately exaggerating them. They complained that no other revenue receivers were required to make such advances, 'much less to so great a degree as Sir Stephen Fox endeavours to impose on us'. They also protested that his proposal as to the running cash was most unfair. 'He alledges that our being in the receipt is the foundation of our credit,' they wrote, yet 'he also proposeth that the running cash shall as it comes in be applied to his tallys, soe that it makes noe credit at all, for noe man will lend us money and at the same time know that we cannot repay them out of that cash because it must be applied to tallys'. They concluded by professing their readiness to do their utmost for the advancement of the King's service, but they trusted that the Treasurer's goodness 'will not suffer us to be exposed to anything unreasonable or unequal for any man's particular advantage'.[1]

Throughout their reply, James, Huntingdon, and Kingdon remained very much on the defensive: possibly they already knew or suspected that they had lost the first round, for it cannot have been very long after he had submitted his paper of 15 August that

[1] Ibid., ff. 402–3.

Fox produced his winning stroke. He proposed to Danby that he should himself, through a nominee, take over the Receiver-Generalship of the Excise on terms more favourable to the government than those by which his adversaries held the office. This would enable Fox to ensure satisfactory arrangements for his Undertaking, but it meant a large extension in the scope of his financial commitments. He would now himself become responsible for raising the weekly or monthly cash which had hitherto been paid to him by the government out of the Exchequer or by other lenders, like the Excise Commissioners, on the government's behalf. In addition, he would also be called on to provide advances to assist in the financing of other branches of government expenditure normally met out of the Excise revenue. His nominee for the Receiver-Generalship was none other than Richard Kent, who was still his chief assistant at the Pay Office, although since 1671 or 1672 he had also been involved in the banking partnership with Duncombe. By this time he must have had his own financial contacts, and this, together with his long experience of Fox's affairs, made him the ideal man for the latter's purposes.[1] So some time early in the autumn of 1674 they made their proposition.

The James syndicate apparently submitted alternative proposals, but they could afford neither such a large advance nor such a low rate of interest. At a meeting with Danby on 9 October they offered to advance £5,000 a month up to a total of £80,000 at 10 per cent for the forces, and perhaps something more for the Household, but it was not enough.[2] Indeed, Danby must have decided to accept the Fox–Kent scheme shortly thereafter, for on 13 November James and his partners were removed from office.[3] The bargain which Fox and Kent had struck with the Lord Treasurer had many provisions, but the essence of it was that the Receiver-Generalship of the Excise and the Paymastership of the Forces and of the Household should all be rolled into one grand Undertaking.[4] Kent was appointed Receiver-General and Cashier of the Excise, and all Excise receipts including the running cash were to be paid to him. In return he, or rather through him Sir Stephen, undertook to advance on the security of Excise tallies at least £3,000 a week for

[1] For Kent's career in Sir Stephen's service see also below, pp. 141–3.

[2] C.T.B. iv (1672–5), pp. 253–4.

[3] Ibid., p. 609; B.L., Add. MS. 28077, f. 77ᵛ.

[4] C.T.B. iv (1672–5), pp. 685–9; B.L., Add. MSS. 28078, ff. 436–7, and 51319, ff. 36–40: draft of Letters Patent.

the payment of the forces, and at the end of each muster to furnish whatever was required to pay them in full up to the whole of the £210,000 per annum at which they were then established. For this money he was to receive 6 per cent interest 'and no more', and a note at the end of Danby's memorandum of the agreement makes it clear that this meant that the customary addition of a few per cent over and above the 'legal' rate was not to be allowed on these advances. The interest was to begin, as it had done since the early days of Fox's Undertaking, two months after the end of each muster, since, it will be remembered, the Paymaster's poundage was reckoned to cover his interest charges that far.

As for the royal household, Kent was to lend £15,000 immediately to pay off arrears due to it, and then to make regular advances of £3,000 a month and as much more at the end of each half-year as was required to pay its expenses in full. Since Fox did not receive poundage on Household payments these advances were to receive interest at 6 per cent plus 2 per cent 'by way of gratuity or reward', from the day of lending until the tallies on which they were secured should be paid off. Furthermore, Kent was to lend, also at 8 per cent, such other sums as the Lord Treasurer should request, provided that the tallies he was given did not anticipate the yield of the Excise 'above 12, or at farthest, 15 months'. Finally, the memorandum of the agreement stated that Kent's interest accounts were to be audited and paid every half-year. Another important provision, which does not appear in the memorandum but which was inserted in the formal instrument by which Kent was appointed, was that his tallies were to be reimbursed 'in course', that is in the order in which they were issued, and in preference to all other payments out of the Excise save certain annuities due to the Queen and the Duke of York. To guarantee that this commitment was honoured Fox successfully persuaded Danby that Kent's appointment should be of the most formal kind, not merely by a warrant from the Lord Treasurer but by Letters Patent bearing the Great Seal of England. This was most important because it added greatly to the security which he and Kent would be able to offer those from whom they would have to borrow to raise much of the money they had committed themselves to lend. However, the Letters Patent subsequently became the subject of much hostile comment when, in the following year, the parliamentary opposition tried to impeach Danby. It was alleged against the Lord Treasurer that through the Letters Patent the long established procedures of the Exchequer had been subverted, since their wording made it possible for him to direct disposal of the Excise revenue simply by verbal instructions to Kent, without having to account for it in the usual way, thus dangerously increasing his personal power. Fox defended him in Parliament, stating flatly that 'the scope of the Patent was only to secure persons that advanced money', and although he can hardly be regarded as a disinterested party in the affair, it is notable that despite the many misgivings voiced about Danby's motives, neither Fox nor Kent themselves came in for any criticism. Indeed, both the Chancellor of the Exchequer, Sir John Duncombe, and the Auditor of the Receipt, Sir Robert Howard, neither of whom had been concerned in the negotiations with Fox and Kent, considered that Danby had struck an advantageous bargain with them. According to Howard, despite the departure from customary Exchequer procedure, 'as good service may arise from this Patent as ever was done to the nation'.[1]

Between the autumn of 1674 and the beginning of 1676 Fox's role in government finance reached its greatest proportions, and there can be little doubt that he was providing loans on a larger scale than any other lender. By undertaking to advance all the money required by the Household he had relieved ministers of worry about the day-to-day financing of that expensive department just as, ever since 1662, he had relieved them of worry about the pay of the forces. What is more, under the agreement with Danby that he would, through Kent, lend additional sums as requested, he was also advancing all that was needed by the Treasurer of the Chamber, and a considerable part of the costs of the garrison at Tangier, and making a smaller contribution towards paying the many pensions charged on the Excise. Since the establishment of the Guards and garrisons was about £210,000, the expenses of the Household about £90,000 a year, and those of the Chamber and Tangier some £30,000 and £55,000 a year respectively, it becomes apparent that Fox was furnishing all the credit needed to support almost a quarter of the Crown's total expenditure, which was some £1,500,000 a year at this time.[2] How much the Crown owed to

[1] Grey, *Debates*, iii. 57–60.
[2] *C.T.B.* iv (1672–5), pp. 681, 767, 827, 875; Ilchester: . . . ledger for 1672–9: accounts of Pensions on the Excise, Sir Edward Griffin (as Treasurer of the

Sir Stephen when he lost office in January 1676 cannot be ascertained with precision, but two months later in March (when the total would already have been considerably reduced) it emerges that £250,580 of loans made since Kent took over the Receivership of the Excise were still outstanding.[1] When what was still unpaid from before November 1674, and interest due on account of loans made both before and after that date, are also considered, then, as we saw in the last chapter, the government's total debt to Fox must have well exceeded £400,000.[2] Kent's share in the partnership with Sir Stephen seems to have been confined to discharging the routine business of the Receivership, and to providing Fox with a continuing loan of £20,000 or £25,000.[3] Otherwise, the whole business was Sir Stephen's, and if there was any doubt that the money nominally advanced by Kent was in reality lent by Sir Stephen, it is removed by the interest account in the latter's ledger which records receipt of the interest money which the Treasury had authorized should be paid to Kent.[4]

Despite the extent to which the government had become dependent on Fox for credit, his position was in some ways less secure than it had been when he was simply Paymaster of the Forces. The flaw in his position was that he had become so important and so powerful in the field of government finance that he was beginning to excite jealousy and distrust. Nor had the last been heard of Sir John James and his partners. Indeed, even before they had lost the Excise Receivership they had turned to the attack, and in a lengthy paper presented towards the end of October 1674 had attempted to undermine Danby's confidence in the probity of Fox's financial behaviour. They began bluntly:

For the better accomodation of his matys service in the payment of the forces, and that yor Lordship may know at all times the state of that affair it seems necessary, 1st. That as soone as may be an audit may pass upon Sr Stephen Fox his account of receipts and payments . . . because otherways the demands of Sir Stephen Fox can never be knowne, whether they be for the King's service or noe.

Chamber), and Samuel Pepys (as Treasurer for Tangier), ff. 159, 246, 281, 283, 327; Chandaman, *English Public Revenue*, pp. 355, 358.

[1] P.R.O., E. 403/2510, ff. 102–4.
[2] See above, pp. 56–7.
[3] See above, p. 82.
[4] *C.T.B.* v (1676–9), pp. 560–1, 765–6; Ilchester: . . . ledger for 1672–9, ff. 334, 349.

They then proceeded to argue that Fox's 'late importunitys for money agree better to the particuler ends of some bankers in Lumbard Street then to any publique service'. They substantiated this accusation by asserting that £20,000, for which he had recently pressed as essential for carrying on his office, had in fact been lent by him to Kent's banking partner Duncombe, who had in turn lent it (or perhaps lent it on Fox's behalf) to the Excise farmers to form part of the advance money on the new farm. The further sums for which Fox was now pressing were, they believed, destined to be used in the same way. They then gave their reasons for thinking that Fox's affairs could not possibly warrant further cash advances, and that he must already hold more tallies than he really needed. Finally, they suggested that steps should be taken to ensure that in future the true nature of Fox's dealings should be revealed, urging 'that a comptroll be appointed upon his receipts and issues, soe the matter of fact as it is transacted may be before yor Ldship as often as you shall think fitt'.[1] Fox's riposte was prepared within a matter of hours of his receiving a copy of the Commissioners' paper. It ignored such peripheral issues as the alleged misapplication of the £20,000, which, incidentally, his ledger suggests was actually paid to Duncombe to reduce his outstanding debt to the banker.[2] Instead, it concentrated on what he clearly considered the most important matter, the assertion that he had been issued with tallies to a considerably greater value than his actual payments in the current year justified. As to the Commissioners' paper in general, he wrote scathingly that 'it ravells irregularly into all my accompts', but since an answer was required he proceeded, with an avalanche of figures, to prove that the apparent excess of tallies in his hands could be completely accounted for by payments he had made to the forces in the previous year, money due to him for interest, and loans for purposes other than the forces.[3] A few days later the point was argued out verbally before the Lord Treasurer, but once again Fox seems to have got the better of it.[4] James's syndicate had not been successful in their effort to shake Fox's reputation for honesty: their first counter-attack had failed.

Less than fifteen months later the tables had been turned. At the

---

[1] B.L., Add. MS. 28082, f. 103.
[2] Ilchester: . . . ledger for 1672–9, f. 177.
[3] B.L., Add. MS. 28078, ff. 171–2.   [4] C.T.B. iv (1672–5), pp. 258–9.

beginning of 1676 not only was Kent replaced as Receiver-General of the Excise by James and Huntingdon, but Sir Stephen himself was dismissed from the Paymastership which he had held for fifteen years and replaced by their nominee Lemuel Kingdon. The explanation of Fox's fall seems to have been entirely political. There was not, for instance, any suggestion that he had failed to furnish the government with sufficient advances and, although James and Huntingdon may have initially agreed with Danby to make their loans on marginally more favourable terms, this was not the real reason why Fox was displaced. For this we must look at the Lord Treasurer's broad political objectives in the mid-1670s. Danby was trying to build up the power of the Crown, and the strengthening of the royal finances was an essential part of his policy.[1] In 1674 he had taken advantage of the dispute between Fox and the three Excise Commissioners to obtain credit on better terms, but in consequence the government had become heavily dependent on a single lender, and we may recall Fox's boast that at this time 'all the credit in the King's affairs center[ed] in mee'.[2] Danby clearly came to consider that this was an undesirable situation, and that Fox had achieved a dangerously strong position. What if he should become difficult about further loans? Evelyn tells us that according to the Bishop of Rochester, whom Danby had consulted, 'the Treasurer's excuse & reason [for Sir Stephen's dismissal] was that Foxe's credit was so over-greate with the bankers & monied men, that he could procure none but by his meanes.'[3] Fox himself confirms this second-hand report when he wrote of his successors, that Danby 'introduced them with hopes to have equalled the credit hee envyed in mee'.[4] Nevertheless, there were advantages to the Crown in continuing the situation in which all advances on the Excise came from a single source, for whilst there was only one borrower raising loans on the money market for this purpose it served to keep the rate of interest down. Fox had declared in the Commons during the debate on Kent's Patent that as a result of the new arrangements, 'no man borrows at interest [on the Excise] but Kent, whereas heretofore they vyed who should get most

---

[1] A. Browning, *Thomas Osborne, Earl of Danby* (3 vols., Glasgow, 1951), i. 128–33.

[2] See above, p. 79.

[3] *Evelyn*, iv. 267.

[4] Ilchester: Family (box 237): autobiography in small volume with green cover.

money from the bankers'.[1] Danby did not, therefore, want to revert
to the old system of competing financiers, but he had decided that
it would be healthy for the Crown to find an alternative to Fox. In
addition, there may have been a further reason why he wanted to
remove Fox from his important position at the centre of public
finance. Danby's own position as the King's chief minister was
never completely secure and he had enemies at Court, particularly
Arlington, who missed no opportunity to try to bring about his
fall. In the spring of 1675 a rumour had circulated that he was to
be dismissed and Sir Stephen put in his place as Lord Treasurer,[2]
which, if it reflected anything, probably reflected a hope on the part
of Danby's opponents that they might be able to replace him with
someone who would confine himself to the technical problems of his
office and would not try, as Danby had done, to establish a political
position independent of those to whom he owed his promotion.
Nothing had come of this, but Danby was not the man to leave any
potential rival in the field if he could possibly be rid of him.

But if he ousted Fox, was there anyone else who was both willing
to accept the assignment and able to command the necessary credit
to carry it through? Danby seems not to have regarded this as a
problem, and to have concluded that Fox's seemingly limitless
ability to raise money in the City ultimately derived from his
possession of the Paymastership, since the constant flow of cash
through his hands provided a basis for credit in the same way as
did the running cash of the Excise. Moreover, Danby believed that
the high rate of profit on his advances, which the poundage ensured, was what enabled Fox to lend to the Crown more cheaply
than his rivals. It was therefore recorded in the minutes of the
meeting on 9 October 1674, when it was made obvious that the
James syndicate could not match Fox's terms for credit, that 'My
Lord Treasurer is of opinion that Sir Stephen Fox may lend at 7
per cent (being enabled to do it by the King) when others can not
afford it at the same rate'.[3] Danby thus had no difficulty in deciding
that any financier who held Fox's office would be able to do what
Fox could do: that by bestowing the Paymastership elsewhere he
could ensure that the financier of his choice would have the credit
required. And if he felt that there was any risk to the royal finances
in getting rid of Fox, the considerably increased yield of the tax

[1] Grey, *Debates*, iii. 60.   [2] H.M.C., *Portland*, iii. 348.
[3] *C.T.B.* iv (1672–5), p. 254.

revenue in the mid-1670s, which made the Crown's financial situation more healthy than at any time since the Restoration, must have encouraged him to take it. Danby therefore entered into negotiations with James and Huntingdon (the third partner, Richard Kingdon, having died) some time towards the end of 1675.[1] By December one may conclude that he was nearing agreement with them, for he was ignoring Fox's complaints that he was getting into difficulties because of delays in the issue of tallies and payment of money which he ought to have received.[2] Finally, on 18 January 1676, Fox was dismissed. He was, according to his own account, taken by surprise: he had perhaps thought that he had become indispensable.[3]

Fox's immediate fear on his dismissal was that the government would not honour its debts to him, and that he would be ruined as the bankers involved in the Stop had been ruined. His dismissal, coming so suddenly and taking effect immediately, had given him no opportunity to reduce the scale of his advances gradually, or make arrangements for bringing his affairs to an orderly conclusion. He tried to obtain some security for the money owed to him by arguing that Kent should remain as Receiver-General until all his tallies had been paid, but his successors replied quite justifiably that this had not been allowed to them when they had been dismissed. Fox also attempted to secure three months' grace for himself as Paymaster, so as 'to leave his busy office in order, but it would not be granted, no not an hour, to the hazard of his utter ruine'. In the end, however, he was not treated too badly. He was allowed to retain part of the Pay Office 'for the dispatch of his affairs and to keep his clerks together till his accounts are declared', and the money he had spent on improvements to the building was refunded to him. More important, all Kent's tallies, amounting to over £250,000 as we have seen, were ordered to be paid off 'in course' as had originally been agreed. Further, in view of the fact that Sir Stephen was no longer receiving poundage on army pay, an extra 2 per cent interest was allowed on that part of the outstanding debt which had been advanced for the forces, so bringing the rate which Fox received for it up to the 8 per cent which was

[1] An undated document containing their proposals is to be found amongst Danby's financial papers. B.L., Add. MS. 28078, f. 418.
[2] Ibid., ff. 237, 244, 246.
[3] Ilchester: Family (box 235, bundle 1, part i): 'Narrative how E. Danby removd Sir Ste. Fox . . .'

paid to him on all his other loans. Finally, the £31,634 owing to
Sir Stephen for interest was made a high priority charge on the
Excise, to be paid immediately after all tallies already struck had
been redeemed. This last concession was, however, only obtained
at a price, and that was an undertaking by Sir Stephen, not only
to lend a further large sum, £40,250, to meet the needs of the
Household up to Michaelmas 1676, but also to re-lend for a period
of one year the whole amount of the interest owed to him as soon
as the tallies securing it should mature.[1] At various times before all
the tallies outstanding at the time of his dismissal were finally discharged, Fox had cause to complain that payments were not being
made to him by the Receivers-General as they should have been.
On one occasion in February 1677, for instance, he complained
that 'in this particular [they] deal with him contrary to what they
practice with other men', suggesting that the personal animosity
between Fox and the James group which had built up during 1674
was still alive.[2] Nevertheless, in the end Fox received everything
that was due to him.

The terms on which James and Huntingdon took over the Receivership of the Excise and the Paymasterships of the Forces and
of the Household seem to have been very similar to those which
Danby had agreed with Fox and Kent in the autumn of 1674.
Nominally, the Paymastership was granted to Sir Henry Pucker-
ing, but he was only a figure-head who never seems to have had
anything to do with the actual running of the office which, in
practice, was in the hands of Lemuel Kingdon, who was probably
the brother of the now deceased Richard Kingdon. There was thus
a neat reversal of the situation previously prevailing when the
Receiver-General had been the nominee of the Paymaster and dependent on him for finance: now it was the Paymaster who was the
subordinate partner.[3] James and Huntingdon had stepped into
Fox's shoes, but they did not find it so easy to take on his enormous
financial commitments. Their credit, Fox recorded smugly and
probably with a considerable degree of exaggeration, was not a
quarter as great as his.[4] Danby had been wrong to assume that

[1] Ilchester: Family (box 235, bundle 1, part i): 'Narrative how E. Danby
removd Sir Ste Fox . . .'; B.L., Add. MS. 28078, f. 286; C.T.B. v (1676–9),
pp. 14–15, 22, 155, 415–16; C.S.P.D., 1676–7, p. 8.
[2] C.T.B. v (1676–9), pp. 37, 422–3, 425–6, 429.
[3] Ibid., pp. 128, 145, 1279, 1306–7.
[4] Ilchester: Family (box 235 . . .), doc. cit.

Fox's ability to raise such large sums was solely due to his possession of the Paymastership. To a greater degree than the Lord
Treasurer had been willing to accept, his credit was a personal one.
Those who lent him money had as their security not only the tallies
he delivered to them but also his personal bond, which was a
valuable additional guarantee in view of his known wealth, and
particularly because it was known that he always paid interest
promptly and had done so even in the aftermath of the Stop. Fox's
contacts with the established financial community were now of
very long standing, whilst with the rising partnership of Kent and
Duncombe he obviously had an especially close connection. Indeed, as we have seen, Fox was to a considerable extent a banker
himself, and the substantial increase in the amounts deposited with
him in the years since 1672 provided him with a further element of
strength which his rivals probably lacked. Whatever the cause,
James and his allies appear to have been unable to raise as much
money as their Undertaking required, and to have got into difficulties quite quickly. The only available commentary on their period
in office comes from the pen of Sir Stephen and so cannot be regarded as impartial, but there seems to be no doubt that for the
first time since 1662 the pay of the forces began to slip into arrears.
What finally broke them was probably the very great increase in
the scale of the Undertaking caused by the raising of a new army
for service against France in 1678. It was only in existence for a
matter of months, but it was much larger than those which had
been mobilized during the Dutch wars: four new regiments of
horse, three of dragoons, and sixteen of foot, besides considerable
non-regimented forces, altogether 27,000 men. The total cost of
this army was over £650,000, and although it is unlikely that James
and Huntingdon were expected to advance the whole of this, the
government certainly looked to them for part of it.[1] In July 1678
Sir Robert Southwell, who had official dealings with the new Under-
takers, told the Duke of Ormonde that 'they have been stoutly
called upon . . . for supplies of money and their credits have been
put to the utmost stretch'.[2] As the months passed their difficulties
increased, and by spring 1679 the pay of the regular forces was ten
months behindhand, so threatening their discipline and, as Fox
remarked, 'making them unusefull & fitter to be disbanded then

---

[1] *C.T.B.* v (1676–9), intro. pp. lii, lviii–lxi; and p. 1227; B.L., Add. MS.
28078, ff. 305–6.   [2] H.M.C., *Ormonde*, N.S., iv. 445.

kept'.[1] Early in February of that year an officer in the Guards, Sir Charles Lyttleton, impatiently waiting for his regiment to be paid, wrote to a correspondent that there was 'not a farthing yet at Mr. Kingdon's office'.[2] If Danby did not come to regret that he had dismissed Sir Stephen, there were probably several thousands of men in the army who regretted it very much indeed.

The system which Fox developed in the 1660s and 1670s, and which James and Huntingdon attempted to continue, is a chapter in the history of government finance which has hitherto been almost entirely overlooked, and it is therefore worth trying to place it in a wider historical context than has been done so far. The seventeenth century was a period in which the English Crown experimented with many new devices for raising revenue and mobilizing credit, and it was eventually so successful in both directions that by the early eighteenth century it had acquired a financial strength unique amongst the European powers. The 'infrastructure of taxation' upon which this strength was ultimately based was largely the achievement of the Restoration decades, but in the field of credit techniques most of the innovations which were to be important for the future came only with the war years after 1689. It is true that several of the most significant of these had their precursors in the preceding period: the Exchequer Bills introduced in 1697 as an instrument of short-term credit were foreshadowed by the Treasury Orders of 1665–72, whilst the practice of funding had been anticipated by the measures adopted to deal with the bankers' debt in the years after the Stop.[3] Yet most of the ways which the English government tried in order to find fresh sources of credit in the three generations or so before the Revolution, proved to be blind-alleys. They proved to be limited in their usefulness either by the political opposition they raised (as in the case of the forced loans of the earlier part of the century), or by their heavy cost (as in the case of the advances made in association with revenue farming), and anyway were not capable of being developed to the extent which the vastly greater credit requirement of the 1690s would have rendered necessary.

[1] Ilchester: Family (box 237), doc. cit.
[2] E. M. Thompson, *Correspondence of the Family of Hatton* (2 vols., Camden Society, 1878), i. 174.
[3] Chandaman, *English Public Finance*, pp. 275–6.

Fox's Undertaking clearly belongs to this category of abortive experiments in methods of meeting the government's need for loans. It was no harbinger of the post-1689 Financial Revolution, but rather represented the ultimate stage in the evolution of an expedient for alleviating the government's financial difficulties which it had first hit upon in the time of James I, if not earlier. That expedient was to appoint as departmental treasurers moneyed men with good contacts in the business world, and to leave them to raise on their own account the funds they needed to discharge their official duties, and to make a profit out of it if they could. In the 1620s the greatest financier of the day, Philip Burlamachi, acted as paymaster to a number of military expeditions abroad, whilst Sir William Russell, Naval Treasurer from 1618 until 1627 and again from 1630 to 1642, was primarily a business man who personally raised at least some of the loans his department required. A further stage in the development of this approach to raising funds for essential services was reached towards the end of the Commonwealth period when responsibility for the pay of the large and expensive garrison at Dunkirk, which was in English hands between 1657 and 1662, was entrusted to Edward Backwell, who was able to draw upon the funds entrusted to him as a goldsmith banker, and to his partner, Sir John Shaw.[1] Then, with Fox, a financier came to provide all the credit facilities required not just for one but eventually for several spending departments, he opening up a private bank specifically *in order* to mobilize the resources required. In the years when Sir Stephen's involvement in government finance reached its height, that is 1674-6, it might perhaps have seemed that a solution had been found to the Crown's credit problem; that given the services of only a handful more such financier-officials able to draw upon both the resources of the City and of the investing public, so that the whole of the government's expenditure could be organized into a series of Undertakings, then it could be sure of obtaining all the loans it needed. The events which followed Fox's dismissal in 1676 must, however, have shattered any such illusions. As we have seen, Sir Stephen's credit, like that of Burlamachi or Backwell before him, was very much a personal

---

[1] A. V. Judges, 'Philip Burlamachi: a Financier of the Thirty Years War', *Economica*, 1926; R. Ashton, 'The Disbursing Official under the Early Stuarts', *B.I.H.R.*, 1957, and his *The Crown and the Money Market*, esp. pp. 165-7, 172, 183; Richards, *Early History of Banking*, pp. 32-3.

one, despite the use he made of government paper, and the eventual failure of James and Huntingdon to meet the demands for credit made upon them showed all too clearly how dependent such a system was upon the particular individuals who held the key positions. It thus became apparent that Undertakings offered a way forward only if the government was prepared to render itself entirely dependent upon those very very few financiers who at any one time were capable of shouldering the enormous burden involved, and whom, in practice, it could be exceedingly difficult, if not impossible, to remove. This was obviously highly undesirable for both financial and political reasons, and so we shall see that although Fox briefly resumed his old financial role in 1679, when he indicated a desire to withdraw after only a short time, no attempt was made to find anyone to continue the Undertaking. By trying to replace Fox with a rival group of financiers, Danby had inadvertently tried an apparently promising system to destruction, and it had been found wanting.

CHAPTER V

Clouds and Menaces; and the End
of the Undertaking

DURING THE fifteen years that Fox was Paymaster of the Forces high finance was naturally his main concern, but it was not his only one. Throughout this time he continued to hold an important administrative post in the King's Household, and doubtless to devote some part of his time to its affairs. We have seen that in January 1661 he had been promoted, on the death of one of his seniors, to be Second Clerk of the Green Cloth, and ten years later he was again promoted in similar circumstances, so becoming First Clerk.[1] There does not seem to have been any significant difference in the functions discharged by the two Clerks, but the promotion was important because it meant that Fox now stood next in line for the considerably more prestigious and much more lavishly remunerated position of Cofferer of the Household, which had eluded him at the Restoration. William Ashburnham, who had secured the Cofferership in 1660 on the basis of a reversionary grant made to him by Charles I, was now an elderly man, and there was every reason to suppose that Sir Stephen, still only forty-four, would outlive him. It should therefore have been only a matter of time before he achieved what was certainly one of his main ambitions, himself to become Cofferer.[2]

His hopes, however, were dashed a couple of years later when, for the second time in his reign, the King decided to set aside the tradition of promotion by seniority in the higher ranks of the Household. In 1663 Sir Winston Churchill had been brought straight on to the Board of Green Cloth as a Clerk Comptroller, but since this was a junior post to the one Fox then held it had not affected him personally. Then in 1673 Charles granted a reversion

---

[1] National Register of Archives: calendar of the Dering–Southwell correspondence, N.R.A. 16180, A/6.
[2] For the functions of the Clerks of the Green Cloth and the system of promotion which operated in this part of the Royal Household, see above, pp. 19–21.

to the Cofferership to Henry Brouncker, who was the younger son of an old courtier of his father's. Brouncker was one of the less amiable figures of the Restoration Court. Though a disreputable gambler, described by Pepys as 'a rotten hearted false man' and by Evelyn as 'a hard, covetous, vicious man', he was friendly with the Duke of York, and it was probably to please his brother that the King acted as he did. This unexpected grant adversely affected the promotion chances of everyone else on the Board, and of the Clerks of the sub-departments who were climbing the ladder towards it, but it affected Fox most immediately. His loyalty to Charles stifled his expressions of grievance, but there is no doubt that he was much disappointed. He wrote that, within the Household, Brouncker's appointment was 'quietly submitted to because it was the King's pleasure', but added that nevertheless it was 'looked upon as an unusual hardship to men without fault who had fitted themselves for that part of His Maties service'.[1] Moreover, there is some evidence that Fox did not submit to Brouncker's intrusion in complete silence, and he seems to have mounted a protest by refusing to yield precedence to him at Board meetings. Brouncker had no active part to play at these as long as Ashburnham remained Cofferer, but he had to attend some of them so that he could learn how business was conducted, and thus qualify himself to take over in due course. However, Sir Stephen, in all likelihood supported by some if not all of his colleagues, refused to vacate his usual place next to Ashburnham, despite two royal directives that Brouncker should be seated there, and eventually, probably through his friendship with the Duke of Ormonde, Lord Steward of the Household, succeeded in getting the ruling reversed. A third warrant, dated 31 December 1674, laid down that Brouncker's seat should be at the lower end of the table, 'where he shall sit, not displacing any of the officers of the Board from their accustomed seats, nor interposing in any debate or business of the Board further than is necessary for his information'.[2] Nor did Sir Stephen abandon his hopes

---

[1] Ilchester: Family (box 235, bundle 1, part i): documents entitled 'A paper concerning the succession of the officers below stairs' and 'Sr Ste Fox his case concerning the Cofferer's office . . .'; *D.N.B.*, under Brouncker, William (*sic*); *Complete Peerage*, under Brouncker of Lyons and Brouncker of Newcastle; Thompson, *Hatton Correspondence*, i. 156.

[2] *C.S.P.D.*, 1673–5, pp. 480, 488. Fox is not actually named in these entries, but since he was the member of the Board who was next in seniority after Ashburnham it is clear that he must have been the officer most intimately concerned in the dispute.

of one day reaching the Cofferership, and when, a few days later, Brouncker became seriously ill, he felt that the moment had come to press his case on the King. The good-natured Charles was always ready to do a favour if it cost him nothing, and to grant the request of an old servant for the reversion after a reversion to an office to which he would normally have succeeded by seniority anyway certainly fell into this category. So in September 1677 Fox was actually sworn in as Cofferer, his appointment to take effect after the deaths of Ashburnham and Brouncker. In fact Brouncker's illness did not prove fatal, as had apparently been expected, and he survived to succeed Ashburnham in 1679. But Fox was a step nearer achieving his ambition, and he seems to have considered that with this reversionary grant he had at last received his real reward for the nearly thirty years of service he had already given to Charles II.[1]

The internal history of the royal Household in the later seventeenth century has not yet been written, and in consequence it is difficult to say much about Fox's work as Clerk of the Green Cloth during the very long period (1661–89) that he held the post, although it is clear that his function was essentially that of maintaining financial control and that he acted as a sort of internal accountant and auditor. The office made a useful contribution to his income, although its relative importance to him declined as he became increasingly wealthy. During the 1670s his receipts from the office averaged some £654 a year, and in addition his right to a share of certain types of surplus provisions made a marginal contribution to the costs of his housekeeping.[2] It was also doubtless by virtue of his Clerkship that for a time in the 1680s he held, in partnership with a merchant named Warren, the position of Purveyor of Wax to the Household. In 1685 he reckoned that this would be worth £300 a year to him, but Warren seems to have proved an unsatisfactory partner and there is reason to believe that this excursion into the field of supply contracts was not a great success.[3] The other advantage which Fox's office conveyed was

---

[1] B.L., Add. MS. 51319, f. 51: royal warrant, 22 Sept. 1677.

[2] Ilchester: Official, Sir S. Fox, Army: ledger for 1672–9, f. 6. See also references to various items 'received from the Spicery' in Fox's own household accounts for the 1670s; ibid.: Accounts, Household (box 210).

[3] In the 1682 Household establishment the Purveyors of Wax are named as Richard Kent and William Warren, but Kent's name was clearly being used (as it often was) by Fox. Ilchester: Official, Sir S. Fox, Charles II's Household (box

the opportunity to secure employments in the Household for his relatives and dependents. Virtually all such posts were bought and sold in normal circumstances in the seventeenth century, the new-comer to office paying a price, which was usually between twice and four times the annual income he expected to receive from it, either to the previous incumbent or to the Great Officer in whose patronage the position lay. Nevertheless, there was brisk competition for most posts, since even the more lowly ones represented the first rung on a ladder of promotion, and thus a willingness to buy would not necessarily be sufficient to secure a purchase unless one had influence in the appropriate quarters.[1] It does not seem that any positions, at any rate any of importance, were actually in Sir Stephen's gift as Clerk of the Green Cloth, but as he gained in seniority within the Household, and as his growing importance as a financier, and later as a member of the government, increased his standing in the world in general, so those higher officials who were able to nominate to vacancies became more ready to listen to his recommendations. In this context we may note that in due course he became very friendly with some of his seniors on the Board, notably with old Cofferer Ashburnham, and with Lord Steward Ormonde, for whom he also acted in his private business concerns.[2] It was thus partly through the good offices of powerful allies that Fox was able, over the years, to secure posts for an impressive number of nominees. The second reason why he was so successful in achieving this is that he seems to have acted as a sort of broker for Court office-holders who wished to sell their places. In 1677, for instance, we find him undertaking to find a buyer for Sir Gabriel de Sylvius's post of Carver to the Queen, and on several occasions he himself bought offices and resold them, or in some instances retained them himself for a considerable period as an investment.[3]

---

269): 'A Booke of Wages and Board Wages . . . payable by the Cofferer.' See also reference to the Wax Purveyance and Warren's debts to Fox, ibid.: Official, Sir S. Fox, Treasury (box 272): vol. marked 'Brullion begun ye 28 of Ober 81'.

[1] See the section on 'Appointment and Promotion' in Aylmer, *The King's Servants*, pp. 69–96, 216 et seq.

[2] Fox's friendship with Ashburnham is suggested by the fact that on several occasions Pepys found Sir Stephen entertaining him: for instance *Pepys*, vii. 406–7, ix. 280, 320. For his relationship with the Duke of Ormonde see also below, p. 177.

[3] Ilchester: Family (box 237, bundle 3): instruction by Sir G. de Sylvius, 15 Nov. 1677; ibid.: Official, Sir S. Fox, Army: ledger for 1672–9, ff. 8, 9, 35. See also below, pp. 161–3.

The extent to which Sir Stephen was able to advance his own people is illustrated by the fact that in 1682 at least ten of his connections held posts in the Household below Stairs which they certainly owed to him.[1] The list was headed by his elder brother John, who had successively been joint Clerk of the Acatery and then sole Clerk of the Spicery in his own right,[2] but had recently resigned the latter office to his son John Fox junior, and probably through Sir Stephen secured a Serjeancy in the Larder to provide himself with an income in his old age. Similarly, John Fox junior did not owe his Clerkship of the Spicery to his uncle, but it is likely to have been through him that he was also Purveyor of Grocery to the Household, and it is quite clear that when in 1688 he was appointed Clerk Comptroller to the ill-fated Prince of Wales, James Edward Stuart, it was Sir Stephen's doing.[3] There were three more of Fox's nephews in the Household of 1682: Nicholas Johnson, a Serjeant of the Bakehouse; Nicholas Fenn, for whom Fox had paid £210 for a Yeoman of the Woodyard's place in 1672, and who had subsequently become a Serjeant in that department; and Thomas Fox, Groom of the Counting House, who had succeeded two other young relatives of Sir Stephen's who had successively held the post and died in it.[4] Then there was Thomas Dunckley, husband of Sir Stephen's niece Elizabeth, who was Closet Keeper in the Royal Chapel and a supernumerary Marshall of the Hall, whilst Dunckley's son-in-law, William Yardley, was a supernumerary Clerk-Assistant in the Kitchen, and some years later became Housekeeper of the royal residence at Greenwich.[5]

[1] Ilchester: Official, Sir S. Fox, Charles II's Household (box 269): 'A Booke of Wages and Board Wages . . . payable by the Cofferer.' Omitted from consideration are those of Fox's connections, such as his nephew by marriage Richard Dalton, who did not owe their places to him. The Edward Fox mentioned in the establishment may have been a relative of Sir Stephen's, but no reason has been found to suppose that he was, and he therefore has not been included.

[2] B.L., Add. MS. 36781, f. 21; C.S.P.D., 1672–3, p. 620.

[3] B.L., Add. MS. 51320, ff. 85–6: warrant for the establishment of the Prince of Wales's Household, 18 Sept. 1688; Hon. G. A. Ellis, *The Ellis Correspondence* (2 vols., London, 1829), ii. 59. Sir Stephen also installed a relative, Mary Johnson, as 'Table Laundress' to the Prince, but none of the other names in the establishment for his Household seem to have been in any way connected with him.

[4] Johnson actually died in April 1682 and so does not appear in the 1682–3 establishment cited in n. 3, p. 113, above, but see E. Chamberlayne, *Angliae Notitia* for 1682 (p. 153) and previous years; Ilchester: Official, Sir S. Fox, Army: ledger for 1672–9, f. 98; B.L., Add. MS. 51324, ff. 21–2: notes by Sir S. Fox on the Johnson family.   [5] *C.T.B.* ix (1689–92), p. 1064.

Not all those for whom Fox found appointments were necessarily related to him, and he also acted on behalf of some of his more deserving servants. In 1682 his steward, Richard Miller, held the post of Yeoman Porter; one of his long-serving assistants at the Pay Office, John Jenyns, was a supernumerary Serjeant of the Pantry; and a former house servant, Arthur Upcott, was installed as a Groom of the Ewery. Some of those whom Fox had advanced had already died or left their posts by 1682. Charles White, another former servant, for whom Fox had bought the office of Yeoman of the Field to the Queen for £200 in 1675, does not appear in the Household establishment of that year.[1] Sir Stephen's cousin John Rawkins, who had been a Yeoman Porter at least since 1668, had resigned in favour of Miller in 1681.[2] Sackville Whittle, Sir Stephen's brother-in-law, had surely owed to him his position as a royal surgeon, and likewise that of Surgeon-General of the Army, which he had briefly held for a few months before his death early in 1681.[3] Nor did Fox's willingness to help his family and servants in this way diminish in later years, although after he ceased to hold Household office in 1689 his ability to do so was substantially reduced. However, even as late as 1691, when John Fox senior died leaving vacant his post of Serjeant of the Larder, Sir Stephen still had enough influence to secure it for John Rawkins.[4] None of the posts in which Fox's clients are found were, it should be said, of any great importance, nor especially lucrative, but they provided their holders with a secure income of a few dozen or a few score pounds a year, and enabled Sir Stephen to discharge part of the responsibility he certainly felt for the material welfare of his very extensive circle of relatives and dependants.[5]

Besides his employment as Paymaster and as Clerk of the Green Cloth, Sir Stephen was also used by Charles II's ministers as one of the main channels through whom the so-called Secret Service funds were dispensed, and this continued down to the time of his

[1] Ilchester: Official, Sir S. Fox, Army: ledger for 1672–9, f. 8. This entry records that White paid £80 and Sir Stephen had paid the other £120.

[2] P.R.O., L.S. 13/35; Ilchester: Family (box 235, bundle 1, part ii): report by officers of the Green Cloth, 16 Dec. 1681.

[3] *C.S.P.D.*, 1680–1, p. 89.

[4] Ilchester: Family (box 237, bundle 3): note of fees for Rawkins's swearing in as Serjeant of the Larder.

[5] For Sir Stephen's family connections see the genealogical tables in Appendix I.

dismissal from the Paymastership. We have seen that a high proportion of the payments he made were in fact salaries and pensions to members of the government and the Court, ranging from the Lord Treasurer to 'Mistress Hellen Gwynn', the nature of whose services was well known to everyone.[1] It is true that there were other recipients of this money whose claim on the royal bounty was less immediately obvious, but it rarely (if ever) justified the sinister interpretation that opponents of the Court placed on it. And even if Secret Service money was occasionally used by ministers for the purpose of political bribery, Fox was in no way concerned in making the decisions about who was to be bought, and how much they were to be paid. There is no evidence that he was ever consulted about the use to be made of Secret Service funds, nor is it likely that he ever offered his opinion. Indeed, in view of the purpose of the funds, it is clear that no occasion would arise for him to be involved in this way. He simply paid out what he was instructed to pay out, and since the money was sometimes redistributed by those to whom he paid it he did not necessarily know who the ultimate recipients were. It is certainly not true to say, as one historian has done, that Fox was responsible for organizing the King's party in the House of Commons.[2]

Finally, in addition to all his other activities, Fox was also a Member of Parliament representing the borough of Salisbury, for which he had been returned, thanks to the patronage of Lord Chancellor Clarendon, at a by-election in November 1661. The campaign cost a modest £87. 10s. 0d., most of which went on 'an entertainment' for the Corporation and on a donation to the town's municipal poor relief fund; and, in addition, Fox apparently thought it prudent to acquire the lease of a plot in the cathedral close on which he could build a house, although, in the event, he never actually did so.[3] Clarendon obviously wanted Fox in the House to strengthen the voting power of the Court party there, and he never played a very prominent part in parliamentary proceedings. On the rare occasions when he is recorded as speaking in the 1660s and 1670s he was invariably non-controversial, even when a highly controversial subject was being debated, and usually

[1] See above, pp. 24–6.
[2] Baxter, *Development of the Treasury*, pp. 179–80.
[3] *V.C.H. Wiltshire*, v. 159 and n. 29; Ilchester: Official, Sir S. Fox, Army: day-book for 1660–4, 30 Dec. 1661, 23 June 1664.

his interventions were simply to provide his fellow members with relevant factual information, or to correct erroneous statements of fact which other speakers had made.[1] On the other hand, Fox was never a 'yes man'. He was not prepared to side slavishly with the Court irrespective of his own feelings, and on at least two occasions in Charles II's reign he risked the royal displeasure, and his own position, by refusing to vote with the other courtiers. The first was the impeachment of Clarendon in 1667. The King had turned against his Lord Chancellor, and having dismissed him and assured Parliament that he would never employ him again in public affairs, was looking on with approval as the Commons scraped together a rag-bag of ill-founded charges against him.[2] Fox owed his original advance in the royal service and his seat in Parliament to Clarendon, and the personal friendship between them since the Restoration is suggested by the fact that Clarendon had agreed to stand as godfather to the young Edward Fox born in 1663. Sir Stephen thus refused to join the parliamentary attack, although it is not completely clear from his own account whether he actually spoke out on Clarendon's behalf or simply voted against the impeachment. He later wrote of this affair that when

... the King took it ill from me, that I went in the Parliament for my Lord Chancellour against him, I took the liberty to say to His Majesty that he knew that I did know my Lord Chancellour so well that I could not in conscience give my vote against him: at which the King turn'd from me and left me to my self, saying I was an honest fellow.[3]

Eleven years later Fox again took his own line in Parliament and again over the impeachment of a leading minister, but this time Charles was less indulgent. The autumn of 1678 had seen the beginnings of a prolonged political crisis which rocked both the kingdom and the throne to their foundations. The allegations of Titus Oates that there was on foot a most dreadful plot by the Catholics against the person of the King and the Protestant regime,

---

[1] Neither of the parliamentary diaries in print for this period, which respectively cover the years 1666–8 and 1670–3, contain references to speeches by Fox: C. Roberts, *The Diary of John Milward, Esq.* (Cambridge, 1938), and D. B. Henning, *The Parliamentary Diary of Sir Edward Dering* (New Haven, 1940). But see Grey, *Debates*, iii. 60, 456.

[2] Ogg, *Charles II*, i. 316–17.

[3] Ilchester: Official, Sir S. Fox, Royal Service (box 267): account-book of exile and Secret Service payments 1660–5, at end; B.L., Add. MS. 51323: booklet relating to Fox's dealing with the 2nd Earl of Clarendon, f. 20.

and the mysterious death of the popular magistrate Sir Edmund Berry Godfrey, had thrown England into turmoil, and aroused a pathological suspicion and hatred against anyone whose conduct in any way aroused distrust. By early December the first victim of the political madness, the Duke of York's secretary Coleman, had already been executed, and as a result of revelations about the secret diplomacy which had been carried on with France, the Commons turned on Lord Treasurer Danby. On 19 December it was agreed by 179 votes to 116 that there were sufficient grounds to impeach him, and on the 21st the articles of impeachment were read.[1] The King was unwilling to dispense with Danby and was greatly incensed at the action of the Commons, the more so because a number of prominent office-holders had voted against the Court, including the Solicitor-General Sir Francis Winnington, and two leading Exchequer officials, Sir Philip Warwick and Sir Robert Howard. Among them was Sir Stephen Fox, who though no longer Paymaster was still First Clerk of the Green Cloth and had been sworn in as Cofferer in reversion. Parliament was prorogued and later dissolved, and the offending placemen were dismissed. Fox's dismissal was especially prompt, as this time there was no question of his action being condoned on grounds of loyalty to an old friend, and because Charles himself saw it as a particular betrayal from one who had gained so much from the royal favour. Nevertheless, Sir Stephen took his loss of office hard. He complained to the Duke of Ormonde that dismissal of Household servants without compensation was almost unprecedented, unless an exceptionally grave crime had been committed, whereas he himself had been guilty of nothing save of voting according to his own judgement, 'and perhaps upon better knowledge concerning that person than most that voted that day'.[2] This account of his own motives was perhaps somewhat disingenuous, for Sir Stephen could hardly claim to have been an impartial observer of Danby's conduct of affairs. He had been, as he saw it, 'maliciously' dismissed by him from the Paymastership, 'without the least pretence of a fault or crime', and this had left him with a lasting sense of grievance against the Lord Treasurer. Fox then went on to tell Ormonde

---

[1] Ogg, *Charles II*, ii. 559–79.
[2] Browning, *Danby*, i. 313; H.M.C., *Ormonde*, N.S., iv. 290–1. Fox possibly meant that he had personal knowledge of the methods the Lord Treasurer had used to enrich himself, some of which were, by any standards, corrupt.

that feeling against himself in Court circles was strengthened by
the inability of those with whom Danby had replaced him to carry
on the Undertaking successfully: '. . . that service from which I
was heretofore dismissed, now failing so dismally as it doth, which
less than half the credit I gave would have prevented, renews displeasure against me, and makes my going out as if sought by me,
who then struggled to keep in with treble the earnestness I do
now . . .'[1]

Sir Stephen's letter to Ormonde was an appeal to him to intervene with the King to secure his reinstatement, for the Duke was
still the titular head of the Household as its Lord Steward despite
his absence from Court in Ireland where he was Lord-Lieutenant.
It might be wondered why Fox was so anxious to recover his
Clerkship of the Green Cloth, with its considerable administrative
and accounting duties and its relatively modest financial rewards,
for he was already over fifty and very wealthy. Probably, he was
less concerned with the office as such, even though dismissal also
meant loss of his expectations of the Cofferership, than that the
King should accept his own interpretation of his vote against
Danby, and that he should recover the goodwill of a master whom
he had known since they both were boys. He told Ormonde that
his dismissal would have produced a debate in the Commons, had
he not taken care to prevent it. 'I would not,' he continued, 'for
twice my value, be an occasion of an angry address to the King,
who, if he will not restore me from his own goodness, I shall have
but little heart to serve, who have ever served him with all my
heart.' Court office was valuable, too, since it provided Fox with
lodgings within the Palace of Whitehall, which he had over the
years turned into a substantial house that was not only home for
himself and his family but also a convenient base from which to
conduct his affairs. Loss of office threatened him with loss of his
lodgings, and indeed he had only averted immediate eviction by
protesting that he had spent a good deal of his own money on them
which ought in justice first of all to be repaid him.[2]

Ormonde apparently did what little he could on Fox's behalf
from across the sea in Dublin, but it was not his representations to

[1] H.M.C., *Ormonde*, N.S., iv. 290–1; Ilchester: Family (box 235, bundle 1,
part i): document entitled 'Narrative how E. Danby removd Sir Ste Fox from
his office of Paymr . . .'
[2] H.M.C., *Ormonde*, N.S., iv. 290–1.

Arlington which obtained Sir Stephen's reinstatement. Nor, in all probability, did it owe much to Sir Stephen's own argument that Household offices were 'usually reckoned a freehold', and that to deprive him of his Clerkship was not only unjust to himself, but would also set a precedent which would prejudice all other officers, present and future, and overturn the strict system of promotion by seniority on which the organization of the Household was, at least in theory, based.[1] Fox was restored to the Board of Green Cloth early in April 1679 almost certainly because the new ministers had decided that they would need his financial services once again, and were anxious lest they might find him in an uncooperative frame of mind. Danby had resigned as Lord Treasurer at the end of March, and had been succeeded by a Commission of five Lords of which the Earl of Essex was the leading member. By the time that they took office the James–Huntingdon–Kingdon Undertaking for the forces, the Household, and the Excise in general, had clearly collapsed, and one of their most urgent tasks was to find a satisfactory alternative. The most obvious one was to bring back Sir Stephen Fox.

Fox's new Patent as Paymaster was issued on 23 May,[2] but on the very same day he found himself at the centre of another and potentially even more serious parliamentary storm. By this time the House of Commons had passed the first Exclusion Bill to prevent the Catholic Duke of York from succeeding to the throne, and were preparing an impeachment of the five Catholic peers who had been sent to the Tower the previous October. It then came to their notice that a number of members of the previous Parliament had received payments out of Secret Service funds, and it was immediately assumed that they had been bribed to vote as ministers dictated.[3] Fox was known to have been the principal, although not the only, dispenser of these funds until a few years previously, and attention was immediately concentrated upon him.[4] He was not present in the House when the affair blew up, and so he was immediately sent for, with instructions to bring with him such account-books and papers as would show to whom he had

[1] H.M.C., *Ormonde*, N.S., iv. 290–1, 296, v. 41.
[2] Ilchester: Official, Sir S. Fox, Army: Letters Patent of 23 May 30 Car. II.
[3] Ogg, *Charles II*, ii. 586–90.
[4] The following account of Fox's ordeal is principally derived from Grey, *Debates*, vii. 316–36. See also H.M.C., *Ormonde*, N.S., iv. 517–18, and v. 111–12.

made payments. When he arrived, without any accounts, he found himself in a very unpleasant dilemma. The Commons were in an ugly mood and determined to have their way, yet to give them the information they were demanding would be to betray the confidence of the King, to whom Fox still felt a deep personal loyalty undiminished by his recent experiences. He tried to play for time, but the temper of the House was such that this proved to be a dangerous tactic. The leaders of the hue and cry felt that they were being trifled with, and Boscawen made an ominous threat that, unless Fox gave them satisfaction, he would bring in a Bill of Attainder against him 'to confiscate his estate and take away his life'. Sir Stephen must have been shaken by this, and he became more forthcoming with his answers. All the same, he insisted that he could not produce the accounts they wanted, for when he had been dismissed as Paymaster he had surrendered the book in which he had recorded Secret Service payments. He admitted that he had also entered these payments in his ledgers, but protested that they would tell the House nothing. 'They are great vast books', he told them, with so many accounts for such large sums intermixed together that they would not be able to get anything from them. The only way in which he could satisfy the House, he said, would be to ask the King for leave to show them the account-book which he had given up on his dismissal. This did not prove acceptable to his interrogators. Mr. Garraway could not believe that so great a 'master of accounts' as Fox had not kept copies of what he had been obliged to give up, and Sir Robert Clayton, himself a financier, thought that the ledgers were likely to prove easier to understand than Fox was trying to make out. In this, incidentally, Clayton was only partly right, at any rate on the evidence of the only one of the ledgers which has survived. With perseverance it is possible to find one's way around it, but on the other hand the Secret Service payments are nowhere gathered under a single head, nor are they differentiated from other non-military payments which Sir Stephen had made on the King's behalf.[1]

After some further debate it was decided to send Fox back to his lodgings in Whitehall in the custody of three other members, to fetch his ledgers and other accounts and papers. They had only been there a few minutes when the Earl of Arlington, who had somehow received information on what was afoot, also arrived, and

[1] Ilchester: Official, Sir S. Fox, Army: ledger for 1672–9.

in his capacity as Lord Chamberlain informed them all that no documents might be removed from the Palace of Whitehall without the King's permission. Fox and his escort thus had to return to the House empty-handed to face a demand that he should tell, from memory, which members of the previous Parliament he had paid money to. He still tried to avoid revealing his royal employer's secrets, protesting that it was now too long ago for him to remember many of the names, and that he could no longer recall whether payments to particular individuals had been on account of Secret Service or on some other account. Again came the threats, and a member named Bennet rose to say that in view of his evasive replies Fox should be required to withdraw, so that the House could 'consider what is fit to do with him'. Eventually it was agreed that the Clerk of the House should read out the list of members, and that as each name was called Fox should say whether or not he had made any payments to him. The first name was the Speaker's, and an immediate stir was caused when Sir Stephen alleged that he had paid him £1,500 at the end of every session. Then, his memory apparently having recovered, he went on to name another twenty-seven members who had received money from him. The following day the House turned to interrogate some of those Fox had indicated. In fact the explanation of most of these payments, in so far as the House got to the bottom of them before the end of the session, was innocent enough. Successive Speakers had received pensions, and Seymour had received his out of Secret Service rather than at the Exchequer because the procedure involved was less troublesome to the recipient, and, it might have been added, not subject to the same deductions for fees. A number of other members had received compensation because they had been displaced from the Excise farm. Certainly, no evidence emerged that Danby, or anyone else, had used the Secret Service money for the purposes of mass bribery. Secret Service, as we have seen, was no more than a simple and flexible method for the Crown to make large numbers of relatively small payments which might be ordered for almost any reason under the sun.[1]

As soon as Fox had provided the House with some names he ceased to be the centre of their attention. It was accepted that he was in no way responsible for the use that ministers made of the funds which he dispensed, and that his role was merely that of a

[1] See above, pp. 24–2, 116–17.

'cash keeper' and accountant. On the second day of the Commons' investigation into Secret Service payments, others therefore bore the brunt of the questioning, but nevertheless Sir Stephen must have been highly relieved when, at the beginning of the following week, Parliament was prorogued before the matter could be taken any further. The prorogation was subsequently turned into a dissolution so that the House of Commons of 1679 did not meet again, and when a new one assembled eighteen months later other matters had arisen to occupy their attention.

Having survived the wrath of Parliament, Fox was able to turn to the problems which faced him now that he was Paymaster again. The actual circumstances of his reappointment he later recalled in the following terms:

> The King sent my Lord Godolphin, then one of the Lords of the new Commission of the Treasury, to propose my reundertaking that affaire & ordered my attendance on His Matie, who began thus, 'Fox thou art my man still, for I am told that you can serve mee if you will', to which I humbly answered that 'If I can I am sure I will.' 'Then' [said the King] 'goe downe to ye Treasury & let them know so much.'

Lemuel Kingdon and his associates were ten months behind in paying the Guards, and it was arranged that Fox should assume responsibility for them from the first day of the preceding January. He thus undertook to pay nearly half their arrears and to discharge them by 1 November.

> The sume necessary [Fox continues] was not les then five musters at 10 callender months amounting to £165,000 wch when computed at the Treasury (particularly by Sir Edw. Deering), & that I said notwithstanding the great sume I would endeavour to doe it, hee said that hee would not beleeve it possible till hee saw it don, for at that time the Treasury was very low & no credit to bee found on the funds, so remote as the anticipations made them. However I had the good luck at my returne into the office to have sufficient credit to perform that great worke, in five months to pay them ten . . .[1]

It is not completely clear whether this claim to have cleared the arrears of the army in so short a time is fully justified, for there is evidence that in early January 1680 at least one regiment had still not received back pay for which Fox was responsible, and indeed

---

[1] Ilchester: Family (box 237): autobiography in small volume with green cover; also P.R.O., E. 403/2576, ff. 128–31.

elsewhere Fox says that it was not until eight months after he had resumed responsibility for the army that he had 'retrieved their being fully paid'. However, at least by early 1680 he had got the pay of the forces up to date.[1]

No explicit statement of the terms on which Fox re-entered large-scale government finance in 1679 seems to have survived, but the indirect evidence suggests that they must have been similar to those which he had agreed with Danby in October 1674. Once again, in order to provide him with a solid basis of credit for raising loans, he was given control of the running cash of the Excise by the appointment of his nominee to the Receivership. Richard Kent was no longer available to act for Sir Stephen, for he was now too deeply involved in lending to the government in partnership with Duncombe, and since May 1677 had held the post of Cashier of the Customs, either on his own account or more probably as Duncombe's nominee.[2] Fox thus had to make use of the man who had succeeded Kent as his chief deputy at the Pay Office, his nephew Nicholas Johnson.[3] Johnson's appointment as Cashier and Receiver of the Excise took effect on 28 May, only a few days after Fox's own re-appointment as Paymaster, and the advances made by the latter in the months that followed were all in Johnson's name. As in 1674–6, Fox provided the money not only for the army but for the Household as well, and contributed towards the requirements of other departments and individuals, this time including not only the Treasurer of the Chamber but also the Victuallers of the Navy and the Colony of Virginia. Interest was allowed him at 8 per cent on most of what he lent, but he received 10 per cent on the £10,200 advanced to the Victuallers, and only 6 per cent

[1] Thompson, *Hatton Correspondence*, i. 214; B.L., Add. MS. 51324, f. 54: document headed 'Losses sustained by Sr Ste Fox . . .' Fox's ledger 'D', which covered this period, does not survive, and so the sources of credit which enabled him to pay off the army apparently so successfully cannot be analysed in detail. However, some abstracts from it are to be found amongst his papers, and these seem to show that he obtained the money he required from much the same sources as in 1674–5. In July 1680 he still owed £46,000 to Kent and Duncombe, either as individuals or as a partnership, and £11,600 to Sir Jeremiah Snow; most of the remaining creditors from outside the financial community were people of the same type (and often the same individuals) as those discussed on pp. 84–8, above. Ilchester: Official, Sir S. Fox, Charles II's Household (box 269): abstract from missing Ledger 'D', 1 July 1680.

[2] *C.T.B.* v (1676–9), pp. 618, 635; B.L., Add. MS. 28078, f. 284; Hughes, *Studies*, pp. 164 and 676 n.

[3] See below, p. 143.

on the £6,114 provided for Virginia. What was the largest figure reached by Fox's advances in 1679–80 does not emerge, but when Johnson left the Receivership on 25 March 1680 the amount still outstanding was at least £163,577. 12s. 5d., all secured on tallies.[1]

The financial aid furnished by Fox under these arrangements seems to have been an important element in the continued solvency of the government at a very crucial time. The political crisis of the Popish Plot continued unabated, and really serious financial difficulties would have put Charles at the mercy of the Commons and possibly have changed the course of English history, but as it was, and despite the failure of his attempt to extract a subsidy from Louis XIV, he was just able to get by. Parliament was prorogued on 27 May, within a fortnight or so of Sir Stephen's return to the Pay Office, and the King was able to avoid the necessity of facing it again until the October of the following year.[2] There were those who might, if they had had their chance, have attempted to destroy Fox at this stage. At the end of September 1679, Sir Robert Southwell told the Duke of Ormonde that, because the opposition had hoped Charles would run aground for want of money, Fox had '. . . new clouds and menaces upon him for being thought the only instrument that has kept things afloat by his credit and supplies, so that all his past accounts are threatened with a Brookhouse'.[3] It was probably as well for him that the new Parliament which met little over a week later was prorogued immediately. But Fox's role in enabling the King to do without Parliament for sixteen vital months was not forgotten, and he was certainly one of those the Commons had in mind when in January 1681 they passed a resolution, 'that whosoever shall accept or buy any tally of anticipation upon any part of the King's revenue arising by Customs,

[1] P.R.O., E. 403/2614, ff. 9–10, 66ᵛ; C.T.B. vi (1679–80), pp. 287, 406, 438, 459, 610–11; Ilchester: Official, William Fox and Nicholas Johnson (box 279): Letters Patent, 25 March 32 Car. II; ibid.: Family (box 237, bundle 3): Johnson's Declaration of Trust. That the £163,577. 12s. 5d. was not the whole extent of the Government's debt to Fox is suggested in Ilchester: Official, Sir S. Fox, Charles II's Household (box 269): abstract of debtors and creditors from missing ledger 'D'. However, some of the items recorded as owing to Fox on his various government accounts may be book-keeping entries rather than genuine credit items.

[2] Ogg, Charles II, ii. 590–3.

[3] H.M.C., Ormonde, N.S., iv. 538. 'Brookhouse' refers to the parliamentary committee which examined the accounts of how the money voted for the Second Dutch War had been spent: it had acquired a reputation for making extremely searching inquiries.

Excise, or Hearth Money shall be adjudged to hinder the sitting of Parliament and shall be responsible for the same in Parliament'.[1]

Nevertheless, the arrangements of May 1679 did not remain in force for very long. In November, only six months after being restored to the Paymastership, Fox accepted an invitation to become a Treasury Commissioner himself,[2] which made it impossible for him to continue in an office which involved constant soliciting at the Treasury for funds, and over whose affairs he would, along with the other Commissioners, have to maintain a watch. He actually remained as Paymaster until January 1680, but then he resigned in favour of Nicholas Johnson (who now had ten years of experience in the work) and his own eighteen-year-old son William. Unfortunately William died within a few months and so Johnson, who had given up the post of Cashier of the Excise at Lady Day 1680, acted as sole Paymaster until his own death two years later. He was then succeeded by Sir Stephen's last surviving son Charles, who remained in office until he was dismissed by James II towards the end of 1685 in circumstances to be discussed later.[3] So Fox was able to keep the Paymastership firmly within his own family, but after his own resignation it was no longer operated as an Undertaking. At some stage between Sir Stephen's promotion to the Treasury Board and his resignation as Paymaster, it was decided that henceforward the Treasury itself should assume direct responsibility for providing the forces with their pay. For the future, such loans as might be required would be raised directly by the Treasury, thus ending the Paymaster's role as an independent financier and limiting his function to the distribution of the funds which were issued to him.[4] There was no reason why Sir Stephen's departure from the Pay Office should in itself have precipitated this change, for had other things remained equal his nephew and sons could presumably have continued to operate the system he had developed, using his capital and his City contacts. They did not do so, and it appears that the explanation lies in Sir Stephen's unwillingness to continue indefinitely exposing the fortune he had made to the risks the Undertaking necessarily involved.

---

[1] *Commons Journals*, 9 (1667–87), p. 702.   [2] See below, pp. 215–16.

[3] Ilchester: Official, William Fox and Nicholas Johnson (box 279); Letters Patent, 31 Jan. 31 Car. II; *C.T.B.* vii (1681–5), pp. 458, 773; and see below, p. 225.

[4] G. Hutt, *Papers illustrative of the Origin and Early History of the Royal Hospital at Chelsea* (London, 1872), p. 127.

The royal warrant which directed the Treasury Lords to take over the advance of money to the forces recited that,

Whereas by agreement betwixt the officers of our Guards and Garrisons and Sir Stephen Fox, Knt., Paymaster-General of our Forces, there hath bin for eighteene yeares past a deduction of twelve pence out of every twenty shillings drawn from the pay of all our said Forces, to enable the said Paymaster to advance their pay by weekly subsistence, and within a short time after the end of every muster to compleat the full pay thereof both to officers and soldiers. Which said payment by way of advance our Paymaster hath declared unto us he can no longer carry on by reason of the present difficulties on our revenue.[1]

It does not seem, however, that this account of the end of the Undertaking should be taken too literally, for Fox had just succeeded in raising a very large sum for the payment of the arrears owing to the troops when he resumed his office earlier in the year; nor were the 'difficulties' on the revenue greater in 1679 than they had been on several occasions in the past. Elsewhere Fox himself tells us that he had been reluctant to get involved in active financing once again and that 'nothing but the King's want of credit could have brought mee back againe into so hazardous an undertaking . . .', words which perhaps carry the implication that he had agreed to it only as an interim measure to help the government over a particularly awkward period. They are also words which suggest that Danby may have been right when he observed that Fox was becoming more cautious as a financier as he grew older.[2] Certainly, the Undertaking was very profitable, especially since its extension to the Household in 1674, but it must always have involved great strain and worry in the continuous negotiations with the bankers for the never-ending series of loans which it required, and in constantly watching political events which might pose a threat to the orderly repayment of moneys advanced. In the crisis-ridden atmosphere of 1679 the element of risk from unforeseen political developments may have seemed unacceptably great. Apart from the danger of catastrophic financial loss if the regime were overthrown, Fox, with his recent parliamentary ordeal still fresh in his

---

[1] G. Hutt, *Papers illustrative of the Origin and Early History of the Royal Hospital at Chelsea* (London, 1872), p. 127.

[2] Ilchester: Family (box 237): autobiography in small volume with green cover; ibid.: Family (box 235, bundle 1, part i): 'Narrative how E. Danby removd Sir Ste Fox . . .'

mind, may well have wondered whether the Commons might not one day turn on him for his financial support for the hated 'Standing Army'.

If there is good reason to think that Fox had concluded that he had gone on with the Undertaking for long enough, there is also reason to suppose that there were others who thought so too. Had the King's ministers considered that a continuance of the Undertaking was essential, they could probably have found another financier or group of financiers with whom to replace Sir Stephen, although it must be admitted that Danby's experience with James, Huntingdon, and Kingdon, did not provide a very encouraging precedent. The decision not to do so may have owed something to the fact that not only Sir Stephen's expertise, but also his financial resources, were now at the disposal of the Treasury itself. It may also have owed something to an appreciation of the fundamental disadvantage of the Undertaking system which has already been referred to, its tendency to make the Crown too dependent on a single source of credit.[1] Indeed, dismantling the Undertaking was in line with the trend in the administration of government finance during the latter part of Charles II's reign, which was away from indirect methods towards more direct and immediate control by the Treasury. Farming of the Customs was abandoned in 1671, although in the case of the Hearth Tax it lasted until 1684. Farming of the Excise continued until 1683, but the terms on which the farms were let had been progressively tightened up since the mid-1670s. Direct collection of the revenues involved many difficulties, but once they were overcome a higher proportion of the taxes paid by the subject actually reached the Exchequer, and the government also saved the interest which it had previously had to pay to the farmers on their advance money. Similarly, ending the indirect system of financing the forces and the Household, whereby the Paymaster was employed as a middleman for the raising of loans, offered the Crown the possibility of saving on the interest it paid out, and ministers like Laurence Hyde, first Treasury Commissioner since the Earl of Essex's resignation in November, who were hostile to the continuance of revenue farming, were doubtless glad of the opportunity to bring the Undertaking to an end.[2]

With the end of the Undertaking the Paymastership ceased, temporarily, to be a source of great profit to its holders. Neither

[1] See above, pp. 109–10.   [2] Hughes, *Studies*, pp. 138–59.

Nicholas Johnson nor Charles Fox made much out of it,[1] although the brevity of their tenures, two years and three months, and three years and seven months, respectively, hardly gave them the time; and they were only Sir Stephen's nominees managing the post on his behalf. But anyway the terms on which they had been appointed precluded the accumulation of a fortune whether by them or by Sir Stephen. From 1 January 1680 the Paymaster received a salary of £365 a year, and although he continued to deduct one shilling in the pound from everything he paid over to the army, he was now allowed to retain only one-third of it for himself, the other two-thirds being at the disposal of the King.[2] Nor was the four pence in the pound which he received from this time onwards by any means pure profit, for out of it he had to pay the fees on all the money issued to him out of the Exchequer, the salaries of the Pay Office staff, and all the other expenses of the office, including the substantial New Year's gifts traditionally payable to Exchequer and Treasury officials by those who had extensive dealings with them. The fees amounted to three halfpence per pound (£6. 5s. 0d. per £1,000), which therefore absorbed more than one-third of the Paymaster's share of the poundage; office salaries probably came to nearly £1,000 a year in the early 1680s, and by 1685 they totalled £1,460 a year; and the remaining expenses were such that, as long as the establishment was still not much over £200,000 a year, the net profit to the Paymaster out of his four pence per pound can only have been a matter of several hundreds of pounds a year.[3] In 1682, for instance, Sir Stephen reckoned on receiving £600 from the place, and in 1684, £660.[4] Not until the great expansion in the size of the army which began in James II's reign did the Paymaster's third of the poundage yield him a really large sum. When in October 1685 the establishment stood at about £600,000 a year, Fox calculated that it was worth £3,614 clear of all deductions to the holder of the office, and by early 1689, when

---

[1] See below, pp. 143, 270–3.

[2] Actually the salary was £1 per day. P.R.O., A.O. 1/51/31, 33, 52/35, 36, 53/38, 39; Hutt, loc. cit.

[3] B.L., Add. MS. 15897, f. 29; C. Walton, *History of the British Standing Army 1660–1700* (London, 1894), p. 656 n.

[4] Ilchester: Official, Sir S. Fox, Treasury (box 272): calculation of income at the back of account-book marked 'Brullion begun ye 28 of Ober 81'; ibid.: Family (box 235, bundle 4): document entitled 'A computation of My owne Estate'.

the pay of the forces was £930,000 a year, Lord Ranelagh put it at £6,910 clear.[1]

As for unofficial opportunities for gain, these too were very restricted in the last years of Charles II's reign. Later Paymasters made great fortunes by investing, to their own profit, the balances of government money which had been issued to them, but which they did not need to pay out immediately. It seems probable that Sir Stephen, or rather his nephew and son on his behalf, did like-wise in the years after 1680,[2] but the size of the balances in their hands were so small by subsequent standards that they cannot have made a great deal in this way either. Fox had made a fortune out of the Paymastership as an Undertaking, but he did not add greatly to it by continuing to hold his old office, through nominees, on a quite different basis for nearly six years more. It was ironical that he finally lost the Pay Office at the very moment when it was once again becoming financially worthwhile with the enormous increase in the scale of its operations. At the time of Charles Fox's dismissal in November 1685 the Paymaster's salary, together with the yield of the poundage, offered the prospect of an income of about £4,000 a year, but it was Sir Stephen's successor Lord Ranelagh who reaped the golden harvest.

[1] B.L., Add. MS. 15897, f. 29; P.R.O., S.P. 8/5, item 9.

[2] This is suggested by comments in an account of the operation of the Pay Office in Nicholas Johnson's time, see B.L., Add. MS. 36148, ff. 137–8.

CHAPTER VI

The Founding of Chelsea Hospital

IF THE last years of Sir Stephen's tenure of the Paymastership were not particularly rewarding in material terms, they were nevertheless worth while from a quite different point of view. The early 1680s saw the establishment of one of the best-known charities and most splendid public buildings in London, the Royal Military Hospital at Chelsea, and Fox played the leading part in its promotion. Posterity has not fully acknowledged what was arguably the greatest of his achievements, and indeed his name has never been connected in the public mind with Chelsea Hospital. Part of the reason for this has obviously been that the Hospital was a royal foundation, and that this has tended to throw a veil of anonymity over those involved in the implementation of the scheme. It is also partly because popular imagination found in Nell Gwyn a far more alluring figure to associate with the scarlet-coated pensioners.[1]

In fact the legend that it was she who was ultimately responsible for the establishment of the Hospital seems to be a complete invention, and probably arose because she had some connections with Chelsea village, and because her good nature made her by far the most popular of Charles II's mistresses.[2] Perhaps the story originated with the earliest pensioners, ex-soldiers whom the Hospital had saved from the terrible fate which must have haunted the minds of many of them as they grew older, and who liked to attribute their salvation to the kindness of pretty, witty Nell. But by the last years of Charles II's reign it did not require the prompt-

---

[1] The fullest account for the foundation and the subsequent history of Chelsea Hospital is given by C. G. T. Dean, *The Royal Hospital Chelsea* (London, 1950). This author does give Fox the credit due to him, and indeed rather more, for he is uncritical in his acceptance of all the claims Fox made on his own behalf, some of which, recorded in narrative accounts compiled in extreme old age, are not altogether justified. Dean's work has not, however, succeeded in securing for Fox the general reputation of a public benefactor enjoyed by such men as Guy and Coram, although his claim to the esteem of posterity is almost comparable to theirs.

[2] T. Faulkner, *An Historical and Topographical Description of Chelsea* (2 vols., Chelsea, 1829), ii. 234–9.

ing of a generous-hearted woman to remind those with eyes to see that there was a pressing need to make some provision for soldiers no longer fit for service. The King had maintained an army continuously in being for twenty years, and some of its strength had enlisted in the 1650s, so that quite apart from those disabled by wounds, every year more and more soldiers were getting too old for their duties. The plight of the latter after their discharge was frequently even more wretched than that of the wounded, many or most of whom did receive at least some compensation, however inadequate: a pension of £6. 13s. 4d. per annum for the loss of an arm or leg, or £4 per annum for the loss of an eye, for instance.[1] But those who survived unhurt, and were finally discharged from their companies on account of age, were simply sent back to their places of origin with little hope of obtaining any employment, and left to beg as best they might. Even officers might be left destitute at the end of their career. In 1684, for example, the case of Captain Graham was brought to the notice of the Treasury. He had served for many years in Tangier, behaving with conspicuous gallantry on one critical occasion, but was now sixty years old, 'disabled by fits from further service, and in great want'.[2]

Fox has left us a fairly explicit account of how the idea arose for a hospital to provide shelter and support for these unfortunates and, although some parts of his narrative are clearly unreliable, there is no reason to doubt the truth of most of what he wrote.[3] At any rate his narratives confirm other evidence that the original impetus seems to have come from the King himself. Charles was probably influenced by a desire to emulate Louis XIV's foundation of the Hôtel Royal des Invalides in Paris which had been begun in 1670. The Duke of Monmouth had visited Les Invalides twice in the years that followed and had even written to Louvois asking for a

[1] *C.T.B.* vii (1681–5), p. 1482. These were the payments laid down for men wounded whilst serving at sea, who formed a high proportion of army casualties in Charles II's reign. Compensation for those wounded on land does not seem to have been so regular, although some of them received something: e.g. P.R.O., A.O. 1/51/30 (1679), 'Pensions to reformed officers and disabled soldiers'. See also Walton, *Standing Army*, pp. 592–4.

[2] *C.T.B.* vii (1681–5), p. 1246.

[3] Fox wrote several accounts of the inception of the Hospital project, apparently at different times. The most important of these are: Ilchester: Family (box 237): autobiography in small volume with green cover; B.L., Add. MS. 51324, ff. 61–2: statement of grievances without date, heading, or endorsement. H.M.C., *Portland*, x. 84–5. The passages quoted in this paragraph are from the first of these sources.

copy of the plans to show to his father, and although there is no evidence that they were ever forthcoming he had doubtless told the King of what he had seen. However, as far as England was concerned, any such schemes had controversial political overtones, for they clearly implied a determination to maintain a standing army into the indefinite future, and this may have dissuaded Charles from attempting to translate them into practice any sooner than he actually did. But by the latter part of 1681 he had been freed from any anxiety about possible parliamentary criticism, and this fact probably explains the timing of the decision to go ahead.[1] But if the King was the ultimate source of inspiration for Chelsea Hospital, Sir Stephen was quick to take up the notion, and make its realization possible. At first, Charles had envisaged the cost of building and subsequent running of the institution should be met out of royal revenue, and he proposed this to the Treasury Lords on several occasions in 1681. However, this was just after the dissolution of the Oxford Parliament and his decision to manage without further parliamentary grants, and the Treasury had thrown cold water on the plan. A hospital able to meet fully the needs it was designed to relieve would have to be large enough to accommodate several hundred men. It would certainly cost many thousands of pounds to build and several thousands more a year to run. Charles was told that his revenue simply could not bear this additional charge, but he was not prepared to abandon his idea, and so turned to Fox, as one of the most gifted financial experts within the circle of government, and asked him to think of a way of finding the large sum of money necessary. Sir Stephen's narrative continues: 'the King said with discontent that he saw nobody in this age for building hospitals but Toby [?Tobias Rustat, Yeoman of the Robes] & himselfe. To which I replyd that I had thought of what His Matie had so often spoken of. To which the King presently told me hee expected helpe from mee. To which I answred I would give His Matie the best thing I could. . . .'

The idea Fox eventually came up with was that a fund to finance the Hospital could be provided out of the shilling in the pound which was still being deducted from the pay of the forces, even though the Undertaking had been brought to an end. Since the beginning of 1680 two-thirds of the poundage had been at the King's disposal, but since it had not been irrevocably committed

[1] Dean, *Royal Hospital Chelsea*, pp. 22–5.

to any other purpose it was, in a manner of speaking, 'spare' money.[1] Fox's original proposal was that only one of the two-thirds available should be devoted to the Hospital, and with the army establishment at something over £200,000 a year this promised to yield getting on for £4,000 per annum, but some time later the other third was also appropriated, thereby doubling the income.[2] Fox supplemented his suggestion as to how the Hospital might be financed with a promise to pay the cost of acquiring a site himself, and, seeing a real prospect of getting things moving, the King instructed him to add to the fund the balance of the Secret Service money he was then holding (some £6,787). So at last the scheme emerged from the realms of royal wishful thinking and became a practical proposition.[3]

The next stage was to consider where to build. The idea that an existing set of buildings should be taken over and enlarged seems to have been briefly considered, but was rejected by the King, who wanted his Hospital to be a completely new foundation. Eventually it was decided that a suitable place would be the site of some twenty-seven acres in Chelsea, on part of which stood the derelict buildings of a defunct theological college.[4] This had once belonged to the Crown, but in 1669 it had been given by Charles to the Royal Society. However, the Society had done nothing with it, and since Fox had promised to provide the land he began negotiations for its purchase. On 14 September 1681 he dined with his friend John

[1] See above, p. 130. On this matter Fox actually wrote: 'I humbly offered to resign up a third part of the twelve pence in the pound which I had agreed with the Forces for their being subsisted . . .', but despite the implication of this remark he was no longer in receipt of the whole twelve pence. He compiled this narrative many years later, when 79 years of age, and was clearly confusing his surrender of part of the poundage when the Undertaking came to an end (31 December 1679) with the measures adopted for the finance of the Hospital. Ilchester: Family, Sir S. Fox (box 237): autobiography in small volume with green cover.

[2] Ibid.; also Hutt, *Royal Hospital*, pp. 127, 133–5.

[3] An adequate fund for the support of the Hospital was eventually provided by supplementing the two-thirds part of the Paymaster's poundage by a levy of a shilling in the pound of the price at which army commissions were bought and sold; by a deduction of a day's pay (two days' every leap-year) from the whole army establishment; and (for a time) by the net profits arising from the licences of Hackney coaches. Hutt, *Royal Hospital*, pp. 136–7, 141; Walton, *Standing Army*, pp. 600–1, and Appendices xlviii and lxxii; *C.T.B.* viii (1685–9), p. 1812. See also P.R.O., A.O. 1/1466/1 etc.

[4] Subsequent additions increased the size of the estate belonging to the Hospital to 72½ acres. Faulkner, *Chelsea*, ii. 236.

Evelyn, a member of the Society, and proposed that he should buy it on the King's behalf.[1] From then onwards things moved quickly. Early in October the Society deputed Evelyn, together with their President, Sir Christopher Wren, to treat with Fox, and although they were initially instructed not to sell for less than £1,400 Fox was successful in beating them down to £1,300.[2] By the beginning of December Nicholas Johnson, Fox's nominee as Paymaster, had been appointed Treasurer of the new concern. During the course of the same month the King's intentions were fast becoming common knowledge in the capital: Narcissus Luttrell records hearing 'discourse' of them on 13 December. During January the details of the purchase of the land were being settled, and on 17 February 1682 the King laid the foundation stone. Soon afterwards work commenced with the clearing of the site. By August the foundations were being dug, and before the end of 1682 the first range of buildings had begun to take shape.[3]

From the moment when Fox and the King had agreed that the project could go ahead, despite the inability of the Treasury to offer any support, it is quite clear that Fox was the driving force behind it. As early as January 1682 he was beginning to consider in some detail how many inmates the Hospital should accommodate, and how it should be organized, staffed, and run, since decisions on such matters had to be made before Wren, who was to be the architect, could draw up plans of the buildings. One source of ideas was the way other large communities managed their affairs, and Fox provided himself with details of the internal organization of both St. Bartholomew's Hospital, and, since Chelsea was to be very much a military institution, of the garrison of Tangier. He also consulted Evelyn on the subject, and one evening they sat down together in Fox's study and compiled a list of the staff that would be required, and how much their salaries would be, from the Governor at eight shillings a day and the Chaplain at six shillings and eight pence, down to the thirteen 'clever women that may be needful to tend the sick, wash the linen, and clean the house', who were to receive ten pence a day each. The scholarly diarist also records that he 'would needs have a library, and men-

---

[1] D. Lysons, *The Environs of London* (4 vols., London, 1792–6), ii. 149–55; Evelyn, iv. 257.   [2] Dean, *Royal Hospital Chelsea*, p. 32.

[3] E. S. De Beer, 'Chelsea Hospital, Charles II, Nell Gwyn, and Sir Stephen Fox', *Notes and Queries*, 1938; *Evelyn*, iv. 289; C.S.P.D., 1680–1, p. 605; C.T.B. vii (1681–5), pp. 383, 790.

tioned several books etc. since some soldiers might possibly be
studious when they were at leisure to recollect . . .' Fox then bore
off the results of their consultation to show to the King, and left
Evelyn to put his mind to the framing of regulations for the inmates of the Hospital, which, it had been agreed, were 'to be in
every respect as strict as in any religious convent'.[1]

By the latter part of May 1682 Wren had produced his designs,
but at this point a hitch threatened to develop. The project had
proceeded so fast that there had been no time to accumulate an
adequate building fund. The King's gift had been in the form of
'remote' tallies on the Hearth Tax, which had not yet matured, and
the third part of the Paymaster's poundage would only become
available very gradually. So Wren did not feel able to negotiate
contracts with the various buildings and other tradesmen who were
actually to undertake the work, since he clearly could not guarantee
when they would receive payment. However, any need to delay
making a start was avoided by Fox's promise to lend, free of interest, as much money as should be required by the progress of the
work. Wren was thus able to make his contracts, and indeed the
work proceeded so fast that at one stage Fox had advanced as
much as £6,000 to meet the payments that fell due, and the cost
of doing so in terms of interest forgone over several years may have
been as much as £2,000. This, together with the £1,300 he had
paid for the site of the Hospital, made him the largest of its private
benefactors, but the time and the trouble which he devoted to the
project were even more valuable gifts. On several occasions in
1682 Evelyn records journeys out to Chelsea which Fox made in
his company on Hospital affairs, and there were obviously others
when Sir Stephen went alone, or with a different companion.[2]
According to his own account his important role in the project was
explicitly acknowledged by the King on his last visit to see the
progress of the work. According to Sir Stephen,

Hee was pleased to say when last ther, the Thursday before his sicknes
(that carryd him off) that Fox and hee had done this great work, upon
wch I made a modest answere, whereupon hee was pleasd to turne to

[1] B.L., Add. MS. 51322, item 9: 'Notes upon ye Royall Hospitall at Chelsey';
Evelyn, iv. 269–70.
[2] *Evelyn*, iv. 281, 289; P.R.O., A.O. 1/1466/1, 4, 6; and sources quoted in
note 3, p. 133. In the autobiography in Ilchester: Family (box 237), Fox puts the
maximum level of his advances on account of the Hospital as high as £10,000.

the company that attended him & told them that I was the person that had performed that work wthout any charge out of the Treasury . . .[1]

Fox remained the guiding hand behind the project throughout the first four years of construction, indeed until the shell of all the main buildings had been put up and covered over. After Charles II's death King James asked Sir Stephen to continue to take care of it as before, but when the Foxes were dismissed from the Paymastership at the end of 1685 it also meant an end, for the time being, of their connection with the Hospital. The new Paymaster, the Earl of Ranelagh, assumed responsibility for it, and it was under his supervision that it was completed: the interiors of the main buildings were fitted up and furnished; the cloister, portico, lantern, and other embellishments added; the offices and outbuildings constructed; and the grounds laid out with gardens, a terrace overlooking the river Thames, and gravelled walks.[2] Ranelagh was still in charge when at last in the summer of 1691 the Hospital was ready to receive its full complement of 472 pensioners,[3] but Fox's part in its creation received proper recognition when, the following year, William III's government appointed him (along with Ranelagh and Wren) as one of the three Commissioners to supervise the administration of its affairs.[4]

Even when it first opened its doors, Chelsea Hospital was not large enough to house all who were technically qualified, by being severely disabled, or by having served for over twenty years and being no longer fit for service on account of age. From the first it was necessary that over a hundred men had to be treated as 'Out-Pensioners' receiving some measure of relief from the Hospital fund, but not living under its care, and the numbers of these were soon very greatly swollen by the wars of the 1690s and later. Nevertheless, the Hospital was one of the great humanitarian feats of the age. For the first time the Crown and the army authorities unequivocally assumed responsibility for at least those veterans who were most desperately in need. For some there was provided a secure place in the type of community to which they were accustomed, housed in a building considerably more splendid

---

[1] Ilchester: Family (box 237), doc. cit.

[2] C.T.B. vii (1681–5), pp. 790, 1077, viii (1685–9), pp. 783, 1446, 1847–8, ix (1689–92), pp. 1262, 1281, 1288–90, 1796.

[3] Hutt, Royal Hospital, p. 189; C.S.P.D., 1689–90, p. 494.

[4] Hutt, Royal Hospital, p. 192.

than the King's own palace in Whitehall. For those who could not be so accommodated there were the Out-Pensions or, from 1698, places in one of the four companies of 'Invalids' organized to provide garrisons for Windsor, Hampton Court, Tynemouth, and Chester. The former in particular were in receipt of an unreliable and unsatisfactory form of relief, but at least they could get some assistance, which was more than their predecessors had done. Despite the greater size of England's army in the eighteenth century, and the frequency of her foreign wars, the destitute ex-soldier begging on the streets of town and village was, if not unknown, a much less familiar figure than he had been in the aftermath of the wars of the sixteenth and seventeenth centuries.[1]

Of course it can easily be said of the role Fox played in the foundation of the Hospital that 'well it became him, who had gotten so vast an estate by the souldiers',[2] but in reality there is no reason to think that his interest and financial contributions were prompted by the stirrings of an uneasy conscience. Fox did not consider that he had anything to reproach himself for in the way he had made a fortune out of army finance, nor did unbiased contemporaries. To the modern mind the taking of a substantial cut from the soldiers' meagre wages as the price for paying them promptly has an unpleasant ring, but we should remember that such a practice was unremarkable to men of the seventeenth century, and that Fox had agreed to pay the army on that basis in response to a request from its commanders. No, Fox was neither trying to buy his way to heaven, nor to redeem a tarnished reputation on earth, and we may believe that in the considerable amount of effort which he devoted to the Hospital and its affairs he was sincerely moved by the feelings of compassion that Canon Eyre attributed to him when he gave the address at his funeral: 'His motive to it I know from his own words, he said he could not bear to see the common souldiers who had spent their strength in our service, to beg at our doors.'[3]

---

[1] *C.S.P.D.*, 1689–90, p. 494; Ilchester: Official, Charles Fox (box 276): minute book of Chelsea Hospital Commissioners, containing report of the Commissioners, 12 September 1712; Walton, *Standing Army*, pp. 602–5; R. E. Scouller, *The Armies of Queen Anne* (Oxford, 1966), pp. 331–5.

[2] The words are those of Fox's friend, Evelyn. *Evelyn*, iv. 270.

[3] Eyre, *Sermon*, p. 8 n.

CHAPTER VII

The Pay Office, 1661–1685

WHERE FOX'S operations as Paymaster were based when he first
began is uncertain, but by the middle of the 1670s they were conducted from a separate two-storeyed building on the Tiltyard site
in Whitehall. This office was next door to the Horse Guards building which had been erected in the early years of the Restoration,
and in all probability it had been put up at the same time.[1] The
Paymaster himself must have spent more time out of his office than
in it. He was mainly concerned with ensuring that he had sufficient
funds at his disposal to meet all demands that might be made on
him, and this involved attendance at the Treasury to discuss which
assignments on the revenue he was to receive, negotiations with the
bankers who made him advances on the security of these assignments, discussions with revenue farmers or officials about dates
and means of payment of the money he was to receive directly,
and the like. Within the office, probably the most important task
Fox had to undertake personally was the examination and approval
of the numerous different accounts which had to be kept—of the
money received at the Exchequer; of the interest due from the
King on money advanced; of dealings with the various bankers
who had lent him money; of the pay of each troop, regiment, and
garrison; and last, but not least, the great ledger in which all
his public and private financial transactions were summarized.
Occasionally, there arose non-routine difficulties or problems which
Fox had to deal with himself, for instance disputes with officers
over pay matters, such as the one which arose in 1667 when the
agent to the King's Troop of the Horse Guards, of which Lord
Gerard was Captain, absconded with a large sum of money. Gerard
tried to throw the loss on to Fox, who was consequently obliged
to spend a great deal of time in consultation with lawyers, on
attendances in court, and on drawing up memorandums and peti-

---

[1] *Survey of London*, xvi, Charing Cross (London, 1935), pp. 7–10, 17;
C.S.P.D., 1676–7, p. 8.

tions.[1] In addition to all this it must be remembered that Fox had other official responsibilities quite distinct from the Paymastership, and so it is not surprising that he left the day-to-day affairs of the office to his subordinates.

At first Sir Stephen employed his nephew John Fox, his elder brother's son, to be in charge of the Pay Office, to have custody of the money coming in, to pay it out as required, to keep the vouchers and accounts, and to do all the routine work. John was only twenty in 1661, and he had a most responsible position because of the very large sums of money he was dealing with: according to his own story, £130,000 had passed through his hands before he was called on to render any sort of account. It was also a difficult position because the business of the office was always being done in a rush, and there was a considerable risk of mistakes and consequent loss by accepting short payment or bad coins, by paying out too much, or in forgetting to enter up what had been paid. John had already performed similar duties for Sir Stephen for several months, first as his 'cash keeper' for the Secret Service money, and then as his deputy at the Green Cloth, but in this new assignment he was not a success. The trouble may have lain partly in his inexperience, and partly (as he claimed) in that his assistant had made errors which were blamed on him, but also he seems to have spent some of the money entrusted to him on gambling and drink. The amount involved cannot have been very large since John was able to reimburse it, but Sir Stephen seems to have had a nasty fright and, concluding that his nephew was a ne'er-do-well, removed him from the Pay Office just the same.[2] In his place Fox appointed John's erstwhile junior, Richard Kent. Kent was the third son of a cadet branch of a minor gentry family who had been neighbours to the Foxes in Wiltshire. He had entered Sir Stephen's service early in 1661, when he was only about eighteen, and naturally had little experience of business affairs. John Fox, who considered that Kent's bungling had been a principal cause of his own downfall, described him with some venom as 'an ignorant country bumpkin' and 'a meer country lad, very ignorant in telling money and keeping

---

[1] B.L., Add. MS. 51319, ff. 21-4, 31, 35: statement of Fox's case in his dispute with Lord Gerard and associated documents; C.S.P.D., 1667, p. 470, 1667-8, pp. 389, 447-8, 1668-9, pp. 146, 261.
[2] B.L., Add. MS. 51324, ff. 10-19: narrative of the life of John Fox junior.

accounts'. But if he was so to start with, he learnt fast and was soon able to take responsibility. After not much more than a year, in April 1662, Sir Stephen sent him to Scotland in charge of a large sum in cash and a consignment of supplies for the troops there, and it must have been soon after this that he replaced John Fox in charge of the office. Kent remained as Sir Stephen's principal deputy for twelve years, and the extent to which he assumed responsibility for the actual conduct of Pay Office business is indicated by the fact that from 1666 onwards an account in his name appears in the ledgers of Alderman Backwell, and many of the transactions which had formerly been entered in Fox's own account were thenceforward recorded in Kent's. By 1671 we even find that on matters of a straightforward nature the Treasury was dealing directly with Kent. At some time in the latter part of that year or in the next, apparently without leaving Sir Stephen's employment, he also started out on his own, establishing a banking business in partnership with Charles Duncombe. This was certainly in operation by 1672, and by 1677, if not from the beginning, was being carried on under the famous 'Grasshopper' sign in Lombard Street.[1] The firm prospered, and soon became very prominent in government finance as both partners came to hold important financial offices. Initially at any rate this success was largely due to Kent's relationship with Fox, for, as we have seen, in November 1674 he was appointed Cashier and Receiver-General of the Excise as Sir Stephen's nominee. On the other hand, Kent's later appointment as Cashier of the Customs (in 1677) seems to have owed nothing to Fox's influence, and his subsequent career in government finance was apparently independent of his former employer.[2] The means whereby Kent had made enough money while at the Pay Office to set up as a banker in the first place must remain a matter for speculation. He must have received a certain amount in the form of 'gratuities' from those to whom he paid out money, probably made a great deal more by lending to officers who wanted to borrow in anticipation of their pay, and it is possible

---

[1] A narrative of John Fox's life, the reference to which is given in the previous note, furnishes several details about the early stages of Kent's career. See also, R. Boucher, 'Kent of Boscombe', pp. 228-35; Ilchester: Family (box 235, bundle 4): R. Kent to S. Fox, Leith, 8 May 1662; Williams and Glyn's Bank: Backwell's ledgers: accounts of S. Fox and R. Kent; C.T.B. iii (1669-72), p. 894; Martin, 'The Grasshopper' in Lombard Street, p. 28.

[2] See above, p. 125.

that as he grew richer he began to make loans to Fox himself for the purposes of the Paymastership.[1]

Kent left the Pay Office when he was appointed Cashier of the Excise, and his successor as Sir Stephen's assistant was another of the latter's nephews, his sister Margaret's son, Nicholas Johnson. Johnson seems first to have attracted his uncle's attention when he had the misfortune, as a young man, to be captured at sea by Barbary corsairs. Sir Stephen sent off £100 for his ransom, but by the time the money arrived he had already been redeemed out of funds provided by the English government. Johnson was thus able to use Fox's money in a trading venture, which was so successful that when he returned home in 1662, Sir Stephen rewarded his enterprise by taking him into the Pay Office as an under-clerk. He was soon given the important responsibility of making payments to the large garrison at Portsmouth, and indeed seems to have acted as a semi-independent deputy paymaster there, handling very large sums of money, especially during the Dutch wars when troops destined for the fleet embarked and disembarked there. At some time in the 1670s he married Kent's sister Jane, and when Kent became Cashier of the Excise he took over some or all of his functions as Fox's principal assistant in London. The final stage in his promotion came in 1679 when Sir Stephen, having recovered the Paymastership, was invited to join the Treasury Board, for it was to Johnson that he resigned the office. At first Johnson nominally shared the Paymastership with Fox's second son William, but after William's premature death in April 1680 he was sole Paymaster until his own death almost exactly two years later. Johnson had started out with nothing save the £100 of surplus ransom money, and although he made a certain amount during his years at the Pay Office, it was hardly a great fortune. He was able to purchase a small country property at Olney in Buckinghamshire and the lease of some houses in Westminster. He also bequeathed legacies totalling £7,000, but they could not be paid in full from what he actually left, and indeed a few years later his family was described as 'but meanly provided for'. Sir Stephen gave them some financial help himself and secured from the King the grant of a small pen-

[1] John Fox refers to these gratuities in a letter or memorandum which he sent to his uncle in Dec. 1663. Ilchester: Family (box 238, bundle 2): document endorsed 'Nephew's proposition refused'. For a possible loan by Kent to Fox, see above, pp. 68-9.

sion for Charles, the eldest son. He also ensured that when Charles was old enough there was a vacancy for him in the Pay Office as a clerk. Charles did indeed work there for a number of years, but his career was not marked by a great deal of success, for which his own failings probably bore as much responsibility as the fact that from the end of 1685 his patron no longer controlled the Paymastership.[1]

Several other of Fox's close relations were also given employment in the office at various times. John Rawkins was there for a while in the early 1670s: he must have been a grandson or great-nephew of the uncle Richard Rawkins who had paid for Sir Stephen's education almost forty years before. In the early 1680s two more of Sir Stephen's own nephews joined the Pay Office. One of these was Thomas Fox, son of Sir Stephen's younger brother Thomas, who was a clerk in Nicholas Johnson's time, may have been Johnson's deputy, and certainly married his daughter.[2] The other was actually only a nephew by marriage: Nicholas Fenn, husband of one of the daughter's of Sir Stephen's brother Henry, who acted as deputy to Charles Fox in 1683. Very little emerges about this aspect of the careers of either man, and they do not seem to have spent very long at the Pay Office. Fenn already had considerable administrative experience, for he had held a post in the royal Household as Yeoman of the Woodyard at least since 1672, and later in 1683 was reckoned fit enough to be named as one of the four Commissioners for Victualling the Navy.[3] As for Thomas Fox, it seems that he, like John Fox, Richard Kent, and Nicholas Johnson before him, was given employment while still very young and inexperienced. However, Sir Stephen's prompt dismissal of John Fox, and his refusal to reinstate him despite his pleas, show that although he was always ready to give his relatives their opportunity, he was not prepared to tolerate inefficiency or dishonesty from them. Nor did he confine his choice of assistants to near relations. Kent was not connected by family with Sir Stephen, and there is no evidence that Charles Toll, the last in the line of deputies at the Pay Office before the Foxes were dismissed in 1685, was either.

[1] B.L., Add. MS. 36148, ff. 137–8; Ilchester: Family (box 244): copy of will of Nicholas Johnson; ibid.: Official, Sir S. Fox, Army: day-books for 1660–72, esp. under 26 Feb. 1661–2; and ibid.: . . . ledger for 1672–9, f. 96 etc.; C.T.B. viii (1685–9), p. 1613; Boucher, 'Kent of Boscombe', p. 233.
[2] B.L., Add. MS. 36148, ff. 137–8.
[3] C.T.B. vii (1681–5), pp. 784, 956; Ilchester: . . . ledger for 1672–9, f. 98. See also below, pp. 248–9.

Moreover, Toll, unlike his predecessors, was already a seasoned financial administrator before he entered Fox's service, for he had been man of business to Cofferer Ashburnham as far back as the mid-1670s, and it was doubtless in that capacity that Sir Stephen had originally come to know him and trust his ability. More recently, in Nicholas Johnson's time, Toll had had considerable financial dealings with the Pay Office so that he must already have been familiar with its affairs. But whether Fox took Toll into the office because he had no suitable relatives left, or because he felt that it needed a really experienced man in view of his son Charles's youth and lack of experience, is not at all certain.[1]

Not a great deal of information exists about the internal organization of the Pay Office in the early days, but by the time of Nicholas Johnson and Charles Fox more records and sources are available. There is a list of employees with their salaries, dated 1685, and some interesting details emerge from papers drawn up in connection with a lawsuit brought by Charles Johnson against Sir Stephen as his father's executor many years after the latter's death. From these sources it appears that the staff had been considerably expanded since the early 1660s when John Fox and Richard Kent had apparently managed everything on their own. There were now seven in the office. There was Charles Toll, who was described as Chief Accomptant and who was paid the substantial salary of £400 a year, and another official with the same salary whose duties are suggested by his title of Auditor of the Muster Rolls. The importance of these two positions is perhaps indicated by the fact that their salaries (which were paid by Sir Stephen) were as large as that paid to Sir Stephen by the Crown between 1661 and 1676. Next in seniority came the Book-Keeper, Mr. Jenyns, and the Cashier, Roger Hewett. Their functions are described at some length in the documents deriving from the lawsuit mentioned above. Hewett was responsible for all the money actually passing through the office, and for entering all the receipts and payments into a cash-book each day. It was then Jenyns's business to post these daily entries to the appropriate accounts in the ledger which recorded everything to do with the payment of the army as well as all Sir Stephen's (or, after 1680, Nicholas Johnson's) other financial affairs. To that extent neither of these two was exclusively

[1] *C.T.B.* viii (1685–9), p. 238; Ilchester: . . . ledger for 1672–9, ff. 215, 280; B.L., Add. MS. 36148, ff. 137–8.

concerned with their master's official business, but in the days of the Undertaking the Pay Office was an entirely private organization and its staff Fox's personal employees, so that there was no reason why this should not be so. Similarly, Richard Kent and Nicholas Johnson successively acted not only as deputy paymasters, although never receiving any official recognition as such, but also as Fox's general men of business. After 1680 the Paymaster was no longer an Undertaker, but even so it was a long time before his staff came to be regarded as public rather than private employees. In the years before 1676, Jenyns's predecessor as Book-Keeper had been paid £200 a year, eventually increased to £300 a year, while Jenyns himself, then holding the less senior position, had received £160 a year. In 1685 Jenyns's salary was £350 a year, and the then Cashier was getting £150. In point of total remuneration, however, there was less of a difference between them, as the Cashier was able to derive a considerable profit by making private advances to officers who wanted to anticipate their pay. Finally, the office staff was completed by two clerks, who were respectively paid £80 and £50 a year, and a door-keeper or caretaker who was paid £30 a year.[1] The clerks must have been increasingly overworked as the size of the army grew in James II's reign, and by the time of the Revolution their numbers had been expanded and the Pay Office salary bill swollen by another £140 per annum.[2]

The procedure for making payments to the army was described in some detail by Sir Stephen in a paper drawn up in 1667, and again in a memorandum over the signature of his son dating from 1683.[3] No significant differences had developed between those two dates, and so the account which follows is probably a fair reflection of the way the Pay Office worked throughout the Fox regime. The main part of the pay due to each unit was advanced by the Paymaster in weekly instalments, or as it was called for, without any formality save for the taking of a receipt, thus furnishing the troops with the means of providing themselves with food and lodging, neither of which was in normal circumstances provided by the authorities.

[1] Ilchester: . . . ledger for 1672-9, ff. 103, 302, 355; B.L., Add. MSS. 15897, f. 29, and 36148, ff. 137-8.

[2] P.R.O., S.P. 8/5, item 9.

[3] B.L., Add. MS. 51319, ff. 21-4: statement of Fox's case in his dispute with Lord Gerard; and Add. MS. 51335, ff. 1-2: 'Method of paying his Maties Forces . . .'

The proportion of total pay thus advanced as subsistence money seems to have varied somewhat from time to time, but it might be as much as three-quarters of the whole: in the case of the King's Troop of the Horse Guards in the mid-1660s it was £250 a week out of £1,372. 18s. 8d. due to them each month. The balance of the pay was known as 'off-reckonings', and out of this regimental clothing and certain items of equipment had to be purchased. This was paid over (less the Paymaster's poundage) at, or soon after, the close of the muster. Under an agreement between Fox and the then Commander-in-Chief, the Duke of Monmouth, the Paymaster was to 'clear' each muster ten days after it had ended, and if he had not done so within a month he was not to take any poundage for that muster.[1]

These musters were the traditional accounting periods of army finance, and until 1675 the year was divided into seven of them, five of fifty-six days and two of forty-two days. After that date there were six of equal length. Once in every muster each unit would receive a visit from the Commissary-General of the Musters, or one of his deputies, and there would be a parade at which he would check that all those named on the muster-rolls, prepared by the colonel and his officers, were duly present and properly equipped. This check was primarily intended to ensure that the officers and men for whom pay was drawn by those in command really were serving with the regiment, and were not merely counterfeit names on the roll. The most common abuse was for the commanders to continue to receive and to appropriate to themselves pay for men who had died, been killed, or who had left the service, and it was one which proved impossible to eliminate entirely. Officers would leave vacancies unfilled and units under strength until immediately before the next mustering day, and were thus able to pocket several weeks' pay on account of each vacancy. The Commissary-General would note that certain names had changed since the previous roll had been compiled, but would have no means of knowing whether or not the new men had only been enrolled the night before. Moreover, captains sometimes went further and tried to prolong vacancies indefinitely by blatant falsification. This finally provoked an effort by the authorities to try and deal with these abuses. One aspect of this seems to have been to encourage informers. Thus in 1673 the army accounts record the payment of £40 by way of

[1] P.R.O., S.P. 44/58, f. 15.

rewards to commissioned and non-commissioned officers who had revealed false mustering by their troop commanders. Again, in January 1675 Captain Reade of the Foot Guards was accused before the Duke of Monmouth by his own lieutenant of procuring other men to answer to the roll-call in the name of soldiers who had been discharged, and of ordering one man to impersonate another before a Commissary, among other offences. The other part of the campaign consisted of tightening up the regulations. In 1673 it was laid down that the Commissary need only give notice of his intention to visit a unit the night before, so depriving officers of time to prepare deceptions (such as impersonation) at the mustering parades. There was also a new set of rules promulgated in August 1674, which imposed on commanders the obligation to produce to the Commissary-General certificates stating the date on which men had died or been discharged.[1] If these last had been enforced they would have provided an effective check on the artificial prolongation of vacancies, but clearly they were not enforced for long, if at all. Ten years later, when the Duke of Ormonde, worried by similar abuses in Ireland, inquired what the practice was in the English army, Fox told him:

As to vacancys that happen here betwixt musters, either by death or running away of private sentinells, the captaines have the advantage of it, and take care of providing another man cloathed against the succeeding muster, soe that in case the roll be full noe notice is taken to the King's advantage of the change of names, and if a commission officer, as a liewt or ensigne happens to dye betwixt a muster the coll. lookes upon those days that he lives short of the muster to be his profitt. . . .[2]

Once verified by the Commissary-General, the muster-roll of each unit was taken into the Pay Office. The roll was a very important document to the Paymaster and Fox described it (in 1667) as his 'principall voucher' for the payments he made, since it enabled him to prove to the King's auditor that he had properly disposed of the money entrusted to him. In fact, Fox seems to have been prepared to pay a regiment in full at the close of a muster before the roll had been brought in, although he regarded this (again in 1667) as being done 'in kindnesse'. He apparently only

---

[1] B.L., Add. MS. 51319, f. 21, doc. cit.; P.R.O., A.O. 1/49/21; *C.S.P.D.*, 1673–5, pp. 334–5, 542–3; Fortescue, *History of the British Army*, i. 318–23; Walton, *Standing Army*, pp. 452–3, 642–4, and Appendix xxiv.

[2] B.L., Add. MS. 51326, ff. 45–8: exchange of letters between Ormonde and Fox, 1684.

refused to do so when he had not yet received the roll of the preceding muster either, and if a commander was really dilatory in sending in the rolls he would even resort to withholding the subsistence money. This seems to have happened in 1668 when Lord Gerard, captain of the King's Troop of Horse Guards, retained the rolls so long that by September of that year the troop was five months in arrears, and the King had to intervene by issuing a warrant instructing Fox to pay them £2,100, to enable them to march to Audley End. It was obviously with such incidents in mind that, when in 1679 Fox agreed to pay each unit in full within ten days of the end of a muster, he made this conditional on the rolls being brought to him within six weeks.[1]

Once the Paymaster had received the muster-roll he could with safety regard the relevant unit as being up to strength, and his clerks were able, by referring to the establishment which laid down the rates of pay and allowances for each rank, to draw up an account of the total sum due to it for the muster in question. A debenture stating the amount would then be sent in, either to the office of the Lord General, during Monk's lifetime and the brief period in 1678–9 when the post was held by the Duke of Monmouth, or when there was no Lord General, to the Secretary to the Forces. A warrant would then be issued, bearing either the signature of the General, or that of the King counter-signed by the Secretary to the Forces, authorizing the Paymaster to make the payment, which in most cases he had already made some weeks before.[2] It was essential for the Paymaster to ensure that these documents were correctly prepared, properly issued, and carefully kept, for when his accounts were eventually audited, possibly several years later, he would have to produce the warrants, as well as the receipts he had taken from those to whom he had actually made payments, and to satisfy the auditor that these tallied with each other, and with both the establishment and the muster-rolls. Only when every penny issued to him at the Exchequer had been satisfactorily accounted for in accordance with this procedure would the auditor grant him his discharge.[3] The work involved in

[1] B.L., Add. MS. 51319, ff. 21–4, doc. cit.; P.R.O., S.P. 29/246, item 142; and 44/58, f. 15.

[2] Walton, *Standing Army*, Appendices xxi and cviii; Mackinnon, *Coldstream Guards*, ii. Appendix 41.

[3] C. M. Clode, *The Military Forces of the Crown* (2 vols., London 1869), i. 73–4.

passing the accounts of former years thus formed a substantial part of the routine of Fox's Pay Office staff, and it had to go on for a long time after Fox had ceased to be Paymaster. Indeed, when he was dismissed at the beginning of 1676 he was allowed to retain part of the accommodation in the Pay Office so that his clerks could continue working on past accounts, and consequently, since his 1675 account was not declared until June 1679, his salary was continued throughout the three years when he was out of office to cover the expenses he had incurred in continuing to pay them.[1]

The rates of pay appropriate to each rank in the forces were laid down in successive 'establishments' which were drawn up by those who advised the King on such matters, and theoretically every soldier was entitled to receive what the current establishment allowed him. In practice, however, the system did not work like that. In the infantry units only field officers seem to have been paid directly from the Pay Office, and junior officers and all other ranks received their money from the captains of their companies, who in turn received it from the colonel of the regiment or the governor of the garrison. In the latter respect things were somewhat different in the cavalry. The three troops of Horse Guards had no colonels and were under the command of captains.[2] As for the Regiment of Horse, which did have a colonel, the captains of its constituent troops seem to have been independent of him in matters of pay, and the Dragoons raised in 1672 followed the same pattern. But throughout the army the pay went to colonels, captains, or governors, and lower ranks received it through them.[3] Moreover, even if these officers were totally honest the men never received anything like the full pay nominally due to them, since officially authorized deductions were made for the Paymaster's poundage and certain other purposes, and an unofficial but customary deduction for the regimental agent, which (in 1685) together absorbed 11s. 1d. out of an infantry private's £8. 8s. 0d. a year, and on top of this came the cost of the man's clothing.[4] Nor were all commanders above

[1] P.R.O., A.O. 1/50/23; C.S.P.D., 1676-7, p. 8; C.T.B. vii (1681-5), pp. 244-5.
[2] But it may be noted that captains in the three troops of Horse Guards had the seniority of colonels in other regiments. Walton, Standing Army, p. 443.
[3] B.L., Add. MS. 51335, ff. 1-2, doc. cit. Also Ilchester: . . . ledger for 1672-9, which contains a series of separate accounts for the payment of each unit in the army.
[4] B.L., Add. MSS. 15893, f. 81, and 51321, f. 78: document endorsed 'Accot of cloathing soldiers'. The full cost of the clothing, including sword, for a private

taking advantage of their men in matters of pay. Charles Fox's paper of 1683 makes it clear that the soldiers did not always receive their subsistence money as promptly as the officers claimed it at the Pay Office, and his suggestion that they ought to be paid what was due to them out of the off-reckonings at least once a year implies that it was common for officers to hold on to the balances owing to their men for very long periods. Up to this date there was still no formal procedure for ensuring that the officers applied the money they received in the proper fashion at all, and certainly the Paymaster had no means of ensuring that they did. Charles indeed proposed to remedy this situation by taking security from captains as a guarantee that they paid their men as laid down. He also suggested that the Paymaster and the Commissary-General should be empowered to hear appeals from private soldiers and to redress their grievances if they did not receive fair treatment from their officers, and that they should also be empowered to investigate the accounts of regimental pay kept by the latter.[1] These would have been thoroughly beneficial reforms for, although it is difficult to be sure how frequent serious abuse actually was, it is certain that complaints reached the surface fairly regularly. The army accounts for 1673 include a payment of £365. 17s. 4d. to men of the Regiment of Dragoons to make up to them money which one of the troop commanders had received but not paid over. In the following August orders were issued to the whole army that no pay was to be stopped from the soldiers' wages, save as a formal punishment, and in the twelve months after that at least two officers who had deprived men of their money were dealt with. One of these was Captain Reade of the Foot Guards, of whom it was alleged that, not only had he falsified the muster-rolls, but that he would not allow soldiers leave of absence unless they made over their pay to him for the period they were away, and that he would never discharge a man from service without obliging him to surrender all his arrears. The second offender was Lieutenant-Colonel Howard, who still owed £101. 17s. 11d. to his lieutenant and several private soldiers on account of their pay nearly ten months after the regiment had been disbanded: in his case a royal order was issued that

---

at this period was £3. 14s. od., but presumably not all items would have to be replaced every year.

[1] B.L., Add. MS. 51335, ff. 1–2, doc. cit.

the money be deducted out of the pension he received from the Crown.[1]

Army pay in the later seventeenth century may have been issued to colonels, captains, or the governors of garrisons, but in practice these commanders did not themselves handle the detail of the financial affairs of their units, and they left this to agents appointed by them specially for the purpose.[2] These agents, who were often referred to as 'clerks' or 'solicitors', formed the vital link between the various units of the army and the Pay Office, bringing in the muster-rolls, receiving the money, and in some cases signing the receipts for it. Sometimes the agent was himself a member of the regiment: in the King's Troop of Horse Guards down to 1667, for instance, and in the Earl of Craven's Regiment of Foot in the early 1670s and in the Coldstream Regiment in 1683, in both of which the function was performed by the major.[3] More often he was a civilian, but either way he was a nominee of the commanding officer, and indeed strictly speaking was a servant who could be appointed and dismissed at will. He had no obligation to keep regular accounts unless his employer required it of him, nor any to ensure that regimental or company pay was applied as the establishment laid down. The agent was, as Sir Stephen put it in 1667, 'lyable to be turn'd out when the captn pleaseth', or, as it was described in a government memorandum of 1695, 'wholly at the Colonell's beck' and consequently obliged to do as he was told to keep his place. Besides, the agent did not necessarily receive all the money due to his unit, since the commanding officer was perfectly at liberty to collect some of it himself without accounting for it either to his agent or to his subordinates. Indeed, in 1695 when there was a parliamentary inquiry into the agency system it was alleged that some colonels repeatedly changed their agents deliberately in order to reduce the accounts of the regiment to confusion, so that they could more easily keep for themselves the arrears of pay due to officers and men who had died or been killed in service. One of the reforms suggested at that time was that *all*

---

[1] P.R.O., A.O. 1/49/21; *C.S.P.D.*, 1673–5, pp. 334–5, 542–3, 1675–6, p. 275. For other examples of army grievances over pay, B.L., Add. MS. 28937, f. 161; and *C.S.P.D.*, 1665–6, pp. 477–8. See also Walton, *Standing Army*, pp. 670 et seq.

[2] Clode, *Military Forces*, i. 74.

[3] B.L., Add. MSS. 51319, f. 21, and 51335, ff. 1–2, doc. cit.; Ilchester: ... ledger for 1672–9, ff. 62, 189.

the regimental pay should be received by the agent, who was to be made to keep regular accounts open to the inspection of all members of the regiment, and who would be empowered to call on captains to produce receipts to prove that every man in their companies had actually received what was owed to him.[1]

Agents were not allowed for in the regimental establishments and were remunerated by a deduction from the pay of both the officers and men. This was already the practice in the King's Troop in 1667 and probably had prevailed from the first establishment of the Guards, but it was never officially approved and was in fact actually declared illegal in 1688, although apparently without effect. The amount of the deduction in the foot regiments was two pence in the pound in 1685. Given the establishment prevailing at that time, this must have yielded to the agent of the Coldstream Regiment, whose pay amounted to £18,076 a year, some £150; the agents to the larger regiments will have received proportionately more. The Foot Guards was the largest of all, with 1,540 privates compared to only 770 Coldstreamers, and a total pay of £35,237 a year which would have produced some £294 to the agent. The agent to the Foot Guards was, moreover, the only one in the army who received an official salary: £72 a year out of the contingency money. In the Horse Guards the agent seems to have been allowed a larger deduction than in the foot regiments, and a calculation of about 1668 suggests that in the King's Troop it was then six pence in the pound, which yielded him £290 on an establishment of £10,568. 2s. 8d. Agents incurred certain unavoidable expenses in the conduct of their duties, but on the other hand they could make considerably larger sums over and above their basic remuneration through the opportunities for profit that arose in connection with purchases of clothing, equipment, and provisions for the regiment, and because they could lend money at high rates of interest to junior officers and soldiers on the security of their future pay.[2] The agency to the King's Troop, for instance, was described by one who had once held it as worth £500 a year 'honestly gotten' in the 1670s. Consequently, the places were much sought after. Some

---

[1] B.L., Add. MS. 51319, f. 21, doc. cit.; Harleian MS. 7018, f. 222; *Commons Journals*, 11 (1693–7), pp. 215, 249.

[2] B.L., Add. MSS. 15893, f. 81, 15897, ff. 74–7, and 51320, f. 35: 'Establishmt of his Maties owne troope of Guards'; P.R.O., A.O 1/48/16, and subsequent accounts for the army; *Commons Journals*, loc. cit.; Walton, *Standing Army*, pp. 644–5.

colonels put them up for sale to the highest bidder, and the agents themselves might try to sell their places when obliged to quit them on grounds of, say, old age or ill health. In the mid-1670s, for instance, the selling price asked by the outgoing agent to the King's Troop was £800.[1] At various times, a number of them were held by Fox's protégés. His nephew, John Fox, was agent to a troop of horse commanded by the Duke of Monmouth in 1667, and temporarily to the King's Troop when Monmouth held its captaincy. The agency for the King's Troop was then filled on a more permanent basis by Richard Dalton, husband of one of Sir Stephen's nieces. John Kent, brother of Sir Stephen's former deputy Richard Kent, was agent to two troops of the Regiment of Horse in the 1670s. As we have seen, the most lucrative post was almost certainly agent to the Foot Guards. For some years down to the beginning of 1672 this had been held by Sir Stephen's brother John, but he was succeeded during that year by John Rawkins, who was later stated to have obtained the position 'by ye choice and recommendation of Sr Stephen Fox'. Rawkins remained with the regiment for nine years, but his story illustrates the fact that an agency, like other forms of money-making activity, also involved certain risks. He suffered serious loss when a goldsmith banker paid some forged bills drawn in his name, and when he tried to recover himself by borrowing he found that he was paying out more interest than he could afford, and he had to resign, owing his regiment £1,912.[2] Rawkins was apparently honest but unlucky, though there were some agents of whom this could not be said. In July 1665 Bulstrode, an earlier 'solicitor' for the Foot Guards, had 'run away' with £600 of the regiment's money, and two years later the agent to the King's Troop defaulted on an even larger scale, fleeing overseas £2,291. 17s. 0d. in his unit's debt.[3] Neither of these men, however, was Fox's nominee.

Much the largest part of the money which passed through the hands of the Paymaster went to the regimental forces and garrisons, but not quite all of it. He also paid the salaries of the Lord General,

---

[1] B.L., Add. MS. 51324, ff. 14ᵛ, 17ᵛ: narrative of the life of John Fox, junior; Walton, *Standing Army*, p. 644.

[2] B.L., Add. MS. 51324, ff. 14–16: narrative of the life of John Fox, junior; Ilchester: . . . ledger for 1672–9, ff. 50, 54, 59, 61 etc., 175, 258; ibid.: Family (box 235, bundle 1, part ii): report on the debts of J. Rawkins by officers of the Green Cloth, 16 Dec. 1681.

[3] *C.S.P.D.*, 1666–7, p. 375; B.L., Add. MS. 51319, ff. 21–4, doc. cit.

the Commissary-General of the Musters and his deputies, the Scoutmaster-General, the Judge Advocate, and the rest of the small army staff. The other item which regularly appeared in the Paymaster's accounts was a sum for 'contingencies'. Under this heading was included a wide variety of expenses incurred by the forces for which no provision had been made in the regimental establishments, such as the cost of medical care and payments to the dependents of those who had been killed; the cost of transport, and of heating and lighting for soldiers undertaking certain guard duties; expenditure on stationery and postage in the Pay Office itself and in the Commissary-General's office; half-pay for officers who could not be provided with regimental postings; the cost of repairs and maintenance to the Horse Guards' building in White-hall; and indeed anything for which the King chose to issue a warrant directed to the Paymaster. There could be no question of misappropriation of the contingency fund since no money had been specifically granted by Parliament for this, or for anything else to do with the army. All the money for it came from the royal revenue in general, and the King was entitled to dispose of it as he wished. Provided that Fox had a proper warrant, he did not need to hesitate in issuing money even for purposes which were not really military at all, and so we find under 'contingencies' not simply small bounties to officers who had specially distinguished themselves, but also pensions to courtiers such as that of £500 a year to Lieutenant George Hamilton 'the better to enable him to support himself and family'.[1]

Sir Stephen's day-books and his single surviving ledger, together with the ledgers of the banker Backwell, provide a great deal of evidence on how payments to the army were actually made, although in a form which it would be exceedingly laborious to analyse thoroughly.[2] However, it is clear that in the early part of Fox's Paymastership only a relatively small proportion of payments were in the form of cash at the Pay Office itself. Despite its name, in the early and mid-1660s the Pay Office was essentially an ac-counting and not a cash-keeping organization, and Fox tried to

---

[1] P.R.O., A.O. 1/48/9, and subsequent accounts for the army.

[2] Ilchester: Official, Sir S. Fox, Army: day-books for 1660–4, 1664–6, 1666–70, 1670–2, 1672–9; and ibid.: . . . ledger for 1672–9; Williams and Glyn's bank: Backwell's ledgers, accounts in the names of Sir S. Fox and Richard Kent.

reduce to a minimum the extent to which his staff had to handle in a physical sense the money for which he and they were responsible. Nevertheless, some cash payments were unavoidable, and although individually they were usually small, and in aggregate they were dwarfed by the amounts transferred in other ways, the absolute sums involved were quite considerable. Fox thus had to ensure that his office was well supplied with coin, a fact which may be illustrated from his account with Backwell:

| 7 April 1666 | To money sent him [i.e. Fox] by Robert ye porter in mild gold . . . and silver | £1375. 0s. 0d.[1] |
| 9 April 1666 | To Mr Kent in mild gold | 537. 10s. 0d. |

For most of the 1660s the principal means Fox employed to funnel money to the forces was to send those due to receive it direct to the bankers who had undertaken to make him advances, or to the revenue officials who had been instructed by the Treasury to provide him with his weekly or monthly instalments of cash. In the latter case he assigned to the officers or agents in question tallies on which immediate payment could be expected, and left them to make their own arrangements for collecting the money. Thus at the centre of his dispute with Lord Gerard in 1667 were two tallies on the Customs for £2,291. 17s. 0d. which the former's agent, William Carr, had received to cover the subsistence of the troop until the next muster. Carr had obtained the money from the Customs farmers, and then disappeared abroad taking it with him.[2] Where bankers were concerned, it is not clear upon what kind of authority they normally made payments on Fox's behalf, but it seems that it was in one of two forms. Either they received written or verbal instructions from Sir Stephen on the strength of which they debited his account with the appropriate sum, transferred a corresponding amount to the credit of an account in the name of the intended recipient, and then issued it as it was called for by the latter; or upon presentation of a 'drawn note' (in modern parlance a cheque) signed by Fox they issued cash immediately. Thus the early entries in Fox's day-books recording his borrowings from the bankers are cast in the form: 'Per John Colville [or Edward Backwell, or whoever the lender was], To accot of acom-

---

[1] Williams and Glyn's bank: Backwell's ledger O, f. 216.
[2] B.L., Add. MS. 51319, ff. 21-4, doc. cit.

modation £3500, borrowed of him . . . which I leave in his hands
to bee att my disposall in part or entier.' Subsequent entries then
record the calls which were made upon the credit which the loan
had established: 'Per King's Troop of Horse Guards, To Jo. Colville £920, assigned to Mr. Carr [their agent] for accot of said
troope as part of what was due to them on the muster of 22
March. . . .'[1] Very large sums reached the forces via transactions
of this nature. For instance, in the six months from Lady Day to
Michaelmas 1664 Backwell paid out no less than £8,058. 3s. 6d.
to Colonel Morgan, probably he of that name who was second in
command of the Lord General's regiment; £5,000 to William Carr,
the agent of the King's Troop; £4,876. 12s. 3d. to Richard Bulstrode, agent to the Foot Guards; £4,800 to Henry Carr, who was
almost certainly another agent; £4,200 to Mr. Bridgeman, who was
probably then, as he certainly was later, agent to the Duke of
York's Troop; and smaller sums to many others.[2]

It was not only the agents of regiments quartered in and around
London who dealt directly with the bankers, but also, sometimes
at least, the agents of units stationed elsewhere. These agents then
had to find means of transmitting the money to the country, which
they would normally have done by obtaining bills on some provincial business man payable in the appropriate place. Their banker
might well be able to provide some, though not necessarily all, of
what they required in this respect. The Foot Guards' agent,
Richard Bulstrode, for instance, obtained from Backwell bills on
Berwick, Newcastle, York, and other places, all within the space
of a few months in 1664.[3] For a commanding officer who did not
have an agent so placed that he could reach either the Pay Office
or Lombard Street, the obvious means of getting what was
due to him was to draw bills on either the Paymaster himself or
on one of the bankers with whom the Paymaster had credit. Even
in the very early 1660s the former of these two alternatives was
sometimes adopted, but the practice became more common in the
latter part of the decade as the Pay Office gradually came to take
over from the bankers the direct function of making the actual cash
transfers to the forces. By 1668 the use Fox was making of their

[1] Ilchester: Official, Sir S. Fox, Army: day-book for 1660–4, 1 May and
24 July 1662.
[2] Williams and Glyn's bank: Backwell's ledger L, ff. 178 et seq.
[3] Williams and Glyn's bank: Backwell's ledger I, f. 578, L, f. 180.

services in this respect had drastically diminished, and it seems that most of their loans were now paid to him in cash, and used by him to pay cash, either directly to officers and agents or to those who presented the bills they had drawn. In the years after 1672 *all* the loans Fox raised appear to have been in the form of cash, and apparently he did not expect any of his lenders to hold money to his account and pay it out on his directions in the old way. The form of the entries in Sir Stephen's day-books does not enable one to say with confidence how extensive the use of bills drawn on the Paymaster actually was, but it had undoubtedly become a common, although probably not the normal, way in which garrisons and other troops quartered outside the capital received their pay. In July 1671, for instance, Mathew Locke, Secretary to the Forces, writing to Secretary of State Williamson, acknowledged receipt of orders for Major Wyndham's troop of horse then stationed in Winchester, and said that he would instruct the Major to take up money in the town by drawing bills on Fox, which seems to imply that without specific instructions he would not have done so. Another example may be cited from 1679 when additional troops were raised in the North to deal with the Scottish rebellion, and the Duke of Monmouth wrote to inform the captains of the new troops of dragoons that they were to receive £120 each and four weeks' subsistence. They were either to appoint persons to receive the money direct from Fox in London, or, if they could find credit where they were, they might draw bills on him. However, the way in which Monmouth put these instructions rather suggests that the practice of drawing bills on the Paymaster was sometimes restricted by the difficulty of finding people to advance money on them in the small and remote places in which troops stationed outside London sometimes found themselves.[1]

Certainly, most of the money issued from the Pay Office in the 1670s seems to have been direct to agents themselves, who were then left, as they had been when they had got their money from a banker, to find ways and means of remitting it to the provinces as necessary. Sometimes, however, Fox himself provided them with the facilities for so doing, although it is not clear why he did not do this on a more regular basis. Thus in the early 1660s he obtained bills payable outside London from the various bankers with whom

---

[1] *C.S.P.D.*, 1671, pp. 376-7; 1679-80, pp. 172-3.

he dealt, as is illustrated by entries on the debit side of his account with Alderman Backwell such as these:

14 August 1663	To a bill for York £1800 and another for Newcastle £450	£2250. 0s. 0d.
14 April 1668	For a bill given him [i.e. Fox] on Isaac Morgan of Bristol[1]	£220. 0s. 0d.

And some of the bankers of the post-Stop era were used in much the same way. When Thomas Price failed in 1685, he had in his hands £4,203. 17s. 0d. which Charles Fox had paid over to him to be remitted to the forces in the West, and, according to Charles, he had been making such payments to Price for a considerable time past.[2] Sir Stephen also gradually built up a network of regular correspondents in the towns to which he most frequently transmitted funds, men like Sir James Stansfield at Berwick, Henry Brabant at Newcastle, James Blackbeard at York, and the brewer Richard Ridge at Portsmouth, on whom he was able to draw bills as and when he needed to, and for whom he provided the same facility in reverse.[3] Another means of making money available to troops serving outside London was provided by the balances held by the local collectors of the tax revenues out of which Fox's advances were due to be repaid, although this was a method which he did not use to any great extent except in periods (notably during the Second and Third Dutch Wars) when he had unusually large payments to make. Thus, during the Third Dutch War when he was regularly receiving large sums from the Country Excise, Fox's ledger records that on a number of occasions money was received from this source at Plymouth, Exeter, Harwich, Hull, Scarborough, and York. Sometimes it seems to have been collected in cash by Fox's own deputies, sometimes paid directly by the collector to some garrison or regiment, but in either case the procedure seems to have been that the Excise Commissioners issued Fox with bills on their collectors, which were then set against his account in the same way as if they had issued him with cash in London.[4] Provincial tax collectors are again found making payments for the army in 1691 as troops passed through the western ports on their way

---

[1] Williams and Glyn's bank: Backwell's ledger I, f. 512, Q, f. 104.
[2] C.T.B. viii (1685–9), pp. 1479, 1522.
[3] Ilchester: Official, Sir S. Fox, Army: day-books, passim.
[4] Ibid.: . . . ledger for 1672–9, ff. 113, 148.

to or from Ireland, although in this instance it was they (acting on Treasury instructions) who drew bills on the Paymaster, Charles Fox, for the settlement of their account with the Exchequer.[1] In times of peace, however, such methods seem to have been less necessary. When, in 1670, a Hearth Tax collector in one of the northern counties inquired whether he could make his returns to London by paying the local garrisons and drawing bills on the Paymaster, he was told that Fox already had satisfactory arrangements for doing this. The arrangements in question illustrate the way in which Sir Stephen was able to make use of his private financial relationships to help discharge his principal public function. He was at this period handling the affairs of the Duke of Monmouth, and so was able to draw bills on the latter's steward in the North, who then made the required payments out of the rents of the estates under his care, and Fox, in turn, credited the Duke's account with the appropriate amount. This method was still being used to pay the garrison of Berwick in 1676, and so may be regarded as a regular part of Fox's system.[2] Finally, if all other means failed, coin could be physically transported in order to make the necessary payments. Thus in the spring of 1662 it was apparently impossible to arrange for more than £5,500 of the £20,000 required for the arrears of the garrison of Leith to be remitted by bill of exchange, and the remaining £14,500 had to be sent up to Scotland in cash on board ship. Later in the same year £1. 10s. 0d. was spent on the hire of a cart 'for conveyance of money to Portsmouth for the garrison', but during most of the time when Fox was Paymaster such measures seem to have been taken only in exceptional circumstances.[3]

---

[1] C.T.B. ix (1689–92), pp. 1089, 1100, 1103, 1114, 1398–9, 1416, 1450–1.

[2] C.T.B. iii (1669–72), p. 662; Ilchester: . . . ledger for 1672–9, ff. 45, 86 etc., 243.

[3] C.T.B. i (1660–7), p. 387; Ilchester: Official, Sir S. Fox, Army: day-book for 1660–4, 17 May 1662.

CHAPTER VIII

The Richest Commoner in Three Kingdoms

SIR STEPHEN FOX grew wealthy during the 1660s by reinvesting in the Undertaking almost everything he made from it, and he did not divert much capital to other ends. In 1663 he bought a house and two acres of land in Chiswick for £1,797. 13s. 4d. in order to provide his family with a country retreat, and over the years that followed he added to its grounds by buying a few adjoining parcels of property as they became available.[1] In the next year he also acquired, for £1,950, a small estate of 229 acres at Bockingfield in Kent which had a rental value of £102 per annum.[2] Fox sold Bockingfield again after a few years, and at this early period in his career he was apparently more concerned with getting a good return on his money than with laying the foundations of a landed property. In May 1667, when wartime conditions had depressed the return from land but forced up interest rates, he told Cofferer Ashburnham that he was in the process of selling some land because it was yielding him only 3 per cent when he could get 10 per cent on his money if he put it out at interest.[3] But even in peacetime the rate of return which could be expected from capital invested in this way was relatively low, and down to 1672 most of the capital which Fox withdrew from the Undertaking went instead into loans to fellow courtiers, or into the purchase of pensions and offices from them. This enabled him to diversify, to avoid having everything tied up in the lucrative but risky business of government finance, yet still to obtain a yield up to twice as high as that which land offered.

Pensions and Court offices offered a greater return than straightforward lending, but they also carried greater risk. Offices were purchasable, but were not normally inheritable unless a reversion

[1] See references given in note 3, p. 256, below.
[2] Ilchester: Official, Sir S. Fox, Army: day-book for 1660–4, 16 Apr. 1664.
[3] *Pepys*, viii. 199.

had been specifically granted, and so the income they yielded would cease on the death of the buyer, who clearly could not rely on them, as he could rely on land, to provide for the future security of his family. He who invested in offices was, therefore, in a sense, taking a gamble on his own expectation of life. For this reason, and because a change of sovereign and other less foreseeable political events potentially threatened the tenure of virtually all office-holders,[1] prices were very low in relation to annual values, and offices usually changed hands at between two and four years' purchase.[2] At different times in the 1660s and early 1670s Fox bought a number of minor Household posts, none costing him more than a few hundred pounds, and several costing less; and although in most instances he acquired them in order to provide for relatives or servants, he did retain a few for himself as income-producing investments. Thus some time before 1667 he paid £590 for the post of Master Cook to the Queen, which yielded him about £224 a year gross, and kept it until after 1679, apparently installing a deputy (whose remuneration reduced the net proceeds of the place to £160 a year) to do the actual work. On another occasion he bought a lowly turn-broach's place for £40, and throughout 1673 and 1674 credited the modest income from it (£13. 7s. 0d. per annum) to his own account.[3] These two offices provided Fox with a very good return on his money, as did a Court pension of £120 a year which he bought from George Hamilton for £500 as early as 1661. The pension seems to have been granted to Hamilton for life and, had he died within four years or so, Sir Stephen would have lost part of his capital. In the event, however, Hamilton lived a good span of years and Fox was still recording payments a quarter of a century later, although no further references to any are found after the end of the 1680s.[4] But two more pensions, both of £273. 15s. 0d. a year, one purchased from the same George Hamilton for £1,500 in September 1668, and the other from Sir Gilbert Gerard for £1,200 a few months later, proved to be most

---

[1] In theory all offices automatically became void at the death of the monarch, although in practice most incumbent holders appear to have been compensated, with a pension or otherwise, if they were not continued in place in the new reign.

[2] Aylmer, *King's Servants*, pp. 216–25.

[3] Ilchester: Official, Sir S. Fox, Army: ledger for 1672–9, ff. 8, 35, 98, 118.

[4] The purchase seems to have been made in the name of Charles Fox. Ilchester: Official, Sir S. Fox, Army: day-book for 1660–4, under 14 Oct. 1661 etc.; ibid.: ... ledger for 1672–9, f. 5; and ibid.: Family (box 235, bundle 4): document entitled 'A Computation of my owne Estate'; P.R.O., L.S. 13/33.

unsuccessful investments. These represented the pay of two lieutenancies in the Horse Guards, which had been removed from the strength as a result of an internal reorganization, but which remained on the establishment to provide an income for the officers who had had to give up their commissions. As such, their continuance was clearly considered to be a matter of doubt by all concerned, not least by Fox, who apparently only bought them as a favour to the Duke of Monmouth, who was supposed to be going to take them off his hands at cost price as soon as he had the necessary cash in hand, and whose influence would doubtless have been sufficient to ensure that they were duly paid. As it happened, however, the Duke was so far up to his eyes in debt that he could never afford the £2,700 required to repay Sir Stephen. Fox still had the title to them in 1672 when the Stop of the Exchequer seems to have sharply depressed their value by putting a large question mark over the Crown's ability to honour its commitments, not only to its creditors, but to those entitled to salaries and pensions as well. He therefore decided to extricate as much of his capital as he could and the following year sold the two pensions for £930. 2s. 0d. and £840 respectively, in both cases entering a loss in his ledger.[1]

Even before the Restoration Fox seems to have made some loans to fellow royalist exiles, and within a few months of his return to England he was again lending. At first the sums were relatively small, early repayment was clearly preferred, and occasionally tangible security such as jewels was insisted upon: for instance, in February 1661 he advanced £100 to Herbert Price, Master of the Household, to be repaid a month later; and in May 1662 he lent George Hamilton £150 on the security of a diamond ring. Indeed, throughout most of the 1660s Fox's private lending continued to consist mainly of small loans, often of less than £100 at a time, although from about 1662 onwards the number of them increased markedly. The loan of larger sums, such as £1,400 lent to the Duke of Ormonde in the June of that year, was unusual, at least until the very end of the decade. How much his advances to private individuals amounted to in these early days is difficult to tell, but even in the mid-1660s it cannot have been more than a very

---

[1] Ilchester: Family (box 235, bundle 4): document entitled 'Acct of ye 2 Lts places of ye Duke of Monmouth's Troope'; ibid.: . . . ledger for 1672–9, f. 9.

few thousand pounds. However, when he began his new ledger on 30 April 1672 the total had increased to some £24,500. There were about fifteen petty advances of £100 or less, including one of £6 to his twelve-year old son Charles, but nearly £24,000 of the total had been lent to seven major borrowers. The list was headed by Lord Cornbury, son and heir of Fox's old patron, the now exiled Clarendon, who owed £8,220. It also included Cornbury's brother, Laurence Hyde, who owed £1,500, whilst Robert Phelipps, a Groom of the Bed Chamber, owed £2,250, and the Countess of Falmouth £2,000. The remaining three were men even more prominent in Court circles. All of them seem to have entrusted an important part of their financial affairs to Fox's care, and to have been allowed overdrafts by him: the Duke of Monmouth's various accounts were £6,629. 1s. 5d. in deficit, Lord Arlington's £2,910. 16s. 5d., and the Duke of Ormonde's £482. 17s. 6d. None of these advances seem to have been on mortgage, and were probably secured by bond. The rate of interest is only specifically stated in the cases of Laurence Hyde and the Countess of Falmouth, who paid 6 per cent, but the rest probably paid the same. Over the next few years Fox made large advances to a number of other individuals, all with Court backgrounds. He lent £1,200 to the Earl of Anglesey in August 1672; £3,750 to Sir Philip Howard in the following month; £1,000 to Sir Edward Hungerford in February 1674; and later in 1674 £2,200 to the Earl of Sunderland; £4,600 to Charles Bertie, then Secretary to the Treasury; £3,500 to William Chiffinch, Keeper of the King's Closet; and he allowed the Duke of Ormonde's son, the Earl of Ossory, to run up an overdraft on his account which had exceeded £4,500 by October 1675. Nevertheless, when repayments of earlier loans are set against these new advances, there does not seem to have been a great increase, and possibly none at all, in the scale of Fox's private lending.[1] Only towards the end of the 1670s, after he had lost the Paymastership, did he shift a significantly larger volume of resources into this field of investment.

Meanwhile, Fox had entered the land market on a much larger scale than before, at last beginning the process of converting his

[1] Ilchester: Official, Sir S. Fox, Army: day-books for 1660–4 and 1666–70, *passim*; and ledger for 1672–9, *passim*, especially ff. 11, 16 etc., 20, 26 etc., 37, 39, 40, 43, 86 etc., 92, 113, 208, 210, 212, 236, and interest accounts on ff. 101 etc.

wealth into a landed estate. This was a step which was taken sooner or later by most moneyed men of the seventeenth century. Despite the relatively low return it yielded, by its very nature land was secure and permanent in a way that no other investment could be. Its value might drop of course, and we shall see that in the last quarter of the century it did, but it was unlikely to drop very far, and whatever befell, even civil war or foreign invasion, it was indestructible. It had, therefore, some positive advantages from the purely investment point of view. But these advantages were not the main reason why moneyed men tended to buy it. They wanted land primarily because ownership of an estate carried with it social prestige, a claim to be admitted to the ranks of county society, and at the same time would also provide the material basis for remaining part of that society for the indefinite future. To purchase land was, therefore, to purchase simultaneously a particular social position and financial security for oneself and one's children. Some moneyed men were clearly very keen to acquire estates so as to be able to live the lives of country gentlemen themselves, to join in country sports, and to sit on the county bench. Possibly such men felt a need to live down their own origins, to become 'respectable' in the manner of the age. Fox was not such a one. Although he became the owner of a very large estate, he never lived like a landowner or made the slightest effort to become part of county society. His career at Court and in government probably gave him sufficient confidence in his own social position, so that he did not feel the need to buttress it by taking up the role of country gentleman. Nor, indeed, did Sir Stephen have the time to indulge in rural pursuits. He was thoroughly immersed in public affairs, and his own financial concerns, well into old age, and when he finally retired he was already seventy-five and a widower, and it was too late to start a new sort of life. So although he acquired a habitable mansion on his estates he never lived in it; he did no more than pay his acquisitions fleeting visits on two or three occasions; and some parts of them he probably never saw.[1] For a country home he preferred the almost suburban Chiswick, where he was not a great proprietor, and where he was only one amongst many wealthy and important residents, several of whom outshone him in rank. One, and possibly

---

[1] Ilchester: Accounts, Personal (box 220): accounts of Sir S. Fox's private expenditure, 1680-1, 1681-4, 1684-97, which record his journeys. Also ibid.: Family (box 238, bundles 6 and 7): loose accounts relating to journeys.

more, of Fox's purchases seem to have been made with the essentially political aim of securing sufficient influence in a nearby borough to ensure his own election to Parliament, in which his important offices made it imperative that he should have a seat. But otherwise it is safe to say that Fox did not buy land for himself, but for his descendants. He had no desire to be a country gentleman, but he looked forward to the prospect of his son and grandson becoming gentry, and his main motive for buying land can be summed up in the single word 'family'.

The first real steps towards the acquisition of an estate were taken by Sir Stephen in 1672, and there can be little doubt that he was spurred on by the Stop of the Exchequer, which must have reminded him how vulnerable was his newly made fortune so long as it remained very largely tied up in government lending. He had already purchased a small property in his native county of Wiltshire in 1670, a single farm in the village of Charlton for £1,100 odd, but in March 1672 he paid no less than £20,000 for the manor of Water Eaton in the north-east corner of the county.[1] The Water Eaton estate consisted of several large farms renting at £1,144. 13s. 4d. a year, but it had the additional advantage of lying within a mile or two of the borough of Cricklade, which returned two Members to Parliament on the basis of a reasonably wide franchise, so that any local personage with a sufficiently long purse had a good chance of securing election for his nominee. This may indeed have been the main reason why Fox wanted the property. He owed his Salisbury seat in the Cavalier Parliament to the influence exerted on his behalf by Lord Chancellor Clarendon, who was now disgraced and in exile, and he probably wanted to be in a position to ensure a seat for himself if, at a future election, no Court influence was forthcoming on his behalf. In the event he was not immediately successful in developing an 'interest' at Cricklade: at both elections of 1679 his attempts to obtain a seat (though whether for himself or his son Charles is not entirely certain) resulted in defeat in the face of the widespread hostility then being felt against candidates associated with the Court. It was not therefore until the more favourable electoral atmosphere of 1685, when Charles was elected, that the borough actually returned a Fox to Parliament.

---

[1] Ilchester: Deeds, Wiltshire (box 133): abstract of title to Water Eaton in booklet marked 'Water Eaton No. 6'; ibid.: Family (box 235, bundle 4): lists of Sir S. Fox's purchases of land.

From the election of 1685 to that of November 1701, however, one of its two members was always either Charles Fox or Sir Stephen himself.[1]

Sir Stephen also invested a considerable sum in fee farm rents in 1672. All over the country there were many thousands of properties which paid small rents, fixed in perpetuity, to the Crown. The origin of most of these rents was either medieval, or a result of the royal policy prevailing in the sixteenth and early seventeenth centuries of selling Crown lands subject to a small annual payment in order to retain at least some income from them. It was, however, a complicated and expensive task to collect such a large number of very small sums, payable by so many different landowners, and so, when the financial needs of the government made it imperative to raise money by selling part of what little remained of the real property of the Crown, it was decided to sacrifice them. The fee farm rents were put on the market in 1671, but the same disadvantages which made them unprofitable to the Crown deterred purchasers, and they did not sell very briskly. An additional disadvantage attaching to many of the rents was that they formed part of the jointure of Charles II's Queen, Catharine of Bragança, so that they could not be sold in present possession but only in reversion after her death. To encourage the sale of these reversionary rents the Crown was prepared to accept eight or eight and a half years' purchase for them. This was little more than half the fifteen of sixteen years' purchase required for the rents sold in possession, even though the normal valuation of a reversion after one life would have been two-thirds of the fee simple, that is ten or ten and two-thirds years' purchase. The reversions, then, were on sale at a knock-down price, but any investment in property reversions was a gamble on how long the life which stood between the purchaser and enjoyment of his acquisition would survive. If Queen Catharine died within a few years the gamble would pay off handsomely, but if she lived for a long time even eight years' purchase might turn out to have been a dear bargain.[2]

Fox bought £424. 14s. 3d. worth of reversionary rents for

<hr>

[1] *Wiltshire V.C.H.*, v. 159, n. 29; Ilchester: Accounts, General Estate: ledger marked 'Sir S.F', f. 13; Sir George Duckett, 'Proposed Repeal of the Test and Penal Statutes . . . in 1688', *Wiltshire Archaeological and Natural History Magazine*, 1879; *Members of Parliament* (H.C. 69, 1878, 2 parts), i, 'The Parliaments of England, 1213–1702'.

[2] Ogg, *Charles II*, ii. 431–2; Chandaman, *English Public Finance*, pp. 112–15.

£3,567. 1s. 7d. in March 1672, one of the few frankly speculative investments he ever made, and one that turned out to be an expensive failure. In the event the Queen lived to a ripe old age, and did not die until 1705, so that Sir Stephen's capital remained tied up for thirty-three years, the interest which it might otherwise have yielded was lost, and no income was received from the purchase in the meanwhile. Later in the year Fox also acquired £319. 14s. 11½d. worth of rents in possession, for the price of £5,023. 6s. 6d. or fifteen and two-thirds years' purchase. However, this was not a cash transaction. Sir Stephen, in his capacity as Paymaster, held an Order for £5,000 charged on the revenue accruing from the sale of fee farm rents, and he was taking advantage of a government decision that, in view of the slowness with which the revenue was coming in, such Orders could be used in the purchase of rents.[1] The rents Fox bought with his Order were all in Wiltshire and Gloucestershire, as were most of his reversionary ones, and unlike the latter they did not turn out to be a bad investment, as we shall see.[2] But possession of an income from fee farm rents carried with it none of the non-monetary advantages of land ownership: social prestige, a place in county society, and ability to influence elections to Parliament. Probably for this reason Fox made no more large purchases of them, although on several occasions in the 1670s he bought small parcels of rents at second hand, from individuals who had themselves been the original purchasers from the Crown trustees. All these later purchases seem either to have been of rents payable out of land in which he himself had an interest, or to have been made so as to enable someone who owed him money to settle his debt.[3] By 1677 he had spent a further £2,842 5s. 0d. in this way, and altogether had an income of about £375 a year from fee farm rents, with the prospect of a further £616 a year whenever Queen Catharine should die.[4]

[1] Ilchester: General Deeds (box 144): conveyance, 5 Mar. 1671, and declaration of trust, 11 Apr. 1672; and General Deeds (box 146): abstract of title to the Earl of Ilchester's fee farm rents; ibid.: Estate, Wiltshire (box 178, bundle 2): document entitled 'An accompt of fee farm rents'; C.S.P.D., 1672, p. 550; C.T.B. iii (1669–72), pp. 932, 937, 1062, 1304.

[2] See below, pp. 202–3.

[3] Ilchester: General Deeds (box 144): conveyances, 29 Aug. 1671, 23 Nov. 1674, 24 July 1676, 4 Oct. 1676 (copy), 9 July 1677.

[4] Ilchester: Accounts, General Estate: ledger marked 'Sir S.F.', ff. 19, 71, 83, 84; ibid.: Estate, Wiltshire (box 178, bundle 2): document entitled 'An accompt of fee farm rents'. The figure given in the text for Fox's income from fee farm

Meanwhile, still in 1672, Fox was buying more land. His new estate at Water Eaton was without any sort of manor house, and so could not be used as a country seat unless a large sum was laid out on building, but the next purchase made up for this deficiency. In June 1672 Fox paid £8,700 for the manor of Redlynch, just across the Wiltshire border in the extreme east of Somerset, from the same Robert Phelipps to whom he had for some time been lending money. This time he acquired a substantial mansion and over 480 acres of demesne land, besides a large number of cottages and small holdings let out to tenants on leases for ninety-nine years determinable on lives.[1] The mansion was nicely situated on one slope of a shallow valley, which was about two miles across, so that it had pleasant views out over enclosed meadows and pastures and patches of woodland. The house itself, however, like the one he had acquired at Chiswick, was old. There was a room known as 'the Castle of Sparrows', which seems to suggest one of those Tudor turret chambers reached by a narrow stairway, but the name may equally well have been an ironical comment on its state of repair. There was a parlour with an oriel window, and one of the remaining rooms had been given the grand title of 'the Lady Marquess's Chamber'. There also seems to have been a private chapel, but few other details about the building have survived. Fox bought the house partly furnished, and he took the livestock on the home farm and the crops standing in the fields too, for which he paid £376. 16s. 3d. over and above the price of the land.[2] The estate was thus a going concern from the first, and the month after the deeds of conveyance had been signed he went down to inspect it for himself.[3] He must have been favourably impressed, for over the next five or six years he made a number of additions to it, costing in all

---

rents excludes the £12. 18s. 0d. and £16. 19s. 1½d. out of his own estates of Water Eaton and Kilmington. These had formerly been outgoings chargeable against the income from those properties, and by their purchase Fox reduced his expenses rather than added to his gross income.

[1] For a discussion of the nature of leases for ninety-nine years determinable upon lives see L. Stone, *The Crisis of the Aristocracy* (Oxford, 1965), p. 312 et seq.

[2] Ilchester: Deeds, Somerset (box 78): conveyance, 4 June 1672, and declaration of trust, 1 July 1672; ibid.: Accounts, General Estate: ledger marked 'Sir S.F.', f. 36; ibid.: Deeds, Somerset (box 295): inventories of goods at Redlynch.

[3] Ilchester: Accounts, Household (box 210): Sir S. Fox's household accounts for 1671–3, under July 1672.

some £10,394.[1] These subsequent acquisitions in Somerset gave Fox possessions of a further 690 acres of demesne land, and 350 acres of leased farms. However, not all of this was immediately adjacent to Redlynch itself. The farm of Piggott's and some other lands, for which Fox paid £2,065 in 1673, had formerly been part of the Redlynch estate, and some of it actually lay within the manor of Redlynch, although the rest lay in the next-door manor of South Brewham. Three of Fox's smaller purchases were also in South Brewham—one of them abutted directly on to the lands of Piggott's—but the rest of the Somerset acquisitions were rather further off, at Kilmington and Norton Ferris, five or six miles north-east of Redlynch House. However, they were little more than half that distance from Fox's purchases in South Brewham, and doubtless could in time have been joined up to them by the acquisition of the intervening land. The fact that in the mid and late 1670s Sir Stephen was buying both large blocks and small parcels of property in this corner of Somerset suggests that he was at that time trying to build up a consolidated estate based on Redlynch. Despite this, he was not prepared to take anything which was offered to him, irrespective of price. In 1677 he allowed a good farm in Kilmington to slip through his fingers, even though it lay next door to land he had bought the previous year; and when he was offered the manor of Kilmington itself in 1682 his refusal to come up to the figure demanded by its owner again caused the deal to fall through.[2] In fact after February 1679 Fox stopped buying in Somerset altogether, and he made no more additions to his estate there until the very end of his life more than thirty years later.[3] The reasons for this will be dealt with shortly, but meanwhile we may note that he had become the owner of eight large farms and five smaller units let at rack-rents, and many other holdings, mostly small, leased for ninety-nine year terms determinable upon lives and yielding only nominal rents. The whole estate yielded about £1,000 a year gross from all sources.[4]

Meanwhile, Fox was also buying property in Wiltshire, and on a

[1] Details of Fox's other purchases in Somerset are to be found in Appendix II.

[2] Ilchester: Estate, Somerset (box 173, bundle 3): documents relating to Farmer Gibbon's land in Kilmington and Beckington farm; and (box 173, bundle 1): Thomas Allen to Fox, 7 and 25 Jan. 1681/2.

[3] See below, pp. 320–1.

[4] Ilchester: Estate, Somerset (box 167): booklet containing a particular of Sir S. Fox's Somerset estate, Aug. 1685.

much larger scale: by 1679 his Somerset acquisitions had cost him
£19,419, whereas between 1670 and 1684 he spent £73,554 in
Wiltshire.[1] But while in Somerset he seems at least to have begun

Map of the West Country showing the location of Sir Stephen Fox's
principal purchases of land there.

to lay the foundations of a compact estate, in Wiltshire he made
no effort to confine his purchases to one district, where he might
in time have become the predominant landowner, and instead,
as the accompanying map shows, bought properties scattered over

[1] For the details see Appendix II.

a wide area. It is true that in February 1675 he paid £1,700 to secure a farm called Jones' Leaze in Water Eaton, to add to his estate there, but that done he seems to have made no further additions to it. Almost without further exception, all Fox's Wiltshire purchases in these years were of complete estates, largely or wholly leased for ninety-nine years determinable upon lives; and having acquired them he did almost nothing to consolidate or to extend them until much later in his life, long after he had ceased to buy land on a big scale.[1] At the same time as he bought the land in Water Eaton he also acquired, from the same seller, Sir Edward Hungerford, another of those to whom he had been lending money, at a price of £5,400, the manor of Maddington up on Salisbury Plain and three or four miles west of Stonehenge. In the summer of 1677 he paid £3,900 for the manor of Erlestoke, which lay about ten miles away on the north-western rim of the Plain; and then the following spring he spent £2,940 on the manor of Allington, which lay further north still in the Vale of Pewsey. His next buy (1678) was in a different area again, a few miles to the east of Salisbury. This was a lease of the manor of Pitton and Farley, which included the village where he had been born and where he had spent his childhood. The freehold of Pitton and Farley belonged to the Dean and Chapter of Salisbury, but they always leased it out *en bloc* on renewable terms, and for £5,200 Fox secured an assignment of the church lease from Sir John Evelyn, the previous leaseholder, together with the freehold of certain lands within and without the manor which Evelyn had owned independently of the Dean and Chapter. Apart from a sentimental desire to become lord of the manor in the place where his parents had had their cottage, Sir Stephen may have had another motive for acquiring Pitton and Farley. Its proximity to Salisbury would usefully strengthen his electoral influence in the city, for which he had sat in the Cavalier Parliament, but, as we have seen, as a Court nominee and not on his own interest. In fact Parliament was dissolved at the beginning of 1679, too soon for him to have developed an independent interest as a local landowner, and in later parliaments he usually represented either Westminster or Cricklade. However, from 1698 until 1713, one of the Salisbury seats was permanently occupied by his son Charles, who was clearly elected because his father was an important local figure through possession

[1] See below, p. 326.

of land in the immediate vicinity.[1] If electoral advantage was a factor in Sir Stephen's decision to buy Farley, it must also have figured in his calculations about a group of farms in the neighbouring parishes of West Grimstead, Laverstock, and Winterbourne Ford, some of which lay even closer to Salisbury and the rest not much further away. He paid £5,502 for this estate in March 1679. Six months later he bought yet another property in yet another part of the county: the manor of Plaitford, down on the Hampshire border, a good seven miles south-east of Farley, which cost him £7,000.

As may be seen from the Table in Appendix II, since Fox made his first major investments in real estate early in 1672, he had been making a continuous series of purchases, with intervals of not more than a few months between each. He had been steadily drawing on the capital fund which he had accumulated as Undertaker for the pay of the army, and was at once converting it into a more solid and durable form, and also running down the resources he had available for lending to the government in the future. By the middle of 1679 he had sunk more than £84,046 in land and fee farm rents, and almost all of this was capital withdrawn from the Undertaking. It is true that in 1673 Sir Stephen had sold two properties which he had acquired in the previous decade, the leasehold estate at East Meon and the manor of Bockingfield, but these had realized only £3,300 between them: everything else which Fox spent on land in the 1670s represented new investment.[2] However, after the middle of 1679, this systematic conversion of a moneyed fortune into a great estate in the West Country received a check, and was never really resumed. Fox made no further purchases in Somerset until the next century, and though after a three-year interval he did acquire more land in Wiltshire, after 1684 he bought no more in that county either. Moreover, his purchases in Wiltshire at that period, the manor of Little Somerford near Malmesbury for £7,000, and various properties in the vicinity of Warminster for a total of £13,100,[3] were made in significantly different circum-

---

[1] *Wiltshire V.C.H.*, v. 219–20; *Members of Parliament*, parts i and ii.

[2] Ilchester: . . . ledger for 1672–9, ff. 13, 40; ibid.: Deeds, Kent (box 69, bundle 2): conveyance, dated 20 March 1672. Fox had also resold one or two parcels of fee farm rents, presumably to oblige the purchasers, but only a few hundreds of pounds were involved. Ilchester: General Deeds (box 144): conveyance, 17 Apr. 1678; ibid.: Accounts, General Estate: ledger marked 'Sir S.F.', ff. 19, 83.   [3] See Appendix II.

stances from those of the 1670s. Fox had lent very large sums of money to Sir Edward Hungerford, who owned both properties, and we shall see that although the evidence is circumstantial, it suggests fairly conclusively that he foreclosed on this part of his security more because he had to than because he wanted to.

The Wiltshire purchases from Sir Edward in 1682–4 were thus the last important transactions that Fox made in the West Country, and they marked the end of his campaign to build up a great estate for himself there. He subsequently made other acquisitions in other parts of England, but, as will be shown, most of these were in order to prevent the ruin of his grandson, the fourth Lord Cornwallis, and not as part of any estate-building activities on his own account. There was, however, one other country property which he acquired for himself at this time. This was the so-called prebend manor of Chiswick, of which he bought a lease in July 1685. Between 1682 and 1684 Sir Stephen had built himself a completely new house on the site of the one which he had owned in Chiswick since 1663.[1] But he had little land in the village, probably not much over ten acres, and some visitors thought that for so imposing a mansion its situation was rather cramped by the possessions of neighbouring owners.[2] It was therefore an opportunity not to be missed when the lease of one of the two manors into which Chiswick was divided came on to the market. The manor actually belonged to one of the prebends of St. Paul's Cathedral, who invariably leased it to the Dean and Chapter of Westminster, who in turn leased it to a private tenant. Like all ecclesiastical property at this period it was leased on renewable terms, the church charging a stiff fine for each renewal but otherwise contenting themselves with an almost nominal rent. Fox paid £3,200 to Mr. Kendall, the previous lease-holder, for his interest in the lease, which was, however, subject to his mother's life tenancy, so that Sir Stephen could only obtain possession by agreeing to pay her an annuity equivalent to the full annual value of the manor (£274 per annum net) until her death at the end of 1687. He also paid £1,200 to the Dean and Chapter for a renewal of the lease, and £55 more for an additional parcel of ground, so bringing the total price of the manor up to £4,455.[3]

[1] See below, pp. 263–4.
[2] *Evelyn*, iv. 294.
[3] Fox was in reality buying a reversion after Mrs. Kendall's death, although by agreeing to pay her the full annual value of the estate he gained immediate possession of it. The instalments to Mrs. Kendall were not therefore strictly

Fox acquired several hundred acres of land by this purchase, although no exact survey of it seems to have survived, and at last had the satisfaction of an estate to go with his fine new residence.[1]

Sir Stephen's interest in building up a great country estate faltered in 1679 and never recovered. Possibly one contributory reason for this was his resumption of the Paymaster's Undertaking in that year, which may have temporarily stretched his capital resources and put an increased premium on liquidity; but the Undertaking was discontinued after only seven months, so that this cannot have been the sole factor. Almost certainly the real explanation is to be found in the tragically early deaths of so many of Fox's children. He and his first wife had had ten in all, seven of them boys, but after nineteen-year-old William succumbed in April 1680, there was only one son, Charles, left alive.[2] Charles, moreover, was growing so corpulent that, even though he was only in his twenty-first year, it was already being assumed that he was unlikely to have any children, nor in fact did he.[3] Sir Stephen was thus faced with the likelihood, which gradually hardened into a virtual certainty, that in the end he would have no male descendant of his own name to inherit his landed property. The main motive for purchasing more land thus disappeared. Of course there were Cornwallis, and later Compton, grandchildren, and there were nephews and great-nephews, between whom his wealth would eventually be divided, but why should he bother to continue building up an estate if it was to be broken up after his death anyway?[4] He did not want to play the great landed proprietor himself, whilst the management of estates was much more troublesome than that of most other types of investment, and even so returned a lower yield to the investor. As long as he had the prospect of founding a landed dynasty, Sir Stephen seems to have been prepared to buy more and more land for the sake of future generations of Foxes, but once it came to look as though the dynasty he had founded was doomed to extinction in the male line his attitude

---

speaking part of the purchase price but were rather payments of rent to a sitting tenant.

[1] The actual purchase deeds, and the original leases, have disappeared, but various relevant documents are to be found in Ilchester: Family (box 236, bundle 10); see also Lysons, *Environs of London*, ii. 191.

[2] See below, pp. 266–9, 333.   [3] *Evelyn*, iv. 248.

[4] For the Cornwallis and Compton grandchildren, see below, chapter XI, parts II and III.

changed. After 1680 or thereabout, as we shall see, he came to regard his estates in the West Country simply as one investment amongst others. He no longer wanted them for their own sake, but only to balance his portfolio, and he was prepared to get rid of them again if financial advantage so dictated.[1]

As Sir Stephen withdrew from the land market, lending to private individuals was a form of investment which was coming to have increasing attractions for him. Provided that he was careful about his securities there was little risk involved, indeed loans on mortgage were virtually as safe as possession of land itself, for the title to the mortgaged property actually became vested in the lender until both principal and interest had been repaid to him. And with agricultural depression settling over large areas of the country at about this time, capital lent on good security might even be safer than that invested in land, for where tenants were unable to pay their rents and farms were standing empty land values necessarily suffered. Moreover, as hard times for farmers adversely affected the landlord's receipts from his estates, so they lowered the rate of return which he received on his original investment. Even in normal times in the later seventeenth century the return on private lending was significantly higher than that on land, though not as high as that on government lending, but now this margin was widening.

The first signs of an increase in the scale of Fox's private lending are detectable before the end of the 1670s, soon after he had been forced out of office by Danby. In July 1677, for instance, he lent £13,000 to Sir Robert Clayton, himself a wealthy financier and a dealer in real estate, and a few months later he increased the advance to £19,000, which was one of the largest sums he had lent to a private person to date. By the early 1680s, however, he was lending even greater amounts: Richard Kent and Charles Duncombe jointly borrowed £20,000 for a period in 1681-2, and Nicholas Johnson, Sir Stephen's nephew and nominee as Paymaster, took up £16,400 from him in the summer of 1681 and a further £10,000 later in the year, probably to provide himself with capital for some financial operation of his own.[2] The advances to Kent, Duncombe, and Johnson seem to have been on bond, but

---

[1] See below, pp. 206-11.

[2] Ilchester: . . . ledger for 1672-9, f. 350; ibid.: Official, Sir S. Fox, Charles II's Household (box 269): abstract of debtors and creditors from ledger 'D';

those to Clayton were secured by mortgage, and it is noticeable that from this period onwards Fox was increasingly inclined to take landed security instead of, or as well as, bond from those to whom he lent. Besides these loans to fellow financiers, he was also continuing to make advances to a number of the important Court personages with whom he now had a long-standing financial relationship. For instance, he lent £3,000 to the Earl of Sunderland in 1682; £10,000 to the Duchess of Monmouth in 1685;[1] and, in November of the same year, £3,000 to the second Earl of Clarendon (formerly Lord Cornbury), on top of the £6,000 which the Earl already owed him. He also lent large sums to the Earl of Ossory, whose debt stood at £11,400 in 1679, and to the Earl's father, the Duke of Ormonde.[2] Ormonde had an enormous income from his Irish estates, but he had never succeeded in throwing off the burden of debt with which he had found himself saddled at the Restoration, and he had suffered more or less serious financial embarrassment ever since. Fox, whom the Duke valued as a personal friend, does not seem to have been a major source of support before the early 1680s, although he had certainly made him occasional advances. However, from this time onwards, the complexity and scale of the dealings between Ormonde and Sir Stephen increased rapidly. These dealings are extremely hard to follow in detail, but from the beginning of 1683 Fox had a £9,000 mortgage on part of the Duke's Irish property, and by September 1685 the debt stood at £14,447. Ormonde died in 1688, leaving his affairs in a state of considerable confusion, and by then Sir Stephen was so deeply involved that he could not easily or quickly withdraw. He therefore continued to have extensive financial dealings with the Duke's grandson and successor until well into the next century.[3] The rate

ibid.: Official, Sir S. Fox, Treasury (box 273): small volume of rough accounts, public and private. For Clayton, see D. C. Coleman, 'London Scriveners and the Estate Market in the Later Seventeenth Century', *Ec.H.R.*, 1951.

[1] This was not a politically motivated loan, for the Duchess was not involved in her husband's rebellion. Fox's continued friendship and financial support for her was known to the King and approved by him. B.L., Add. MS. 51326, ff. 35–6: account of Fox's relationship with the Monmouths without date, heading, or endorsement.

[2] Ilchester: Family (box 237, bundle 3): Richard Kent's declaration of trust, 25 Mar. 1681/2; ibid.: Official, Sir S. Fox, Treasury (box 272): account-book marked 'Brullion begun ye 28 of Ober 81'; ibid.: . . . ledger for 1672–9, ff. 26 etc., 43; B.L., Add. MSS. 51326, ff. 35–6, and 51323, *passim*.

[3] T. Carte, *The Life of James, Duke of Ormond*(6 vols., Oxford, 1851), iv. 393–422; Ilchester: Deeds, Norfolk (box 71): document endorsed 'An Abstract

of interest Fox obtained from the Duke, and from all, or at any rate most, who borrowed from him at this time, was 6 per cent. By July 1681 Fox's private advances amounted to £84,530, and nearly five years later, in the early part of 1686, they certainly exceeded £130,000, although an exact total is not to be had.[1] One of the largest debtors in 1681, and much the largest in 1686, was Sir Edward Hungerford. Hungerford was the son of an active Royalist, himself a Knight of the Bath, and a prominent, if disreputable, figure in Court circles. His family had been important landowners in the West Country since the end of the fourteenth century, and he had inherited from his father an estate in Wiltshire and Somerset worth £4,000 a year or more. He had added to this by his own marriage to an heiress who had brought him property in Devon, Dorset, and elsewhere, and his total income in the early 1660s must have exceeded that of many peers of the realm. But large though Sir Edward's income was, his expenditure was larger still, and as he grew older he developed into one of the most notorious spendthrifts of the age. There are a whole series of stories about his reckless extravagance, some more credible than others, but the principal cause of his ruin was probably a compulsive addiction to gambling. In the 1660s he was able to satisfy his need for money by selling the lands of his first wife, but his way of life was already worrying his relatives, for when his aunt, Lady Margaret Hungerford of Corsham, made her will in 1672 she bequeathed him a set of diamond buttons with the recommendation that 'he doe not by improvident courses lessen the estate of his family, but leave itt faire to him that shall come after him'. Sir Edward ignored this advice, and in the years that followed ran up an enormous debt by mortgaging his inherited lands, until eventually all of them had to be sold.[2]

Fox's financial dealings with Hungerford seem to have begun

---

of ye Duke of Ormonde's security . . .'; ibid.: Official, Sir S. Fox, Treasury (box 272): account-book marked 'Brullion begun ye 28 of Ober 81'; ibid.: Accounts, Personal (box 221): account-book of Fox's dealings with the second Duke of Ormonde; B.L., Add. MS. 51326, ff. 63–5: 'A representation of Sr Ste Fox's friendship to the Duke of Ormonde . . .' See also below, pp. 322–3.

[1] Ilchester: Official, Sir S. Fox, Charles II's Household (box 269): abstracts of debtors and creditors from ledger 'D . See also below, p. 188.

[2] Library of the Wilts. Arch. Soc., Devizes, Hungerford Family Collections: Personal History, iii. 34–63.

early in 1674 when he lent him £1,000 on bond, and then only a matter of days later bought from him two properties in Wiltshire for a total of £7,100. A few years later, in March 1677, Fox lent him £3,000 on a mortgage of his London mansion, Hungerford House. This second loan was quickly followed by others, and from about this time Sir Stephen seems to have become his main source of funds. Every few months over the next six or seven years Hungerford borrowed more, usually one or two thousand pounds at a time, until by July 1683 his total debt to Fox was £40,000. In addition to this he also owed substantial sums to other creditors, and was inexorably being forced to sell some of his outlying estates. He sold one property to his cousin, Sir Giles Hungerford, in 1681, and in 1682 Fox himself bought the manor of Little Somerford in north Wiltshire for £7,000. Probably by now the speed at which Sir Edward was increasing his debt was beginning to worry Fox, and he was feeling that the time to call a halt was approaching. At any rate in early 1684, by which time the debt was well over £40,000, Sir Stephen insisted that it be reduced, and he obliged Sir Edward to convey to him the freehold of lands worth a total of £38,100. The property Fox thus acquired consisted of five manors, Codford St. Peter, Sutton Magna, Warminster Scudamore, Upton Scudamore, and Dilton, all of which lay near to the town of Warminster, and 120 acres of woodland in the same neighbourhood. These properties were valued at £11,600 and £1,500 respectively, and the remaining £25,000 was accounted for by Hungerford House and its grounds. The Wiltshire manors were already mortgaged for £7,500 to another of Sir Edward's creditors, and this had to be discharged out of the purchase money, so that only £30,600 remained to be deducted from what he owed to Sir Stephen. However, when all had been settled, by June 1684 his debt had been brought down to a round £13,000. It did not long remain at that figure, for Hungerford continued to press for fresh advances, and Fox also paid off a number of the other creditors, so that by February 1686 it was back to £38,500. Clearly the end could not be much longer delayed. Besides his sales to Fox, Sir Edward had sold a further large block of Wiltshire land, including the Corsham estate, to Richard Kent, and he was now mortgaging his ancestral home of Farleigh Castle and even the household goods and furniture inside it. The final act in the Hungerford drama was played out before the end of 1687 when Farleigh itself, and all the estates which still remained to Sir Edward, were sold to Henry Bayntun of Spy Park for £56,000, and out of this money Fox's mortgages were paid off in full.[1]

Sir Stephen had seemingly allowed Hungerford all the rope he needed to hang himself, and this, together with the fact that Hungerford's estates lay in the very part of the country in which he had so recently been buying land, might seem to suggest that from the first he had hoped to incorporate Sir Edward's property into his own, and had decided that the best way to ensure that he got it was to put himself in a position to foreclose. And yet on a closer examination the sequence of events does not support this interpretation. When it came to it Fox absorbed only a very small part of the huge Hungerford estate. The properties which he did take were not the choicest ones, Corsham and Farleigh, which Sir Edward naturally parted with last, but outlying estates sold at an earlier stage. There was little or no land out of lease, either at Little Somerford, or in any of the five manors, so that his acquisitions would not be susceptible of any 'improvement' for many years to come. Nor did they even lie close enough to any of the other lands owned by Fox to introduce an element of consolidation to his extremely scattered estate. It is difficult to see that Sir Stephen can have had any strong reasons for wanting those particular manors: indeed, he sold most of them again within a few years, and the chance survival of a letter he wrote to Lord Weymouth about one of them reveals that he had contemplated selling it even before the purchase deeds had been signed. The same letter also shows that he knew very little about what he was buying before it had actually become his.[2] There cannot be much doubt that Fox only took the Wiltshire manors from Sir Edward in 1682–4 in order to prevent the latter's mortgage debt from exceeding all bounds. He may well have hoped that some modest capital gain might be made by reselling, sufficient to compensate for the drop

---

[1] Ilchester: . . . ledger for 1672–9, f. 208; ibid.: General Deeds (box 150): two bundles of deeds relating to Fox's loans to, and purchases from, Hungerford; ibid.: Deeds, Wiltshire (box 133, bundle 1): purchase deeds, 4 Mar. 1683/4, 21 May 1684, and valuation of the five manors; ibid.: Deeds, Wiltshire (box 132): copy assignment of trust term, 29 June 1692; ibid.: Estate, Middlesex (box 162): volume of Hungerford Market estate accounts, also containing a loan account of Fox's advances to Hungerford; B.L., Add. MS. 51332: schedule of deeds. See also Table of Fox's land purchases in Appendix II.

[2] Library of the Wilts. Arch. Soc., Devizes, Hungerford Family Collections: Personal History, iii. 60.

in yield he would experience by exchanging mortgages for land itself, but he did not want the manors for their own sake.

If Fox had his eye on any part of Sir Edward's estate it was not his country manors, but Hungerford House in London. Hungerford House occupied a site which stretched between the Strand and the river, more or less where Charing Cross Station now stands. The mansion had apparently been seriously damaged by fire in 1669, and as Sir Edward's financial troubles had worsened he had converted the property from residential to commercial purposes. He enlarged the estate by buying and leasing from neighbouring owners, and obtained a licence from the Crown to hold a thrice-weekly market there. The ruins of the great house had been demolished, and part of the site was converted into a market-place, which took the form of an open space surrounded by a sort of colonnaded cloister with dwellings above, and stalls and stands for retailers beneath. Most of the remaining part of the site was covered with shops and houses, either built at Hungerford's expense, or by tenants to whom he had granted forty-one-year building leases.[1] These changes were only commenced in about 1680, and so when Sir Edward was forced to convey the property to Fox four years later his investment had hardly begun to bear fruit: some of the places in the market were still unlet, and some of the building plots still vacant. Nevertheless, the prospects for the market were most promising, for it was situated so close to Whitehall that it attracted custom from the vast army of royal servants, government officials, and hangers-on, who lived in or near the Palace. It therefore promised to be a lucrative income-yielding investment, and its acquisition would add diversity to Fox's portfolio, for hitherto he had bought no urban property at all. Such large blocks of real estate, with so good a situation, cannot often have come up for sale in later seventeenth-century London, and since Sir Stephen lived only a few hundred yards away it was so eminently desirable a possession that he may well have felt it worth going to a good deal of trouble to get it. It therefore seems reasonable to conclude that a principal motive for his earlier loans to Sir Edward was to ensure that it became his. And

---

[1] *Pepys*, ix. 534–5; B.L., Add. MS. 51324, f. 80: notes on land leased from the Dean and Chapter of Westminster; Ilchester: Estate, Middlesex (box 162): volume of Hungerford Market estate accounts, also containing copies of other documents concerning the property.

yet, two months after he had acquired Hungerford Market, Fox sold a quarter share in it to the architect Sir Christopher Wren, whom he had recently worked with on the establishment of Chelsea Hospital. Wren paid £6,250, which was exactly a quarter of the price Fox had himself paid, so that there was no question of the latter seizing an opportunity for a quick capital gain.[1] Why then his partial disinvestment? One possibility is that part of the money which Fox had been lending to Hungerford had in fact been Wren's, and that from the start there had been an agreement that they should go into partnership in the management of the estate as soon as it had been prised from Hungerford's grasp. It is also possible, of course, that Fox felt that £25,000 was too large a sum to have invested in a single London property of this type, which was very much at risk from damage or destruction by fire. Unfortunately, there is no means of knowing which explanation is correct, or whether Fox had some quite different reason for wanting part of his money back. He may simply have wished to recover some of the liquidity which he had lost by lending such a large sum to Sir Edward over so short a period. However, he made no attempt to sell his remaining three-quarters share, and there is no evidence to suggest that he had come to regret his purchase, nor that the assumption that he had been very anxious to secure it in the first place is incorrect.

To return to Sir Edward, we have seen that Fox did not cease to lend money to him after he had obliged him to part with Hungerford Market, and as long as the latter had any security left to offer he was able to obtain loans from Sir Stephen.[2] One might suppose that Fox was being forced to extend further credit in order to ensure the safety of his outstanding investment, that he was unwillingly but inexorably sucked into deeper and deeper involvement with this man whose need to spend had now reached pathological proportions. Yet the fact that Fox not only made him new advances, but also took over the debts which Hungerford owed to others, suggests that this was not so, that he was perfectly content to put out large sums on mortgage, even though he had no desire to acquire any more of the lands being mortgaged. Whatever may

---

[1] Ilchester: Deeds, Middlesex (box 70, bundle 2): articles of agreement between Fox and Wren, 15 July 1684.

[2] Ilchester: Estate, Middlesex (box 162): volume of Hungerford Market estate accounts, also containing a loan account of Fox's advances to Hungerford.

have been his main motive in his earlier dealings with Sir Edward, in the later stages it is difficult to see any other than a positive preference for investing in mortgages. It was certainly not to obtain any more Hungerford property, for once he had secured Hungerford Market Fox showed no interest in the remaining country estates, and when the final crash came he bought none of them and extricated his capital completely.

Meanwhile, Fox had not withdrawn entirely from lending to the Crown once he had ceased to finance the army, but he had progressively reduced the proportion of his fortune which was invested in conventional loans. In fact it was not for several years after he had abandoned the Undertaking at the end of 1679 that all the money owed to him in that connection had been fully repaid. His various military and interest accounts remained open at least until 1684, and possibly into 1685, while he awaited the final settlement of them by the government, and as late as January 1686 he still held £48,441 worth of 'old' tallies, which almost certainly represent the last of what was owed to him from his time as Paymaster. In the meantime he was also making fresh advances, or at least re-lending part of what was being paid back to him, on a substantial scale in 1682 and 1683, although on a more modest one by the middle of the decade. Some of these loans were made on the security of tallies, but the largest of them are recorded as having been made to Robert Squibb. Squibb was a Teller of the Exchequer and a Treasury Clerk, and, although no details of the transactions emerge, it is probable that he was named simply as the recipient of payments made directly into the Exchequer. At any rate the sums recorded against his name rose from £11,000 on 1 October 1681 to nearly £70,000 fifteen months later, before declining to £17,900 by the middle of 1685, a level which was maintained in 1686. This decline was only partly offset by an increase in the sums lent on tallies from £6,441 in early 1683 to £34,000 three years later, by which time the total of Fox's 'new' loans to the government was thus £51,900. The rate of interest he received on most of this money is not recorded, but it was 7 per cent in the case of the £20,000 he lent on the security of tallies charged on the Linen and East India duties of 1685, and in all probability was usually either at this rate or at 8 per cent.[1]

---

[1] Ilchester: Official, Sir S. Fox. Charles II's Household (box 269): abstracts of debtors and creditors from ledger 'D'; ibid.: Official, Sir S. Fox, Army (box

However, while Fox gradually reduced his involvement in government finance of the traditional type during the 1680s, he was becoming increasingly concerned in one of its more esoteric byways. This arose from the interest he developed in the purchase of annuities. As has been seen, on several occasions since the beginning of the 1660s he had bought pensions and offices from needy courtiers, but from the later 1670s the sums he laid out on this account became much larger. In 1677 Sir George Hamilton, from whom he had already made two purchases of this type, and who was as acutely in need of ready money as ever, sold him a pension of £300 a year for £1,500. This, like the £120 per annum he had bought from Hamilton sixteen years earlier, seems to have been granted to the seller for his life and so was a speculative investment, particularly since Hamilton was that much older and the likelihood of his death occurring before Fox had made a reasonable profit had correspondingly increased. On the other hand, by this later period Sir Stephen's influence in Household circles was much greater, and he probably considered that, if Hamilton did die unexpectedly, he had a good chance of securing continued payment of the pension to himself. In fact it is not clear when Hamilton's death occurred, but whenever it did Fox succeeded in retaining the annuity until the early years of the eighteenth century, and he only lost it after his retirement from public life when he no longer was in a position to influence affairs at Court.[1] Indeed, Sir Stephen's renowned 'dexterity' (to use the phrase of an admiring observer) in ensuring that payments due to himself, or to others on whose behalf he was acting, were forthcoming from the Exchequer or elsewhere, provided him with an important element of security denied to most others when he acquired this type of asset.[2] It was doubtless for this reason that, although he bought no annuities payable out of the estates of private persons, he invested very large sums in those payable out of Crown revenues. Certainly £300 a year was small beer com-

---

266): declared account for interest on money advanced for the forces, 28 Oct. 1684.

[1] Ilchester: . . . ledger for 1672–9, f. 29; B.L., Add. MS. 51324, ff. 52–3: document endorsed 'Proceedings at the Greencloth agst Sr Stephen Fox'. In the latter narrative Fox refers to a pension of £350 per annum, but there is little doubt that it was the one purchased in 1677 that he meant. See also below, p. 317.

[2] H.M.C., *Ormonde*, N.S., v. 387.

pared to the other annuities which Fox acquired at this period, but on the other hand, the later purchases, being for fixed terms of years, were much less speculative. In 1677, for instance, he bought from the Earl of Ossory, for £6,000, an annuity of £1,600 payable for five and three-quarter years out of two pensions which the Earl had obtained from the King.[1] This transaction secured for Sir Stephen an effective return on capital invested of no less than 18 per cent per annum, which surely encouraged him to look for similar opportunities elsewhere, and early in the next decade several duly presented themselves. Thus in 1684 he acquired an interest in a pension of £1,000 per annum payable out of part of the royal revenue known as the First Fruits and Tenths, which had originally been granted to the Earl of Sunderland for twenty-one years from 1680. Sunderland had sold seven years of his pension immediately, and the remaining fourteen years of it some time later. The buyer of the fourteen-years reversion was a certain Captain Hinde, who had also come into possession of a moiety (i.e. £500 per annum) of the pension for what was left of the seven-year term, and it was from Hinde that Fox purchased. He paid £1,200 for a half share in the remaining three years of the original seven, and £1,150 for the same share in the fourteen-year term which was due to commence when the seven had expired. Altogether, therefore, he laid out £2,350 in order to purchase £500 a year for seventeen years, thereby securing returns of about 12½ and nearly 24 per cent respectively on the two transactions. Then in 1687, just as the seven-year term was about to expire, Fox also bought the other half share in the remaining fourteen years, paying £2,800 for it which ensured him a handsome 17 per cent.[2] Meanwhile, in 1685, he had acquired an even larger pension: £5,000 per annum, to be paid half-yearly out of the Crown's Irish revenue until £21,000 had been received. This too had been granted in the first instance to the Earl of Sunderland, and was immediately sold by him in order to raise a lump sum. Fox paid him £15,000, which should have secured him a return of just over 15 per cent during the four and a half years during which he would receive payments,

---

[1] Ilchester: Legal, Ireland (box 254): document endorsed 'The case of Mr Richd Kent'; ibid.: Official, Sir S. Fox, Treasury (box 273): small volume of rough accounts, public and private.

[2] Ilchester: Family, Robert Earl of Sunderland (box 243, bundle 17): deeds relating to the pensions payable out of the First Fruits and Tenths; B.L., Add. MS. 51320, f. 76: agreement between Fox and Sir Tho. Duppa, 15 Oct. 1684.

which was very much in line with the anticipated yield on most of the other pensions and annuities he had purchased.[1]

The rates of return Fox received from these annuities were clearly very much higher than those he obtained from the rest of his investments. From lending to the government on tallies at this time he got 7 or 8 per cent; from lending to private individuals on bond or mortgage normally 6 per cent; from fee farm rents in possession acquired at sixteen years' purchase he could expect to make $6\frac{1}{4}$ per cent gross, with few deductions; and from his country estates which he bought at various rates between twenty and sixteen years' purchase, 5 or 6 per cent gross, but significantly less net. This difference between the return on annuities and all other securities may have owed something to the incomplete diffusion of sound accounting techniques, so that the sellers, extravagant aristocrats pressed for ready cash, were not fully aware of how poor was the price they had agreed to. Furthermore, all the annuities were payable out of Crown revenues, and like all payments made by the Exchequer were attended with delay, trouble, and expense to the recipient, the inevitable result of the cumbersome way in which the Exchequer operated and the fees which had to be paid to its officials.[2] Indeed, some years earlier (though in a different context) Fox had complained that, partly because of this inefficiency, 8 per cent from the Crown was worth no more than 7 per cent from a private borrower.[3] Over and above this was the danger that payments might not be made when they fell due. Even for a man with Fox's influence and contacts, any investment which relied on payments by the Crown involved something of a gamble on continuance of royal solvency and political stability, neither of which could be taken for granted at this time, and payments which were made by virtue of grants of pensions to needy courtiers were particularly likely to suffer interruption if things went seriously wrong. Fox, who had lived through 1672 when not only did the Crown withhold interest on its debts but allowed payment of many salaries and pensions to fall badly into arrears, can hardly have needed any reminder of the very real nature of these risks, but the events of

---

[1] See references given in note 2, p. 187.

[2] All the rates of return on annuities quoted in the text are *gross* rates. Net of fees the rates would be slightly lower.

[3] B.L., Add. MS. 28078, f. 286. This paper is in the name of Richard Kent, but the argument is Sir Stephen's as it dates from a time when Kent was his nominee as Cashier of the Excise.

1688 served to underline the point most forcibly. The new government did not, in fact, repudiate the debts of its predecessor, but it was not prepared to continue to pay unquestioningly the pensions which had been enjoyed by James II's principal supporters, nor was Parliament prepared to allow it to do so. The Earl of Sunderland, who had fled abroad in December 1688, was one of those whom the new regime had to regard as potential enemies, and in 1689, and again in 1691, Fox found that his investment in Sunderland's £1,000 per annum out of the First Fruits and Tenths was in jeopardy from anti-Jacobite feeling in the Commons. He was obliged to mount campaigns, which in 1689 included a formal petition to Parliament, to make it clear that he had bought the title to the annuity outright, and that if it was stopped it would be he, not Sunderland, who suffered.[1] He was successful in saving the £1,000 a year, but the larger £5,000 annuity caused him even more serious trouble. One consequence of the 1688 Revolution was that the government in London temporarily lost control of Ireland, so that the collection of the royal revenue there came to an end, and it was several years before it could be resumed. Hence the last few instalments of the £5,000 per annum were not paid as expected, and when peace was finally restored to Ireland Fox's attempt to recover the £6,473. 7s. 8d. which was still owing to him was blocked by the Countess of Dorchester. She held a reversionary grant of the same pension to commence immediately after the expiry of the four and a half years, and she claimed that payments to her were now due to begin. The question of whether Fox ought to be allowed to receive the full amount owing to him, even though the period in which it should have been paid had expired, was considered by his fellow Treasury Lords in 1693, but they refused to come to a decision and in effect told Sir Stephen and the Countess to take their dispute to the courts.[2] Fox eventually recovered his arrears, placating the Countess with a loan to tide her over

---

[1] *Commons Journals*, 10 (1688–93), p. 229. See also J. P. Kenyon, *Robert Spencer, Earl of Sunderland* (London, 1958), pp. 249–50. It should be noted, however, that Professor Kenyon has not correctly interpreted the documents relating to Sunderland's annuities before 1688.

[2] Ilchester: Legal, Ireland (box 254): document entitled 'A state of the case between Sr Stephen Fox and My Lady Dorchester'; ibid.: Family (box 237, bundle 3): declaration of trust, 25 July 1692; B.L., Add. MS. 51319, f. 109: royal warrant, 25 Feb. 1691; Add. MS. 51331: schedule of deeds, f. 17; *C.T.B.* x (1693–6), pp. 206, 356.

until her pension payments began,[1] but nevertheless these episodes do illustrate the hazards involved in the purchase of Court pensions and, by implication, the justification for the high rate of interest that moneyed men required before they were prepared to invest in them.

Nowhere does Fox provide us with a complete analysis of his investment portfolio for a given date, but it is possible to reconstruct one for the beginning of the year 1686 with a reasonable degree of confidence that nothing of importance has been omitted. It is inevitable that assets are valued at their original cost since a current valuation is not to be had, but values in general had not altered a great deal in the relatively short period since most of the items had been acquired, and the distortion introduced by this procedure is not very serious. It is true that the value of the Somerset estate, and to a lesser degree that of the Wiltshire estate also, had fallen; and that the capital value of the annuities must also have been less than their original cost price owing to the reduced life expectancy of the individuals on whose survival some of them depended, and in the case of the others because part of a fixed term of years had expired. On the other hand, the value of the fee farm rents which Fox had purchased in reversion after the death of Queen Catharine had probably increased, now that the latter was nearly fifteen years older. A further reservation that must be made is that a precise total of Sir Stephen's advances to private individuals cannot be calculated, for in the highly compressed summary accounts which have survived from the mid-1680s formal loans cannot always be distinguished from other types of 'creditor' entries. However, the true figure cannot have been significantly higher than the £140,000 entered in Table X, and it may well have been as much as £10,000 lower, and some deduction should probably also be made for a proportion of bad debts. The valuation of assets arrived at in the Table may, therefore, be a little too high generally, but not by more than 4 or 5 per cent of the total sum involved, and in all probability by less.[2]

A more important proviso is that the figure of £383,248 shown

[1] Ilchester: Family (box 238, bundle 25): abstract of Mr. Robinson's account, 1693–1700.
[2] The acquisition of most of the items in Table X has been discussed in the text, and references given as appropriate. Additional references are given in the notes to the Table itself.

as the total value of Fox's investments should not be taken as his net worth. To arrive at this it is necessary to add in all his other assets, the most important of which were cash in hand; his household goods and plate; his coaches and horses; the money owed by the tenants on the estates; and his Court offices. From this grand total all liabilities must then be subtracted. Unfortunately there is insufficient information to undertake these calculations with any degree of precision. The amount of cash Sir Stephen kept, and allowed his servants and his banker to keep, is unknown, but it is unlikely to have exceeded a few hundred pounds. He does not seem to have spent lavishly, by the standards of the day, on the furnishing of his houses, and he certainly did not collect art treasures, or amass gold and silver plate, or precious stones. Yet even so, the value of his personal possessions, including the contents of his stables, can scarcely have been worth less than £3,500 or £4,000.[1] He was certainly owed many hundreds of pounds of rent arrears by his tenants, particularly those in Somerset, and many hundreds more which he had lent to them to tide them over difficult times. Altogether about £1,700 was due to him in this way in 1686, but much of this, although by no means all, was certainly lost for ever.[2] Finally, Fox still held the office of First Clerk of the Green Cloth, and that of Purveyor of Wax to the Household, and although one cannot estimate the price the latter would have commanded, the former should definitely be valued in any complete calculation of his wealth, for there is little doubt that he could have sold it had he wished to, probably for about £2,000.[3] All these items together are thus more or less sufficient to counter-balance the element of overvaluation in Table X, so that we can say that altogether Fox's assets must have been worth approximately £380,000, if not a little more. However, against his assets must be set his liabilities, which were considerable since he was still accepting interest-bearing deposits from other investors, and to a large extent relied on

---

[1] See below, pp. 261-4. [2] See below, pp. 200-1.

[3] Fox reckoned the Wax Purveyance to be worth £300 a year to him (see above, p. 113). The Clerk of the Green Cloth's place was worth about £580 p.a. net at this time (see below, p. 197), and in view of the fact that Sir Stephen was nearing sixty, it would hardly have sold for more than three or four years' purchase. At different times he had also bought a number of minor offices (see above, pp. 114-16), but by the mid-1680s these seem all to have been either sold or bestowed on relatives. The reversionary grant of the Cofferer's place, which Fox had secured in 1677 (see above, pp. 112-13), was presumably valueless after the death of the sovereign who had made the grant.

borrowed money to maintain his liquidity. It is impossible to be sure of the exact amount he owed to others in the early part of 1686, but it was not more than £150,000 and was probably rather less.[1] It is therefore safe to conclude that Sir Stephen's net worth was between £230,000 and £240,000.[2] For a man who had started with only a few pounds in his pocket twenty-six years earlier, he had accumulated a truly colossal fortune by seventeenth-century standards.

Table X setting out Fox's investments at the beginning of 1686 indicates that Sir Stephen had put some capital into almost every type of investment vehicle then available, except for the securities of the joint stock trading companies. Despite his extensive purchases of land the country estates comprised only about a quarter of his gross assets, a proportion which rises to just over a quarter (about 27 per cent) if the £7,117 spent on the new mansion at Chiswick is added to the £96,347 laid out on the estates themselves. Urban property, that is his three-quarter share in Hungerford Market and his own apartments in Whitehall, accounted for nearly $5\frac{1}{2}$ per cent, and fee farm rents for less than 3 per cent, of his total portfolio. Altogether, therefore, not much more than one-third (about 35 per cent) of Fox's capital was invested in real estate, whether in lands, in buildings, or in rents. A similar proportion, between 36 and 37 per cent, was in loans to private individuals, secured either by bond or by mortgage, whilst the remainder was in government securities of one sort or another—either lent to the Crown by Fox himself, or in the form of annuities which, although purchased from private individuals, were paid out of Crown revenues. Sir Stephen thus had a well-balanced spread of investments which distributed his risks almost as widely as was feasible, a precaution which, in the event, was thoroughly justified, since several of his acquisitions turned out to be less successful than he had had reason to anticipate. We have seen that his speculative gamble in buying fee farm rents in reversion, after the death of Charles II's Queen, had backfired, and that in respect of the £5,000

[1] Ilchester: Official, Sir S. Fox, Charles II's Household (box 269): abstract of debtors and creditors from ledger 'D', 23 Mar. 1685/6; ibid.: Official, Sir S. Fox, Treasury (box 272): account-book marked 'Brullion begun ye 28 of Ober 81'.

[2] However, it should be noted that Fox had settled the Water Eaton estate on his son Charles at the time of the latter's marriage in 1679; it was not, therefore, in his own possession at this time. See below, p. 268.

TABLE X

Sir Stephen Fox's Investment Portfolio, January 1686

(£. *s. d.*)

Country Property[1]			
Somerset		19,419 ⎫	
Wiltshire	Water Eaton	21,908 ⎪	
	South Wilts. Manors	49,720 ⎬	103,464
Chiswick	Estate	5,300 ⎪	
	House	7,117 ⎭	
Town Property[2]			
Whitehall apartments		2,000 ⎱	20,750
Hungerford Market, three-quarter share		18,750 ⎰	
Fee Farm Rents[3]			
In possession		5,897 ⎱	10,983
In reversion		5,086 ⎰	
Annuities etc.			
£120 p.a. ⎫ purchased from		500 ⎫	
£300 p.a. ⎰ Sir G. Hamilton		1,500 ⎪	
Moiety of £1,000 p.a. out of Clerical			
Tenths		2,350 ⎬	21,710
£5,000 p.a. out of Irish quit rents		15,000 ⎪	
Other annuities (£141. 12s. 0d. p.a.)		2,360 ⎭	
Loans to the Government[4]			
Old tallies		48,441 ⎫	
On East India Commodities			
(Act of 1685)		20,000 ⎬	86,341
In the name of Robert Squibb		17,900 ⎭	
Loans to Private Individuals[5]		*c.* 140,000	*c.* 140,000
		TOTAL	*c.* 383,248

[1] The total cost of the Wiltshire estates had been £73,554. 9s. 1d., but two farms had been sold in 1682 (see below, p. 207). These had been valued at £1,800 and £126 respectively so that the cost price of what remained was £71,628. 9s. 1d. For the cost of the house at Chiswick see below, p. 263.

[2] This was the value of the Whitehall apartments in 1691. C.T.B. ix (1689–92), p. 1372.

[3] Fox had also bought fee farm rents, costing £207. 15s. 9d. and £285 respectively, which were payable out of his own lands at Water Eaton and at Kilmington. These have been treated as additions to his landed property and are included in the figure for that species of investment. Rents in possession to the value of £4. 10s. 0d. p.a. had been sold for £76. 10s. 0d., and some in reversion

annuity purchased from the Earl of Sunderland he had suffered a lengthy delay in recovering part of his money. But hardly less serious was the fact that the performance of his principal country estates, particularly those in Somerset, had already proved to be disappointing, and after a good beginning Hungerford Market also failed to fulfil the promise of a lucrative return which it had seemed to offer at its acquisition.[1]

Any attempt to calculate the annual income which Fox received from his great fortune at this time is fraught with difficulties, some of the most serious of which arise from the fact that it involves making a computation which Sir Stephen himself probably never made. There are, amongst his papers, numerous estimates, often in his own hand, of the income which had in the past accrued from his offices, pensions, and estates, or which could be expected from them in the future.[2] However, we have just seen that in the mid-1680s nearly two-thirds of his assets consisted of government securities and loans to private individuals, and he never reckoned the return from these on an annual basis. The main reason for this was probably that in his operations as a financier of the government and as a moneylender he did not maintain a clear distinction between capital and income, and indeed the way he had become rich

---

for £372. 12s. od., both in 1678. Ilchester: General Deeds (box 144): conveyances, 29 Aug. 1671, 9 July 1677, and 17 Apr. 1678. Also ibid.: Accounts, General Estate: ledger marked 'Sir S.F.', ff. 19, 83.

[4] This figure is actually for 23 March 1686, but a comparison between the summary account for that date and the previous one in the series (for June 1685) does not suggest that it is likely to have been very different in January. Ilchester: Official, Sir S. Fox, Charles II's Household (box 269): abstracts of debtors and creditors from ledger 'D'. The figure given for tallies excludes £938. 19s. 8d. of accumulated interest.

[5] See references cited in note 1, p. 190.

[1] For the performance of the Somerset and Wiltshire estates in the latter 1670s and 1680s, see below, pp. 197–211. Hungerford Market failed to live up to its early promise for various reasons. One was that the market itself failed to withstand the competition from Covent Garden Market. A second was that the fire which burnt down most of the old palace at Whitehall in 1698 swept away a large proportion of the potential customers for the market and the shops which surrounded it. See J. Strype, *Stow's Survey of London and Westminster* (2 vols., London, 1720), ii, Westminster, p. 76. Also Ilchester: Family (box 236, bundle 10): document entitled 'A Memoriall for the Dean and Chapter . . .'

[2] The estimates relating to the 1680s are those contained in Ilchester: Official, Sir S. Fox, Treasury (box 272): account-book marked 'Brullion begun ye 28 of Ober 81', at back; ibid.: Family (box 236, bundle 4): booklet marked 'Abstract of Sr Stephen Fox's estate', and document marked 'A computation of my Owne Estate'.

in the 1660s and 1670s was by treating virtually all the income accruing from his financial activities as additions to his operating capital, and to a degree he continued to do this in the later phases of his career. Certainly, the interest on the money which Fox had out on loan was not invariably, or even normally, paid to him regularly every quarter or half year, but at irregular intervals and sometimes not at all for long periods. Interest due on tallies was often not paid until the securities themselves were redeemed, when it was forthcoming as a lump sum added to whatever principal was due for repayment; and some private borrowers similarly allowed unpaid interest to accumulate until they discharged their debt. Others avoided the immediate need to service their borrowings from Fox by having unpaid interest periodically added to the principal outstanding, so that it too came to bear interest, which in turn remained unpaid. For example, between February 1688 and April 1700, the Earl of Clarendon paid no interest at all on the £3,000 Sir Stephen had lent him in 1685, by which time the unpaid arrears amounted to £2,188. 12s. 0d. This was, perhaps, an extreme instance, but the surviving accounts of Fox's loans to Sir Edward Hungerford for the years 1683 to 1687 show that Hungerford paid little of the interest when due, and most of it was simply carried on and periodically added to the principal of his debt. Similarly, the record of the loans to the second Duke of Ormonde in the late 1680s and early 1690s shows that he made no effort to pay the interest, and it too was added to the debt which, in consequence, mounted steadily over the years.[1] Sir Stephen was thus, in effect, obtaining from a number of those who borrowed from him not simple, but something nearer to compound, interest. Because his great resources enabled him to do without regular income from some of his loans he was able to secure a considerably higher rate of return in the end. His courtier clients seemed to regard it as a favour to be allowed to leave their interest unpaid, but it cost them more than they probably realized. We may therefore note that nominally Fox received 7 per cent per annum on the £20,000 he had lent to the government on the security of the

[1] B.L., Add. MS. 51323: booklet on Fox's relationship with the second Earl of Clarendon; Ilchester: Family (box 238, bundle 20): document endorsed 'The Earles of Clarendon & Rochesters accompt . . .'; ibid.: Estate, Middlesex (box 162): account of Fox's loans to Hungerford contained in a volume of Hungerford Market estate accounts; ibid.: Accounts, Personal (box 221): volume of accounts of Fox's loans to the second Duke of Ormonde.

East India Commodities Act, 8 per cent on the £48,441 of old tallies, and an unknown rate (probably 8 per cent) on the £17,900 lent through Robert Squibb, and that these rates implied receipt of some £6,707 in a full year. Similarly, the 6 per cent per annum which he charged private borrowers on the £140,000 odd he had lent them should in theory have yielded him £8,400 a year.[1] In both cases, however, the reality was very much less straightforward. There are also problems involved in the case of the two fixed-term annuities which Fox enjoyed in 1686.[2] It is true that these were paid to him on a regular basis, at least until political complications led to an interruption of payments on the £5,000 per annum out of the Irish revenue, but of course the annual instalments represented a combination of repayments of capital and a return on capital. Only the latter can properly be regarded as income, and the sums entered in Table XI are therefore arrived at by eliminating the former. However, in practice Sir Stephen probably made no clearer distinction between capital and income in the case of annuities than he did with his lending on tallies, or with his complicated financial dealings with Hungerford and the Duke of Ormonde. Hence it is unlikely that he thought in terms of an annual income from them at all.

There is therefore a certain artificiality about Table XI, which purports to show Sir Stephen's gross income in 1686. A second element of artificiality derives from the fact that there was a considerable gap between the gross and the net return from the landed estates. This was particularly marked in the case of the Somerset property (for reasons which will shortly be explained), and the contribution made by the estates to Fox's total income was thus somewhat smaller than Table XI appears to suggest.[3] Nevertheless, the figure arrived at there does serve to indicate Sir Stephen's relative standing *vis-à-vis* other men of great wealth in the late seventeenth century. The gross income of some £22,062 from his estates, fee farm rents, annuities, and loans was, moreover, in addition to the £1,140 or so from Water Eaton, which had been settled

---

[1] It is possible that some of the loans were at 5 per cent rather than 6, but all those for which the rate charged can actually be established were at 6 per cent.

[2] The purchase price of the two annuities on the life of Sir George Hamilton, bought in 1661 and 1677 respectively, had been recouped in full well before 1686, so the whole amounts received can legitimately be regarded as income without any intermixture of capital repayment.

[3] See below, pp. 199–206.

TABLE XI

Sir Stephen Fox's Gross Income, 1686[1]

(£. s. d.)

Estates

Somerset (average of 1680–7)	892 15. 4.	
Wiltshire (average of 1685–9)	1,370 9. 6.	
Chiswick (1689)	379 13. 1.	3,759, 1. 11.
Hungerford Market, three-quarter share (average of 1685–6)	1,116 4. 0.	

Fee Farm Rents[2]   375 15. 8¾.   375 15. 8¾.

Annuities etc.

On the life of Sir G. Hamilton	420 0. 0.	
Moiety of £1,000 p.a. out of Clerical Tenths	150 0. 0.	2,820 0. 0.
£5,000 p.a. out of Irish quit rents	2,250 0. 0.	
Other annuities	*	

Loans to the Government

£48,441 on old tallies at 8 per cent	3,875 5. 7.	
£20,000 on East India commodities at 7 per cent	1,400 0. 0.	6,707 5. 7.
£17,900 in name of Squibb, ? at 8 per cent	1,432 0. 0.	

Loans to Private Persons

     c. £140,000 at 6 per cent   c. 8,400 0. 0. c. 8,400 0. 0.

Court Offices

Clerk of the Green Cloth	580 0. 0.	880 0. 0.
Wax Purveyance	300 0. 0.	

Miscellaneous

     Reward for managing the finances of the Duchess of Monmouth, and others   ?   ?

TOTAL   c. 22,942 3. 2¾.

* Nominally 14 1. 12. 0. p.a., but in fact not being paid regularly.

1 For the Somerset and Wiltshire estates, see the references cited in note 1, p. 203, and note 2, p. 204; for Chiswick and Hungerford Market, see Ilchester: Estate, Middlesex (box 162): separate volumes of estate accounts for the two properties; for Chiswick alone, ibid.: Family (box 236, bundle 10): document entitled 'A Rentaile of Prebend Manor . . .'; for the fee farm rents, ibid.: Accounts, General Estate: ledger marked 'Sir S.F.'

2 In addition to the income Fox was receiving from fee farm rents, he held the reversion to a further £616 per annum, so that once Queen Catharine was dead his income would be increased by that amount. See above, pp. 167–8.

on his son Charles at the time of his marriage in 1679,[1] and the
£616 a year of fee farm rents purchased in reversion which would
produce nothing so long as Queen Catharine remained alive. On the
other hand, from the £22,062 must be deducted interest on the
£150,000 or so of borrowed money which Fox still held. Since
1684 he seems invariably to have paid his depositors 5 per cent, so
that expenditure on interest will have amounted to some £7,500 in
1686. A deduction must also be made on account of £376. 10s. 0d.
of outgoing annuities with which certain of Fox's lands were
encumbered as a result of the terms on which he had bought them.[2]
It may therefore be said, subject to the reservations already discussed, that Sir Stephen Fox's fortune was yielding him approximately £14,186 a year, before deduction of the costs of management, direct taxation (which, it may be remembered, was negligible
in the 1680s), repairs to the estates, and such like. This was roughly
twice the income obtained by the East India Company magnate,
Sir John Banks, from the fortune he made over a slightly longer
period: it is reckoned that his gross receipts averaged about £6,363
a year in the early 1680s and about £7,580 a year in the later 1680s.[3]
It is possible that one or two of the other leading financiers of the
day, Sir Josiah Child perhaps, or Charles Duncombe, were, or
shortly became, richer than Fox, but otherwise only a handful of
the greatest landed aristocrats, such as the Earls of Bedford,
Devonshire, and Clare, had larger resources. For instance, the last
of these three, who became Duke of Newcastle in 1694, had a gross
income from real estate of £25,000 a year, although his net income
after deduction of interest on debts cannot have exceeded Sir
Stephen's by more than three or four thousand.[4] Besides, Fox also
received something from office on top of the income deriving from
his investments, although at the beginning of 1686 it was less than
at almost any other time before his retirement in 1702. He had
ceased to be a Treasury Lord on James II's accession in February

---

[1] See below, p. 268.

[2] The rent charges were £274 p.a. on Chiswick, and £77. 10s. 0d. and £25
p.a. on Milford and West Grimstead in Wilts, respectively. For the first, see
above, p. 174; for the two latter, Ilchester: Estate, Wiltshire (box 178): series of
half-yearly accounts for the Wilts. manors.

[3] Coleman, *Sir John Banks*, p. 186.

[4] R. Grassby, 'The Personal Wealth of the Business Community in Seventeenth-century England', *Ec.H.R.*, 1970; O. R. F. Davis, 'The Wealth and
Influence of John Holles, Duke of Newcastle', *Renaissance and Modern Studies*,
1965.

of the previous year, and his son Charles had been dismissed from the Paymastership in November, so that his post at the Green Cloth and the Wax Purveyance were his only remaining sources of official income.[1] At this time these were worth about £580 a year and £300 a year respectively, so bringing his receipts up to at least £15,000 a year. In fact they were certainly even more than this because Sir Stephen continued to handle the private finances of the Duchess of Monmouth and a number of other important personages, from whom he received some form of remuneration, although not necessarily on a regular basis. However, before February 1685, and again after January 1687, he had enjoyed a Treasury Commissioner's salary of £1,600 a year, and a share in the New Year's gifts traditionally paid to the Lord Treasurer, worth perhaps a further £150 per annum, while down to the previous November (i.e. of 1685) he had also drawn up to £1,000 a year from the Pay Office.[2] A year or two earlier Sir Stephen must, therefore, have had a total income approaching £18,000 a year. His nephew, John Fox, was neither flattering nor exaggerating when he called him 'the richest commoner in three kingdoms'.[3]

By the beginning of the 1680s Sir Stephen, as has been noted, had lost his principal motive for building up a great landed estate, and certainly in the years that followed he did not show any signs of interest in the country properties he had acquired, save in the case of his birthplace, Farley, where he built a church and an alms-house, and tried to establish a grammar school.[4] He maintained no household at Redlynch, and allowed the mansion to be occupied successively by his elder brother John, and his younger brother Thomas, who acted for him in some more or less formal managerial capacity. He spent no more on it than was necessary to keep it, and its various outhouses, in reasonably good repair, and hardly ever visited it himself: indeed the accounts of his personal expenditure seem to show that after his brief stay in 1672 he did not see the place again for thirty years.[5] Nor did he particularly concern him-

[1] See below, pp. 216, 225.

[2] Ilchester: Official, Sir S. Fox, Treasury (box 272): account-book marked 'Brullion begun ye 28 of Ober 81', at back.

[3] B.L., Add. MS. 51324, f. 16: narrative of the life of John Fox junior.

[4] See below, pp. 308–10.

[5] Ilchester: Accounts, Personal (box 220): accounts of Sir S. Fox's private expenses, 1680–1, 1681–4, 1684–97; ibid.: Family (box 238, bundles 6 and 7): accounts relating to journeys undertaken by Sir S. Fox.

self with problems of estate management. Judging from the correspondence of his agent in Somerset, Thomas Allen, Sir Stephen was kept well informed of what went on, and was consulted before important decisions were taken, but he seems almost invariably to have accepted Allen's advice on what to do, and rarely, if ever, to have given instructions unless they had been specifically requested.[1] He certainly did not pursue any consistent policy of improvement on his property, although where individual farms called for significant expenditure to meet the changing needs of tenants, he was quite prepared to authorize it. In September 1675, for example, he allowed £100 to the tenant of the large demesne farm at Maddington, Wiltshire, to pay for a new barn and granary; and in 1683 he agreed to the building of a completely new farm house at Plaitford farm at a total cost of £155. 3s. 2d., a figure which was more than twice the annual rent of the holding.[2] Nevertheless, such instances were exceptional, and for the most part both the Wiltshire and the Somerset properties seem to have been on a care-and-maintenance basis. Sir Stephen's passive attitude to his estates is further illustrated by the case of the West Grimstead enclosure. There was a piece of common within the manor whose enclosure would increase the value of all the principal farms there, not least those belonging to Fox, thus providing an opportunity which one might have expected a new owner, especially a moneyed man who was well able to meet the costs of the scheme, to have seized upon with alacrity. As it was, however, the initiative came not from him, but from the tenants: as early as 1693 some of them approached his Wiltshire agent to inquire whether he would be prepared to give his consent to an enclosure proposal, although the plan was not actually carried into effect until 1706.[3]

There can be little doubt, therefore, that from the 1680s Fox regarded his West Country estate as simply one investment among many, valuable as part of a balanced portfolio, but no different in status from any of his other capital assets. Since it had become apparent that he was unlikely to leave a male heir he not only lacked

[1] Ilchester: Estate, Somerset (box 173, bundle 1): letters from Thomas Allen to Sir S. Fox.

[2] Ilchester: Accounts, General Estate: ledger marked 'Sir S.F.', ff. 27, 101, 102.

[3] Ilchester: Family (box 236, bundle 2): W. Smith to Sir S. Fox, 28 June 1693; ibid.: Deeds, Wiltshire (box 128, bundle 4): articles of agreement relating to W. Grimstead enclosure, 20 May 1706.

strong motives for buying more land in Somerset or Wiltshire, but he did not even have any particular reasons for keeping what he had already acquired if it proved to be a poor investment judged from a strictly financial point of view, or if some other use for the capital presented itself. And a poor investment much of it did indeed prove to be, at least in the short and medium term, the return from it turning out even lower than Fox had anticipated when he acquired it. He had bought Redlynch, and the freehold part of the Pitton and Farley estate, at twenty years' purchase; most of the other Wiltshire properties at seventeen or eighteen years' purchase; and those of the remaining Somerset lands for which the rate can be ascertained at between sixteen and seventeen years' purchase.[1] On that basis he should have received a return of 5 per cent gross for the more expensive acquisitions, and proportionately more for those bought at lower rates, up to just over 6 per cent for those obtained at sixteen and a half years' purchase, with the net return, after deduction of taxes, costs of repairs and administration, and occasional losses from tenants unable to pay their rents in full, at least 1 per cent less. We shall see, however, that these expectations were not fulfilled, at least during the 1680s, and that not only was the annual income from the estates falling but the capital value too was affected. This was not because Fox had chosen his purchases badly, or paid more for them than they were really worth, but because of the impact of adverse economic conditions whose advent he could not possibly have foreseen. There were times in the seventeenth century when land, normally the very symbol of security, was a less than gilt-edged investment.

Agricultural depression, mainly resulting from low prices but periodically aggravated by adverse weather conditions, affected many parts of England in the later seventeenth century. It seems

---

[1] The rates mentioned are those Fox gave for freehold land 'in possession', i.e. unencumbered by leases for 99 years determinable upon lives. Especially in Wiltshire, much of what he bought was, of course, not in possession but leased to tenants for one, two, or three lives, but the rates at which leased property changed hands were derived from that which had been agreed for whatever there was out of lease, i.e. the sometimes complicated calculations of the landlord's reversion to property subject to leases took the price agreed upon for land in possession as their starting point. Ilchester: Manorial, Somerset (box 18): survey and valuation of the Redlynch estate, 1681; ibid.: Manorial, Wiltshire (box 19): valuations of Allington; ibid.: Family (box 236, bundles 2 and 10): valuations of Pitton and Farley, and lands in W. Grimstead etc., Maddington, and Plaitford.

to have hit south-eastern Somerset very soon after Sir Stephen had made his main series of purchases there, and then to have persisted right through the 1680s and into the early 1690s. The area was essentially a pastoral one, where the smaller farmers relied mostly on dairying and paid their rents from the sale of cheese, and the larger ones fattened sheep and cattle for the butcher.[1] Such people may not have suffered as severely from falling prices as did farmers in grain-growing districts, but nevertheless things became extremely difficult and, as one bad year succeeded another, many of them were simply not getting enough for their products to make ends meet. Tenants on Fox's estate, and on those of neighbours like Lord Fitzharding, were unable to pay their rents in full, began to accumulate arrears, and sometimes failed altogether, so that farms stood unlet and the income accruing to landlords fell heavily. An early symptom of the trouble ahead was Fox's own decision to give up operations on the home farm at Redlynch. This had been in hand when purchased in 1672 and, under his brother John's supervision, considerable efforts had been made in the first few years to build it up into a profitable mixed enterprise, producing both grain and fatstock for sale to local markets. More draught animals and equipment had been acquired, including six yokes of oxen and two wains; soap ashes had been carted from nearby Bruton to serve as fertilizer; and not only clover, but also 'French grass' (sainfoin) had been sown to improve the pasture. Then Sir Stephen abruptly changed his mind. In 1675–6 the scale of the operation was being reduced, and by April 1678 what remained of the sheep and cattle had been sent off to stock a temporarily untenanted farm at Water Eaton, and the lands were all let out at rack-rents.[2] Fox was able to cut his losses and withdraw from farming altogether, but his tenants were not so fortunately placed. As their difficulties increased towards the end of the decade, he was obliged to lend money to them one after another to enable them to buy the livestock they needed to continue in business. By May 1679 he had lent a total of £456, and by Michaelmas 1682 six tenants owed him £568 on this account, and

[1] J. Thirsk (ed.), *The Agrarian History of England and Wales 1500–1640* (Cambridge, 1967), pp. 79–80. See also Thomas Allen's correspondence in Ilchester (box 173, bundle 1), doc. cit., and the entries for 'Redlynch' in Ilchester: Accounts, General Estate: ledger marked 'Sir S.F.'

[2] Ilchester: Accounts, General Estate: ledger marked 'Sir S.F.', ff. 35, 36, 41 et seq.

it was already clear that much of this money would never be repaid. Down to 1680, perhaps because of this financial help from their landlord, few of the tenants had run up substantial arrears, but from the Michaelmas rent day of that year they began to fall more seriously behind. At Michaelmas 1681 arrears of rent amounted to just over £300 on a rental of roughly £783 per annum, and a year later to £568. By 1687 they had risen to nearly £1,370, and by 1691, after more than a decade of depression, the tenants owed no less than £1,718. 18s. od. of back rent, more than a third of which was written off as irretrievably lost two years later.[1] All this was despite constant pressure to pay up exerted by the steward Thomas Allen who was, to use his own terminology, for ever 'dunning' them for money.[2]

Allen's letters to Sir Stephen in the 1680s, as he excused the disappointingly small sums he was able to remit to London, returned again and again to the plight of the tenants, and the difficulties of getting rent out of them. 'Never worse tymes and tenants heere for making and paying rent than now', he wrote in April 1682, and some months later, 'the tymes are hard for getting money, the dairy trade being here soe extremely low'. More than five years later, nothing had changed: 'these tymes are very ill for tenants, all things being soe plentifull and cheape.' It was not only small, inefficient, or lazy tenants who were getting into difficulties. One Edward Gaspar, who rented a farm of £78 a year in Kilmington, 'found he ran more and more in debt, though a very laborious man', and despite a substantial reduction in his rent when he died, he left his wife and children 'in low condicon'. John Phipping had once occupied the largest farm on the estate, several hundred acres for which he had paid the large rent of £140 a year, and which must have required several hundred pounds to stock, yet, when he died in 1685, several years after being forced to give it up, he left his family so poor that Allen told his employer that they would probably 'come to the parish'. Even William Masters, who, according to Allen, had 'gained the repute here of a very sober, thrifty, careful, man', and who was actually employed by Fox as a bailiff, owed

---

[1] Ilchester: Family (box 235, bundle 4): document relating to assignment of bonds by John Fox to Sir S. Fox, and summary account of money due and actually received from the Somerset estate, 20 July 1687; ibid.: Estate, Somerset (box 173, bundle 3): papers concerning rent arrears; ibid.: Accounts, General Estate (box 191): volume of Somerset estate accounts for 1678–83, pp. 29–31.

[2] See Ilchester (box 173, bundle 1), doc. cit., *passim*.

more than a year's rent by 1691. As early as March 1682 Allen informed Sir Stephen that around Redlynch 'rents are fallen a quarter part at least in general', and sooner or later the rent of every farm on the Fox estate had to be reduced at least once, or a rebate allowed to its tenant to avoid the need for a formal reduction. Nor were reductions only necessary upon a change of tenant. 'Tenants that are worth anything are exceeding scarce', Allen wrote in August 1687, and this made it very important to retain those who were paying their way. When, later that autumn, Edward Penny, who was successfully farming most of the Redlynch demesnes at £140 a year, told Allen that he would quit unless his rent was reduced by £10, there was little that the agent could do save advise Sir Stephen to allow it. 'It will be a great losse to yor Honor to loose such a tenant as Penny is', he reminded Fox, after negotiations had dragged on for three months and it looked as though Penny was on the point of leaving. Some years earlier, in 1681, when the large demesne farms at both Redlynch and Kilmington had fallen vacant simultaneously it had proved impossible to let them at all. They had to be broken up into smaller holdings, and even so it was not until Lady Day 1683 that tenants had been found for all of the holdings. In the meanwhile, Allen had had to make what he could from the untenanted land by buying cattle himself to fatten for sale in London, a venture which did not prove conspicuously successful.[1]

The force with which the agricultural depression struck the Somerset estate is perhaps best illustrated by the fall in the total rental of the farms let out at rack-rents from £732. 10s. 0d. per annum in 1678 to £569. 7s. 8d. in 1690. Neither of these figures represents what Fox actually received since, as we have seen, rents were not being paid in full, and there were the costs of taxes, running repairs, and management to be deducted from what was paid. On the other hand, there were other sources of income than rack-rents, notably the small quit rents paid by those tenants who held for ninety-nine years determinable on lives, occasional fines for the grant or renewal of such tenancies, and profit from the sale of wood and timber. In fact the sums Fox received from the estate fluctuated sharply from year to year, largely because in some years

[1] The foregoing paragraph is based on the letters of Thomas Allen, Ilchester: Estate, Somerset (box 173, bundle 1); and the various documents cited in note 1, p. 201. See also Ilchester: Accounts, General Estate: ledger marked 'Sir S.F.'

important farms stood empty for want of tenants and so yielded near to nothing, and in others substantial arrears of rent were discharged all at once from the sale of stock seized from a bankrupt tenant, but over the six and a half years from Michaelmas 1680 to Lady Day 1687 net receipts amounted to £3,218. 18s. 5½d., or an average of about £495. 1s. 0d. per annum. This was not much over half of the gross figure for which the agent was accountable,[1] and represented a return of little more than 2½ per cent on the £19,419 which the estate had cost to purchase. By contrast, Sir Stephen's fee farm rents were paid almost without arrears, were subject to deductions neither for repairs and maintenance, nor on account of most forms of taxation, and were collected by an agent who charged no more than one shilling in the pound. Fox's principal purchase of rents, some £321 per annum out of properties in Wiltshire and Gloucestershire, had cost him £5,023. 6s. 6d. He had sold off a few of them in 1678, so reducing his capital investment to £4,946. 16s. 6d., on which, taking the 1680s as a whole, he received a return of 6 per cent net.[2] Fee farm rents may not have given the buyer any dividend in the form of social prestige, nor have offered any long-term prospect of capital appreciation, but in the conditions of the later seventeenth century Fox, for one, found them a far better income-yielding investment than land itself.

Land values were also falling on Sir Stephen's Wiltshire properties in these years. This is seen most clearly in the case of Water Eaton, which was the only one of them wholly let out at rack-rents and where, as early as 1679, it had already proved necessary to lower the rent on six out of the seven main farms, thereby reducing the total rental by about 8 per cent from £1,244. 13s. 4d. per annum to £1,141. 6s. 8d. Most of these reductions had been postponed until the end of the 1670s, but the tenants' difficulties were by then of several years' standing, and the nominal rent-roll had only been maintained so long because substantial rebates had been

[1] Parts of a series of half-yearly accounts for the Redlynch estate covering the years 1667–91 is to be found divided between Ilchester: Estate, Somerset (box 173, bundle 3), ibid.: Family (box 235, bundle 4), and B.L., Add. MS. 51324, ff. 64–7. See also Ilchester: Accounts, General Estate (box 191): volume of Somerset estate accounts for 1678–83; and with the same reference, but unboxed, ledger marked 'Sir S.F.'; ibid.: Family (box 235, bundle 4): booklet marked 'Abstract of Sr Stephen Fox's Estate . . . to Lady Day 1689', and summary account of money due and actually received from the Somerset estate, 20 July 1687.

[2] Ilchester: Accounts, General Estate: ledger marked 'Sir S.F.', ff. 19, 83.

allowed to them on a number of occasions, notably in 1674 when the majority seemed to have sustained heavy losses and a total of £419. 16s. 8d. (37·7 per cent of what was owed that year) was entirely written off. Altogether the rebates made to the Water Eaton tenants between 1672 and 1676 involved the sacrifice of £823. 1s. 11d. or more than 14 per cent of the gross income that should have been forthcoming from the estate in those five years, and a considerably higher proportion of the income net of taxes, repairs, and costs of administration. No information is forthcoming about Water Eaton in the 1680s and 1690s because in 1679 Sir Stephen had conveyed it to his son Charles on the occasion of his marriage, and it remained in the latter's custody until his death in 1713; but it is clear from rentals surviving from Charles's later years that there had been a further fall in rents during these last two decades of the seventeenth century, although the extent of it cannot be precisely established.[1] Certainly, on the rest of the Wiltshire manors the position seems to have been little better in the 1680s than it had been at Water Eaton in the 1670s. The tenant of the very large demesne farm at Maddington, whose rent was £300 a year, began to fall into arrears from 1681 onwards and by the end of the decade owed £442, although he apparently remained solvent and Fox did not feel it necessary to reduce his rent. In nearly every case where the tenant was paying a rack-rent a similar story can be told. The farmer of the demesne at Plaitford quitted owing more than a year's rent in 1681, and his successor also came to grief three years later; the tenant at Charlton had his rent reduced from £52. 10s. 0d. per annum to £47 per annum in 1685 or 1686, but nevertheless had accumulated arrears of £138. 5s. 0d. by 1689; and at various times tenants at both Laverstock and West Grimstead too owed money to their landlord.[2]

The disappointing financial performance of these rack-rented holdings was doubtless the reason why Fox decided to convert several of them into tenancies for lives. Outside Water Eaton there

[1] Ilchester: Accounts, General Estate: ledger marked 'Sir S.F.', ff. 1–12; ibid.: Accounts, General Estate (box 191): estate account for Charles Fox's properties, 1699–1713.

[2] The latter part of the foregoing paragraph and the whole of the following one are derived from Ilchester: Estate, Wiltshire (box 178): half-yearly accounts for the Wiltshire manors 1681–95, successively by F. Hill and W. Smith; and ibid.: Accounts, General Estate: ledger marked 'Sir S.F.' Little correspondence from the Wiltshire agents survives for this period.

were only nine full-sized farms on the Wiltshire estate which were not already leased for lives when he acquired them, and between 1682 and 1685 he sold leases for ninety-nine years determinable on three lives to four of them, raising a handsome £2,924 in fines, but turning £279 per annum of rack-rent into a mere £25 per annum of quit rent. As this comparison shows, the quit rents or 'old' rents owed by life-leaseholders were so small in relation to the full value of their land that they virtually never had any difficulty in paying them in full, even in the worst times, and even if some of them occasionally did fall into arrears the sums involved were relatively trivial. For the same reason the question of the landlord having to reduce the annual rents to help his tenants through a crisis never arose. Holders of leases for ninety-nine years determinable on lives made their main contribution to the landlord's income through the fines they paid for the grant of a new lease, or when they 'renewed' or exchanged a life in an existing one. Thus once the owner had taken his fine he was almost completely secured against losses through defaulting tenants, vacant farms, and the need to allow rent rebates or to make formal reductions in rent which, in a time of agricultural depression, were so serious a matter on estates let at rack-rents. But of course the basis on which the fines were calculated was the notional rack-rent value of the holding to be leased, so that as these values declined so inevitably did the level of fines. The owners of estates occupied by life-leaseholders were thus not entirely insulted against the effects of bad times for farmers, but they were likely to suffer less severely. For whereas on a rack-rented estate the income from every single farm was potentially liable to shrink, or even to dry up altogether, in every year of a period of depression, only a small proportion of lifeholds would come up for renewal in any one year, and even over a period of, say, ten to fifteen years, there would still be many from which no occasion to take a fine had arisen. Only if acutely depressed conditions lasted for a very long time was the loss of revenue likely to be equivalent on the two types of property. Fox's receipts from fines on his Wiltshire manors do seem to have suffered in the late 1670s and the 1680s as a result of the decline of the underlying annual values, although it is not easy to illustrate this by specific examples. It is noticeable, however, that during the early 1680s there was a marked increase in the number of tenants who, having agreed on a fine, did not pay in the instalments as promptly as they ought to have done, and so were for a time entered in the rentals as being in arrears; and in the later years of the decade there were several instances in which tenants failed to honour the agreements at all, presumably because they had been unable to raise the money. The information available is not in a form which makes it practicable to calculate the net return on the capital invested in the Wiltshire estate as a whole, in the way that it is possible to do for Somerset, but a comparable calculation can be done for some specific manors, all of which were wholly leased out for terms of ninety-nine years determinable on lives. These calculations raise certain problems of method and the results should be treated with caution,[1] but they seem to suggest that the rate of return Sir Stephen received from the capital he had invested, though rather higher than in the case of the Somerset estate, was still lower than he ought to have received given the prices he had paid. Gross receipts from the manor of Allington between 1678 and 1690 amounted to £1,364. 4s. 5d., a return of nearly 3·6 per cent per annum on £2,940, compared to the 5½ per cent which a purchase price based on eighteen years' purchase would have led Fox to expect. Actual receipts were hardly different from gross income because, on a property let wholly on lives, there were virtually no arrears, no repairs undertaken by the landlord, and only the trivial management costs involved in the holding of manor courts. The net return was thus virtually identical with the gross return. Similarly, over much the same period Fox received 2·9 per cent per annum on the £3,900 invested in the purchase of Erlestoke, and 3·8 per cent over the years 1682–9 on the £7,000 invested in Little Somerford.[2]

With matters on his country properties turning out so badly from a financial point of view, and getting worse rather than better with every year that passed, Fox began to think about extracting his capital. As early as October 1682 he was contemplating the sale of the Somerset estate, and Allen told him that the Duke of Southampton was interested in buying Redlynch and Kilmington,

---

[1] The principal methodological problem is whether fines may legitimately be regarded as income, or must be treated as repayments of capital. Modern accountants would doubtless regard them as repayment of capital, but contemporary owners tended to treat them as income, especially on estates like Fox's where a sufficiently large number of holdings were let on lives for the receipts from fines to be a regular rather than an occasional source of revenue. I have therefore counted them as income in the calculations which follow.

[2] Ilchester: Accounts, Estate General: ledger marked 'Sir S.F.', ff. 76–8, 81–3, 135–6, 173.

adding significantly, 'as affaires now stand heere you have little encouragemt to keepe it if on reasonable termes you can have a chapman.'[1] In the event nothing came of it, but at about the same time Sir Stephen actually did sell two Wiltshire holdings which he had bought only three and a half years earlier, a big farm at Laverstock which rented at £100 a year and a small one at Winterbourne Ford which let for only £7 a year. Reasons why these two rack-rented farms were sold outright, while other holdings were only leased out for ninety-nine years determinable on three lives, do not appear, but it may well be that Fox would have sold the rest too if he could have found a buyer, and that he only leased them *faute de mieux*. The smaller of the two farms sold went off at eighteen years' purchase, which was the rate at which it, along with the rest of the West Grimstead property, had been acquired, and the larger was probably sold on the same terms, so that although Sir Stephen made no profit he at least avoided any loss.[2] Later in the decade came more extensive sales in Wiltshire. Next to go was the manor of Warminster Scudamore, sold to Lord Weymouth early in 1687 for £1,550. Weymouth had long wanted this manor which lay so close to his Longleat estate, and some years earlier had asked Fox if he was prepared to part with it. He had been refused because its sale would have broken up the relatively compact estate which Sir Stephen had acquired from Sir Edward Hungerford, but now Fox had determined to sell, not only his Hungerford estates, but others elsewhere. Two farms in Warminster Scudamore were sold separately from the manor to the tenants who held the leases of them, but even so the total price obtained for the property seems to have fallen short of the figure at which it had been valued prior to the sale. Nevertheless, dismantling manors and selling off as many of the holdings as possible to the leaseholders was clearly the way to get the best possible price for estates let on leases for ninety-nine years determinable on lives, for the reversion after the expiry of a lease was always worth more to the occupying tenant than to anyone else. In the circumstances of the middle and later 1680s, indeed, it was probably the only way in which land bought in the recent past could be resold without

---

[1] Ilchester: Estate, Somerset (box 173, bundle 1): Thomas Allen to Sir S. Fox, 21 Oct. 1682.

[2] Ilchester: Accounts, Estate General: ledger marked 'Sir S.F.', ff. 105, 107; ibid.: Family (box 236, bundle 2): particulars of Laverstock etc.

serious capital loss. So in 1689 and 1690 Upton Scudamore and Sutton Magna were sold piecemeal in this way, and the manors almost completely dismembered, and at Dilton and Little Somerford a number of holdings were disposed of separately, although the rest were sold together to single buyers.[1] At Codford St. Peter, however, the plan to sell the leaseholders their farms ran into difficulties. The tenants, perhaps hearing of the sales that Fox was making elsewhere in the county, concluded that he must be short of money and obliged to sell in a hurry. They therefore determined to reject the offers made to them in the belief that this would force their landlord to lower his price. The agent advised that they should be left alone for a while so that they might, as he put it, 'come to their senses'. Fox took the advice to leave them alone, but he did not give them another opportunity to buy. Codford thus remained in his possession.[2]

Fox sold five out of the six manors he had bought from Hungerford between 1682 and 1684. The price he obtained for Little Somerford does not emerge, but the information available about the other sales confirms that he was making the best of a bad job and cutting his capital losses rather than realizing any capital gain. The record of the sales of Warminster Scudamore, Upton Scudamore, Sutton Magna, and Dilton is not quite complete, but unless there are far more omissions from it than appears probable, Fox must have sold them for less than the £10,300 they had cost him in 1684. Although it must be remembered that in the meanwhile he had raised a certain amount from fines for the renewal of lifeholds, even if the whole of his net receipts from the four manors until the time of their disposal (£2,045. 0s. 2d.) is added to the aggregate of the sums recorded as received on account of the sales (£8,295), the resultant figure of £10,340. 0s. 2d. is still barely more than the 1684 price. Fox can, therefore, be regarded as either having

---

[1] Ilchester: Deeds, Wiltshire (box 132, bundles 3 and 6): conveyances 5 June 1690 and 22 June 1689; ibid.: Deeds, Wiltshire (box 308): conveyances 10 Jan. 1686/7 and 27 Nov. 1689; ibid.: Family (box 236, bundle 2): document endorsed '26 Octr 89. Received by Mr Smith of livings sold'; ibid.: Estate, Wiltshire (box 178): half-yearly accounts for the Wilts. Manors for 1689 and 1690. Library of the Wilts. Arch. Soc., Devizes, Hungerford Family Collections: Personal History, iii. 60, and Everett Collection: Sutton Veny 5, Deeds, pp. 27–8, 29–31, 32–3, 43, 68, 88, 98. Wilts. Record Office, 212B (We.5), conveyance 25 July 1689, and ibid.: 132/21, conveyance 22 June 1689.

[2] Ilchester: Estate, Wiltshire (box 177, bundle 1): W. Smith to Sir S. Fox, 6 Nov. 1689.

got a reasonably good annual return from these manors as long as he held them, but to have sold at a loss, or to have recovered his capital intact but to have made almost nothing from it during the years it had been invested. Certainly he is unlikely to have done better, and in all probability he did worse, than in the case of Erlestoke which was also sold at this time. He had paid £3,900 for it in 1677, received a total of £1,839. 12s. 7d. (net) by way of income since then, and sold it again in 1689 for £3,300. If the capital loss sustained at the time of sale is deducted from the net profits, the annual rate of return Fox had made on his investment drops from the 3·9 per cent it appeared to be prior to its disposal, to only about 2·6 per cent. Another capital loss was involved when the farm at Charlton was sold, for Fox had paid £1,100 for it in 1670 but could get no more than £830 in 1689. Perhaps these unpromising results deterred Sir Stephen from putting any more of his Wiltshire property on the market in these years, although he certainly contemplated doing so. The disposal of Plaitford was under discussion in November 1689, and a start seems to have been made with the dismemberment of Maddington, although the reversion to only one farm was actually sold.[1] In addition, Fox also made a further attempt to get the Somerset estate off his hands.

The timing of this second attempt to sell the Somerset lands owed a good deal to the development of a crisis in their management. Allen, the agent, collected rents and negotiated new lettings, but was too busy with his own affairs to supervise the tenants in detail, and during most of the 1680s this function had been shared by Sir Stephen's brother Thomas, who had lived at Redlynch House, and a tenant bailiff. Early in 1689 Thomas died, and when Fox sought opinions on how to fill the gap it became clear that the bailiff had been worse than useless, and that a great deal had been going on behind Thomas's back. 'As to old Penny' (the bailiff), wrote one neighbour, 'he hath been a long time bed-rid, nor can I imagine what use he ever was to yor Honour. It is true while Mr Fox was alive he was the less able to defraud you, but of what beneficiall use he was I cannot learn.' He continued: 'it is a certaine rule of wisdome among countrey people to devour absent landlords, and if you put a bayliffe in that is a renter of any part

---

[1] See references cited in note 1 to p. 208, and also the record of receipts from the manors mentioned in Ilchester: Accounts, General Estate: ledger marked 'Sir S.F.' Also W. Smith to Sir S. Fox, 9 Nov. 1689, doc. cit.

of yor estate, you are to take it for granted that he will prey upon it himselfe, and then must connive at the rest that doe the like'. Another correspondent wrote in similar terms:

I find Sr Stephen hath been advertized of ye necessity of a bayliff, and great necessity there is of a very good and just one. Infinite matter there is for ill dealing in Sr Stephen's estate, and men were bold enough while Mr Fox was alive, knowing how to impose on ye quietness and levity of his temper. But now they will play all ye Devil . . . if a careful and uncorrupt bayliffe be not gotten . . . As I have said formerly so say I still, Sr Stephen's estate here will be beggered and utterly defaced without a steadfast care.[1]

The problem of supervising the tenants was much more acute in Somerset than in Wiltshire because there were so many more tenants holding for short terms and paying rack-rents, and thus lacking the life-leaseholders' long-term interest in maintaining the value of their farms. Left to themselves, tenants who only held from year to year, or on short leases, might well neglect repairs and injure the land by careless or unscrupulous husbandry practices, because the ultimate loss would be borne by the landlord, not by themselves. But the dilemma which faced Sir Stephen was that his estate was too small to warrant a full-time salaried steward, whilst a bailiff chosen from amongst the tenants would probably be either inefficient or corrupt, and possibly, as 'old Penny' had apparently been, both. Hitherto Sir Stephen had been able to rely on the presence of a member of his family at Redlynch House, his brother John in the later 1670s, Thomas in the 1680s, to keep an eye on things, but now apparently he had run out of relatives who were both suitable to manage the estate, and willing to bury themselves in the depths of the country. This problem, coming on top of the very poor performance of the estate over a long period of years, was surely a major factor in inducing Sir Stephen to put it on the market again in 1689.

The asking price for the whole Somerset estate was £18,000, which was significantly less than the £19,419 which it had cost Fox to build up, and this was only in a small part due to the fact that in the meanwhile reversionary leases had been sold to a number of the tenants who held their land on lives. Nevertheless, Sir Stephen's

[1] Ilchester: Estate, Somerset (box 173, bundle 1): W. Barnsby to Sir S. Fox, 16 Feb. 1688/9, and S. Hill to John Fox, with the same date.

agent did not expect the property to fetch so much, and he commented that 'as the estate is now fallen badly it may not sell for more than £16,000'. At that figure there could be no disguising the fact that it had been sold at a loss, and yet Sir Stephen was prepared to accept this, for he actually agreed with Lady Howe to sell Redlynch, which had cost him £8,700, for £7,600. In the end this transaction fell through, but other potential buyers continued to come to look around the property until the autumn of 1690, when eventually Sir Stephen changed his mind and decided to keep the estate after all.[1] But, even though he had sold nothing in Somerset, Fox's sales in Wiltshire in 1682 and 1687–90 had meant the disposal of rather over one-third of the estate he had acquired there, £26,246 worth of land out of the £73,554 which he had originally purchased in the county.

The sales and contemplated sales of West Country property clearly owed much to Sir Stephen's dissatisfaction with their financial performance, and to the emergence of managerial problems, but there can be little doubt that the final decision to put so large a part of them up for sale more or less simultaneously was precipitated by the fact that in 1689–90 he found that he needed to mobilize capital for other uses. At the beginning of the year he was successful in securing the post of Cashier of the Customs for his nephew Thomas, who held it as his nominee and on his behalf. The price of Thomas's appointment was that Sir Stephen should make an immediate loan to the government of £30,000, and this was only the first step in a deliberate swing back towards a much greater involvement in government finance in the 1690s.[2] Moreover, the latter part of the year also saw a crisis in the financial affairs of his son-in-law, Lord Cornwallis, which required his intervention. The long and complicated story of Fox's relationship with the Cornwallises is told in another chapter, and here it is only necessary to note that over a period of several decades Sir Stephen provided the financial support which enabled the family to survive its difficulties without irrevocable damage being done to the future prospects of his daughter's descendants. Thus when he realized that Cornwallis was determined to sell a substantial part of his

---

[1] Ilchester: Estate, Somerset (box 173, bundle 1): letters from T. Allen to Sir S. Fox, 22 June 1689, 29 Mar. and 25 Oct. 1690; ibid.: Family (box 235, bundles 1, part i, and 4): from Allen to Fox, 1 Oct. 1690, and 'An acct of my estate in Somersetshire'.

[2] See below, pp. 234–44.

estates, Little Bradley in Suffolk, and the manors of Waborne and Hemblingham in Norfolk, in order to pay off his debts, he stepped in and bought them himself for £16,000 early in 1690 so as to protect the interests of his two grandsons.[1] By doing so he did in fact re-invest in land much of the capital he had realized by his sales in the West, and indeed during the later years of his life he collected a number of important pieces of real property. None of them, however, were purchased wholly for their own sake and as deliberate acts of estate building: instead with only one partial exception, Fox acquired them as a by-product of his efforts to uphold the sagging fortunes of his Cornwallis son-in-law and grandson, or as a means of enabling those who owed him money to discharge their debts.[2]

The partial exception was the leasehold manor of Lambeth Wick which he bought for £7,500 in 1695, from a man who was certainly in debt to him, though not for so large a sum that the transaction can be represented as a foreclosure. Lambeth Wick, moreover, was a very different type of estate from those which Fox had been buying in Somerset and Wiltshire in the 1670s and early 1680s. It lay only a mile or two south-east of the Surrey bank of the river Thames, and was easily reached from Whitehall by means of the horse-ferry and a short road journey. It would thus be possible for Sir Stephen, or at least those whom he employed to look after such matters, to keep a much stricter eye on it than was feasible in the case of the distant country properties. There were two substantial mansions on the estate, one of which, Loughborough House, seems to have been a very grand affair with a separate banqueting house attached to it, and both of which were eminently lettable because of the easy access they enjoyed to both Westminster and the City. Surrounding the mansions were 240 acres of land or more, which was leased in small parcels to farmers and horticulturalists who produced for the great metropolitan market which lay on their doorsteps, and whose rents were likely to be more reliably paid than those of farmers who depended on sales in the small and easily glutted markets of the south-west. It may be also that Sir Stephen's acquisition of the lease of Lambeth Wick was connected with his part-ownership of Hungerford Market since, as landlord, he would be able to bring pressure to bear on the gardeners there to bring their produce to sell at his market, thereby increasing its turnover and

[1] See below, pp. 280–1.   [2] See below, pp. 289–90, 292, 319, 326.

the income it produced.[1] However, this was the only piece of landed property which, during more than twenty years after 1686, Fox acquired because he really wanted to add it to his own portfolio of investments.

During the course of this chapter it will have become clear that at different times Fox was pursuing quite different objectives in the way in which he invested his money. It has been possible to detect a series of distinct phases in his investment policy, which roughly coincided with the decades of the later seventeenth century. In the 1660s he ploughed back almost everything into the Undertaking; in the 1670s he was mainly interested in building up a landed estate; and in the 1680s he was more concerned to develop a diversified portfolio in which land was only one element amongst several. From about the end of the 1680s he changed tack again, and for ten years or so was once again to be found lending to the government on a large scale, whilst the other principal end to which he was devoting his wealth, now that it had become a moral certainty that his son Charles was not going to give him a male heir, was to support the fortunes of the families into which his two surviving daughters had married. Then in the early eighteenth century he wound down first his government, and then, after an interval, also his private lending, and concentrated on helping the Cornwallises and the Comptons until, towards the end of his life, the arrival of a second family of children as a result of his very late second marriage, once again gave him the prospect of leaving descendants in the male line. Only in this final phase of his career, after about 1709 or 1710, did Sir Stephen again begin to buy property for its own sake to extend and consolidate the estate he would hand on to the son of his old age. We shall not follow these later stages of Fox's financial dispositions in quite the same way that we did the earlier ones, for after the 1680s the way in which he used his wealth becomes increasingly difficult to separate from other aspects of his life. His renewed involvement in government finance will thus be considered in the context of his role as a Lord of the Treasury; his major acquisitions of property in the 1690s

[1] Ilchester: Family (box 238, bundle 4): articles of agreement for the purchase of Lambeth Wick, 8 Apr. 1695; ibid.: Family (box 236, bundles 9 and 10): documents marked 'A perticuler of Lambeth Wick . . .' and 'Mr Andrews his acct of Hungerford Market & Loughborough House etc.', and also accounts of the debts of Dionisius Andrews to Sir S. Fox.

and 1700s in that of his relations with his two sons-in-law and their families; and the renewed interest he showed in estate building in connection with his remarriage and the arrangements he made for the disposal of his fortune after his death.

CHAPTER IX

Lord of the Treasury

FOX'S ELEVATION to the Treasury towards the end of 1679 proved to be the beginning of a new chapter in his already lengthy career as a royal servant. After the fall of Danby early in that year the office of Lord Treasurer had been put into commission, and its duties were being performed by a board of five members of whom the Earl of Essex was the most senior. Essex had been a successful Lord Deputy of Ireland, but he does not seem to have taken to Treasury business, which was at once highly demanding yet largely routine, and it was for this reason as well as because he disapproved of the King's action in immediately proroguing the new Parliament which had met at the beginning of October, that he resigned in the following month. He had made his intentions clear to his fellow ministers some days before he broke the news to Charles, and they had had to find a substitute Commissioner to take his place. By no means everybody was prepared to accept appointment. Lord Halifax refused, as did the Earl of Shaftesbury, a former Chancellor of the Exchequer and a survivor of the Treasury Commission of 1667–72. Technically, Shaftesbury was admirably qualified to fill the vacancy, but doubtless he saw the offer as an attempt to woo him from opposition and, playing for higher stakes as he was, he avoided the trap. It was only after these two prominent political figures had refused to come into the Commission that ministers turned to consider the possibility of bringing in an outsider.

Fox was an expert on financial methods in general, was recognized as particularly skilful in the negotiation of loans, and had special experience of the problems of both the royal Household and the army. His personal loyalty to the King was beyond question, and he was known to be acceptable to Charles. Finally, if he were to become a member of the Treasury, the government would be able to rely on his continued financial support, and, in the circumstances of 1679, that represented a political advantage comparable to the adherence of a Halifax or a Shaftesbury. Once Sir Stephen's name had been suggested the King's advisers knew they had the answer, and even before Essex had actually tendered his resignation they had agreed amongst themselves that he should replace him. He apparently kissed the King's hand the very day that Essex finally resigned, 16 November 1679, and a new Treasury Commission including his name was issued five days later.[1] It was rumoured that he was to be made a Baron to mark his promotion, but when the Commission appeared he was still Sir Stephen, and though it is more than possible that he was offered, but refused, a peerage, this cannot be verified.[2] However, it is certain that he had mixed feelings about joining the Treasury. He was flattered by the honour, but had no illusions about the nature of the work he would be undertaking. He, of all people, knew too much about government finance to be dazzled by the prospect of being in 'the place where money groweth', for nearly twenty years experience had taught him that the Treasury was usually almost empty and those responsible for its management at their wits' end. Both in his autobiography, which was written later, and in a letter to the Duke of Ormonde written at the time, Fox makes it clear that he would have preferred to remain as Paymaster, but he allowed himself to be persuaded by a friend who was already on the Board, the young Sidney Godolphin.[3]

Fox remained at the Treasury from November 1679 until May 1702 with only two short intervals: the first two years of James II's reign when the Earl of Rochester was Lord Treasurer, and for a little less than a year between April 1689 and March 1690. Altogether he was a Commissioner for nineteen years and eight months in a period of twenty-two years and six months, serving on no less than seventeen different Commissions; he briefly acted as First Lord of the Treasury in the winter of 1696–7 during the culminating stages of the most desperate financial crisis faced by the English government since 1672. Throughout this period Fox, together with Godolphin, provided the main element of continuity in the direction of the Crown's finances, but down to his retirement at the beginning of Anne's reign not even Godolphin could rival his length of service, and no other Treasury Commissioner came any-

[1] Ogg, *Charles II*, ii. 390, 593; R. W. Blencowe, *Diary of the Times of Charles the Second by the Honourable Henry Sidney* (2 vols., London, 1843), i. 183, 185, 186, 189.

[2] H.M.C., *Seventh Report*, Appendix, p. 477.

[3] Ilchester: Family (box 237): autobiography in small volume with green cover. H.M.C., *Ormonde*, N.S., v. 238–9.

where near doing so.[1] It was, moreover, a period which was extremely important in the development of the Treasury as an institution, during the course of which the collection of the revenue was brought more firmly under its control than ever before and a series of financial innovations of far-reaching importance were introduced. Yet unfortunately there is very little that can be said about the role which Fox, or any single Treasury Lord, played in these changes. The minutes of the Commissioners' meetings survive for a number of years, but they rarely distinguish the contributions of separate individuals, and since the Board held its deliberations in private there are almost no other records of what took place. The Treasury acted as a corporate body, making collective pronouncements or decisions, and it is hardly ever possible to penetrate the veil of anonymity which its members cast over themselves.[2]

For this reason, we cannot trace the story of Fox's years at the Treasury in any detail, but there is no doubt that throughout he took a full share of the work. The work, moreover, was extremely hard, and Godolphin compared his existence whilst a member of the Board with that of a galley-slave.[3] The Commissioners did not meet every day of the week, but they usually met on at least four and often on five of them, sometimes both in the morning and afternoon, and very occasionally for a third session in the evening as well. In a busy period such as April 1690 there were meetings on twenty-four out of the thirty days in the month, with additional afternoon sessions on nine of them. During the summer, and particularly during the holiday month of August, the Board tended to come together less frequently but, if business was pressing, even August was not sacred. They may have met on only six days in August 1695, but in the same month of the following year they had twenty-four meetings on seventeen separate days. Sir Stephen, moreover, was an extremely conscientious Commissioner. Between 19 March 1690, when he rejoined the Treasury at the invitation of William III, and 4 May 1691, the Board met 324 times on 245 separate days, and according to the minutes Fox missed only four of these meetings, which was a substantially better attendance record than that of the remaining Lords. His only period of absence

---

[1] S. B. Baxter, *Development of the Treasury*, Appendix I; P. G. M. Dickson, *The Financial Revolution in England* (London, 1967), pp. 348–57.

[2] Baxter, *Development of the Treasury*, pp. 23–4.

[3] Roseveare, *The Treasury*, p. 79.

during this time was during August 1690 when he made a brief visit
to see his daughter Jane and her family at Castle Ashby in Northamptonshire, a holiday which lasted only six days including more
than two days' travelling. On the morning of the seventh day he
was back at work at the Treasury chambers. At the end of the
month he got up to Northamptonshire again, once more for six
days, without missing any meetings, but these two expeditions
were the only real breaks from Treasury routine which he took in
the whole of the thirteen and a half months in question. At Christmas 1690 only a single day free of meetings was allowed. A few
years later Sir Stephen's capacity for business was still unimpaired.
In the year from May 1695 to April 1696 he missed only six out of
the 160 meetings recorded in the minutes, again by far the best
attendance amongst the Commissioners: Godolphin, for instance,
missed thirty-two in the same period, Montague forty-five, Smith
twenty-four, while Trumbull, who ceased to attend meetings altogether after his appointment as Secretary of State in 1695, had
already become more conspicuous by his absence than by his
attendance. Not until 1696, when he was in his seventieth year and
the strain of a long career in public life was at last beginning to tell,
did Sir Stephen allow himself a rather less strict schedule. In that
year he was away for a full month, allowing twenty-four consecutive meetings between the beginning of August and the beginning
of September to be held without him. The explanation for this
particular absence was almost certainly the death of his wife on
11 August after a prolonged illness: they had been married for
forty-five years and it was clearly a heavy blow. But the following
summer, 1697, he again took several weeks' holiday, and thereafter
did the same every year until his final retirement in 1702, even
though it meant being away from a succession of meetings on each
occasion. Work, however, could not be altogether forgotten even
in the peaceful surroundings of Castle Ashby. For instance, during
his visit there in September 1701 he writes of a morning when after
he 'had scribbled many letters ther cam . . . a messenger from the
Treasury wth many orders & warts [i.e. warrants], for his signature.
Holidays, moreover, were always liable to be cut short, as in 1698,
by a hurried summons back to London to deal with some matter
which required the presence of all members of the Board.[1]

---

[1] The surviving minutes of the Treasury Commissioners are printed in *C.T.B.*
x (for 1689–90), x–xvi (for 1696–1701), and xvii (for 1691 and 1702). *C.S.P.D.*,

So week after week, month after month, for nearly twenty years, Fox took his place at the table in the cramped tapestry-hung room, with its crimson velvet chairs and silver candlesticks, which the Treasury Lords used as an office.[1] Perhaps the most important routine business which had to be discharged was the never-ending series of decisions about how to allocate funds between the various spending departments of the government. Each had its establishment, which laid down what its expenditure ought to be, but since there was rarely, if ever, enough money to meet all their requirements in full, a 'weekly distribution' became essential. Decisions on such matters clearly could not be made without hearing the various Treasurers and Paymasters present their departments' cases, and so much time had to be spent seeing the Treasurer or the Commissioners of the Navy, the Paymaster of the Army, the Treasurer of the Ordnance, the Commissioners of Navy Victualling, of Army Clothing, and of Transportation, the Cofferer of the Household, and others. The Treasury Lords had to listen to their pleas for more money, read the papers which they submitted, and try to judge which services really might collapse if they did not get what they demanded. An important aspect of their Lordships' routine was of course attempting to ensure that there was at least some money to distribute. They therefore had to supervise the collection and administration of the various sources of revenue, particularly the direct taxes over which they exercised an extremely close control. In the case of the principal indirect taxes, the Customs and the Excise, more was left to the Commissioners concerned, but even so the Treasury Lords had to see them regularly once a week and the matters arising could be complex and time-consuming. Throughout the later seventeenth century the government could only make ends meet by anticipating its revenue, and so the problem of ensuring that there was something in the Exchequer was in practice largely a question of arranging a continuous succession of short-term loans: especially in the 1690s the scale of this borrowing was so great, and the problems connected with it so involved, that it absorbed a great proportion of the Board's ener-

---

1696, p. 338; Ilchester: Accounts, Personal (box 220): account of Sir S. Fox's private expenses for 1684–97; ibid.: Family (box 238, bundle 6): account of Sir S. Fox's journeys; Gloucestershire Record Office, D. 1799/C. 9; Sir S. Fox to T. Povey, 11 Sept. 1701; *C.T.B.* xiv (1698–9), p. 104.

[1] Baxter, *Development of the Treasury*, p. 19.

gies. Finally, there was the flood of petitions, for money, for the grant of offices, for leases of Crown land, with which the Treasury was deluged, and which had to be dealt with; and there were disputes between subordinate officials, or departments of the administration, which had to be resolved. Indeed, the range of matters which the Treasury Lords had to cope with was immense, and varied from those on which the survival of the state depended to the ludicrously trivial, but the form in which these matters presented themselves had a monotonous sameness. Whatever the issue there were people to be interviewed, written statements to be read, and then a debate amongst themselves out of which a decision would emerge.[1]

Treasury business not only involved regular and lengthy meetings, it also involved the reading of innumerable papers on all aspects of the royal finances all copied out in long-hand by the clerks, and a good deal of worry. The strain of it all was further increased, especially for an elderly man as Fox now was, by the considerable amount of travelling made necessary by the King's desire to attend a certain proportion of meetings. He would sometimes come to the Treasury Chambers in Whitehall, but more often the Commissioners would have to go to wherever he happened to be staying. In the 1680s, under both Charles II and James II, this was most often at Windsor. Sir Stephen had an apartment in the Castle, possibly by virtue of his post at the Green Cloth, and his personal accounts are full of references to the journeys he made there and back, at some periods several times a month. He normally travelled in his own coach, often providing Godolphin with a lift it would seem, crossing the river Thames by the ferry at Datchet. He must have got to know the road extremely well, a familiarity which apparently extended to the ferryman's daughter, to whom he once gave a present of half-a-crown! The ride to Windsor may have been pleasant enough in summer, especially when Sir Stephen could indulge his passion for cherries, which he bought by the basketful from wayside vendors, but in wet wintry weather it must have been a dreary expedition. In the 1690s King William was more often to be found at Hampton Court, which was not only much nearer to Fox's house at Chiswick but could be conveniently reached by water, a much smoother and less exhaust-

---

[1] For the nature of Treasury business see the minute books, *C.T.B.* ix–xvii, cited above in note 1, p. 218. Also Baxter, *Development of the Treasury*, chapters iii–v, *passim*.

ing method of travel at that period. On occasions Treasury Lords had to make altogether more distant and prolonged journeys on official business. Charles II in particular liked to go to Newmarket, and some, if not all, of the Commissioners had to attend him. Fox went there at least once a year in the early 1680s, sometimes managing to make a visit to his Cornwallis daughter and son-in-law at nearby Brome at the same time. In the summer of 1687 Fox travelled for several weeks accompanying the King on his 'progress' through the western counties which the latter undertook to try to rally opinion against the Test Act.[1]

It was highly advantageous to the Crown if the Treasury Commissioners were also Members of Parliament, so that they would be available to explain the Crown's financial problems to the House and to press for additional supplies. Nevertheless, Fox was not an M.P. when he joined the Board in November 1679. In the previous Parliament, which had met in March and had been dissolved four months later, he had sat for the Borough of Westminster, but at the August election feeling against candidates closely associated with the Court was running high on account of the Popish Plot, and he had either been defeated at the polls or had decided not to stand.[2] Nor was he returned to the short-lived Oxford Parliament of 1681, and though he was returned for his old seat of Salisbury to James II's only Parliament in 1685, he was then no longer on the Treasury Board. He also missed the Convention Parliament, which met at the beginning of 1689, shortly after James's flight abroad. His son Charles was returned at Cricklade, where the Foxes had a strong, though not dominant, interest on account of their ownership of the nearby Water Eaton estate, and he could doubtless have had the seat himself if he had really wanted it. His decision not to stand was almost certainly because, realizing that he was unlikely to be continued at the Treasury under the new regime, he had de-

[1] Ilchester: Accounts, Personal (box 220): account of Sir S. Fox's personal expenses for 1680-1, 1681-4, 1684-97; ibid.: Family (box 238, bundle 15): warrant allocating lodgings in the new tower at Windsor to Sir S. Fox, 10 Feb. 1682; ibid.: Family (box 235, bundle 1, part i): note by Fox on his relations with Godolphin.

[2] In 1679 Fox financed campaigns at Cricklade in both the spring and the autumn, but whether for himself or his son Charles, who represented the borough in every Parliament between 1685 and 1698, is uncertain. Ilchester: Accounts, General Estate: ledger marked 'Sir S.F.', f. 13. See also references quoted in note 1, p. 222.

termined to retire from public life. Elections for William III's first full Parliament took place just over a year later, and once again Sir Stephen did not contest a seat and allowed Charles to be returned for Cricklade. On this occasion his decision was a little unfortunate, for by the time the Members actually assembled on 20 March 1690 he was, after all, back at the Treasury, and the government's need for unprecedentedly large grants of money to fight both James II in Ireland and Louis XIV at sea and on the Continent, made it more desirable than ever to have in the Commons as many well-informed spokesmen on financial matters as possible. Another general election was clearly not imminent, so that Sir Stephen had to wait for a suitable by-election, and it was not until November 1691 that he got back to the House, once again as one of the Members for Westminster. From this time until the end of William III's reign he was continuously an M.P.[1]

The seat which Fox had won in 1679 and 1691, and which he was to win again in 1695, was of a very different nature from either Salisbury or Cricklade. It was the largest urban constituency in the country, with an electorate approaching the 9,000 which it numbered in Walpole's day, and one in which large and menacing mobs could easily be mobilized. The Court had a powerful interest there, because so many office-holders of different types lived within its boundaries, and because of the 'servile expectations' of the numerous tradesmen who depended for their livelihood on the patronage of the royal Household. Yet in the later seventeenth century Westminster does not yet seem to have become quite 'the King's borough' into which it later developed. Elections were invariably contested, contested hotly, and their outcome could not necessarily be forecast with any certainty at the start of a campaign. Nevertheless, it was recognized that the results tended to set the national trend, and so the ministry usually made great efforts to secure favourable results in order to influence opinion elsewhere in the country.[2] Fox could therefore count on powerful assistance in his efforts to capture or retain the seat, and it was duly forthcoming: in 1695, for instance, Narcissus Luttrell specifically records that Princess Anne instructed the members of her Household

[1] Sir G. Duckett, 'Proposed Repeal of the Test and Penal Statutes . . . in 1688', *Wilts. Arch. and Nat. Hist. Magazine* 1879, pp. 363, 372; *Members of Parliament*, i. 536, 555, 556, 562, 567, 570, 574, 577, 584.

[2] Romney Sedgwick, *The House of Commons, 1715–1754* (2 vols., London, 1970), i. 285–7; W. Speck, *Tory and Whig* (London, 1970), p. 95.

to vote for Sir Stephen.[1] He also had some independent influence in the constituency through his ownership of the Hungerford Market estate. All the same it was not an easy way into Parliament, and it was perhaps characteristic of Sir Stephen that he preferred to fight hard for a prestigious seat, and one in which he lived and had property, rather than to slip into the House as representative for some obscure borough with a few dozen voters.

The by-election of 1691 was contested by a certain Mr. Owen, and certainly involved Sir Stephen in a strenuous battle. At any rate it was an expensive election, for it cost him £630 16s. 6d. to secure his victory, which was an unusually large sum for a contest of this period. The money was inevitably spent mainly on providing free alcoholic refreshment for electors at taverns and ale-houses all over the constituency, and the total quantity of drink consumed at Fox's expense must have been colossal. At the 'Five Bells' in the Strand where his bill was a mere £48 10s. 6d. no less than eighty-two gallons of port, fifty gallons of canary, and eight gallons of hock were charged to his account. Perhaps his opponent could not match this lavish treating, for before the poll was taken it had become clear that Fox would win and, despite the fervour of his supporters, Owen conceded as much in a speech in which he declared he was unwilling to put his friends to further trouble and to the risk of injury or even death from 'the presse and crowd at the barr'. Owen thereupon resigned his pretensions to Fox, describing him as 'this honble & worthy gentleman, whose high station in the governmt, besides his own great worth, & personal accomplishmts justly recomend him to yor choice, as a person much better & fitter to serve you'.[2] At the general election of 1695 Sir Stephen was involved in an even more ferocious battle at Westminster when he and Charles Montague, the Chancellor of the Exchequer, were challenged by that vocal critic of the ministry, Sir Walter Clarges, and Macaulay has vividly described the mounted parades through the streets made by the candidates and their adherents, the jeering mobs, and the broadsheets filled with invective against the 'two courtly upstarts' which were scattered all over the city.[3]

---

[1] N. Luttrell, *A Brief Historical Relation of State Affairs* (6 vols., London, 1857), iii. 537.

[2] Ibid., ii. 304–5; B.L., Add. MS. 51319, ff. 103–4, 107–8, 146–7: accounts of election expenditure, and summary of polling-day speeches.

[3] Lord Macaulay, *The History of England* (8 vols., London, 1858–62 edn.), vii. 244–5; Luttrell, *State Affairs*, iii. 533, 537, 541.

In the end Clarges came bottom of the poll, and so Fox again sat for Westminster in the new Parliament. By the time of the 1698 general election, however, he seems to have felt that at seventy he was getting too old for such vigorous contests for he declined to fight the seat yet again.[1] He therefore replaced his son Charles at Cricklade, where campaigning was not only quieter but also cheaper: the two elections of 1701 apparently cost him only half the sum which he had been obliged to spend on one at Westminster ten years before.[2]

Once back in the Commons in 1691 Sir Stephen, as a Treasury Lord, had to play a somewhat more active role than he had done in his earlier years in the House. Throughout most of the decade the government's principal spokesman on financial matters was Charles Montague, whether as Chancellor of the Exchequer or later as First Lord of the Treasury, and it was he who bore the main responsibility for securing from an often reluctant assembly the taxes needed to carry on the war, and for dealing with the Parliamentary Commissioners of Accounts, whose inquiries into the way money had been spent tended to be hostile, if not downright malicious. His fellow Treasury Lords, however, had to support him, and although a detailed account of the debates is only available for part of the decade, it is enough to show Fox doing his duty in this respect. He rarely spoke unless the matter in hand directly concerned government revenue or expenditure, and when he did get to his feet his speeches were usually short, but they were to the point and delivered with authority. We find him intervening in debates on the raising of supplies in order to try and instil a sense of urgency to the proceedings; trying to prevent wrecking amendments to vital bills, such as the attempted 'tack' of a clause about the taking of the public accounts to the Poll Bill in February 1692; and providing factual details about the yield of taxes or about army pay. During the winter months of 1696–7 when he was First Lord of the Treasury he probably had to speak more often and at greater length, and perhaps on a wider range of subjects, but few details about the debates of that period have survived.[3]

Yet though Sir Stephen was a government spokesman in the

[1] *C.S.P.D.*, 1698, p. 331.

[2] Ilchester: Family (box 236, bundle 7): account of election expenses.

[3] H. Horwitz, *The Parliamentary Diary of Narcissus Luttrell, 1691–1693* (Oxford, 1972), pp. 77, 82, 105–6, 112–13, 114, 137, 187, 230, 248, 260, 283, 287, 360, 420, 445.

parliaments of the 1690s, he was not prepared to sacrifice his own independence completely and to vote with the ministry on any and every issue, regardless of his own feelings in the matter. He already had what was for so prominent a placeman a rather remarkable record of voting against the Court in important divisions. He had voted against the impeachment of Clarendon, and for that of Danby.[1] A further occasion had been in 1685. When the Commons reassembled in the November of that year James II made a determined effort to obtain supplies for the support of his newly expanded army, but making it quite clear that he had no intention of excluding Catholic officers from it. At this even the subservient assembly of that year began to show signs of alarm, and opposition to the Court began to develop. When, on 13 November, Secretary of State Middleton proposed that the question of supply should be the first to be considered in committee, the opposition contended that the usual practice was that grievances should be redressed first, and the matter of Catholics in the army was a serious grievance. There was a division on whether Middleton's motion should be put, and the government was defeated by one vote. Many members on whom the Court had believed it could rely had voted against, including both Sir Stephen and his son Charles. The King was furious, and though Sir Stephen was left undisturbed as Clerk of the Green Cloth, Charles was dismissed as Paymaster and the Earl of Ranelagh appointed in his place.[2] In fact this bore on Sir Stephen as much or more than on his son, for the latter only held office as his nominee and certainly passed over to him a large share of the profits. The recent expansion in the size of the army had greatly increased the scale of those profits, and whereas the Paymastership had probably not yielded more than £1,000 a year in the early 1680s, by the autumn of 1685 its holder could look forward to an income of at least four times that sum.[3] The financial sacrifice that Sir Stephen and Charles made by their determination to vote 'against ye power of Papists to be equall with Prodestants' was thus very great, and they knew full well when they cast their votes what the likely consequences would be.[4]

[1] See above, pp. 118–20.
[2] Macaulay, *History*, ii. 271–2, 276–80; D. Ogg, *England in the Reigns of James II and William III* (Oxford, 1955), pp. 158–62; B.L., Add. MS. 28875, f. 426; *C.T.B.* viii (1685–9), p. 500. [3] See above, pp. 130–1.
[4] B.L., Add. MS. 51324, ff. 57–60: autobiographical narrative endorsed 'Recollections relateing to my self . . .'

In the 1690s he did not go to the lengths of actually opposing his ministerial colleagues, but on at least one, and probably two, occasions he withheld his support. In January 1696 his attitude to the forthcoming division on the proposal to establish a new Council of Trade was considered doubtful by the compiler of a list of the voting intentions of the Members of the Commons, even though the government needed every vote it could muster, and it is likely that in the event he abstained. Fox's motives in this instance are obscure, for the issues do not seem to have been ones about which he is likely to have felt strongly, but the reasons for his other abstention are clear. Towards the end of the same year a more bitterly controversial affair broke, the attempt to pass a Bill of Attainder against the conspirator Sir John Fenwick. Fenwick was undoubtedly guilty of treason, but the disappearance of the key witnesses would have made it impossible to convict him in an ordinary court. The government therefore proceeded against him in a way which avoided the necessity for a normal trial, and in doing so raised fundamental questions about the rule of law and the liberty of the individual which made many M.P.s, who had no sympathy with conspiracy, extremely unhappy. Fox kept away from the House when the vital vote was taken, as did a number of other important figures in the government, including Secretary of State Trumbull and the Attorney-General, Trevor. His son Charles, however, was one of those office-holders who actually voted against the government, and it is clear that for him and his father the issue was the same as in the vote on supplies for James II's army eleven years before: the danger to the constitution and the liberty of the subject, which could be threatened as seriously by laws to deprive individuals of their lives as by an army whose officers were Catholic.[1]

By the end of the seventeenth century the Treasury Board lay at the very centre of English government, but it was essentially an administrative rather than a policy-making body. First Lords, especially the longer-serving ones such as Rochester and Godolphin, were leading ministers concerned in taking the major decisions of state. They were also members of the Privy Council and its principal committees, and enjoyed direct access to the

[1] I. F. Burton and others, *Political Parties in the Reigns of William III and Anne* (special supplement of the Bulletin of the Institute of Historical Research, 1968), pp. 12, 24, 25.

sovereign. Junior Treasury Lords, however, had neither of these two advantages, and their function was very much restricted to the management of the Crown's finances. Sir Stephen Fox, in particular, was an administrator, not a politician, and he never seems to have sought a share in determining government policy. To the end he found sufficient satisfaction in efficiently discharging tasks allotted to him, just as he had done in those far-off days on the Continent with the exiled Court in the 1650s. 'Faire sans dire' was the motto he had adopted to go with the coat of arms he had been granted at that time, and he always remained true to it. In the earlier part of his Treasury career his political stance was determined by an intense personal loyalty to Charles II, but he did not transfer this loyalty wholeheartedly to the latter's brother. We have seen that he joined the parliamentary opposition on a crucial vote in November 1685, and it indicates the respect that James II had for his ability and experience that only fourteen months later he was again appointed a Treasury Commissioner. Indeed, by the latter part of his short reign, the King seems to have set considerable store by Fox's support. Sir Stephen accompanied him on his 'progress' through the West in 1687, and in the following year Fox was one of those prominent personages to whom the King exhibited his new-born son in order to try to scotch rumours that the Queen's pregnancy was a pretence and that any child she produced would be a changeling. He was also one of the last people with whom James consulted before his precipitate flight from London early in the morning of 11 December 1688, although what advice he offered or what instructions he received must unfortunately remain a a mystery.[1] Fox has left no specific statement of his attitude towards James and his policies at this time, but his action makes plain what it was. He disapproved of the advancement of Catholics and Catholicism, but nevertheless was prepared to serve his lawful sovereign to the best of his ability. On the other hand, once that sovereign had 'abdicated' by deserting his throne and going overseas, Fox felt absolved from his allegiance and was therefore ready to make his peace with the new regime.[2]

[1] Ilchester: Official, Sir S. Fox, Charles II's Household (box 269): Cofferer's account from Lady Day 1679; H.M.C., *Portland*, iii. 419; *Memoirs of the Earl of Ailesbury* (2 vols., Roxburghe Club, 1890), i. 194.

[2] As we have seen, Sir Stephen did not sit in the Convention of 1689, and so was not obliged to make public his attitude by having to vote on such issues as the offer of the throne to the Prince and Princess of Orange.

Indeed, by the time of the Revolution Fox already had a long-standing relationship with the Prince of Orange, for as far back as 1680, and perhaps earlier, he had acted as the latter's London banker, and when William visited England in July of the following year it had been Sir Stephen who had entertained him upon his arrival in London. Nevertheless, in the early months of the new reign he was under some suspicion because of his close association with the deposed ruler. He was omitted from William III's first Treasury Board, and not until February 1690 could Narcissus Luttrell report that 'Sir Stephen Fox hath lately kist his majesties hand, and is received into favour'.[1] Like James before him, William came to appreciate that Fox was too valuable a servant to be dispensed with, and a month later he was back at the Treasury. During the 1690s he was a firm adherent of Godolphin's, an old associate by this stage and a personal friend. Both men were moderate Tories, unwilling to tie themselves closely to any one party or faction, and principally concerned to serve the Crown. Both were competent and conscientious administrators and clearly respected each other's abilities. According to Fox it was Godolphin who was responsible for his return to the Treasury after the Revolution. He wrote that 'His Lordsp. thought it necessary for him to be sum times out of yt comision whoes absence [sic] could not be well dispenced wth, as he told me, unless I would come in'. Sir Stephen was at first unwilling. Having left public life after nearly thirty years in important government positions, he seems to have relished the idea of peace and quiet. Nor is there any need to suppose that his reluctance to return to the Treasury was anything but genuine. Persons selected as Commissioners tended to regard their appointment with mixed feelings, and Sir John Lowther, who was named as First Lord in the Commission of March 1690, has also made it plain to posterity that he had little enthusiasm for his task.[2] Eventually, however, Fox was won over by Godolphin's persistence and the King's promise that, if he would return to the Treasury, his son Charles should have the place of Joint-Paymaster of the Forces in Ireland. Under this combination of pressure and

---

[1] N. Japikse, *Correspondentie van Willem III*, Tweede Gedeelte ('s Gravenhage, 1935), ii. 347, 352; *C.S.P.D.*, 1680–1, p. 371; H.M.C., *Ormonde*, N.S., vi. 106; Luttrell, *State Affairs*, ii. 16.

[2] C. H. Firth, 'The Memoirs of the First Lord Lonsdale', *Eng. Hist. Rev.*, 1915.

bribery he agreed to serve, or, as he commented some years later, 'I did weakly alter my resolution of retiremt.'

Godolphin's concern to have Sir Stephen at the Treasury in 1690 is not surprising when the dearth of experience amongst the others named in the Commission issued in March is considered: Lowther, the First Lord, was a complete novice, so was Pelham, and Hampden had been a Commissioner for less than a year. By comparison Fox had already spent nearly seven and a half years at the Board. Ogg's comment that after the Revolution Godolphin, alone of those available to serve on the Treasury, had knowledge of the national finances may not be a great exaggeration, but Fox was just as knowledgeable as he and could therefore in effect deputize for him.[1] Eight months later Godolphin was back, this time as First Lord, and he remained as such until his resignation in October 1696. During these years the two worked closely together. For instance, early in 1691 it was they, apparently without consulting their colleagues, who took the decision to encourage moneyed men to lend on the security of the recently granted Land Tax by promising, privately and 'underhand', a higher rate of interest than the authorized 7 per cent.[2] Some time later, indeed, a hostile observer (Sydney) noted that Sir Stephen deferred to Godolphin's opinion in everything.[3] This was certainly an exaggeration, for if he considered the matter important Fox was quite prepared to speak his mind, even if it meant a disagreement with his colleague. Thus in July 1695, when the King's controversial grant of the lordship of Denbigh to the Earl of Portland came before the Treasury for the Commissioners' signature, it was reported by their secretary, Lowndes, that 'there was not a word said by any one for a while; then Lord Godolphin spoke for doing [i.e. signing] it, but Sir Stephen Fox violently against it; the others said nothing, and so went off to other business without coming to any sort of resolution'. Fox moreover won the day. He held the grant up for long enough for political pressures from other quarters to develop sufficient weight to oblige William to rescind it. His motives in this successful piece of obstruction are, it must be said,

[1] Ilchester: Family (box 235, bundle 1, part i): note by Fox on his relations with Godolphin. B.L., Add. MS. 51324, ff. 46–7: document endorsed 'Relating to the persons that were Lords Comisionrs of the Treasery'; Ogg, *James II and William III*, p. 229.
[2] *C.S.P.D.*, 1690–1, pp. 241–2.
[3] *C.S.P.D.*, 1691–2, p. 365.

not clear, but the incident confirms that he was no mere 'yes man'.[1]

Sir Stephen's non-involvement in 'party' was even more complete than Godolphin's, and is underlined by the fact that he remained continuously at the Treasury from 1690 until 1702 despite the repeated ministerial changes which took place around him. When Godolphin resigned as First Lord in late 1696, Fox automatically succeeded him at the head of the Commission on grounds of seniority, but he seems to have had no wish to hold this inevitably politically sensitive position on a permanent basis. Macaulay writes of an open rivalry between Fox and Montague for first place in the new Commission which would have to be issued when a new member was added to the Board, but without question this was a figment of his imagination. Sir Stephen does not refer to the incident at all in his own writings, and far from wanting fresh responsibilities to contend with a few months before his seventieth birthday, he was beginning to tire of public life altogether. Narcissus Luttrell reports that he offered to resign a few days after Godolphin had done so, but 'his Majestie said he could not spare him'. Twice more in the later 1690s, in April 1697 and again in September 1698, Luttrell refers to Fox's desire to give up the Treasury, and the record of his attendances and absences at meetings show that the strain of a lifetime of hard work was beginning to tell on him. We have seen that from 1696 onwards he began to take longer summer holidays. In August and September 1698 he was absent from twenty-five consecutive meetings which enabled him to spend nearly twelve weeks at Castle Ashby, and in 1699 he took almost three months off Treasury business. His health was less good than formerly, and long periods of absence in the winters of 1697–8 and 1701–2 clearly indicate illness.[2] By the last years of the seventeenth century Fox was getting old and tired, and there is little doubt that he was only too glad to shed the position of First Lord to the much younger Montague in April 1697.[3] And when

---

[1] Japikse, *Correspondentie van Willem III*, ii. 58–66.

[2] Macaulay, *History*, vii. 411–12; Luttrell, *State Affairs*, iv. 134, 211, 431. See also the minutes of Treasury meetings for the years after 1696 printed in *C.T.B.* x–xvii.

[3] I came to this conclusion despite Vernon's rather obscure remarks to the Duke of Shrewsbury on which Macaulay bases his belief that Fox wanted the first place in the new Commission and was seriously upset at not getting it. Vernon was very hostile to Sir Stephen and not an impartial witness. G. P. R. James, *Letters Illustrative of the Reign of William III* (3 vols., London, 1841), i. 227.

at last at the beginning of Queen Anne's reign he was able to bow
out altogether it was with a great sense of relief. In August 1702
in a letter to Sir Robert Southwell he refers to his recent retirement
as 'now happily com upon mee'.[1]

Fox's conscientious attention to duty and his freedom from party
affiliations were necessary conditions for his regular appointment
to the Treasury Board over nearly a quarter of a century, while
colleagues came and went, but they are hardly a sufficient explanation for the value which successive governments attached to his
services. The principal reason for his unprecedentedly long tenure
of office was surely because the government was thereby able to
enlist the gifts of one of the most successful financiers of the age,
and to ensure that his skills and his experience were deployed on
behalf of the Crown. Like Lionel Cranfield before him, Fox had
made a huge fortune at the Crown's expense and then had turned
from poacher to gamekeeper, undertaken the administration of the
royal finances, and done what he could to remedy the defects and
weaknesses which had made his own rise to fortune possible. The
Treasury's decision to take over responsibility for advancing money
to the forces at the beginning of 1680[2] clearly must have owed
much to the fact that the man who had formerly made the advances as a private Undertaker had recently become a member of
the Board. After he had ceased to be Paymaster Fox thus continued
to be involved in the financing of the army, but as a Treasury Lord
his aim was now to save the Exchequer as much interest as possible.
And in general the raising of loans and negotiations with the
moneyed men of the City was an aspect of Treasury business in
which Fox was able to play an especially active role. We have seen
that, in concert with Godolphin, he was involved in the attempt to
encourage lending on the Land Tax in 1691 by making private
promises to potential lenders that they would receive a higher rate
of interest than the 7 per cent which was publicly offered. Another
example is provided by the negotiations with Charles Duncombe,
the Excise Cashier, in February 1697. When Duncombe proved
unwilling to lend an additional £50,000, which the Treasury wanted
to extract from him, it was Fox who told the King that he was sure

[1] B.L., Add. MS. 51319, f. 179.
[2] See above, pp. 127-9.

there were others who would gladly lend the sum required if they had Duncombe's place, and who in due course came up with a substitute Cashier in the person of Bartholomew Burton.[1]

What contribution Fox made to the series of important innovations in the financial methods of the government which were introduced in the 1690s it is unfortunately impossible to say. The beginning of the long-term public debt with the 'Million Loan' of 1692-3; the establishment of the Bank of England in 1694; the introduction of Exchequer Bills in 1696: these were crucial elements in the early development of a modern system of government borrowing, the so-called 'financial revolution', and all were introduced while Sir Stephen was at the Treasury. At this period most new financial expedients originated in proposals submitted by members of the public and were not devised by the Treasury itself, but the Commissioners had the task of sifting through the large number of suggestions which reached them, and of selecting those which seemed the most promising. Most of the credit for their choice has been given to Charles Montague, perhaps because as Chancellor of the Exchequer he was the Treasury's principal spokesman in the Commons and responsible for introducing the legislation which gave effect to the various schemes. Yet there does not seem to be a great deal of evidence for attributing to him a role in their inception so much more important than has been allowed to his colleagues. Fox in particular was also on the Board during the whole of Montague's membership of it, and, with his unrivalled knowledge of the London money market, it is hard to believe that his was not a very influential voice in the discussions which took place on the many alternative proposals which the Treasury considered during these years.[2]

Fox's reputation for honesty and competence provided a further reason why he was considered so valuable a member of the Treasury Commission. His own success as a financier had been based on maintaining an untarnished personal credit with his fellow dealers in money, and no serious accusation of malpractice or corruption was ever made against him. The respect with which he was regarded amongst moneyed men is suggested by the ironical phrase applied to him by his nephew John Fox: Sir Stephen, he said, was

[1] C.T.B. xi (1696-7), pp. 353-4, xii (1698), p. 5.
[2] Dickson, *Financial Revolution*, pp. 46-57; Roseveare, *The Treasury*, pp. 67-71; Baxter, *Development of the Treasury*, p. 57.

'the darling of the City'.[1] His membership of the Board was thus
something of a guarantee to those on whom the government relied
for loans that its affairs were being properly managed, and therefore it substantially increased the Crown's creditworthiness. Fox
was not the only Treasury Lord who inspired trust in this fashion,
but there were some who clearly did not. In 1680 the Prince of
Orange was advised that it would be safe to lend money to the
Treasury whilst it was 'in its present hands', implying that in
other hands it would not necessarily be so.[2] In the early part of
1690 the composition of William's first Commission, which was
headed by the Earl of Monmouth, appears to have deterred would-
be lenders, but when in March the King replaced Monmouth,
Delamere, and Capel, with Lowther, Pelham, and Fox, the climate
of opinion in the City changed abruptly, and within a fortnight
over £150,000 was subscribed to the loan then being floated.[3]

Fox's personal wealth also contributed to the inspiration of
confidence and the improvement of the Treasury's image, and it
may be noted that the other new Commissioners of 1690, too, were
very rich, though as landowners rather than as moneyed men.
Wealthy Treasury Lords could be useful to the government, since
in an emergency they could pledge their own assets to provide
collateral security when the Crown's own credit was insufficient
for it to raise the loans it needed.[4] The other advantage, from the
government's point of view, in employing men of great means was
that they would themselves lend substantial sums, and at this
period the government's financial requirements were still not so
large that loans by one or two wealthy individuals could not make
an important contribution towards satisfying them. During Sir
Stephen's early years at the Treasury considerable sums remained
owing to him on account of the Undertaking, and as late as the
beginning of 1686 he still held £48,441 of 'old' tallies, which appear
to represent the remnant of that debt. However, he had also been
making fresh advances, of which some £76,000 appears to have
been outstanding in January 1683, and £37,900 three years later.
As at earlier periods, Fox was only able to lend on this scale because
he was himself operating with borrowed money, although by the

[1] B.L., Add. MS. 51324, f. 18ᵛ: narrative of the life of John Fox junior.
[2] Quoted by Ogg in *Charles II*, ii. 442.
[3] H. Horwitz, *Revolution Politicks* (Cambridge, 1968), p. 110.
[4] H.M.C., *Lindsey*, Supplementary Report, p. 24; Luttrell, *State Affairs*, iv.
92.

mid-1680s he no longer needed to draw on the resources of fellow financiers and was able to get all he needed from the savings deposited with him by private investors.[1] We have seen that early in 1686 he may still have held as much as £150,000 of their money, but he reduced the amount substantially in the latter part of the decade and on 1 January 1691 held no more than £69,187. At that date he owed sums ranging from £20 to £10,000 to seventy individuals, to whom he paid interest variously at 4, 5, or 6 per cent, and, as before, he seems to have been drawing mainly on those in some way connected with the Court.[2] In fact even after his withdrawal from government lending soon after the turn of the century, he was continuing to accept deposits, albeit on a reduced scale, and a few months before his death in 1716 he still had £26,819 of borrowed money in his hands, although whether it was from force of habit, as a service to his clients, or because it provided him with a useful degree of liquidity, is uncertain.[3]

Immediately after the Revolution most of Sir Stephen's lending was done in connection with the post of Receiver-General, or, as it was more often referred to by this time, Cashier of the Customs, which he had secured for his nephew Thomas Fox shortly before he was dropped from the Treasury board in 1689. The outgoing Cashier was Richard Kent, who had been in office ever since 1677, and he, of course, had originally been a protégé of Sir Stephen's. In this later stage of his career he was no longer acting on Fox's behalf, although he may have been acting on Charles Duncombe's, but nevertheless some kind of relationship undoubtedly continued between him and his old employer. All the documents relating to Thomas Fox's appointment refer rather pointedly to Kent's 'voluntary resignation' from office, and it is likely that he gave it up through ill health, for two years later he was dead. The evidence is circumstantial, but it looks as though some arrangement was

---

[1] See above, pp. 189–90. Also Ilchester: Official, Sir S. Fox, Charles II's Household (box 269): abstract of debtors and creditors from missing ledger 'D'.

[2] B.L., Add. MS. 51324, ff. 74–9: list of Sir Stephen's debts and credits, 1 Jan. 1690/1; Ilchester: Accounts, Personal (box 221): parchment volume recording debts owed by Sir S. Fox, 1691–8. The money owed by Sir Stephen in 1691 includes sums due from him as executor of Nicholas Johnson; £3,000 which he had settled on his nephew Thomas; and a £5,000 mortgage which he had taken over with one of the estates he had purchased from his son-in-law Lord Cornwallis.

[3] Ilchester: Family (box 227, bundle 2): schedule of Sir S. Fox's debts at 25 Mar. 1716, attached to deed, 2 June 1726.

arrived at between Kent and Sir Stephen whereby Kent handed over to the latter's nominee, perhaps selling him the place for a lump sum. Any such transaction would have required the approval, not only of Fox's colleagues at the Treasury, but of leading ministers as well. If they had misgivings about it in view of Sir Stephen's close association with James II, these will have been over-ridden by an appreciation that his possession of the post would ensure his financial support for the new regime. And there is no doubt that in reality the Cashiership was Sir Stephen's, not Thomas's, and that Thomas merely discharged the office duties on his uncle's behalf: his ledger shows that he retained for himself only £300 a year out of the Cashier's salary and expense allowance of £1,300 a year, and that he paid over the rest to Sir Stephen. It was not, however, the salary for which the Cashiership was chiefly valuable to its holder, but still (as had been the case in the 1670s) because the enormous sums of money which passed through his hands provided an excellent credit base for private financial operations; and this in itself would suggest that Sir Stephen had taken a deliberate decision to resume something of his earlier role as an active financier. Moreover, the Cashier was expected to make a large loan to the Crown, theoretically to provide security for the money he would be handling, but in fact as the price of his appointment. Sir Stephen, using Thomas as a mouthpiece, at first offered £20,000 at 6 per cent, but his Treasury colleagues stood out for more and eventually £30,000 was agreed upon. Later in the year Fox lent another £20,000 in Thomas's name, so bringing his total advance on account of the Customs Cashiership up to £50,000. On top of this, between May and September 1689 he lent at least a further £18,400 on the credit of various parliamentary grants made to the Crown in the earlier part of the year, and as these sums were repaid he re-lent as much or more, so that the total sum he had invested on this account was at least in the region of £70,000.[1] During the course of 1691 Thomas died prematurely, but the threat which this accident posed to Sir Stephen's control of the Customs Cashiership was averted when he succeeded, through the, influence of Godolphin, in obtaining the post for John Knight

---

[1] *C.T.B.* viii (1685–9), p. 2168, ix (1689–92), pp. 21, 59, 182, 287, 289, 348, 402, 403, 551, 694, 697, 729, 742, 970, 1744, 1971–2008, xvii (1702), pp. 581, 599; Ilchester: Official, Thomas Fox (box 279): volume relating to Thomas Fox as Customs Cashier, and his ledger for 1689–91.

Thomas's assistant, who then assumed the role in the conduct of Fox's affairs which had been filled by his former principal.[1]

It was a feature of Sir Stephen's government lending in these years that none of it was done in his own name, even when the loans were not made in connection with a revenue post held by a nominee. This was not in order to conceal the fact that he was making advances, and certainly not in order to deceive anyone, for his employees and agents were well known in government and City circles, and in most cases, although not by any means in all, it must have been readily apparent whose money they were investing.[2] The use of pseudonyms was simply a convenience dictated by Sir Stephen's close involvement in Treasury affairs. It was a convenience to him personally for it made it unnecessary for him to be repeatedly signing the many documents which were generated by each loan that he made, and did away with the need to grant powers of attorney to his employees. Instead the person who lent his name executed a simple deed declaring that he was acting in trust for Fox, and he could then be left to handle the entire transaction without Sir Stephen being further concerned. Operation through the medium of men of straw was also convenient in that the Treasury naturally often discussed matters to do with government loans which might bear directly on the interests of individual lenders, and hence sometimes the presence of lenders was required by the Commissioners. Indeed, often lenders came of their own accord to argue their case for a higher rate of interest or earlier repayment than they had originally been promised. Early in 1690, for instance, Sir Stephen was pressing for the rate of interest on his advances on account of the Customs Cashiership to be raised from 6 to 8 per cent, and in such cases it was desirable to preserve the fiction that the money belonged to Thomas, and not to a member, or in this case a former member, of the Board.[3] And just as a Treasury Lord could hardly appear before his own colleagues, as established procedure would have demanded had his loans been in his own name, so it was also necessary to avoid a

[1] H.M.C., *Finch*, iii. 220; *C.T.B.* ix (1689–92), pp. 1302, 1373, 1862.

[2] The use by major investors of pseudonyms, however, might deceive historians using central government records to analyse the sources of government credit in this period. Fox's name does not, for instance, appear among the major lenders of the 1690s in Dickson's *Financial Revolution*.

[3] Ilchester: Official, Thomas Fox (box 279): volume relating to Thomas Fox as Customs Cashier.

situation where he would have to go to the Exchequer officials, revenue commissioners, or those concerned with the actual mechanics of payments of interest and repayments of principal, and solicit payment from those who were subordinate to him in his official capacity. Thomas Fox's was the name which Sir Stephen used most often between 1689 and 1691, but even in those years some money was lent through his son Charles, through Nicholas Fenn who was a nephew by marriage, and probably also through Charles Toll who had certainly served Fox in this capacity earlier in the 1680s. After Thomas's death in August 1691 his successor in office, John Knight, and Fox's cousin John Rawkins, who were his business assistants for most of the decade, filled the gaps, together with Knight's associate Bartholomew Burton. However, the large Irish loan of 1693 (which is discussed below) was made in Charles's name, and Sir Stephen made occasional use of a variety of other people, including his house steward, Richard Miller, as circumstances rendered desirable.[1]

The employment, not of one agent at a time but of several simultaneously, considerably complicates the task of following the course of Fox's financial activities in the 1690s. The accounts of the most important agents do survive, but they tend to be very difficult to follow in detail. This is partly because they are set down in a highly compressed form, partly because they contain the record of many other matters which only indirectly concerned Sir Stephen, and partly because of the constant change-over of securities as successive batches of government paper came to maturity, were redeemed, and were in turn replaced by others.[2] Nevertheless, it seems clear that Fox increased the size of his advances fairly rapidly during 1689 and then more slowly until about 1696, after which his total investment remained roughly stable. How much he had out on loan to the government at the time of James II's flight

[1] Ilchester: Accounts, Personal (box 220): account-book kept by John Knight, 1691–8; ibid.: Accounts, Household (box 216): two account-books wrongly ascribed to Ridge (recte J. Rawkins); ibid.: Official, Sir S. Fox, Treasury (box 273): cash account for 1691–7 marked 'No. 1', and for 1697–1702 marked 'No. 2'; B.L., Add. MS. 51324, ff. 74–9: list of Sir Stephen's debts and credits, 1 Jan. 1690/1. £6,000 of loans made through Nicholas Fenn in 1690 were on account of the Commissionership of the Wine Licence revenue which Sir Stephen had secured for him. For the Irish loan, see below, pp. 242–3.

[2] See the account-books kept by Knight and Rawkins, and the cash accounts, referred to in the previous note. Also Ilchester: Official, Sir S. Fox, Treasury (box 272): paper volume marked 'A collection by Mr Abbot in 1694'.

abroad does not emerge, and although in all probability it was very much less than the £86,341 which had been owed to him at the beginning of 1686,[1] it must have been still a substantial amount. Some part of what he lent to the new government therefore represented the renewal of old loans rather than the extension of additional credit, but the total quickly far exceeded any sum likely to have been outstanding in December 1688. A list of Sir Stephen's securities drawn up at the beginning of 1691 yields a total of £53,127, but this does not include the first £30,000 advanced through Thomas Fox, so that the true figure for the principal of his loans would be at least £83,127. By the summer of 1693 they stood at a minimum of £93,825 and three years later in 1696 the total was at least £100,940.[2]

Fox's willingness to lend to the government did not depend on his being at the Treasury, and the suggestion that he 'purchased' his reinstatement in 1690 is unfounded, since he had continued to lend while out of office and did not greatly increase the scale of his lending at the time he recovered it. The contemporary rumour that he, like Pelham, had paid £200,000 'upon the nayle' for his place at the Board was thus certainly ill-informed, and probably malicious because of the implication that he had paid handsomely in order to get his hands back into the national till.[3] In fact far from being eager to return to harness, Fox did so with reluctance, and we have seen that it required not only Godolphin's cajoling, but a bribe, in the form of one of the Paymasterships of the Army in Ireland for his son Charles, before he would agree to serve.[4] Nevertheless, if a seat at the Treasury Board did not affect his fundamental readiness to lend one way or another, nor even influence much the size of his loans, it did come to have some bearing on the form his lending took.

In the first few years after the Revolution virtually all Fox's advances were paid directly into the Exchequer in return for tallies

[1] See above, pp. 183, 191.

[2] B.L., Add. MS. 51324, ff. 74–9, doc. cit.; Ilchester: Accounts, Personal (box 220): account-book kept by John Knight, 1691–8; ibid.: Official, Sir S. Fox, Treasury (box 272): paper volume marked 'A collection by Mr Abbot in 1694'; ibid. Official, Sir S. Fox, Treasury (box 273): cash account for 1691–7, marked 'No. 1'.

[3] C.S.P.D., 1689–90, p. 517.

[4] See above, p. 228. Also Ilchester: Family (box 235, bundle 1, part i): note by Fox on his relations with Godolphin.

or Orders charged by parliamentary authority on specific sources
of tax revenue, which he accepted at par, and which therefore must
have been first-class securities, for those on which prospects of
repayment were at all remote normally bore a substantial discount.
There are few references to discounts in any of the accounts kept
on Sir Stephen's behalf, and down to the end of 1696 the highest
rate mentioned is a mere 2 per cent. Possibly Fox felt that as a
Treasury Lord he ought not to make a profit from the Crown's
financial embarrassment, which it was his official duty to try to
alleviate, and therefore normally rejected the opportunities for
acquiring government paper at less than its par value. Certainly
this is what he implied to his colleagues in July 1690 during the
course of a discussion about the terms on which a fresh advance
of £20,000 would be made by Thomas Fox, the Customs Cashier.
Thomas, who was no more than his uncle's employee and spokesman, is reported in the Treasury minutes to have told the Commissioners, in order that they might not think he was trying to
impose on them, 'that he might have had £1,000 for lending
£20,000 [i.e. a discount of 5 per cent] and interest at 8 per cent,
to commence some time past, which he refused because he hath
never dealt that way but reserved himself to be directed by your
Lordships'.[1] On the other hand, at the height of the financial crisis
in the early months of 1697, when government credit was under
severe pressure, Sir Stephen did buy £4,000 worth of tallies at
discounts of 10 and 15 per cent, even though he was then acting as
First Lord of the Treasury, and in 1701 he is to be found investing
in Exchequer Bills which he had acquired at no less than 21 per
cent below their face value.[2] It may be, therefore, that in the early
1690s he was not concerned with high returns but rather with
maintaining an adequate rate of capital turnover taking in 6, 7, or
most often 8 per cent, whilst running the minimum or risk. However, if there was a good reason for venturing into less familiar
territory, he was still prepared to undertake other forms of finance,
notwithstanding a greater sacrifice of liquidity and greater risks.
It was characteristic both of Fox in particular, and the personalized
nature of the late seventeenth-century money-market in general,

---

[1] C.T.B. ix (1689–92), p. 403.
[2] Ilchester: Official, Sir S. Fox, Treasury (box 273): cash account for 1691–7,
under February 1696/7, and for 1697–1701, under March 1700/1: ibid.: Family
(box 237, bundle 3): document endorsed 'Benjamin Levey'.

that one of his principal forays in this direction was prompted by the financial difficulties of a member of his own family. One of Sir Stephen's nieces, Jane, daughter of his elder brother John, had become the wife of a Portsmouth brewer named Ridge, who had built up a considerable business in supplying beer to the fleet. Ridge died late in 1691 or early in 1692, leaving his widow to carry on his business, and she, faced with long delays before the navy paid for what she delivered, and perhaps also with the disruption of previous credit arrangements as a result of her husband's death, ran out of capital within a few months. She must have appealed to her uncle for assistance, and Fox, working through John Rawkins, came to an agreement whereby he discounted the bills she received from the Victualling Commissioners and so provided her with the ready cash she needed for her operations. He also seems to have come to an agreement with the Treasurer of the Navy, on whom the bills were drawn, that instead of waiting until the bills became due for payment and receiving cash for them, he should be reimbursed by being assigned tallies on various branches of the revenue. This did not necessarily mean that he got his money back any sooner, but that he exchanged a form of paper which was not secured on any specific tax for a form which was. To that extent it was a valuable concession, and the cash loan of over £11,000 he made to the Treasurer at this time may well have been the price he paid to obtain it. Between August 1692 and September 1693 Fox accepted bills from Mrs. Ridge to the value of £29,990, which at a discount of 8 per cent ensured him a profit of some £2,400.[1] Beside this he also got interest at 6 per cent per annum on the face value of the bills up to the time when they were redeemed by the issue of tallies, so that the full rate of return on the capital invested was very high indeed.[2] Nevertheless, after the autumn of 1693 he only continued to supply Mrs. Ridge with credit on a much reduced scale. Possibly she had by then made other arrangements, and certainly Sir Stephen's resources were suddenly stretched by the large loan which he had been called upon to make in order .

---

[1] The nature of the transactions involving Mrs. Ridge (Mrs. Shea as she became, presumably on remarriage) can be pieced together from the references to them in the account books of J. Rawkins, Ilchester: Accounts, Household (box 216), doc. cit.; and in 'A Collection by Mr. Abbot in 1694', Ilchester: Official, Sir S. Fox, Treasury (box 272), doc. cit.

[2] It was very high because the 8 per cent discount was not per annum, but rather, it would seem, on an average for a period of perhaps six months.

to extricate the government of Ireland from its financial difficulties.

As a member of the Treasury Board, Fox periodically found himself in a position in which it was necessary to set an example to other lenders, and he was always liable to come under pressure from his colleagues to provide help in an emergency. For instance, during the 1690s the English government began to experiment with the raising of long-term loans, devising a series of expedients, including tontines, lotteries, annuities, and the grant of corporate privileges, to induce lenders to part with their funds for an indefinite period, and Fox, who was deeply involved in the decisions to adopt these schemes, must have been extremely anxious that they should succeed. His participation in them as a private investor was thus probably undertaken, at least in part, in order to inspire confidence in the rest of the investing community. The first long-term loan was that of 1693, when an attempt was made to raise £1m. by means of a tontine. In fact the tontine itself did not prove particularly attractive to subscribers, but this possibility had been anticipated and the Act authorizing the loan contained a provision that, if the sum required could not be raised on that basis, then the rest might be taken up by the sale of life annuities yielding 14 per cent, and in the end much more money was obtained by this means. Fox only put £500 into the tontine, either in the name of his nephew Charles Johnson, or possibly on his behalf, but he spent £2,500 more on the purchase of annuities in the name of seven of his relatives, a tactic obviously intended to spread his risks. This made his total investment £3,000, one of the largest in a fund which, perhaps because of its novelty, did not attract the wholehearted support of investors. In the following year he bought tickets to the value of £2,349. 14s. 7d. for a lottery with which the government was trying to raise a further £1m., but the most important loan of 1694 was, of course, that for £1,200,000 which led to the establishment of the Bank of England. Fox undertook to subscribe £5,000, and actually paid in £1,250 of this on the first day that the books were opened, although it should be noted that like other original subscribers he never had to provide the last 20 per cent of the price of his stock, which was eventually credited to him out of the profits earned by the Bank. Fox's £5,000 was a considerably smaller subscription than that of some of the other great moneyed men of the day, but it was comparable to the £6,000 put up by his Treasury colleague Godolphin, the difference in amounts perhaps reflecting the fact that the latter was his senior on the Board.[1]

There were two occasions when Fox came to the government's rescue during a financial emergency. The first was in 1693 when he was induced by Godolphin to lend more than £40,000 to the hard-pressed government of Ireland. The financial difficulties of the recently established Williamite administration were largely derived from the fact that the country had suffered severely during the war following the 1688 Revolution. However, these problems had been aggravated by the terms the Lord Deputy, Sydney, had accepted a year earlier in order to raise the money necessary to carry on the government. To secure from three London financiers (Sir Joseph Herne, Sir Stephen Evance, and Sir William Scawen) an immediate £30,000, and the promise of further sums in the future, Sydney had not only mortgaged to them the Crown's revenue from quit rents but also agreed that their agent, Elnathan Lumm, should be appointed Deputy Receiver-General of Ireland under the Great Seal, with a provision that he should not be removed until the loan had been repaid. The English Treasury Lords had opposed Sydney's deal because they feared to set a precedent that large lenders should receive a grant of an office over and above normal interest, but in the event it proved to be unfortunate in a quite different manner. As Deputy Receiver-General, Lumm's position was analogous to that of the Customs or Excise Cashier in England, in that incoming revenue passed through his hands as it was collected, but unlike them he handled not just one, but all branches of the revenue. Thus the credit which this flow of money generated was transferred from the Irish government to Lumm and to the bank which he and some associates had opened in Dublin. The government, therefore, found it hard to raise any further loans, save through Lumm and his backers, and it was not long before it realized the urgent necessity of paying them off to free the revenue from their thrall. The problem, however, was not merely to find someone to advance the £41,000 which by the summer of 1693 was owed to them, but to find a lender whose terms for so doing would be significantly easier, since there was

---

[1] Ilchester: Accounts, Personal (box 220): account kept by J. Knight; and ibid.: Official, Sir S. Fox, Treasury (box 272): 'A Collection by Mr. Abbot in 1694'; Dickson, *Financial Revolution*, pp. 48–9, 52–7, 254–8.

obviously no point in exchanging one Lumm for another. Fox was already involved in Irish affairs because his son Charles was, with Lord Coningsby, one of the two joint Paymasters of the Army in Ireland, and that, together with his own official position, meant that, unlike other potential lenders, he had no need to demand the grant of a strategic office as additional security. He was therefore willing to put up the sum required (or rather the larger part of it, for he had a partner in the enterprise) on terms which enabled the government of Ireland to recover control over its own finances. He always regarded this action as one of his most valuable services to the Crown, but in fact it was still a very profitable one for himself. He got a larger return than on his lending to the English government at this time, for interest rates were higher in Ireland on account of the relative scarcity of capital and the greater risks, and, in addition to 10 per cent on his principal, he also secured a pension of £600 a year payable for as long as any of the money remained outstanding, which was until the end of 1698. The adverse rate of exchange between Dublin and London somewhat reduced his net profit, but even so there is no doubt that the arrangement he concluded, although convenient for the government, was very satisfactory from his own point of view.[1]

The second occasion when Sir Stephen is to be found living up to his responsibilities as a Lord of the Treasury, and providing help at a time of difficulty, was in 1697 when, prior to a new issue of Exchequer Bills, whose circulation was to be guaranteed by the Bank of England, the Bank's directors undertook to raise a fund to finance the operation. The matter was debated in the General Court of the Bank, but the directors' recommendation that the money be raised from the shareholders was defeated, and it was decided to leave it to a voluntary subscription whose prospects, in the tight financial climate of that year, were not very promising. The directors themselves were thus obliged to subscribe heavily to the fund, and Sir Stephen on behalf of himself and his son did likewise, putting up £10,300 between April and August, and a

---

[1] B.L., Add. MS. 51324, ff. 57–60: autobiographical narrative endorsed 'Recollections relateing to my self . . .'; Add. MS. 51335, f. 50: undated petition of Charles Fox to the King; C.S.P.D., 1691–2, pp. 364–5, 399, 548–9, 1693, pp. 333–4, 365–6; C.T.B. ix (1689–92), pp. 1759–60, 1764, x (1693–6), p. 340; Ilchester: Family (box 238, bundle 25): abstract of Mr. Robinson's accounts 1693–1700; ibid.: Family (box 235, bundle 3): document marked 'Heads of an answer'.

further £1,700, as part of a new subscription, in September. His money, however, was all refunded to him fairly promptly, presumably because the emergency had passed and the Bank had accumulated a sufficiently large sum for its purpose from other sources.[1]

The direct financial rewards of a place on the Treasury Board in the later seventeenth century were substantial but not princely. The Commissioners divided between themselves the £8,000 a year salary which Lord Treasurers had received since the Restoration, and since there were usually five of them they were paid £1,600 each. In addition each also received a share of the New Year's gifts made by members of the royal family other than the King himself, and by the officials of the Exchequer and the revenue. How much these amounted to is uncertain and probably varied over time, but at New Year 1683 Fox recorded that they had received 220 guineas from the various Exchequer officers and 500 guineas from the farmers of the Hearth Tax, of which his own share was 144 guineas. Various 'gratuities' were doubtless also offered to the Treasury Lords, as in the past they had been offered to the Lord Treasurer, in respect of favours sought or already performed, but in view of Fox's attitude to such *douceurs* it is unlikely that he accepted any of them.[2]

Treasury Lords could also normally look forward to the grant of a substantial pension, or some other kind of reward, bestowed as a mark of the King's appreciation for the service they had given. In a number of cases this took the form of promotion to the peerage, in others appointment to important government office when they left the Board, and sometimes retiring Commissioners were given a present of money as well. Fox did, in fact, secure the grant of a pension of £1,000 a year for twenty-one years from 1701, but since this was a renewal of the one originally bestowed on the Earl of Sunderland and which he had bought as an investment in the 1680s, he seems to have regarded it, with what justification it is impossible to say, as no more than his due and not in any way connected with the service he had given at the Treasury. Thus

---

[1] Ilchester: Accounts, Personal (box 220): account kept by John Knight 1691–8; Sir J. H. Clapham, *The Bank of England* (2 vols., Cambridge, 1944), i. 54–5.

[2] Baxter, *Development of the Treasury*, pp. 17–18; Ilchester: Official, Sir S. Fox, Treasury (box 272): at back of account-book marked 'Brullion begun ye 28 of Ober 81'.

when he finally retired he was keenly conscious that he had not received his just deserts. He felt that he had been slighted and gave vent to his feelings in a number of papers, apparently drawn up for his own satisfaction, in which he recalled all the honours and advantages which had been bestowed on his colleagues and compared their experience with his own. Of all the twenty-six Commissioners appointed to the Treasury since 1679, Fox concluded that besides himself only Sir Dudley North and Henry Thynne, both of whom had served for a few months only, had gone unrewarded.[1]

In fact Sir Stephen, who was apt to harbour his grievances, was being less than fair to those of William III's and Queen Anne's ministers whom he blamed for neglecting him. For instance, although it is true that Fox received nothing for himself other than the £1,000 pension, we have seen that some important and highly lucrative offices were bestowed on his son Charles, his nephew Thomas, and his protégé John Knight. Charles Fox was appointed one of the two Paymasters of the Forces in Ireland in 1690. He was dismissed in July 1698, probably for party reasons, for he was a High Church Tory and the ministry was predominantly Whig, but was eventually granted a pension of £1,500 a year in partial recompense for his loss of office, probably because William did not wish to see Sir Stephen, who was still valuable as an administrator and a source of loans, withdraw from the Treasury Board in dudgeon at the way his son had been treated. Then, at the beginning of the new reign in 1702, Charles was made Joint-Paymaster of the English forces operating on the Continent.[2] Thomas Fox was made Cashier of the Customs in 1689, and after his death in 1691 Sir Stephen succeeded in securing the post for Knight.[3] It is true that the Customs Cashiership had to be bought by the making of a large loan, and the Irish Paymastership also involved an

[1] B.L., Add. MS. 51332: schedule of deeds, f. 44; Add. MS. 51324, ff. 45–53: documents endorsed 'Observations on the 26 persons that were Comissrs of the Treasury', 'Relateing to the persons that were Lord Comisionrs of the Treasery', and 'Proceedings at the Greencloth agst Sr Stephen Fox . . .'

[2] B.L., Add. MS. 51324, ff. 57–62: autobiographical narrative endorsed 'Recollections relateing to my self . . .' and statement of grievances without date, heading, or endorsement; Add. MS. 51335: petitions of Charles Fox to the King and to the Queen; C.T.B. xiii (1697–8), p. 397, xiv (1698–9), pp. 2, 109, 114, xvii (1702), p. 425.

[3] See above, pp. 234–6; H.M.C., *Finch*, iii. 220; C.T.B. ix (1689–92), pp. 1302, 1373.

obligation, albeit less formal and explicit, to provide financial help for the discharge of the office as and when the need arose, but there was plenty of competition for both. The Irish Paymastership, it may be added, was worth about £2,720 a year, and the English post carried a salary of £1,500 a year and lavish unofficial opportunities for the holder to enrich himself, although Charles did not take advantage of these. As for the Customs Cashier, he received a salary of £1,000 a year, £300 a year to pay his clerks, and all the benefits that accrued from the fact that the entire Customs revenue passed through his hands.[1]

As far as personal rewards to Fox himself are concerned, it is highly likely that once, if not several times, he was offered a peerage but refused it. Rumours that he was to be made a lord were circulating at various times although nothing ever came of them, and an unauthorized biography published shortly after Fox's death specifically states that he turned down the offer of a hereditary title in James II's reign. Finally, at his funeral his old acquaintance Canon Eyre commented that, as a Treasury Commissioner, Sir Stephen 'could not have [had] any thing greater, unless he had been rais'd above the degree of a *commoner*, which he would never have yielded to'.[2] With Fox unwilling to become a peer, and successive ministers probably feeling that it would be inappropriate to grant a large sum of money to someone who was already a byword for wealth, the only way he could have been rewarded was with an important and honorific office for himself.

The office that Sir Stephen wanted, indeed had wanted ever since it had eluded him in 1660, was that of Cofferer of the Household. We have seen that he had secured a reversionary grant of the post from Charles II and had even been sworn in as Cofferer in reversion,[3] but such a grant did not bind a new sovereign, and so, when Brouncker died a few months after Charles, Fox could not expect to succeed him. Nor did he, for James brought in his own man, Sir Peter Apsley, who had been Treasurer and Receiver-General to him as Duke of York. However, when the post of

---

[1] B.L., Add. MS. 51321, ff. 1–5, 9–10, 17–20: Charles Fox's accounts of the profits of the Irish Paymastership; Ilchester: Official, Thomas Fox (box 279): Thomas Fox's ledger; *C.T.B.*, ix (1689–92), p. 21, xix (1704–5), p. 97. See also below, pp. 270–2.
[2] H.M.C., *Seventh Report*, Appendix, pp. 406, 477; H.M.C., *Portland*, iii. 368; Anon., *Memoirs of the Life of Sir Stephen Fox*, p. 80; Eyre, *Sermon*, p. 9.
[3] See above, pp. 112–13.

Cofferer again became vacant at the Revolution Fox seems to have considered that his title to the office ought to have been respected, and it was an unlucky coincidence that at the moment when the reversion might have taken effect he was temporarily out of favour. He had been too closely associated with James II to receive preferment from his successor immediately, and so the vacancy went not to him but to one of William of Orange's staunchest supporters, Lord Newport. The loss of the Cofferership was a blow which never ceased to rankle in Fox's mind. The office had clearly acquired a value in his eyes over and above the income of £4,000 or £5,000 a year that it yielded to its holder, perhaps because having entered the King's Household at the lowest level of the hierarchy it was psychologically important to him to reach the highest post attainable by the normal course of promotion. He also regarded his reversionary grant of it as his true reward for his loyalty during the exile, and, as he saw it, his exclusion thus made it appear '. . . that my long and very acceptable services to my master King Charles is as if it had never been, for the recompence was the Cofferer's place in revertion, which made me not ask any [other] marke of his good will, which might have bin easily obtain'd, for he was graciously satisfied with my diligence and integrity . . .' Fox was especially bitter that Newport (later made Earl of Bradford) should combine the place with that of Treasurer of the Household, so joining two offices whose functions were incompatible with one another. He considered that Newport had thereby gone contrary to the oath taken by all royal servants to uphold the constitution and ordinances of the Household, and moreover had undermined its internal organization in such a way as to permit substantial extravagance by subordinate officials. Indeed, Fox was so incensed that he felt unable to remain as Clerk of the Green Cloth, since it meant serving under Newport and his ally, Devonshire (the titular head of the Household as its Lord Steward), and he resigned his place to his nephew John, who as Clerk of the Spicery, was in line for promotion in his own right. This was a tactical error, for not only did John completely lack his uncle's authority and prestige, but he was an unreliable scapegrace whom Newport and Devonshire had no difficulty in getting dismissed on a charge of drunkenness within a few months.[1]

---

[1] Ilchester: Family (box 235, bundle 1, part i): 'Sr Ste Fox his case concerning the Cofferer's Office'; B.L., Add. MS. 51324, ff. 54-5, 61-2: document

The events surrounding the succession to the Cofferership in 1689 did not make it easy, even for those who wished Fox well, to do very much on his behalf. His lack of political experience meant that he could hardly be rewarded by promotion to one of the great offices of state, and, in view of his background, the most suitable post for him was obviously one in the higher ranks of the royal Household. But the office he wanted was not available, and because of his grievances against Newport and Devonshire and his unwillingness to break his oath (to uphold the constitution of the Household) as they had done, he was not prepared to accept any other post. Sir Stephen admitted that Godolphin had offered him the Comptrollership of the Household at some stage, probably at the beginning of Anne's reign when Godolphin became Lord Treasurer, but he refused it. This refusal may have been due to a sense of pique at the wrong he felt he had suffered many years before, or it may have been due to a genuine abhorrence of perjuring himself; either way, however, he had rejected a mark of royal favour which his long service at the Treasury had earned him, and his complaints that he had been passed over must therefore be regarded with some reserve. Nevertheless, as late as April 1704 when the Cofferership was once again vacant he was still pressing his claim, and provoked the unfortunate Godolphin into complaining to the Duchess of Marlborough of the 'persecution' he was experiencing at the hands of his old colleague.[1]

Fox may not have got the appointment he desired, but he certainly enjoyed his share of the patronage which the Treasury Commissioners had at their disposal. They were able to nominate to numerous lucrative posts in those branches of the administration under their direct control, and were able to influence selection in others, such as the revenue departments, where they could not actually dictate it. Sir Stephen only had one son living during his time at the Treasury, but he had a very large family of nephews, nieces, and cousins, their spouses and descendants, and he was able to secure official positions for many of them. The relative who benefited in this way most frequently was Nicholas Fenn. In 1683

---

headed 'Losses sustained by Sr Ste Fox and his son', and statement of grievances without date, heading, or endorsement.

[1] Ilchester: Family (box 235, bundle 1, part i): document endorsed 'Duke of Marlborough'; H. L. Snyder, *The Marlborough–Godolphin Correspondence* (3 vols., Oxford, 1975), i. 288.

he was appointed Housekeeper at the Excise Office at a salary of
£400 a year and, though he was removed at the Revolution, he
recovered the post in 1690, thanks to Fox's intervention with
Secretary of State Southwell. In 1683 too, Fenn was named as one
of the Commissioners for Victualling the Navy, and he remained
a member of successive Commissions into the 1690s. In this decade
he served on several Commissions for the levying of new taxes and
the raising of loans upon them. In September 1690 and again in
1701 he was one of five Commissioners of Wine Licences with a
salary of £200 a year; in 1694, one of twenty-one Commissioners
to administer the Million Lottery Loan; and in 1697, one of ten
managers of a further lottery.[1] John Rawkins, a cousin of Sir
Stephen's on his mother's side, was appointed Receiver-General of
the new tax on hackney coaches in 1694. Richard Dalton, a nephew
by marriage, became Comptroller-General of the Accounts of the
wine licence revenue in 1690, a post which carried a salary of £200
a year. John Knight, an employee, although not a relative, of Fox's,
surely owed his appointments as Comptroller of the revenue from
First Fruits (1687) and Receiver of revenue from vacant bishoprics
(1691) to Sir Stephen, as he certainly owed to him his later elevation to the post of Customs Cashier. It is also probable, though this
was not a matter of patronage in the strict sense, that Knight's
Directorship of the Bank of England was not unconnected with the
fact that at the time the Bank was established he was Fox's right-
hand man in financial matters. Thomas Allen, also an employee
as land steward at Redlynch, obtained a Collectorship in the Excise
through Sir Stephen in 1683, a post in which his son (who eventually absconded owing £800) succeeded him. The elder Allen was
subsequently named as Receiver-General for Somerset and Bristol
for a succession of parliamentary taxes. From 1689 onwards Charles
Brawne, a third of Fox's nephews by marriage, shared these appointments, and then from 1692 until his death in 1702 held them
on his own. John Baber, who was a 'kinsman' (and heir) of the
husband of Sir Stephen's younger sister Elizabeth, was successively
Clerk of Securities in the Excise Office and Solicitor for prosecu-
tions before the Excise Commissioners. The last post, however,
required a degree of legal expertise and general competence which

---

[1] *C.T.B.* vii (1681–5), pp. 924, 956, viii (1685–9), p. 50, ix (1689–92), pp. 62,
118, 698, 817, x (1693–6), pp. 552–3, 983, xii (1697), p. 126, xvi (1700–1). pp.
409, 425.

was beyond him, and he was removed from it in 1697 and compensated with the Comptrollership of the revenue from First Fruits, which Knight's disgrace had rendered vacant. Baber also obtained an appointment in the colonial administration of Jamaica, although this was a sphere in which Fox did not normally exert influence and it may have been obtained through the good offices of some other patron. James Pavey, a member of Sir Stephen's mother's family and later steward of his Wiltshire estates, was appointed Customs Searcher at Ipswich in 1696, and Housekeeper to the Trustees for Exchanging Exchequer Bills in 1697. William Yardley, a great-nephew by marriage, obtained a Customs Surveyor's place at Rochester in 1680 but lost it again the following year for some misdemeanour. Richard Miller, Fox's house steward and later his general man of business, was a Tidesman in the port of London in the 1680s, and in 1692 was promoted to the more important place of Customer and Collector of duties on woollen cloth at London.[1] We have also seen that Fox used the patronage available to him as a member of the Board of Green Cloth in a similar fashion, securing the appointment of relatives and servants to a wide range of positions in the royal Household; indeed, some of those, such as Fenn, Rawkins, Dalton, Yardley, and Miller, who gained posts through Fox's influence as a Treasury Commissioner, also held Household offices at various times.[2] Well might one of the more distant members of Fox's family circle write, towards the end of his life, 'Lord of his mercy long preserve that usefull person for a great blessing is he to all his relations young and old.'[3]

Before we finally leave the subject of the material benefits which Fox derived from his service at the Treasury, there is the question of whether he ever abused his position in order to enrich himself by methods which were either irregular or actually corrupt. Some

---

[1] *C.T.B.* vi (1679–80), pp. 608, 659, vii (1681–5), pp. 250, 299, viii (1685–9), pp. 439, 1637, ix (1689–92), pp. 131, 252, 423, 459, 567, 605, 610, 873, 976, 1175–6, 1471, 1541, 1847, x (1693–6), pp. 34, 152, 465, 590, 661, 933, 1042, 1249, 1308, xi (1696–7), p. 283, xii (1697), pp. 59, 284, xiii (1697–8), pp. 43, 166, 171; xvii (1702), pp. 56, 242; *C.S.P.D.*, 1697, p. 202; Ilchester: Estate, Somerset (box 173): letters from Thomas Allen to Fox; B.L., Add. MS. 51319, f. 167; Somerset R.O., DD/X/SR, p. 55.

[2] See above, pp. 115–16. For those of the above who are stated to be relatives of Sir Stephen, see also the Genealogical Table in Appendix I.

[3] Ilchester: Family (box 236, bundle 8): Janet Home to Richard Miller, 6 Apr. 1706.

seventeenth-century Lord Treasurers certainly did not scruple to do so, and Danby in the 1670s seems to have been particularly venal.[1] Among the malpractices laid at the latter's door was that of buying up desperate debts from government creditors at a heavy discount and then paying them to himself in full, and a similar accusation was made against Sir Stephen in the 1690s. Whatever may have been the truth in Danby's case, in Fox's the charge need not be taken too seriously. Everything that emerges about Fox's personality makes it seem highly improbable, and it should be noted that the accusation derives from the Earl of Ailesbury who, like his master the exiled James II, regarded Sir Stephen as an arch-traitor, and who was making no attempt to be impartial. Ailesbury recounted how, early in 1691, army officers in England were ordered back to their posts in Flanders, and, in order to raise some money for that year's campaign, were obliged to sell the tallies issued to them in lieu of pay at a great discount. He alleged that Fox cynically took advantage of their poverty by buying up their tallies in vast quantities. 'Sir Stephen Fox,' he wrote, 'sold a great part of his land to have ready money, and he had a goldsmith in or near Hungerford Market, I have forgot his name, that was his broker, and Sir Stephen, having vast sums for that purpose, got prodigiously, for he, being of the Treasury, knew well how to make valid his tallies.'[2] It is true that Fox did sell some land in 1690, but what he sold was a very small part of his estate and was part of a series of sales which had begun several years earlier.[3] Moreover, although the accounts of his dealings in government securities do not survive for the early part of 1691, the most important of those covering the period September 1691 to December 1698 do, and they show no sign of any similar attempt to profit by the necessities of impoverished government creditors, despite the fact there were many occasions when their tallies might have been had at a sufficiently large discount to make it worth while.[4]

Fox has also been implicated in the notorious Exchequer Bills scandal at the end of 1697. Exchequer Bills were interest-bearing, transferable, paper securities, similar in nature to the Treasury Orders introduced by Downing a generation earlier. During 1697

---

[1] Baxter, *Development of the Treasury*, p. 18.
[2] *Ailesbury Memoirs*, i. 241.   [3] See below, pp. 206–9.
[4] Ilchester: Accounts, Personal (box 220): account kept by John Knight, 1691–8. Also see above, p. 239.

they were changing hands at a 10 per cent discount but were accepted at par if used for the payment of taxes, in which case the bills were endorsed accordingly by those who had made the payment. This provided an opportunity for several leading financial officials, Charles Duncombe who was Cashier of the Excise until early in that year, his successor in the post Bartholomew Burton, and John Knight, the Cashier of the Customs. Using the funds in their hands they purchased bills at the going discount, had them fraudulently endorsed so that it appeared that they had received them on account of the taxes for which they were responsible, and then paid them into the Exchequer where they were credited with their full face value. By this means they used the King's tax money to make a nice profit for themselves. When their activities accidentally came to light it caused a great stir. The guilty financiers were dismissed from all their posts. Duncombe and Knight as Members of Parliament were expelled from the House and, together with Burton, imprisoned on parliamentary authority. However, a bill to impose a colossal fine on Duncombe was defeated in the Lords by a single vote and, since none of the three had committed any offence for which a conviction could be obtained in an ordinary court of law, they had to be released at the end of the session and escaped any further punishment.[1] No one at the time suggested that Sir Stephen was in any way implicated in their fraud, but he has subsequently fallen under suspicion because of his very close association with both Burton and Knight.[2] He had arranged the former's appointment only six months earlier, and had nominated the latter as Customs Cashier in succession to Thomas Fox back in 1691 and had since then, and probably before, entrusted an important part of his private financial business to him. However, the account-book recording Sir Stephen's dealings with Knight, which is extremely detailed, provides no ground for suspecting that he was involved in his protégé's malpractice.[3] Nor do Sir Stephen's actions, once the scandal had broken, seem to be

---

[1] W. Cobbett, *Parliamentary History of England* (36 vols., London, 1806–20), v. 1171; *C.T.B.* xiii (1697–8), pp. 4–36; B.L., Add. MS. 29588, f. 9.

[2] Baxter, *Development of the Treasury*, p. 77. Professor Baxter's suggestion that Charles Fox's dismissal from the Irish Paymastership was connected with the Exchequer Bills affair is mistaken: for the apparent explanation see below, p. 270.

[3] Ilchester: Accounts, Personal (box 220): account kept by John Knight 1691–8.

those of a man with anything to hide or to fear. He freely admitted before the King and the Privy Council that he had put bills into Knight's hands to dispose of, and he risked coming under attack himself by speaking up on his behalf before both Council and Parliament. He did not try to excuse what Knight had done, but he asked that he might be allowed to keep his lesser appointments in recompense for the good service he had given to the Crown in the past. However, Sir Stephen's eloquence was of no avail, for outrage was general, and the plea that 'till now he never made the least slip' received the crushing reply from Sunderland that ''tis not likely this is the first fault, though not discovered til now'.[1] Fox loyally stood by Knight in the hour of the latter's disgrace, but secretly he may have agreed with Sunderland's verdict for he did not continue to use him in his private affairs for much longer.

C.T.B. xiii (1697–8), pp. 35–6; C.S.P.D., 1698, p. 65.

CHAPTER X

Sir Stephen at Home

FROM THE Restoration until the end of his working life Sir Stephen Fox's home was a set of apartments inside the royal palace of Whitehall, which he originally occupied by virtue of his then position of Second Clerk Comptroller. When they were allotted to him they were not a particularly desirable residence, being situated in the furthest corner of the palace precinct (a fact which saved them in the Whitehall fire of January 1698) and consisting only of three 'very inconvenient low roomes', with some garrets and two small closets. However, Fox obtained permission to extend them at his own expense, a practice courtiers often resorted to when they did not find their official accommodation adequate to their needs. Indeed, the habit became so prevalent that some years later an effort was made to check it for by then it was leading to overcrowding in some parts of the palace. Fox's accounts for March 1661 contain an item recording the expenditure of £239. 13s. 4d. for 'buildinge, altring, beautifying, and repairing' his new home; and at various times he made further additions and alterations, in all costing over £1,000, and also succeeded in taking in adjacent rooms formerly occupied by the servants of the Old Bottlehouse. By the end he had quite a large house on two floors, and a plan of it by Sir Christopher Wren, in his capacity of Surveyor-General of the Works, shows that it had a river frontage of nearly a hundred feet, about twenty rooms on the principal floor, and no fewer than five separate staircases. Several of these rooms were used as offices from which Fox discharged his duties as Clerk of the Green Cloth, and such business that was not transacted there he conducted a few hundred yards away at the Pay Office.[1] The rest of the building was given over to the family and its servants, but considering the numbers of both there can have been little space to spare. Three

---

[1] Ilchester: Estate, London (box 161): bundle of papers relating to the Whitehall lodgings; ibid.: Official, Sir S. Fox, Army: day-book for 1660-4, 30 Mar. 1661; B.L., Add. MS. 51319, f. 11: certificate from the Gentlemen-Ushers, 29 Jan. 1660; C.T.B. iv (1672-5), p. 553, viii (1685-9), pp. 2126, 2129, ix (1689-92), pp. 1372, 1727; C.S.P.D., 1698, p. 19.

children had already been born before the Foxes returned to England, and more followed at regular intervals during the 1660s. The seventh and eighth died in infancy, but the first six all survived the perilous early months, as did the ninth born in 1669, so that there was a very full nursery.[1] As for the servants, there were at least ten and probably a dozen by the end of the decade, although it seems inconceivable that they all lived under Sir Stephen's roof. Indeed, it may have been partly for reasons of space that two of the older Fox boys were boarded out to school with a certain Mr. Hern.[2]

Fox valued his Whitehall 'lodgings', as he described them, because they were so conveniently situated, close to the Pay Office, the Horse Guards, the Treasury, and to Whitehall Stairs from which he could take a boat, either down-river towards the Temple and the City, or up-river to Chelsea and beyond. The lodgings were perhaps less ideally suited to the needs of his wife and children, for Whitehall was a congested, noisy, and sometimes smelly, place. However, they had a small walled garden, looked after by a part-time man for fifteen shillings a quarter, and the windows on one side of their house overlooked the river. Moreover, for the children there were compensations in living where they did: the sight of small craft passing to and fro on the Thames, of vessels unloading supplies for the palace at Scotland Dock just to the north of the house, and of the soldiers at the guard house which adjoined them on the west.[3] Later on there could be more grown-up entertainments which they could not have experienced if they had lived in the country: puppet shows in the Strand, exciting events like the arrival of the Moroccan ambassador at Court in 1682, for which thirteen-year-old Jane Fox had a ticket, and above all the theatre. On 22 January 1669, for instance, Sir Stephen's house steward entered in his account book:

> Pd Mr Stephen, Mr Charles, Mr Wm, & my selfe goinge to ye playhouse twice—£1. 5s. 0d.

The three boys were then aged ten and a half, eight, and seven respectively, but Charles in particular seems to have developed a

---

[1] Ilchester: Official, Sir S. Fox, Royal Service (box 267): account-book of exile and Secret Service payments 1660-5, at end.

[2] Ilchester: Accounts, Personal (box 221): cash accounts of Elizabeth Fox.

[3] A map showing the situation of the Whitehall lodgings will be found in *Survey of London*, xvi, Charing Cross (London, 1935), Plate 92.

taste for plays for he was taken on three other occasions over the next few weeks. Trips on the river were another source of amusement: for instance on 25 September 1669 the steward recorded expenditure of a shilling, 'pd by water etc to see the great fish'.[1] Possibly the 'fish' was an unfortunate whale or porpoise which had come up the Thames and become stranded on the shore.

Nevertheless, there could be no substitute for the fresh air of the countryside and, as soon as he could afford it, Fox secured a *pied-à-terre* far enough away from Westminster to ensure a real change of environment. He chose the village of Chiswick, which, like Hampstead and Highgate, was already becoming fashionable as a refuge for the better-off inhabitants of the capital. However, unlike the villages to the north of London, it was easily accessible from Whitehall by water. It was then a quiet, clean, place where, behind the cottages of the fishermen and boatmen which fronted the river, there was a broad street of gentlemen's residences with pleasant gardens and, beyond those, some larger country houses standing in more substantial grounds.[2] In August 1663 Fox bought one of these, paying the sum of £1,797. 13s. 4d. for the house and two acres of ground which were copyhold of the manor, and thus subject to a small annual rent.[3] No evidence survives as to the age or size of Sir Stephen's new country seat, but it was probably a Tudor or Jacobean building, and the price suggests that it was of middling size. However, he used it very much as an occasional retreat, mainly to be visited in summer, and for most of the time he kept his family around him in Whitehall, leaving at Chiswick permanently only a small group of servants to look after the place with the assistance of a guard dog.[4] Only in the terrible plague year of 1665, when the bills of mortality soared to unheard of heights, and the infection spread to Westminster itself, did the Foxes remain at Chiswick continuously over a long period.[5]

---

[1] Ilchester: Accounts, Household (box 210): Sir S. Fox's household accounts 1667–71; ibid.: Accounts, Personal (box 220): account of Sir S. Fox's private expenses 1681–4, under 28 Jan. 1681/2, and similar account for 1684–97, under 19 Feb. 1686/7.

[2] W. P. W. Phillimore and W. H. Whitear, *Historical Collections Relating to Chiswick* (London, 1897), pp. 11–14.

[3] Ilchester: Family (box 235, bundle 4): lists of Sir S. Fox's purchases of land; B.L., Add. MS. 51332: schedule of deeds, f. 43; Add. MS. 51324, f. 217: document headed 'Sr Stephen Fox's coppey hold land in Cheswicke. . . .'

[4] Ilchester: Accounts, Household (box 210): Sir S. Fox's household accounts, 1667–71.   [5] H.M.C., *Ormonde*, N.S., iii. 204.

By the later 1660s Fox was fast becoming a very wealthy man, but almost everything he made from the Undertaking was being ploughed back into it, and he was not diverting a large part of his resources either into investments in other fields, or to support a more lavish style of living. His domestic, household, and personal expenditure had risen from less than £900 a year in 1662–3 to an average of £2,790 a year in 1667–70,[1] but this was almost completely covered by his income from office, Court pensions, and land, which by the end of the decade was approaching £2,370 a year.[2] The interest he received on private lending may not yet have been sufficient to account for the difference, but any gap which remained between his private income and his private spending was, his own financial memorandums clearly demonstrate, to be met out of that part of the Paymaster's poundage which was intended to defray his expenses, and not out of the part which represented interest on money advanced.[3] It is true that his way of life and that of his family could hardly be described as modest, even at this relatively early stage of his career. They clearly lived in considerable comfort, well attended by servants, and able to enjoy any luxury or convenience which the age could afford. Yet there was no extravagance and no waste in their household, and their housekeeping was

[1] Ilchester: Official, Sir S. Fox, Army: day-book for 1660–4, 28 Feb. 1662/3; ibid.: Accounts, Household (box 210): Sir S. Fox's household accounts, 1667–71.

[2] Sir Stephen's private income (£.s.d.) in 1669 was as follows:

Clerkship of the Green Cloth, approx.	630	
Salary as Paymaster	400	
Annuity of £120 purchased from Sir George Hamilton, net	117	
Office of Queen's Master Cook, net	160	
Two pensions of £273 15s. 0d. p.a. each, net	542	2. 6.
Out of a pension of £1,000 p.a., net	233	
Manor of East Meon, net	180	
Manor of Bockingfield, net	95	
Miscellaneous	10	
	2,367	2. 6.

Ilchester: Accounts, Personal (box 221): cash accounts of Elizabeth Fox; ibid.: Official, Sir S. Fox, Army: day-book for 1666–70. See also above, pp. 161–3. The £233 p.a. out of a larger pension, the rest of which Fox received on behalf of a number of other individuals and paid over to them, seems to have been allowed him by the King as a reward for his services. He had been in receipt of it since 1665.

[3] See his calculations in his wife's cash-book of how certain of his domestic expenses could be met. Ilchester: Accounts, Personal (box 221): cash accounts of Elizabeth Fox.

still at this time, and probably later on as well, as careful as it had been when they had lived in near-poverty during the 1650s. Lady Fox, for instance, received a regular allowance of £50 per month from her husband, with some additional payments which raised it to £700 or £750 a year. But this was not mere pin-money, for out of it she was expected to pay the wages of seven or eight women servants (which in 1667 she reckoned would come to £65); to buy clothes for herself (reckoned at £150), and for the five children who were then living at home (£130); to meet the cost of keeping two boys at boarding-school (£120), and of her daughter's singing and dancing lessons (£37); to buy all necessaries for the family washing (£30); and to keep the household provided with linen (£39). She did not therefore have a great deal of scope for extravagance, but her personal account-book shows that she had no inclination that way. She had perhaps two mild vices. One was to stake a few pounds on a game of cards, and the other, which cost her considerably more, was drinking tea, for which she had to pay three guineas a pound as late as 1684 and 1685. But in other respects she retained the habits of thrift she had acquired when young, and she was meticulously careful of her money. She carefully recorded the details of even relatively trivial purchases:

2 petticoats for Willy—5s. od.
5 capps for my 3 boys—9s. od.
for 7 pieces of fine china viz = one pare of large dishes, 3 other dishes, 1 little basin, 1 sacer—£4. 2s. 6d.

Besides this she watched carefully to see whether any economies could be made in the aspects of the housekeeping for which she was responsible. Thus on 26 March 1672 she wrote in her book: 'Taken in six half barrills of soape for Chiswick and 2 half firkins for Whitehall at 3 pence half penny per pound. A half barrill did use to last six or 7 weeks & now I may observe whether old soap or new will goe farthest.'[1]

Sir Stephen himself applied to his own domestic affairs the same strict financial control which had enabled him to keep the exiled Court afloat. His steward was obliged to keep an extremely detailed record both of expenditure on supplies for the household, and of

---

[1] Ilchester: Accounts, Personal (box 221): cash accounts of Elizabeth Fox; ibid.: Accounts, Household (box 210): Sir S. Fox's household accounts, 1667–71; ibid.: Family (box 238, bundle 17): bills for tea and chinaware supplied to Lady Fox.

the quantities of the various items which had been drawn from stocks. Control of the cellar was particularly careful, and every month a table was compiled showing how much of each type of drink there was at the beginning, followed by a record of what had been received, and what had been consumed. If some wealthy men of the period were cheated by their servants, Fox was not among them. Nor did he allow the tradesmen to take advantage of him. With the more important ones he negotiated contracts, which were to run for at least a year at a time, and which laid down in considerable detail the prices at which goods were to be supplied. These contracts were probably modelled on similar ones used by the purchasing authorities of the royal Household, but doubtless Fox took care that the prices he agreed to pay were the most favourable which could be secured. Copies of the contracts with the butcher and the poulterer were written into the household account-books, and, although no others are to be found there, it is likely that others were made, perhaps with the suppliers of fuel and lighting materials. The butcher's contract lays down the prices not only for the main types of meat, with some allowance for seasonal alterations, but even covers such items as marrow bones, sweetbreads, and udders. Nothing was left to chance.[1]

It was important to Sir Stephen to get his supplies of food, drink, coal, wood, lights, and other household necessaries at good prices, because the cost of these things accounted for just about a third of his domestic expenditure in the late 1660s, averaging some £908 a year out of £2,800 in the period 1667-9.[2] Much the largest part of this was spent on food and drink, and this certainly reflected the fact that Fox kept a good table, though not a lavish one by the standards of the day. The diaries of both Pepys and Evelyn confirm that Fox entertained generously and often, but on a fairly small scale. Pepys indeed began to develop the habit of calling in towards mealtimes, secure in the knowledge that he would be offered hospitality. Thus on 3 February 1661 he noted: '. . . to Mr Foxes unbidd, where I have a good dinner and special company'; and on 21 September 1662, '. . . I [dined] with Mr Fox, very finely; but I see I must not make too much use of that liberty, for my honour's

[1] Ilchester: Accounts, Household (boxes 210, 211): Sir S. Fox's household accounts for the 1670s (several volumes).

[2] Ilchester: Accounts, Household (box 210): Sir S. Fox's household accounts for 1667-71.

sake only—not but that I am very well received.' Nevertheless, he continued to receive invitations and some years later, in December 1666, wrote: 'I home with Sir St. Fox to his house to dinner, and the Cofferer with us. . . . A very gent. dinner, and in great state and fashion, and excellent discourse.' On the occasion of yet another visit, in September 1668, Pepys recorded 'mighty kind usage', and again good conversation.[1] On the other hand, the scale of Fox's expenditure on 'diet' also reflected the size of his household, with so many children and servants, and a fair proportion of it must have gone towards feeding the latter. Indeed, it is probable that the cost of the servants' food was considerably greater than the cost of their very modest wages. The Chiswick servants, who did not get free meals, were allowed five shillings each per week 'board-wages' in lieu. Their board was thus reckoned to cost £13 a year each, and even if it could be supplied more cheaply to the servants who lived with the family, the likely figure would still be far greater than the wage most of them received. It is difficult to be sure exactly how many servants the Foxes kept at any one time in the 1660s, but by the early 1670s the household accounts include regular listings and there were then seven women and six or seven men at Whitehall, and a gardener and two maids at Chiswick. The wage bill for this very considerable staff, which of course does not include those who helped Sir Stephen at the Pay Office or at the Green Cloth, was only £134 in 1673, to which must be added £39 for the board-wages of the three at Chiswick. Only Lewis Maidwell, the house steward, and 'Madamoizelle', the French governess, were paid as much as £20 a year, and the others received considerably less. For instance, Mistress Dearing, the housekeeper, received £10 a year, 'Bess ye cookemaid' £8, William the coachman £6, James the groom £5, and the footmen and the lowest category of female domestics only £4. Some of these servants had also to be provided with liveries, but the cost of these was also very low: an average of only £18 a year is recorded as being spent in this way in the years 1667-9.[2]

In all other respects the pattern of Fox's domestic expenditure seems to confirm that at this stage he was living a life of great comfort, but one not yet aspiring to the magnificence of the truly great

---

[1] *Evelyn*, esp. vol. iv; *Pepys*, ii. 29, iii. 202, vii. 406, ix. 320.
[2] Ilchester: Accounts, Household (box 210): Sir S. Fox's household accounts for 1667-71 and 1671-3.

figures of the Restoration Court. He kept a coach and four horses, but that seems to have been the full extent of his stable, the running costs of which averaged only £92 a year (excluding wages) in the late 1660s. He himself frequently travelled by hired coach or by sedan-chair, Lady Fox usually by chair. His personal expenditure averaged £357 a year, but this too is not very much when it is considered that it included his clothes, a good deal of expenditure on the children, and much casual and spontaneous charity. Nor was he laying out large sums on furniture or works of art. Indeed, in 1667 and 1668 there was almost nothing spent on such items, although in 1669 £115. 10s. 0d. was spent on new bedding, £110. 5s. 3d. on table linen, and £22. 16s. 0d on 'cabbinetts'. Presumably both the Whitehall and the Chiswick houses had been fully furnished before 1667 and their further embellishment was as yet felt to be unnecessary.[1]

During the early years of the 1670s Fox's domestic expenditure rose markedly, the average of 1674 and 1675 being £4,241. Thereafter, the upward movement of his outlays continued, but more slowly, so that they averaged £4,835 a year between 1682 and 1688.[2] This steady increase coincided with Sir Stephen's acquisition of a large landed estate, and it looks as though it was only when a substantial part of his profits from government finance was securely invested, and yielding an income which could be firmly relied upon, that he permitted his expenses to rise significantly above the level which his pensions and offices could support. The increase was not, as might have been supposed, a reflection of the fact that his family was beginning to grow up, for so many of the children had died in the years after 1669 that they were a lesser rather than a greater expense in this later period.[3] On the other hand, part of it was certainly due to the fact that after the eldest daughter, Elizabeth, had got married in 1673, she and her new husband, Lord Cornwallis, moved in with Sir Stephen, bringing their servants with them. They continued to live with him for many years, so that from this time onwards he was supporting two households

---

[1] Ibid.: also Ilchester: Accounts, Personal (box 221): cash accounts of Elizabeth Fox.

[2] Ilchester: Accounts, Household (boxes 210 and 213): Sir S. Fox's household accounts for 1673-6, and a summary of household accounts for 1682-8. The accounting years in these and Fox's other household accounts run from Michaelmas to Michaelmas.

[3] See below, pp. 266-7.

rather than one, and he reckoned the additional cost involved at £500 a year in the 1670s and £600 a year in the 1680s.[1] But in addition there is no doubt that Fox was beginning to live in a grander, more expensive, fashion. He was, for instance, employing more servants: by the beginning of 1676 there were seventeen or eighteen at Whitehall and five at Chiswick. He was also keeping up a much larger stable, the cost of which, including the purchase of new horses, had risen to an average of £281 a year by 1674 and 1675. By the early 1680s Fox was keeping no less than eleven horses, and besides his own coach there was also a 'charriott', and possibly other vehicles as well. The Foxes also had their own sedan-chair by this time, and a principal duty of the additional footmen on their staff was presumably to carry it. The chair cost £36, exclusive of the interior trim, in November 1674, but wheeled vehicles were more expensive. Sir Stephen paid £139. 4s. 4d. for a new coach and four horses in 1670, and £60 for a replacement, or perhaps additional, coach in 1674. In 1687, however, he paid his coach-maker no less than £450 for what must have been a truly opulent equipage! Much larger sums were also being spent on furniture and furnishing fabrics for the two houses: in 1674 and 1675 the totals under this heading were £338. 12s. 4d. and £429. 11s. 0d. respectively, and in the 1680s the average over a seven-year period was £350 a year. It is not altogether clear how these sums were made up but, judging by the inventory of the Chiswick house made towards the end of Fox's life, probably wall-hangings were a major item. A good many pieces of modern furniture and ornamentation were also purchased, and the accounts occasionally give details which enable us to visualize the interior of Fox's houses more clearly. Thus in April 1674 £26. 10s. 0d. was paid for 'a japan table, a gilded couch and chaires & a glass walnutt-tree table'. Sir Stephen, however, seems to have had little interest in art and did not spend significant amounts on paintings or antiques. The Chiswick inventory mentions landscapes and seascapes, but almost all the references to pictures in the accounts clearly concern family portraits. Lely was employed on several occasions to do Sir Stephen himself, his wife, and his children: in 1682, for instance, he was paid £42. 10s. 0d. 'for pictures'. The prices paid for the few works of a different type which were purchased do not suggest

---

[1] See below, pp. 275–8.

that they were of very great merit: thus in 1687 a 'Wisdom of Soloman' was acquired for a mere £2. 3s. 2d.[1]

An aspect of the more lavish life-style which Fox permitted himself in the 1670s and later was expenditure on building, but as might be expected of one so eminently sensible and moderate he kept within relatively narrow bounds, and he did not pour out the gigantic sums which some contemporaries spent in this way. In 1675 he spent £881. 19s. 6d. on additions or alterations to one or other of his two houses, but the accounts unfortunately do not make clear which.[2] However, his major project was the building of a completely new house at Chiswick a few years later. The old building was taken down in 1682, and a fine modern one, designed by Hugh May, Comptroller of the King's Works, was finished inside and out in just over two years at a total cost of £7,117. 4s. 3d. Evelyn makes plain that it was largely to please his wife that Sir Stephen had gone to this expense, and the diarist was distinctly critical of the architecture which he thought 'somewhat heavy & thick; & not so well understood'. He also thought that the position of the new house was poor, for it was without water, and had little land about it, being rather too close both to the main road and to a large house nearby belonging to Lord Burlington. 'But', he wrote philosophically, 'women will have their will.' Fox was able to do something about one of these criticisms for he later acquired more property in the neighbourhood, but he could do nothing about the others. Not all visitors, however, agreed with Evelyn's judgement. King William III was much struck with the house and its grounds, and he paid it what was from him a very great compliment: 'this place is perfectly fine. I could live here five days.' The author of an early eighteenth-century work on the antiquities of Middlesex also described it in favourable terms as 'a very beautiful seat . . . after the modern manner . . . large and extraordinarily well finished'. No visual record of the interior decorations seems to have survived, but they were undoubtedly sumptuous. There were paintings on the main staircase, and perhaps elsewhere, by

[1] Sir S. Fox's household accounts in Ilchester (boxes 210 and 213), doc. cit. Also Ilchester: Official, Sir S. Fox, Treasury (box 272): account-book marked 'Brullion begun ye 28 of Ober 81', estimate of domestic expenses at end; ibid.: Household (box 186): undated inventory of one of Sir S. Fox's houses (internal evidence shows that this must relate to Chiswick).

[2] Ilchester: Accounts, Household (box 210): Sir S. Fox's household accounts for 1673–6.

Verrio, who was paid £160. 5s. 0d. for his work, and Grinling Gibbons carved a number of chimney-pieces and cornices.[1] Outside the house Sir Stephen and his wife laid out an extensive garden. There had only been a single gardener at Chiswick in the old days, but by the early 1690s four men and a boy were employed, and they received such additional help from one or more 'weeders' as the season required. The plan of the garden was probably traditionally formal: there was a lawn in front of the house; a gravel walk between yew hedges; many beds planted with roses, tuberoses, and clove gillyflowers; walls covered with honeysuckle; a well-stocked orchard and fruit garden, where peaches, figs, strawberries, and raspberries were grown. In a greenhouse were probably housed the numerous orange and bay trees which were grown in tubs. Evelyn had thought the garden was too narrow, but several others who saw it commented more favourably and one, writing only five years after its establishment, described it as having been 'brought to great perfection for the time'.[2]

The new house at Chiswick thus provided Fox with a fine residence, suitable to his dignity as a Lord of the Treasury, but which was by no means ostentatious, and one whose situation made it almost a suburban rather than a country seat. However, its proximity to London meant that Fox was able to spend a good deal of time there, even though he continued to hold an exacting public office into his old age. His personal accounts for the 1680s and 1690s are very full of references to travel to and from Chiswick, and it seems that he divided his time more equally between his two houses than he had done earlier on. For instance when, in September 1697, he laid on a special entertainment for his fellow Treasury Lords, hiring a special chef and musicians for the occasion, it was at Chiswick that it was held.[3] Not until after his final

---

[1] Ilchester: Estate, Middlesex (box 162): various documents, including account-books, relating to the building of the new house; *Evelyn*, iv. 294; D. Defoe, *A Tour Through the Whole Island of Great Britain* (ed. G. D. H. Cole, 2 vols., London, 1928), ii. 13; Phillimore and Whitear, *Chiswick*, pp. 12–13. The Chiswick house was sold after Sir Stephen's death and eventually demolished in the early nineteenth century and its grounds incorporated into those of Lord Burlington's famous villa.

[2] Ilchester: Accounts, Household (box 212): Sir S. Fox's household accounts for 1693 and 1694; T. Faulkner, *The History and Antiquities of Brentford, Ealing and Chiswick* (London, 1845), p. 381.

[3] Ilchester: Accounts, Personal (box 220): accounts of Sir S. Fox's private expenses for 1681–4 and 1684–97.

retirement in 1702, however, did he at last give up living partly at Whitehall and settle permanently at Chiswick to end his days there in quiet.[1]

[1] Phillimore and Whitear, *Chiswick*, p. 13.

CHAPTER XI

The Family

I. THE HEIR APPARENT

CHILDREN MUST have played a very important part in Sir Stephen's private life, for throughout the fifty-six years from the Restoration until his death there was only one very brief period when there were none living under his roof. In the 1660s the White-hall apartments were full of his own progeny. An entry in the house steward's accounts for November 1667, 'for scourges for ye children—4d.', seems to suggest that Sir Stephen may have been a hard disciplinarian, but as one reads further through the items of expenditure this becomes increasingly difficult to believe. On 18 December 1667, 4s. 2d. was spent on 'battledores and topps etc' for the children, and on 31 January 1669 'for 4 oz of coryander comfitts—5d.' is followed by 'for 1 lb of sugar candy—1s. 4d.'. Finally comes an entry which confirms that the scourges were for use *by* the children themselves to whip up their tops, and not for use *on* the children: 'for shuttle-cocks, battledores, topps, scourges etc [at] severall times for ye children—6s. 6d.'[1] Indeed, all the evidence is that Fox was kind and indulgent, both as a father and later as a grandfather, and that his was a happy household. On one of his many visits to it Pepys referred to 'seven of the prettiest children . . . that ever I knew', and on another occasion wrote that Sir Stephen and Lady Fox's was 'a family governed so nobly and neatly as doth me good to see it'.[2] But from the end of the 1660s domestic happiness was clouded by tragedy as one child after another died. Six-year-old Neddy succumbed in October 1669, and in the following year there was an even heavier blow. The two elder boys, Stephen aged twelve and Charles aged ten and a half, set off on an expedition to Paris in the company of Fox's nephew Nicholas Fenn from which Stephen was never to return. Probably he picked up some acute infection in the strange city, for his father sadly recorded that he was buried in the Protestant burial place in the faubourg Saint Germain. Four years later Lady Fox's tenth

[1] Ilchester: Accounts, Household (box 210): Sir S. Fox's household accounts for 1667–71.   [2] *Pepys*, vii. 406, ix. 280.

and last child, also named Stephen to replace the lost heir, died after only a fortnight of life, and in 1677 smallpox took twelve-year-old James. There were then only four left, and two of those were destined to die almost as soon as they had grown up.[1]

After the death of young Stephen, Charles, born in 1659, was heir to the Fox fortune, and his father therefore took particular trouble in launching him into the adult world. In 1676, when he was seventeen, he was dispatched in the company of a tutor on a European tour which lasted two years and took him to Italy, Germany, Holland, and France.[2] Then, within months of his return, his marriage was already under consideration. Sir Stephen seems to have intended that Charles should forthwith be established as a landed gentleman on the estates he had recently purchased, while his other surviving son, William, was to be trained to follow himself in the path of financial office-holding. To fulfil this intention it was desirable that Charles's wife should be a member of, or better still heiress of, a well-established landowning family. At one moment it was rumoured that Lady Margaret Russell, daughter of the Earl of Bedford, would be the one, and it would have been a fine match indeed for the Foxes, since it was much less common for the daughter of a great aristocrat to marry the son of a self-made moneyed man than it was for an aristocrat's son to marry a moneyed man's daughter.[3] In the event the Russell match came to nothing and the bride selected was Elizabeth Carr Trollope, the only daughter and heiress of a wealthy Lincolnshire baronet, Sir William Trollope, whose uncle and guardian, Sir Robert Carr, Chancellor of the Duchy of Lancaster, was a political associate of Sir Stephen's at that time, a fact which may have had something to do with the choice. Elizabeth's portion was £6,000, which was supposed to be paid over to Sir Stephen in return for the estates which he settled on the young couple, although in the event part of the money was apparently never paid owing to default on the part of Sir Robert in his capacity as trustee for his niece.[4] Moreover,

[1] Ilchester: Official, Sir S. Fox, Royal Service (box 267): account-book of official and Secret Service payments, 1660–5, at end; ibid.: Accounts, Household (box 210): Sir S. Fox's household accounts for 1667–71.

[2] Ilchester: Family (box 236, bundle 6): letters from Charles Fox and Mr. Younger to Sir S. Fox; ibid.: Official, Sir S. Fox, Army: ledger for 1672–9, f. 355.

[3] H.M.C., *Seventh Report*, Appendix, p. 472.

[4] This fact emerges only from a reference in Sir Stephen's will of 1700. Ilchester: Family (box 237).

since both her parents were already dead she also brought with her a considerable landed property in and around Bourne and Witham-on-the-Hill on the edge of the Fens, and further east towards the Wash in the Fenland parishes of Weston and Whaplode.[1] Altogether these lands yielded a yearly income of something over £650, but there was also the prospect that Elizabeth would one day inherit even larger properties through her mother, although in 1679 when Charles married her these still belonged to Sir Robert and they did not become hers until the latter's death, and that of his unmarried son, in 1683. The Carr estate had been considerably reduced in size by sales over the preceding half-century, but it still extended over a wide sweep of Lincolnshire countryside, including the town of Sleaford and lands in numerous Fenland townships around about it. The rents amounted to about £600 a year in 1685, but most of the holdings seem to have been let on beneficial leases and the real value of the estates was a great deal more, probably between £1,500 and £2,000 yearly. As a result of a complicated series of family settlements, trusts, lawsuits and so on, culminating in a private Act of Parliament to sort things out, Elizabeth was due to inherit a half-share of this (one-third of the share to be hers in fee simple, two-thirds for life only).[2] Charles Fox thus acquired a considerable landed property by his marriage, and he was further endowed with lands by the settlement his father made on him and his issue by Elizabeth. Under the terms of this he was to have the large estate at Water Eaton, worth about £1,140 a year, and later, after Sir Stephen's death, he would inherit all the remaining Wiltshire properties, the whole Somerset estate, and all the fee farm rents. Together his wife's inheritance and his father's settlement ensured Charles Fox a landed income of about £1,790 a year immediately, with the expectation that this would (when allowance was made for renewal fines on leases as well as rents) increase to well over £2,500 a year when the Carr inheritance came up, and the ultimate prospect that after Sir Stephen's death he or his heirs would have more than as much again.[3]

[1] Ilchester: Deeds, Lincolnshire (box 69): rental of Lincs. estate for 1689.

[2] Ibid.: copy of private Act of Parliament of 16–17 Car. 11, briefs for counsel in the cases of Vaughan v. Burslem, and Scroope v. Burslem, articles of agreement, 24 July 1694, and particulars of Sir Robert Carr's estate, 1685.

[3] Ilchester: General Deeds, Somerset and Wiltshire (box 149): marriage settlement, 27–28 June 1679; ibid.: Deeds, Somerset (box 306): revocation,

Sir Stephen had sent Charles on the Grand Tour, found him a wife, and provided him with an estate. All that remained, before he could be considered well and truly launched into the world as an independent country gentleman, was a seat in the House of Commons. In the climate of hostility towards candidates associated with the Court which prevailed in 1679 Fox was unable to secure his election at Cricklade, but his son-in-law Lord Cornwallis had a powerful interest at Eye in Suffolk, and was prepared to put it at Charles's disposal. Charles stood for election in August and was duly elected, although still only nineteen. Indeed, from that date onwards he sat in almost every Parliament until his death, although he never took a very active part in the proceedings of the House, because, according to one contemporary, 'his modesty made him backward in attempting set speeches'.[1] However, despite all these preparations, Charles never did live the life of a country landowner. He never took up permanent residence on any of his estates, never built himself a country house, or attempted to consolidate and extend his properties. This may have been partly because his own inclinations did not really lie that way, and the fact that his wife never had any children removed one potentially powerful incentive for settling in the countryside. But a further factor was that two unexpected deaths upset the plans that Sir Stephen had laid for his family. When the latter had resigned the Paymastership at the end of 1679 he ensured that the place should be kept in the family by nominating as replacements his nephew Nicholas Johnson, who had long worked in the office, and Charles's younger brother William, not yet eighteen.[2] However, William died only a few months later, and then after two years as sole Paymaster Johnson also died, in April 1682. At this point, rather than drawing in another of his nephews, Sir Stephen decided to keep as close a hold as possible on his old place and installed Charles,[3] who after all found himself destined to a career of financial office-holding, and perhaps for that reason spent much of his married life living under his father's roof.

---

15 Jan. 1704. For the value of the properties settled on Charles by his father, see above, pp. 166–8, 195.

[1] *Members of Parliament*, i. 544, and references cited in note 1, p. 274; Anon., *Memoirs of Sir Stephen Fox*, p. 77.

[2] See above, p. 127.

[3] *C.T.B.* vii (1681–5), p. 458.

In all Charles held office three times. He was his father's stand-in at the English Pay Office from 1682 until late 1685, when he was dismissed by James II because both he and Sir Stephen voted in Parliament against the Court on the crucial question of whether supplies should be granted before grievances had been redressed. He was Joint-Paymaster of the Forces in Ireland from 1690 to 1698, responsible for the English end of the business whilst Thomas Coningsby managed affairs in the field, an appointment which we have noted was made in order to induce Sir Stephen to return to the Treasury Board, and to enlist his financial support for William III's efforts to subdue his Irish dominions. Once again his eventual dismissal seems to have been connected, albeit perhaps less directly than in 1685, with his and his father's behaviour in Parliament, for he actively opposed the government's Act of Attainder against Sir John Fenwick, whilst Sir Stephen avoided having to support it by staying away from the House when the final vote was taken.[1] Then, at the beginning of Anne's reign, Charles was made Joint-Pay-master of the English forces operating on the Continent. This he unquestionably owed to his father's old friend and colleague Godolphin, and it probably represented payment by the Crown of such debt of gratitude as it felt it owed to Sir Stephen for his long service as a Treasury Commissioner. Charles remained as Pay-master from 1702 to 1705, and then was for a third time removed for voting against the Court on a major issue. In this instance the issue was 'Occasional Conformity', the practice whereby Non-conformists could escape the operation of the Test Act, which would otherwise bar them from office, by taking the Anglican communion just once in a while. Charles was a High Church Tory, much more a man of party than his father, and the staunch Angli-canism which had led him to oppose James's attempts to get parliamentary grants for an army partly officered by Catholics, also led him to support the attempt to 'tack' to the Land Tax bill a clause outlawing the practice.[2]

On none of the three occasions when Charles was Paymaster does

---

[1] See above, pp. 225–6. Also B.L., Add. MS. 51324, ff. 57–62: autobiographical narrative endorsed 'Recollections relateing to my self . . .', and statement of grievances without date, heading, or endorsement; Add. MS. 51335, ff. 50, 53: petitions of Charles Fox to the King, and to the Queen; C.T.B. xiii (1697–8), p. 397, xiv (1698–9), pp. 2, 109, 114.

[2] B.L., Add. MS. 51324, f. 59: autobiographical narrative endorsed 'Recollections relateing to my self . . .'; C.T.B. xx, part ii (1705–6), p. 236.

he seem to have been much more than a figure-head, under whose authority the complicated business of paying the forces was carried on, but who did relatively little of the work himself. In the early 1680s he was an inexperienced novice, and indeed during his tenure of the place spent many months travelling abroad,[1] and there is no doubt that he left almost everything to the well-seasoned staff bequeathed to him by Sir Stephen. In the 1690s he came to rely very heavily on Edward Pauncefoot, who had been a relatively menial servant in charge of his stables, became his man of business, then his official deputy, and eventually indeed his creditor. Pauncefoot combined the post of Deputy-Paymaster with that of agent to several regiments, and in that capacity he was so assiduous in enriching himself at the expense of the officers and men that it was he, together with his brother, who was singled out for attention when the Commons investigated the corrupt practices of the army agents in 1695. He was subsequently employed by Ranelagh as his deputy in the English Pay Office and, after the latter's dismissal, again acted in the same capacity for Charles Fox, having by this time been elected Member of Parliament for Malmesbury and accumulated considerable wealth. Eventually he became Cashier of the Excise, a post which required possession of, or access to, very large sums of money. Charles, it was later asserted, 'did greatly intrust & rely upon ye sd Edw. Pauncefoot in ye management of ye said offices', so much so that 'Mr. Fox . . . took only his salary & left all the managemt of the money & other profits of the office out of which very great estates . . . have been raised, wholly to . . . Pauncefoot. . . for his own sole benefit without account.' It was even said, apparently with considerable justification and with reference to the 1690s as well as to 1702–5, that though the Paymastership was in Charles's name it was effectively in the hands of Pauncefoot.[2] At least for the later years this does not seem to have been any exaggeration. The letter-books recording correspondence between the Pay Office and the Deputy-Paymasters abroad, in the Peninsula and the Low Countries, show conclusively that Pauncefoot was

[1] C.T.B. vii (1681–5), pp. 784, 1415.

[2] Ilchester: Family (box 235, bundle 3): two documents concerning Charles Fox's dealings with Pauncefoot, one without heading or endorsement, the other endorsed 'Heads of an answer'; ibid.: Accounts, Household (box 215): Charles Fox's stable account for 1682–3; Commons Journals, 11 (1693–7), pp. 236, 239, 283, 320; C.T.B. x (1693–6), p. 1045, and xxiv (1710), p. 304; Members of Parliament, i. 584, 591, 598, 605.

handling virtually all aspects of the business. Charles's role seems to have been restricted to 'soliciting' for funds and dealing with the Treasury in other ways, and even so the Treasury minutes show Pauncefoot attending on matters of army finance more often than Charles did, and the Treasury frequently communicated directly with him without any pretence of doing so through his nominal superior.[1] It may have been because he was glad to be relieved of most of the work that Charles allowed Pauncefoot to take advantage of the financial possibilities of the Paymastership, of which the most important by this time was the opportunity to invest privately the temporarily unemployed balances of government money held by the Office. But had he wished to, Charles could surely have found someone willing to do the work without passing over to him almost the whole profit deriving from the post. It is much more likely that in taking only his salary, £2,000 a year in the 1690s, and £1,500 a year between 1702 and 1705, Charles was following his father's example of strict financial probity, and that he did not relish making money by means of doubtful propriety.[2] It may be true that contemporaries accepted the ways employed by some Paymasters (such as Charles's immediate successor, James Brydges) to make spectacular fortunes, but they did not applaud them.

Charles did not, therefore, greatly enrich himself, by the offices he held, and indeed by the end of his life he was considerably less well off than he had been earlier on. In 1694 he disposed of his wife's interest in the Carr estate for £12,550 to John Hervey of Ickworth, whose own wife Isabella was already entitled to the other moiety of it. The first sale seems to have been made under the supervision of the Court of Chancery, and to have been necessitated by the fact that the property was encumbered by debts incurred years before by Sir Robert Carr, which had to be discharged.[3] However, in 1703 we find him selling more of his wife's lands, this time a large part of what she had inherited from her

---

[1] Ilchester: Official. Charles Fox (box 277): entry books of letters, bills of exchange, etc., relating to Holland, Portugal etc. For Pauncefoot's appearances before the Treasury, see the minutes of Treasury meetings printed in *C.T.B.*, especially volumes for 1700 onwards (e.g. xviii (1703), pp. 11, 14, 15, 22, 32, 42, 43 etc.).

[2] *C.T.B.* x (1693–6), pp. 119–20, xix (1704–5), p. 97.

[3] Ilchester: Deeds, Lincolnshire (box 69): articles of agreement dated 24 July 1694; *The Letter Books of John Hervey, first Earl of Bristol* (3 vols., Wells, 1894), i. 40; *The Diary of John Hervey, first Earl of Bristol* (Wells, 1894), p. 22.

father, for an unknown sum, which was probably about £7,000.[1] None of this capital seems to have been re-invested in real estate elsewhere, and it is not clear what happened to it, save that little remained by the time Charles died in 1713. By these later years of his life, moreover, there are indications that Charles's finances were becoming distinctly unhealthy, though it would be too much to say that he was in difficulties. He was borrowing money, and some time before 1710 he made an unsuccessful attempt to sell what was left of his wife's property in Lincolnshire. Perhaps because he failed to find a buyer he also resorted to further borrowing: £1,000 on the security of jewels in 1708, and in 1712 £5,000 on a mortgage of one of the estates conveyed to him by Sir Stephen, probably in order to consolidate earlier borrowings. By the time he died Charles owed his principal creditor, who was Edward Pauncefoot, some £7,190, and he had £8,000 of other debts. His assets, including the unsold part of the Lincolnshire estate, were enough to cover these, but they were not enough to pay the £5,900 of legacies which he bequeathed to friends and relatives, so that his father, who survived him by three years, had to pay about half of them.[2]

A document drawn up in connection with Charles's affairs shortly after his death tells us that 'ye said Cha. Fox's expenses exceeding his income his estate was gradually impaired'. But it does not tell how it came about that he overspent. Charles and his wife had no children. They did not build themselves an expensive house in either the town or the country, and indeed for a long time they seem to have lived with Sir Stephen, for by 1700 the latter reckoned that 'housekeeping' for his son and daughter-in-law had cost him £6,000.[3] The reasons why Charles had to borrow money do not emerge at all clearly, but some possibilities suggest themselves. He may have spent more than he could afford on his long series of

[1] The conveyance does not survive, but the lands disappear from Charles's rent-book in 1703. Ilchester: Accounts, General Estate (box 191): estate account for Charles Fox's properties, 1699–1713.

[2] B.L., Add. MS. 51336: volume containing abstract of Charles Fox's will and statement of his debts; Add. MS. 51324, f. 218ᵛ: notes on Sir Stephen Fox's will; Ilchester: Family (box 238, bundle 23): documents endorsed 'Abstract of the estate of Charles Fox Esqr' and 'Mr. Le Bass's report'; ibid.: . . . (box 235, bundle 3): document without heading or endorsement on Charles Fox's dealings with Pauncefoot.

[3] Ilchester: . . . (box 235, bundle 3), doc. cit.; and ibid.: Family (box 237): unexecuted will of Sir Stephen Fox, 6 July 1700.

election campaigns at Cricklade and Salisbury. After 1698 he sat continuously for the latter, but he seems to have maintained the family interest at the former, probably at considerable expense. In July 1710, for instance, his agent at Cricklade assured him that 'all the chife of the inhibatance are really for yor friend and are desirous to know who yor friend is'. But he went on to remind Fox that it could not be done cheaply: 'if yor Honr do not fear yor money we do not fear the election'.[1] He also seems to have had a weakness for speculative investment. He invested £645 in the Newcastle Water Company, and even more surprisingly became involved in overseas commerce. An account of money owed to him at the time of his death include two items which reveal that at one time he had been dabbling in the East India trade: £200 lent to a Captain Gifford in 1694 'to accot for at his return from India', and £60 advanced to Captain Hammond and 'sent as an adventure to the East Indies in 1698'. These particular ventures had clearly been unsuccessful, but the scale of investment had been small. Considerably larger was Charles's involvement in the Portugal trade, for in 1713 some £8,286 was owing to him from various merchant houses in London and Lisbon, much of which was probably in the form of bad debts. It is probable that his concern with this branch of commerce arose out of the fact that large sums of money were being remitted to Lisbon in his name to finance the English army sent out in 1704, although no details of his dealings emerge save that cloth was being exported. It is difficult to believe that he himself had the necessary knowledge or experience to make a success of it, and he must surely have had a partner or agent. His associate may not have been well chosen, for there is at least some evidence to suggest that he was rather gullible, and had experienced other losses through trusting the wrong people. Thus the biggest amount owed to him when he died was £2,400, which he had advanced to provide the necessary security for a customs post for John Kent, a relative by marriage, who had never repaid the money.[2] Further evidence comes in a letter written to him by his wife in October 1703, shortly before she died:

[1] *Members of Parliament*, i. 584, 591, 598, 605, ii. 6, 15, 25, 34; Ilchester: Family (box 238, bundle 11): R. Painter to Charles Fox, Cricklade, 22 July 1710, and also Painter to Fox, 15 July 1710, and W. Davis to Fox, 30 Sept. 1710.

[2] Ilchester: Family (box 238, bundle 23): documents endorsed 'Abstract of the estate of Charles Fox Esqr' and 'Accot of the Lisbon trade due to the estate of Charles Fox Esq.'

I feel my self so visibly every day decay that I am sure it is impossible I can last long. . . . I pray God to bless you in every thing, health of body and easiness of mind; and now once take my advise, be govern'd by no body, your temper is not fitt to have to do with designing people, that have something else at the bottom than what appears uppermost, and such you have generally most heard.[1]

To what, and to whom, she was referring must, however, remain obscure, and so, in the last analysis, do the causes of Charles's financial problems.

II. ELIZABETH AND THE CORNWALLISES

Sir Stephen Fox and his wife must have suffered much from seeing so many of their children die at a pathetically early age, but they did have rather better fortune with their daughters than with their sons, for two out of their three girls reached adulthood, whereas out of seven boys only the same number survived so long. The eldest daughter, Elizabeth, was their first child and had been born at Breda in 1656.[2] By the time that she was growing up, Sir Stephen was already well known as a man of great wealth, and the question of her marriage must have excited a good deal of speculation in Court circles. It was a sign of Fox's rapid social advancement, and of his integration into the ranks of the governing class, that he was able to secure a peer of the realm for a son-in-law in the person of Charles, third Baron Cornwallis. The Cornwallis peerage was, it is true, a recent one, but as a landowning family they were very well established. They also had a long tradition of Court service, which had been carried on in the time of Charles I by Sir Frederick Cornwallis, who fought for the King in the 1640s and spent the Interregnum in exile. At the Restoration he was rewarded for his loyalty with a barony and the lucrative post of Treasurer of the Royal Household, but died in 1661. His son and heir, Charles, second Lord Cornwallis, had shared his father's exile and he too received the rewards of the courtier: the Order of the Bath, and appointment as a Gentleman of the Privy Chamber and Surveyor of the Customs. The second Baron died in April 1673 and was succeeded in his title and estates by his eighteen-year-old son,

---

[1] B.L., Add. MS. 51335, f. 55: letter from Elizabeth Carr Fox to Charles Fox, 21 Oct. 1703.

[2] Ilchester: Official, Sir S. Fox, Royal Service (box 267): account-book of exile and Secret Service payments 1660–5, at end.

another Charles, as third Lord Cornwallis, and it was he who married Elizabeth Fox in the December of that year.[1]

One is hardly being cynical if one assumes that the size of Elizabeth's portion was the main factor in bringing Cornwallis to the match, and Sir Stephen himself had no illusions on that score. The Cornwallises seem to have been one of those actively royalist families who weathered the storm of the Civil War and its aftermath without suffering any serious diminution of wealth, but who contracted a burden of debt which proved extremely difficult to get rid of. While the second Lord was alive the family finances were probably fairly sound because he was receiving a considerable income from his posts at Court and in the Customs, but when this was lost at his death the prospects did not look so promising for his heir. The third Lord had a gross income from land of about £3,500 per annum at this stage, but his net income must have been substantially less and his debts apparently amounted to about £20,000, on which the interest alone would have been at least £1,000 a year.[2] So he needed, if not to marry for money, at least to marry someone who had money, and he might hope to do best in this way by marrying the daughter of someone whose wealth was newly made. The well-established landowning family might be able to provide a sufficiently large cash portion, but they would possibly be less ready to ally themselves with the debt-ridden Cornwallises, and if they were they should be likely to insist on a higher ratio of jointure to portion than would a new man who was keen to acquire the social prestige of an aristocratic connection. The characteristic marriage contracted by a peer looking for a fresh injection of wealth into his coffers, was with the daughter of a London alderman, but the Cornwallises and their connections tended to move in Court rather than in City circles and so it was that the third Lord's aunt, Lady Grimston, made the approach to Sir Stephen on her nephew's behalf.[3] Her negotiations were successful, and Fox agreed to provide his daughter with a portion of

[1] For the Cornwallis family see *Complete Peerage* and *D.N.B.* Also A. Simpson, *The Wealth of the Gentry* (Cambridge, 1961), chapter iv.

[2] The figure for the Cornwallis rental is arrived at by estimating the likely product at this date of estates whose yield is definitely known for the beginning of the eighteenth century: see reference cited under note 3, p. 287. The figure for his debts is given by Fox in a document entitled 'A state of the late Lord Cornwallis's circumstances'. Ilchester: Family (box 236, bundle 10).

[3] Ilchester: Family (box 237, bundle 3): booklet headed 'The case of my Ld Cornwallis . . .'

£12,000, which was clearly to go towards the reduction of his Lordship's debts.[1]

Sir Stephen had made a socially brilliant match for his eldest daughter, but his new son-in-law seems to have had some of the worst failings of aristocratic young men of that period. According to Anthony Hamilton, Cornwallis was an extravagant spendthrift who loved gambling and was ready to lose as much as anyone would trust him for, and who frequently had to go to the disapproving Sir Stephen for money to pay the debts thus incurred.[2] He was also given to drinking bouts with his cronies, and after one of these an accident happened which led to his prosecution, before his fellow peers, as an accessory to a murder which, it was alleged, his companion, Lord Gerard's son, had committed.[3] He was acquitted, but the shock of finding himself on trial for his life apparently led him to mend his ways, an intention he certainly expressed from the dock, for after this we hear no more of his faults for a considerable period. Perhaps also the fact of living in his father-in-law's household began at last to have a sobering effect on him, for throughout their married life Elizabeth and her husband lived under Sir Stephen's roof. This arrangement was not because they had nowhere else to live: Cornwallis had two houses on his Suffolk estates, Brome and Culford, the first of which his father had reno-vated at some cost. It seems to have been originally agreed on because the couple were so very young, and to have been continued as an economy measure to last until all Cornwallis's debts had been paid off. At any rate they moved in with Sir Stephen immediately after the wedding, bringing five servants with them, and they lived free of charge, so that Fox reckoned that their 'entertainment' cost him £500 per annum in the years down to the death of his daughter in February 1681. By that time there had been four children born, all boys. Fox paid for the confinements; he paid for the christen-ings; and he paid for the burial (in the Close at Westminster) of the two who died in infancy. Nor, after Elizabeth too was dead, did he cease to support her family. Cornwallis himself, with his two surviving sons, and his servants, continued to live with Sir Stephen

---

[1] B.L., Add. MS. 51325: note-book summarizing financial help given by Fox to his sons-in-law, f. 5.

[2] A. Hamilton, *Memoirs of the Count de Grammont* (London, 1906), pp. 222–3.

[3] *A Complete Collection of State Trials* (London, 1730 edn.), ii. 721–6; Ilchester: Family (box 238, bundle 10): copies of Cornwallis's evidence, with counsel's comments; Thompson, *Hatton Correspondence*, i. 127–8, 134–6.

for seven years more, until May 1688, at a cost which the latter reckoned to have been at least £600 per annum. The two boys were virtually adopted by their grandfather, who brought them up with his youngest daughter Jane, and educated them as though they had been his own sons. The younger one, John, lived a short life, one of unfulfilled promise as was so common in those days when death was such a frequent visitor to every family. As Sir Stephen put it, he was 'bred up at Oxford to the civil law until 19, and then buried at Brome'. Charles, the elder son, survived and eventually succeeded to the title, but while his father was alive, he followed a military career which was likewise financed by Sir Stephen. Altogether Sir Stephen recorded that the support of his daughter, son-in-law, and their children over this period cost him £15,500, over and above gifts of jewels and furniture worth £2,100 and the original marriage portion of £12,000.[1]

So for a long period Cornwallis was relieved of virtually all household and family expenses, and the bulk of his income could be applied to the discharge of the £8,000 of debts which still remained after Elizabeth's marriage portion had been used to pay off the others.[2] This operation, and the general management of the Cornwallis property, was certainly carried on under Sir Stephen's detailed supervision. One of the two mansion houses, Culford, was leased out for rent to the Duke of York, and a determined effort was made to improve the yield of the rest of the estate. The gross yield in the late 1680s was about £4,760 a year, and under Sir Stephen's guidance Cornwallis was aiming to raise it to a round £5,000. The lands at Brome were apparently in fine condition: there were extensive and valuable woods, containing thousands of pounds worth of timber; the park contained a large dairy herd, and there were two flocks of sheep containing between them 3,000 animals which presumably grazed on the rough Breckland pastures of the district.[3] As a result of Cornwallis's period of free residence with Fox, therefore, his debts had been much reduced, his financial

[1] B.L., Add. MS. 51325: note-book summarizing financial help given by Fox to his sons-in-law, ff. 5–9; Ilchester: Family, Sir S. Fox (box 237): small volume with purple cover, ff. 17–21. Some details of Charles Cornwallis's military career are recorded in Ilchester: Family (box 238, bundle 21): document entitled 'Coppy of a memoriall sent to Mr. Hill'.

[2] H.M.C., *Ninth Report*, Part ii (Appendix), pp. 37–8.

[3] Ilchester: Family (box 236, bundle 10): 'A state of the late Lord Cornwallis's circumstances . . .'

health had been greatly improved, and a few years more of economy and improvement would have seen it completely restored. In the event, however, the gradual recovery of Lord Cornwallis's fortunes was cut short by his second marriage in 1688 to the Duchess of Buccleuch. She was the thirty-six-year-old widow of the ill-fated Duke of Monmouth and, in that she was an extremely wealthy heiress, Cornwallis could be said to have made himself a very good match. His wife had an estate in Scotland yielding £5,000 a year and a royal pension worth another £4,000 a year, but of course none of this would go to Cornwallis's children by his first wife. So although this marriage enabled Cornwallis to begin living on an altogether different scale, it would not mean any improvement in the long-term prospects of his family, unless the Duchess were ready to allow some of her income to be used to pay off his debts. In fact no such thing was done, and indeed the prospects of his heirs rapidly deteriorated as, under the influence of his new wife, Cornwallis reverted to his early tendencies to extravagance.[1]

Her wealth apart, the Duchess was not really a very suitable wife for Lord Cornwallis. Fox himself certainly did not approve, and the pair must have known it, for they did not tell him about their engagement until two days before the wedding ceremony.[2] He already knew the Duchess well, for their acquaintance went back nearly a quarter of a century, and at regular intervals during that period he had, originally at the King's request, spent a good deal of time and effort straightening out her finances, and those of her late husband, which seemed to be continually sliding into chaos. He liked her too, doubtless for her well-known vivacity, wit, and intelligence. But he knew that she was recklessly extravagant, quite incompetent at managing her affairs, and that she had a generally unstable personality given to bouts of penitence and despair, and to rages when she brooked no opposition to her will. He can have had no doubts that her influence on Lord Cornwallis was likely to be unfortunate.[3]

---

[1] The Duchess held the Buccleuch title in her own right. W. Fraser, *The Scotts of Buccleuch* (2 vols., Edinburgh, 1878), i. chapter 17. For her income at this time see B.L., Add. MS. 51326, ff. 24–8: volume marked 'A narrative of facts betwixt Sir Stephen Fox and the Duchess of Bucclugh', and Add. MS. 51327A.

[2] Ilchester: 'A state of the late Lord Cornwallis's circumstances . . .', doc. cit.

[3] B.L., Add. MS. 51326, ff. 24–8, 35–6, and 51327A, *passim*. All these documents are narratives by Fox of his dealings with the Duchess since he first met her in 1665. Both Evelyn, and later, when the Duchess was considerably older, Lady

The immediate result of Cornwallis's marriage was that all economy measures were thrown to the winds. In order to make Brome Hall fit for a Duchess to live in, new buildings were started, and the park enlarged at the expense of rent-yielding farm land. Then the Duchess decided that she liked Cornwallis's other seat, Culford, so the letting agreement which had brought in £200 a year was ended, and the house left empty, whilst the couple amused themselves with landscaping the gardens. This, however, was only a beginning. Cornwallis and his Duchess proceeded to celebrate their union with an exorbitant spending spree, for soon after the Revolution when Sir Stephen examined their financial situation he found that they were already in debt to the tune of £30,000. At this juncture he suggested a scheme whereby the couple should confine their outgoings to the still princely figure of £8,000 a year, leaving £5,000 or more out of their combined income of £13,000 for the discharge of debts and to provide portions for any children that they might have. Although this was all 'much to their liking', they did not succeed in holding themselves to it for long 'but contrary to this method agreed to by themselves, they ran into such wild & extravegent expences, that their accompts many years exceeded their whole income, so that their debts encreased upon them'. Cornwallis decided to try to extricate himself from his difficulties by realizing capital, and it may well have been at this stage that he felled some £6,000-worth of timber on his estates. In 1690, moreover, he concluded that some of the estates themselves should go, namely Little Bradley in Suffolk and the Norfolk properties of Waborne and Hemblingham, which together produced about £810 a year in rent. Seemingly, this was in part to pay off the debts he had had before his second marriage, rather than merely to raise cash for current expenditure, and it is true that the lands were not old hereditary Cornwallis property but had been a windfall inheritance in the recent past.[1] All the same the sales could certainly have been avoided if Cornwallis had adhered to his earlier economies, and, as a result, the estate that his heir would

---

Cowper, were struck by her personality, though in rather different ways. Their comments are quoted in *Complete Peerage* under 'Buccleuch'.

[1] They had been bequeathed to them by Dame Jane Bacon, mother of the first Lord Cornwallis. For Little Bradley see C. G. A. Clay, 'Two Families and their Estates' (Cambridge University Ph.D. thesis, 1966), p. 8, n. 6. For the other lands, Ilchester: Deeds, Norfolk (boxes 71 and 72): title deeds to Waborne and Hemblingham.

inherit would be considerably reduced in size. Fox was obviously much distressed at the courses his former son-in-law had fallen into: he saw the future prospects of his grandson being sacrificed in order that Lord Cornwallis and his Duchess could continue to indulge in their wasteful fancies, but he could not stop the sale since the lands in question had not been comprised within his daughter's marriage settlement. The only way in which he could protect the interests of future generations of Cornwallises was thus to buy the properties himself, and this he did in January 1690 for £16,000, a sum which was much more than sufficient to pay off all Lord Cornwallis's long-standing debts. Little Bradley Sir Stephen settled on his own son Charles, but intended, if Charles died without issue, as by 1690 appeared to be virtually certain, that it should then pass (as it eventually did) to Cornwallis's elder son who would, in due course, succeed to the title and the remainder of his father's estates. Waborne and Hemblingham, he envisaged, would provide for the second Cornwallis boy, John, but, as we have seen, the latter died young, and in the end he gave it to his brother as a wedding present.[1]

However, the expenditure of the newly married couple still exceeded their income and their own debts continued to accumulate apace, and by January 1694 these were 'so clamorous and uneasy' that lack of cash and credit interfered with the ceremonies at the wedding of Lord Dalkeith, the Duchess's eldest son. Sir Stephen had to make them considerable advances in the few months following, but by May things had come to a crisis: all the money that could be raised had been spent, and the tradesmen were apparently refusing to grant any further credit. The Duchess sent for Fox and showed him a letter from her steward,

. . . the substance of which was that without ready money no dinner could be provided for the family. And thereupon bursting out into tears, she told him that no case could be more miserable than her's, who besides her self, her lord, & her chiledren, had above fifty servants all

---

[1] Ilchester: Family (box 237, bundle 3): booklet headed 'The case of my Ld Cornwallis . . .'; B.L., Add. MS. 51326, ff. 24–8, and Add. MS. 51327A, doc. cit.; Ilchester: 'A State of the late Lord Cornwallis's circumstances . . .', doc. cit. The purchase deeds do not survive but are listed in two schedules of documents, B.L., Add. MS. 51331, ff. 6ᵛ–8, and 51332, f. 41ᵛ. For Sir Stephen's intentions for the manors see his unexecuted wills of 1700 and 1703 in Ilchester: Family (box 237), and B.L., Add. MS. 51324, ff. 167 et seq. And see below, pp. 287–8.

without bread . . . [that] she knew no way out but by his assistance . . .
& that in order to it she would submitt to live as low & near as her sad
condition should make it adviseable for her to doe.

As a result of this scene, Sir Stephen drew up another 'establishment' for the Cornwallises which fixed their joint expenditure at
£4,000 a year, and their remaining income, except for some un-
specified sum out of Lord Cornwallis's own estate which was to
go towards the maintenance of his own children and to provide
him with pocket-money, was to be applied to the reduction of
debts. That, five or so years after the previous 'establishment', Sir
Stephen had to reduce their annual budget by half suggests that
their total indebtedness must have more than doubled from the
£30,000 of 1689 to over £60,000.[1] He appreciated that they would
find this cut in their disposable income hard, but, he told the Earl
of Melville, the Duchess's brother, 'a gangreen must be cured by a
violent operation'. He went on to remark that in the trouble he
was taking over the Duches's affairs, 'I have a double sattisfaction,
for it was ever my pleasure to serve Her Grace and hers, and by
this way I hope to do it effectually for them, and at the same time
have an eye to preserving my own grandchildren, who are equally
tender to me, that they may come to their father's estate without
troublesome debts upon it. . . .'[2] Sir Stephen tried to ensure that
this time the Cornwallises did live within the income allotted to
them by having the £4,000 a year, which was derived from the
rents of the Duchess's Scottish estates, sent to him in the first
instance, and then paid over to their steward by weekly instalments,
so that neither the Duchess nor her husband could divert the money
to some end not provided for in the establishment. This scheme
was partly successful, for in the next couple of years they overspent
much less disastrously than they had been doing before, and in
1697, by which time a considerable amount of debts must have
been paid off, it was agreed that their establishment could be increased to £5,200 a year. At last Sir Stephen seems to have got the
financial affairs of his troublesome charges on to a fairly even keel,
and down to Cornwallis's death in April 1698 there were no further
crises 'and all their expenses were regularly carried on'.[3]

The death of the third Lord Cornwallis did not, however, end

[1] B.L., Add. MS. 51326, ff. 24–8, doc. cit., and Add. MS. 51327A.
[2] This letter is printed in full by Fraser, *Scotts of Buccleuch*, i. 457–8.
[3] B.L., Add. MS. 51326, ff. 24–8, doc. cit., and Add. MS. 51327A.

Fox's involvement in the affairs of the family, and indeed since the title and estates were inherited by his grandson as fourth Lord, he became more closely concerned than ever. The first consequence of his son-in-law's death was an unexpected crisis in his relationship with the Duchess of Buccleuch. Initially, the Duchess leant on him for support more heavily than ever. Sir Stephen himself tells us that he 'afforded her . . . all the consolation she was capable of, mingling his tears with hers for the common loss they had sustained, & never failing to be with her twice or thrice in a day'. Also he promised to those who undertook the funeral arrangements that he would see that their bills were duly paid, 'without which nothing could have been done, all [her] credit being at that time as dead as her lord'. As part of these arrangements, Sir Stephen, according to the custom of the period, had Lord Cornwallis's coat of arms set up above his door in the form of a funeral escutcheon, the achievement being the arms of Cornwallis crossed with those of both his wives, Elizabeth Fox and the Duchess of Buccleuch. When the latter saw the Fox arms were included with hers she seems to have given way to previously suppressed resentment against the benefactor to whom she owed so much, but who had chided her again and again for her irresponsible extravagance, and whose conduct and values were so different from her own. Without saying anything to him about the offending escutcheon, she

grew so far enraged (when grief, one would have thought, should have been prevailing passion) that she sent in the night for the persons who had set it up, and caused it immediately to be torne down and the arms of the first lady to be rased out, & set it up again without her arms; and all this was done with a command so violent, and with such words in contempt of the present Lord Cornwallis's mother, that the persons concerned durst not scruple to obey her.

This was a most wounding insult to Sir Stephen, who clearly held the memory of his daughter Elizabeth very dear, and he was profoundly hurt. He wrote that the incident 'gave me a deeper stroake of trouble than I thought I was capable off . . . that this way should be so suddenly found out to spurne away in a moment a friendship that had lasted above 30 years. . . .' Up to this point his relationship with the Duchess had been 'a friendly contest of civility', but now perhaps because she realized that she had done the unforgivable, she broke with him completely. Not only did she make

no effort to apologize, but she added injury to insult by intervening to stop her agents from paying Sir Stephen another penny out
of her revenues. Her action was taken despite the fact that he had
provided all the money needed for the funeral, in addition to his
regular advances of the Cornwallises' weekly allowance; and altogether she owed him £1,500. Whether or not Fox ever got this
money back is unclear, but certainly his friendship with the
Duchess was gone for good.[1]

The incident which gave rise to this quarrel was so closely
associated with the rank, standing, and family origin of the parties
involved, that it is highly revealing of their social attitudes. On the
one side there was the grand aristocrat, heiress of a distinguished
Scottish noble house, formerly indeed allied by marriage to the
royal family itself, enormously wealthy yet always pinched for
ready cash and chronically in debt. On the other side there was Sir
Stephen, *nouveau riche* if anyone ever was, a man who had begun
near the bottom of the ladder yet who had risen to distinction and
wealth even greater than that of the Duchess. It was bad enough
for the Duchess to find herself relying on this parvenu for her
weekly subsistence, but it was intolerable for her to see his armorial
bearings on top of her own on her late husband's achievement. Her
outburst surely tells us something of how the established ruling
class felt about the rise of vastly rich 'new men' in this period, even
when they were as almost universally liked and respected as was
Sir Stephen Fox. Fox himself seems to have been almost as deeply
puzzled as he was hurt by the whole affair. He referred to it as 'a
contrivance . . . to break all manner of friendship & correspondence between Her Grace & her steady, obliging, old friend, who
had never fail'd her in her frequent difficulties & extremities',
adding that whether the Duchess's behaviour was more a matter
of malice, avarice, or scorn he could not tell.[2]

The quarrel with the Duchess had, however, another and quite
different dimension. She was now a hostile party, and her unhelpful
attitude towards the affairs of her dead husband's family considerably increased the difficulties his son and Sir Stephen experienced
in sorting them out. For from the moment that his father died, the

---

[1] Ibid. Also Ilchester: Family (box 236, bundle 7): memorandum of Fox's
relations with the Duchess.
[2] Ilchester: Family (box 238, bundle 21): undated memorial by Fox about the
Duchess.

new Lord Cornwallis was in deep financial embarrassment, largely as a result of his father's immoderate and short-sighted behaviour in his last years. He inherited an estate whose rental had been seriously reduced by the sale of Little Bradley, Waborne, and Hemblingham; whose outgoings had been increased by the house-building and landscaping projects undertaken to please the Duchess; and whose capital reserves had been exhausted by extensive sales of timber. The gross income from the Cornwallis lands must have been about £4,000 a year when the fourth Lord inherited them, but net income was nothing like so much. By the time Land Tax at four shillings in the pound had been paid on the whole rental, local taxes and rates paid on the lands kept in hand, the cost of repairs and administration met, and some allowance made for arrears of rent, net proceeds were down to about £2,500 a year. This income was, moreover, heavily charged with payment of annuities mostly to relatives and creditors of his father, totalling about £440 a year.[1] Out of what remained, about £2,060, the fourth Lord had to support himself, and, should he marry, his wife and children. Also out of it he had to set about discharging the mountain of debt, unmatched by any substantial liquid assets, which he had inherited from his father. The largest single item was the portion of £6,000 which the latter had bequeathed to Isabella, the surviving child of his second marriage, and which was charged on the unsettled estate at Wilton in Yorkshire. One day this sum would somehow have to be raised, and meanwhile interest on it would have to be paid. The major part of the debt, however, was comprised of sums large and small owed to a variety of people (including Sir Stephen himself), who had advanced money to the third Lord in his later years, and to tradesmen who had supplied goods and services on credit. Altogether, in June 1701, including unpaid arrears of interest up to that date, these sums amounted to £13,641, so that the total debt that the fourth Lord had inherited was nearly £20,000. A debt of this size on a net income of little more than £2,000 a year was clearly a very serious matter, especially since interest had to be paid on about two-thirds of this sum, thus absorbing about one-third of the income. Besides, many of the creditors who had already waited a number of years for their

[1] See a summary of the fourth Lord's income and outgoings for 1706 in Ilchester: Accounts, Yorkshire Estate (box 209): volume marked 'Memorandoms relateing to Wilton etc. in Yorkshire'.

money were not prepared to wait much longer before taking steps to enforce payment. Clearly Cornwallis was in grave difficulties, which were increased by the fact that he had already accumulated some debts of his own, partly it would seem because his father had not been very prompt in paying him his allowance. By the time of his marriage in 1699 he himself owed a further £2,500.[1]

Fox kept a close watch on his grandson's affairs, and was concerned that both the honour and the solvency of the Cornwallis family should be saved,[2] but he was not prepared simply to pay off all his debts and leave him to enjoy an unencumbered inheritance. His means were not unlimited, and Elizabeth had not been his only daughter, nor was Cornwallis his only grandchild: there was also the family of his younger daughter Jane.[3] And although it seemed fairly certain that his son Charles would leave no children, Sir Stephen wished to leave an heir of his own name and had come to regard his great-nephew Stephen as such.[4] However, short of bailing Cornwallis out completely, he gave him a great deal of help and support.

For a start Fox seems to have continued to provide Cornwallis with a home, as he had done throughout the latter's boyhood and youth, and after his marriage this arrangement was continued for several years, so that he was relieved of the cost of maintaining his own household, just as his father had been relieved a generation earlier.[5] Fox also tried to enlist the help of the Duchess of Buccleuch in paying the third Lord's debts, an attempt which was thoroughly justified since these had been jointly incurred by him and the Duchess, and indeed some, though standing in his name, had in reality been incurred wholly for her benefit. The Duchess, however, having quarrelled with Fox, was in no mood to co-operate and washed her hands completely of any responsibility for the affairs of the Cornwallis family. She refused to act as her late husband's executor, although named as such in his will; she refused to pay any of his debts with her own money; and when Sir Stephen

---

[1] P.R.O., Prob. 11/448, f. 260: will of third Lord Cornwallis. Schedules of debts of third and fourth Lords in 'Memorandoms relateing to Wilton etc. . . .', doc. cit.; Ilchester: Deeds, Somerset (box 74, bundle 3): Lord Cornwallis to Sir Stephen Fox, 8 May 1704.

[2] Ilchester: 'A state of the late Lord Cornwallis's circumstances . . .', doc. cit.

[3] See below, pp. 294–302.

[4] See the unexecuted will made by Fox in November 1703. B.L., Add. MS. 51324, f. 172.

[5] Ilchester: Family (box 237): small volume with purple cover, f. 19.

came up with a scheme whereby she could have helped her stepson, whilst reaping considerable advantages for her own children, she would have nothing to do with it. Fox's plan was that she should assign £2,000 a year of her income from royal pensions for the discharge of her late husband's debts, in return for which the same amount of pension would be continued for twenty-one years after her death. Sir Stephen's influence in high places was sufficient to secure the King's consent to the second part of this scheme, but in view of the Duchess's hostility his success in this respect was wasted.[1]

Better success attended Sir Stephen's efforts in respect of Cornwallis's marriage, for he was able to provide his grandson, from within his own circle of connections, a well-endowed yet unquestionably aristocratic bride, and thus provide a measure of relief to his hard-pressed finances. This bride was Lady Charlotte Butler, the only surviving child and heiress of Richard Earl of Aran. The Butlers were one of the greatest of Irish families, and Fox's acquaintanceship with them stretched back nearly half a century to the days of exile which their then head, the Marquess of Ormonde, had shared. After the Restoration, Fox had become not only a man of business and creditor, but also friend, to the Marquess, who was created Duke of Ormonde in 1661, and to his sons the Earls of Ossory and Aran. Since the first Duke's death in 1688 Fox had become even more deeply implicated, as both creditor and financial ally, in the tangled financial affairs of the grandson who had succeeded as second Duke. Sir Stephen was thus very well placed to bring about a match between Lady Charlotte who, as Aran's daughter, was a first cousin of the second Duke, and his own grandson.[2]

Cornwallis married Charlotte in 1699 and Sir Stephen celebrated the event by settling on his grandson the estate at Waborne and Hemblingham in Norfolk which he had purchased from the third Lord some ten years earlier.[3] This meant an addition of £350

---

[1] Ilchester: 'A state of the late Lord Cornwallis's circumstances . . .', doc. cit.; B.L., Add. MS. 51326, ff. 37–8, 41: 'A memoriall given by my Lord Chancellor Somers to his Majtie . . .', and copy of letter from Fox to the Duchess of Buccleuch, 4 Aug. 1710.

[2] *Complete Peerage*, under 'Ormonde' and 'Aran'; B.L., Add. MS. 51326, ff. 63–5: 'A representation of Sr Ste Fox's friendship to the Duke of Ormonde'.

[3] Ilchester: Deeds, Norfolk (box 71): settlement, 11–12 Apr. 1700. This actually provides for the estates to come to Cornwallis only after the deaths of

a year to the fourth Lord's income, and Charlotte herself brought an even larger increase. It was, however, only because of Sir Stephen's intervention that this was forthcoming at the start of their married life. The Earl of Aran had in fact died back in 1685, leaving very large debts about which nothing could apparently be done until his daughter came of age, which was not until the year of her marriage. Mainly for this reason, her financial affairs were extremely complicated and closely tied up with those of the second Duke, who had inherited most of Aran's lands and now assumed responsibility for his debts. But despite these debts, Charlotte stood to inherit a large fortune: a cash portion of £12,000, together with the accumulated interest on it for the fourteen years since her father's death, which brought the total to over £21,000, less what had been spent on her upbringing over that period and a few other items. In addition she stood possessed of some real estate in the form of the Isles of Aran in Galway Bay, off the west coast of Ireland. In fact, however, these distant islands were the only part of what her father had left her which Charlotte actually enjoyed at the time of her marriage, for the lands on which her money fortune was secured were held by her mother as her jointure, and no part of it could be raised from them until after her mother's death, an event not thought to be imminent at the time of her marriage and which indeed did not occur until 1716.[1] Charlotte's wealth was thus potential rather than actual, and her ability to help her new husband out of his financial troubles would have remained slight for many years but for Sir Stephen's help. Many details of the transactions are obscure, but it is clear that Fox used his own resources to so rearrange her affairs that Cornwallis could draw the maximum immediate advantage from her inheritance instead of having to wait for his mother-in-law to die.

The most promising of the properties in which Charlotte had

both Sir Stephen and Charles Fox, but the former apparently put him in possession immediately. See reference to this effect in his unexecuted will of 1703, B.L., Add. MS. 51324, f. 169. For the rental of these lands, Ilchester: Family (box 238, bundle 25): notes on the yield of the Cornwallis estates.

[1] B.L., Add. MS. 51326, ff. 49, 69, 71, 73–8: documents relating to the debts of the Earl of Aran, and 'Lady Charlotte Butler's case . . .'; Add. MS. 51328: volume relating to the affairs of Lord Cornwallis and the Countess of Aran, *passim*; Ilchester: Deeds, Ireland (box 134): conveyance, 12 Apr. 1700, recitals in assignment of mortgage term, 12 Aug. 1717, and abstract of title to Black Castle, 23 Oct. 1716. And ibid.: Family (box 238, bundle 25): abstract of settlement, 11–12 Apr. 1700.

an interest was a large leasehold estate at Leighton in Huntingdon-shire, and it was from this that most of the money due to her would one day be raised. For the moment Leighton was held by Charlotte's mother the Dowager Countess of Aran, but the ultimate reversion to it, after the portion money and all arrears of interest had been paid, belonged to the Duke of Ormonde. Sir Stephen arranged for Cornwallis and his wife to buy out both these interests, of which the latter was worth very little because it would be so many years before the very large sum due to Charlotte could be paid off out of the rents it yielded; and to enable them to raise the price he bought from them the Isles of Aran for £8,000. Fox thus enabled his grandson to exchange an Irish estate and the expectation of £17,500 (and accruing interest) at some uncertain future date, for immediate possession of an English estate worth £1,400 a year, which increased his landed income by one-third. Leighton, how-ever, was not completely free from encumbrances: there was a debt of £3,441 charged on it, which represented loans raised by Charlotte's mother to pay for her maintenance and upbringing, and to clear this and some lesser charges, Cornwallis eventually raised £4,000 by mortgaging his own estate at Wilton in Yorkshire. On the other hand, there was a part of his wife's portion still outstand-ing. This was charged on the Black Castle estate in Ireland which, like Leighton, belonged to the Dowager Countess as long as she lived, with an ultimate reversion to Ormonde, who would have to pay the money, together with interest, before he could enjoy the inheritance. In this case Fox's solution for enabling his grandson to get what was due to his wife in advance of old Lady Aran's death was simply to put up the £3,809. 8s. od. in question himself, and take over the security as mortgagee to the Duke of Ormonde, and this he did in 1708. Neither of the two assets Sir Stephen ac-quired during the course of these transactions was a very satisfac-tory investment from his own point of view. No interest could be expected on the money sunk into the Black Castle mortgage, nor was any received, until the Dowager Countess's death, which was not until a month after that of Fox himself. As for the Isles of Aran, they lay in the most wild and remote part of a land where violent political convulsions were liable to break out at any time, were very poor, produced an uncertain income, and were exposed to attack from privateers whenever there was a war with France. Moreover, Fox had not only bought them, he had done so for the sum at which they had been valued by Charlotte's representatives before her marriage, and which he reckoned was £2,000 more than they were really worth. It is not possible to substantiate this latter claim, but there is no doubt that a few years after Fox had become their owner (in 1704) the rent paid for them had to be reduced by one-third, from £600 a year to £400 a year; that the incursions of the French in the two following years seriously affected the ability of the tenants to pay even this reduced amount; and that Fox, as landlord, had to bear considerable expense in providing some means of defence. He remained in possession of Aran throughout the war, but as soon as an opportunity arose to discard them without sustaining a heavy loss he seized it, and in 1713 succeeded in selling them for £8,200 to the Galway agent who had been responsible for their management. This good price was not, however, much compensation for the poor return he had received from the islands during the thirteen years he had owned them, especially as the adverse exchange rate between Ireland and England more than wiped out the small capital gain he had apparently made. In short, there need be no doubt that what Sir Stephen did in the matter of Charlotte's fortune, he did for his grandson's sake, and not to advance his own interests.[1]

To return to the period immediately after Cornwallis's marriage, His Lordship had, thanks to Sir Stephen, added considerably to his landed income; but he had also added to his indebtedness to the extent of the encumbrances on Leighton, and his position remained a very exposed one. He owed a great deal of money on short-term securities but had very little in the way of liquid assets out of which to pay it, and the creditors were suing him in Chancery.[2] It is true that there was no danger of foreclosure on his

---

[1] In addition to the references cited in the previous note see also Ilchester: Family (box 238, bundle 25): document entitled 'An abstract of the articles of marriage as by Mr. Foulks his calculation . . .'; ibid.: Family (box 237): booklet marked 'Cop. of the state of account . . . Duke of Ormonde and Sr Ste Fox'; ibid.: Accounts, Personal (box 221): volume entitled 'Mr. Wm. Watson of Dublin his accompt . . .'; ibid.: Deeds, Ireland (box 134): copy conveyance, 24 Dec. 1713; B.L., Add. MS. 51328: volume relating to the affairs of Lord Cornwallis and the Countess of Aran, esp. ff. 5ᵛ–6; Add. MS. 51326, ff. 120, 149: documents marked 'Totalls of what hath been received by Lord Cornwallis . . .', and 'A state of the D. of Ormond's deed . . .'; H.M.C., *Ormonde*, N.S., viii. 318–19.

[2] There are several references to these suits. See, for example, Ilchester: Family (box 237, bundle 3): narrative of Fox's dealings with the Duchess of Buccleuch.

estates, since they had been settled and were not legally liable for the payment of personal debts, but the movable property which he had inherited was so liable, and this included the large amount of livestock on the lands kept in hand in Suffolk, as well as all plate, furniture, linen, and other household goods, together worth almost £9,000. If money to this amount could not somehow be found, then the fourth Lord would have to realize it by selling, which would leave his lands unstocked (thus sharply reducing his annual income), and his houses bare and uninhabitable. Nor were things made any easier by the behaviour of his new mother-in-law, to whom various sums were due out of Charlotte's fortune. She was pressing hard for the payment of one particular bond for £900, sending her attorney along (according to Sir Stephen) no fewer than five times at a moment when 'Lord Cornwallis was in the greatest streights that he was ever in, his goods being in danger and his horses threatn'd to be seized'.[1] In the end Cornwallis seems to have been saved from losing at least part of his movable possessions by timely advances from Sir Stephen, which enabled him to pay to his father's creditors the amount at which the latter's goods had been valued. By 1704 Cornwallis owed his grandfather a total of £10,750, but by no means all the debts he had inherited had been paid, and the disappointed creditors had succeeded in persuading Chancery to rule that, since the third Lord had been entitled to raise £3,000 on mortgage out of his own estate at Wilton in Yorkshire (although he had never done so), this should be taken as part of his personal estate and so become liable to satisfy their claims. The fourth Lord thus found himself obliged to raise £3,000, with interest since a year after his father's death in 1698, out of the Wilton property.[2] He could perhaps have borrowed this money, but coming on top of his other major debts—£4,000 borrowed to clear his wife's estate; £6,000 (together with accumulated interest) for his stepsister Isabella's portion; and the large

---

[1] B.L., Add. MS. 51328: volume relating to the affairs of Lord Cornwallis and the Countess of Aran, f. 4.

[2] Ilchester: 'A state of the late Lord Cornwallis's circumstances . . .', dic. cit.; ibid.: 'Memorandoms relateing to Wilton etc. . . .' (see abstract of deeds, 10–11 July 1704), doc. cit.; ibid.: Family (box 238, bundle 25): document entitled 'Totall of what is due from Ld Cornwallis to Sr Ste Fox . . .'; ibid.: Deeds, Yorkshire (box 311): 'Mr. Aubery's Bond of Indemnity', enclosed within deed, 22 Apr. 1702; B.L., Add. MS. 51326, f. 41: Fox to the Duchess of Buccleuch (copy), 4 Aug. 1710.

advances made by Sir Stephen—it was probably what finally made him decide to sell the estate a few years later (1709).

It was not a very propitious time to try to sell, nor had it been for several years past, since land prices had dropped heavily in response to a renewed bout of agricultural depression, heavy wartime taxes, and the diversion of investment capital into government lending, also in connection with the war.[1] But in the end Cornwallis could wait no longer, and he was therefore fortunate that, as on earlier occasions when he or his father had needed to sell, Sir Stephen once again agreed to buy, thus ensuring that his grandson did not have to wait for a purchaser and that he got a respectable price. He paid £20,000 for the estate, which enabled Cornwallis to set aside £3,000, plus £1,800 of accumulated interest, as a fund for settling the remainder of his father's debts, to pay off Isabella's portion and the £4,000 mortgage, and to repay some of what he owed to his grandfather.[2] However, in this instance Fox did not, as he had done when he bought the Isles of Aran, pay more than the going rate.[3] Nor did he buy Wilton in order to restore it to its former owner at a later time, although he half apologized to Cornwallis for not doing so, referring to it as a 'noble estate', as indeed it was, being well tenanted and producing a gross income of some £1,130 a year, almost all from rack-rents. Fox then continued, 'If I had not been under vast losses by your father's second marriage it should not have gone out of your family at any rate.'[4] Whether the alleged vastness of these losses was the only reason for the terms on which Sir Stephen bought is doubtful, although certainly at this late stage in his career his resources were more limited than once they had been. Of at least equal importance was the fact that in 1703 he himself had married a second time, and that his young wife had produced several children for whom it was

[1] C. Clay, 'The Price of Freehold Land in the Later Seventeenth and Eighteenth Centuries', *Ec.H.R.*, 1974.

[2] Ilchester: Family (box 238, bundle 25): draft letter from Fox to Lord Cornwallis, 17 Mar. 1710; ibid.: 'Memorandoms relateing to Wilton etc. . . .', doc. cit.; Also Ilchester: Deeds, Yorkshire (box 311): release, 31 Dec. 1714.

[3] Fox paid rather over seventeen and a half years' purchase of the gross rental. This is in line with prices paid by other buyers for comparable estates in the years on either side of 1710: see Clay, 'The Price of Freehold Land . . .', op. cit.

[4] Ilchester: Family (box 238, bundle 25): Fox to Lord Cornwallis (draft), 17 Mar. 1710; Ilchester: 'Memorandoms relateing to Wilton etc. . . .', doc. cit. Also Ilchester: Accounts, Yorkshire Estate (box 209): account-book marked 'An accompt of Wilton estate in Cleavland York-shire'.

necessary for him to make financial provision for the future.[1] The prospect of direct male descendants, to whom he could leave the landed property he acquired, thus also influenced his decision about what to do with Wilton after he had bought it. At first he intended to sell it, although he was apparently content to wait until property prices had recovered sufficiently to avoid any possibility of loss, but in the end he did not do so and bequeathed it to the eldest of his two new sons.[2] As the little boys of his old age began to grow up, Fox recovered an interest in estate building which he had lost when it began to appear that Charles was unlikely to have any children, and the decision to keep Wilton was only one of several manifestations of this which are apparent in the last few years of his life.[3]

After the sale of Wilton the Cornwallis finances seem at last to have been on a fairly stable basis: the third Lord's debts had been provided for, and of the other debts all had been paid save for £7,400 owed to Sir Stephen.[4] When the latter died in 1716 he could have the satisfaction of knowing that his grandson was out of danger, and that his affairs were in a more prosperous condition than those of any of his ancestors had been since before the Civil War. Back in 1681 Evelyn had been premature in assuming that Fox had already 'restored that intangled family',[5] but by the end of his life he had succeeded in doing so. The final instalment of advantage that the Cornwallises derived from their Fox connection was, moreover, delayed until after Sir Stephen's death. In fact if Fox had died without marrying again Cornwallis would have been one of the principal beneficiaries in the division of his property since he would have received, besides much else, £10,000 in cash and the whole of Fox's Wiltshire estate. As it was, Fox completely recast his will when a second family began to arrive, and left the bulk of his possessions to his two young sons, Stephen and Henry; but even so he bequeathed to Cornwallis the remainder of the lands he had bought from the third Earl in 1690, that is the Suffolk

[1] See below, pp. 319, 327–9.
[2] Evidence for the intention to sell is from B.L., Add. MS. 51325: note-book summarizing financial help given by Fox to his sons-in-law (see calculations of income etc. at end of this volume). For the deed under which it passed to young Stephen Fox, see Ilchester: Deeds, Dorset and Other Counties (box 290): settlement, 25 May 1716.
[3] See below, pp. 320–1, 327–9.
[4] Ilchester: 'Memorandoms relateing to Wilton etc. . . .', doc. cit.
[5] *Evelyn*, iv. 219.

manor of Little Bradley. This was now worth about £350 a year, and thus went some way to filling the gap in the Cornwallis rent-roll caused by the sale of Wilton.[1]

It is not easy to summarize just how much financial help, not to mention advice and personal support, Sir Stephen gave the third and fourth Lords Cornwallis over a period of more than forty years. But the story which has unfolded does seem to justify the judgement that it was largely thanks to him that they were able to retain for themselves, and hand on to their descendants, the place amongst the wealthy landed aristocracy of the country which they had inherited.

III. JANE AND THE EARL OF NORTHAMPTON

Sir Stephen's only other surviving daughter, Jane, was much younger than Elizabeth. She was not born until 1669, and was still little more than a child when her elder sister died in 1681. But such was the wealth and distinction of her father that later the same year, several months before her twelfth birthday, the question of her marriage was already being discussed. It was not Sir Stephen, it should be said, who was in a hurry to find a husband for his daughter, but a portion-hungry mother who was on the look-out for a wealthy bride for her son and hoped to snap Jane up before any competition materialized. The mother was the Countess of Sunderland, whose husband, the Earl, had just been dismissed as Secretary of State and was in considerable financial embarrassment as a result of this loss of office coming on top of earlier extravagance. The Sunderland estates were heavily mortgaged and a good marriage for their seventeen-year-old son, Lord Spencer, seemed to offer the surest way to a restoration of their affairs.[2]

The Countess began by approaching John Evelyn, a mutual friend of theirs and Sir Stephen, to sound the latter out. Evelyn in fact had well-founded doubts about both the soundness of the Sunderlands' finances and the character of their son, but with some reluctance he agreed to act as intermediary. Sir Stephen professed himself flattered at the proposal, and was not unduly concerned that his daughter's portion was to be used to clear the debts

---

[1] B.L., Add. MS. 51324, ff. 167–75: unexecuted will made by Fox in Nov. 1703; Ilchester: Deeds, Somerset and Wiltshire (box 306): copy of Fox's final will, 25 May 1716. For the value of Little Bradley, see Ilchester: Accounts, General Estate (box 191): accounts of the estates of Charles Fox.

[2] Kenyon, *Sunderland*, pp. 75–7.

from the estate of her father-in-law to be. He wanted an aristocratic marriage, as Evelyn appreciated, 'both to fortfie his interests
and better his allyance', and he well knew that for a man of his
background this was only to be had at a price. However, he was
unwilling to make Jane's portion the £20,000 for which the Sunderlands were pressing, and anyway considered her much too young.
He was determined not to marry her to a man she did not like, and
did not consider that she could properly express her own preference in the matter until she was sixteen or seventeen. Evelyn did
his best for the Sunderlands, working on Fox's good nature and his
vanity, by arguing 'that he would do an act of greate generositie, &
as already he had [by marrying his eldest daughter with a vast
portion] redeem'd my Lord Cornwallis's intangled estate . . . so
it would be his glory to set up the Earl of Sunderland's family
againe'. At first Fox asked him to put Lady Sunderland off as
civilly as he could, but she persisted and several weeks of negotiations ensued. There was hard bargaining over the amount of the
portion to be paid, with the Countess half apologizing to Evelyn
for her efforts to get a larger sum, telling him that 'nesesity com-
pells us to insist on yt wch otherwise wee should wth joy have left
to ye good nature of so kind a father, for I am sure my Lord nor
I nether love to bargain, especially wth a man wee have so good an
opinion of as Sr Steven. . . .' However, she went on to suggest,
rather disreputably, that if Sir Stephen was reluctant to offer more
because of what his son Charles might think, there was no need
for Charles to know the amount paid. 'He may be sure', she wrote,
that 'nothing shall be publicke but as he shall direct.' In the end
they were able to agree on the portion, £14,000, but Sir Stephen
resolutely refused to commit Jane irrevocably until a further four
years had elapsed, and even then the marriage would not take place
unless she was agreeable. However, the Sunderlands' financial
position did not permit either the delay or the uncertainty, and
lamenting their ill luck in encountering a father so tender of his
daughter's wishes, they reluctantly decided that they would have
to look elsewhere.[1]

There is no record of any more suitors for Jane's hand for nearly
five more years, but by 1686 she was in her seventeenth year and
Sir Stephen can no longer have felt it necessary to discourage proposals. The middle-aged and corpulent Lord Feversham, certainly

[1] B.L., Add. MS. 15889, ff. 59–68; Evelyn, iv. 245–8.

no Adonis, although the nominal victor, as Lord Churchill's superior, of the battle of Sedgemoor, appears to have been interested in her; and the second Earl of Clarendon, too, had designs on her for his son. Clarendon was the son of the great Lord Chancellor, brother to Lord Treasurer Rochester, and currently held office as Lord-Lieutenant of Ireland. On the other hand he was not a wealthy man and, like Sunderland before him, an eldest son of marriageable age was his main financial asset. 'You will believe I would be very glad to have him married, and the sooner the better, whilst I am in some seeming credit', he wrote to his brother. 'I wish it might be with Sir Stephen Fox; I had rather there than any where I can think of: and methinks, if it were well proposed to him, he might think it of advantage to him.' As an additional inducement he suggested that the King might be persuaded to raise Fox to the peerage. 'The giving him a little honour might, I believe, go far, and has been as undeservedly bestowed; you can manage it better than anyone, if you approve it, and to you I leave it, not having mentioned it to anyone.'[1] In fact, Clarendon was almost certainly misinformed about Fox's interest in a peerage,[2] and despite the high positions held by the Hydes, he may well have considered that a marriage connection with them would align him too closely with one particular political faction. At any rate whether for this reason, or perhaps because Jane did not take to the young Lord Cornbury, Clarendon's overtures did not prove acceptable. Two months later, however, a marriage for her was at last arranged, with the twenty-two-year-old George Compton, fourth Earl of Northampton.

Socially this was possibly an even better match than one with the Sunderlands or the Hydes would have been. The Comptons were a medieval family who had come into great wealth as a result of royal favour in the reign of Henry VIII. They had acquired a barony in 1572 and an earldom in 1618, and had been distinguished for their loyalty to the Crown in the Civil War. Royalism had, however, cost them dear, and the losses they incurred in the 1640s, coming on top of what might otherwise have been a manageable level of debt, eventually involved George's father, the third Earl, in selling some £40,000 worth of his inherited lands, so that

---

[1] S. W. Singer, *The Correspondence of the Earls of Clarendon and Rochester* (2 vols., London, 1828), i. 304.
[2] See above, p. 246.

although the family survived this period of crisis, its wealth had been permanently reduced.[1] So financially the marriage of the fourth Earl to Jane Fox was as fine a one for the Comptons, as it was socially for Sir Stephen. The latter provided the portion of £20,000 which he had been unwilling or unable to put up five years earlier, and which was certainly a very large one for a girl who was not an heiress. It was considerably more than Jane's elder sister had been endowed with thirteen years before, which probably reflects the fact that the Earl of Northampton stood higher in the social order than did Lord Cornwallis.[2] It may also be noted that the ratio between Jane's portion and the jointure of £1,200 a year which Northampton settled on her in the marriage settlement was unusually unfavourable to Jane (sixteen and two-thirds to one, at a time when eight or ten to one was normal), and this too is surely to be accounted for by the disparity in the social standing of bridegroom and bride.[3]

Finally, what of the political implications of the marriage? In what sense did it, to use Evelyn's phrase, fortify Fox's interests? The Earl of Northampton himself was too young to be much of a political figure in his own right, but his uncle, the formidable Henry Compton, Bishop of London, with whom the marriage seems to have been actually negotiated, was very much one.[4] His political stance, moreover, was one which Fox must have warmly approved of. Bishop Compton had fought for the King in the Civil War, and after the Restoration had held a Cornet's commission in the Horse Guards before becoming ordained. More recently he had opposed the Exclusion Bill, and there could be no doubt of his devotion to the Crown and the dynasty, but his loyalty to the constitution of Church and State was as great or greater. Thus in the November of 1685 he had spoken out in the House of Lords against King James's army and its Catholic officers, and in consequence he had been removed from the Privy Council and dismissed from his post as Dean of the Chapel Royal, at the same time as Charles Fox had been dismissed as Paymaster for his vote upon the same

[1] Marquess of Northampton, *History of the Comptons* (London, 1930), chapters viii–x; H. J. Habakkuk, 'The Landowners in the Civil War', *Ec.H.R.*, 1965, pp. 131, 140 n., 144.

[2] See above, pp. 275–7.

[3] Ilchester: Family (box 223): marriage settlement, 7 May 1686; Stone, *Crisis of the Aristocracy*, pp. 642–5.

[4] Ilchester: Family (box 237): small volume with purple cover, f. 23.

issue. Bishop Compton was shortly to become even more prominent amongst those hostile to James II's policies, but he was already sufficiently so for an alliance with his young nephew to be liable to interpretation as an expression of sympathy with the constitutional opposition to the King.[1] However, whether or not Fox saw it in this light remains uncertain, and it did not deter the King from offering him a post on the Treasury Board the following year.[2]

Northampton had succeeded his father to the family estates in 1681, but he had spent most of the years between then and his marriage travelling on the Continent. He was thus not very experienced in business matters or in supervising the running of his own properties. Sir Stephen was clearly determined to ensure that his new son-in-law managed his affairs properly, and in the November after the marriage we find him going through his estate accounts and making suggestions on how they should be kept for the future. 'If yr Lopp approves of the method observed in making them up,' he wrote, 'then that way may be the rule for ye future. The abbreviating the acctt at ye end of every month is to tempt yr Lopp to looke over yr acctts often without much pains, by wch yr Lopp wilbe soone knowing in all yr expenses and therby find sattisfaction that you doe not exceed by surprise.' A few weeks later he told Northampton that, while looking at the accounts,

I tooke a little pains to informe my selfe how much yr Lopp may relye on (after all charges incident to an estate is taken out of it) to carry on ye expences of support & maintenance, and at ye end I found my selfe sufficiently recompenced for my pains because it concludes better than I could be assured it would doe, & answeres the question I so often troubled yr Lopp wth [vizt] what would be ye cleere incom after all charges were deducted. . . .

This was a question which, it would seem, Northampton had been unable to answer satisfactorily, but Sir Stephen had now established for himself that his son-in-law had £4,400 a year clear from land, plus the interest on Jane's portion money. Seven years later Sir Stephen was still keeping a close eye on the Earl's financial and estate concerns, and the latter was constantly referring to him for advice. Thus in May 1693, when Northampton had reason to doubt the honesty of his agent in Warwickshire, he wrote to Sir Stephen: 'Mr. Stocker [the agent] being now come to town, I beg

[1] Macaulay, *History*, ii. 286, 289, 347–8; also *D.N.B.*
[2] See above, p. 227.

that his account may be examined & all things settled as you shall
judge best, whether by continuing him or by employing an other.'[1]
The Earl and Countess of Northampton took up residence at
their seat of Castle Ashby in Northamptonshire, and it was there
that they brought up the large family of children that soon began
to arrive. The first was already on the way in November 1686
when Dr. Pierce, Dean of Salisbury, wrote to Sir Stephen to con-
gratulate him. 'Glad we are both yt yr daughter the Countess of
Northampton is very sick, because of a disease wch argues very
good health, and such as some Queens are wont to pray for. . . .'
Six months later a son was born, and Sir Stephen's accounts record payment of a five-shilling gratuity 'to Patrick, my Ld Northampton's futtman who brought you news of a Ld Compton'.[2]
Eventually Jane bore ten children, nine of whom were still alive
when Sir Stephen made his will in 1716. 'Nine lovely children',
their grandfather called them, and clearly he was very fond of
them.[3] He visited Castle Ashby almost every year in late summer
or early autumn, although, as we have seen, until a few years before
his final retirement from the Treasury, he could never stay for very
long. The account of his expenditure when he went up in June
1692 begins with the following items:

Toyes for ye children	6s. 6d.
Shugar plumbs	4s. 0d.
A travelling ink bottle	0s. 6d.

entries which conjure up a picture of the busy Lord of the Treasury
buying presents for his grandchildren, and then remembering that
there would be work to be done, papers to be read, and letters to
be written, even when he was taking a short holiday with his
family.[4] A year later Lord Compton was six and perhaps learning
to ride, for Sir Stephen took with him not only a pound of comfits
and eight shillings' worth of toys, but also a leading rein.
Moreover, the upbringing of one of the Compton children,

[1] Marquess of Northampton, *The Comptons*, p. 131; Castle Ashby MS. 1093,
Fox to the Earl of Northampton, esp. 9 Nov. and 18 Dec. 1686, and Northampton to Fox (draft), 30 May 1693.
[2] Ilchester: Family (box 238, bundle 22): Thomas Pierce to Fox, 27 Nov.
1686; ibid.: Accounts, Personal (box 220): account-book of Fox's private
expenses 1684–97, 2 May 1687.
[3] Ilchester: Deeds, Somerset and Wiltshire (box 306): copy of Fox's will,
25 May 1716.
[4] See above, pp. 218, 230.

George, the second son, was wholly taken over by Sir Stephen and Lady Fox, who seem in effect to have adopted him. George was born on 21 June 1691 and 'was given to his grandmother the 16 of July following and continued under her care to her death in July 1696'. So he spent his earliest years in the Fox household, filling the place left empty now that the Cornwallis grandchildren were beginning to grow up. At the age of seven George was sent off to Eton, then to Froubert's Academy, and when he was old enough there was a Cornet's commission in the Horse Guards for him. In fact joining the army did not mean the end of his education, for in August 1710, when he was still only just nineteen, he received leave to go abroad for eighteen months 'for his improvement'. During this time he attended the Military Academy at Wolfen-büttel, near Brunswick, in the company of an English tutor. Some time after his return to England in November 1713 Sir Stephen advanced his military career one step further by buying him a Guidon's commission[1] in the most aristocratic and exclusive regiment of all, the Life Guards. Fox calculated that George's upbringing and education, up to the time of his departure for Germany, had cost £1,464, besides a further £1,036 for the Cornetcy, £500 to buy him an Exchequer annuity of £70 a year, £1,500 towards the difference between the price of the Cornetcy and the Guidoncy, and miscellaneous gifts, so that altogether he spent some £4,622 on promoting his career. This was an expense which the Earl of Northampton, with so many other children, could ill have afforded.[2]

The only other of the Compton children to benefit much from Sir Stephen's bounty whilst he was alive was one of the girls, Mary, who received an addition of £2,000 to her portion when she got married in 1709, which must have made it that much easier for her parents to find her a husband of appropriate rank. The Northamptons themselves, however, received a great deal. Quite apart from her marriage portion, Sir Stephen gave Jane jewels worth £2,100 and furniture worth over £940, and to her husband he gave straightforward financial help. In 1702 he paid off a £4,000 mortgage on

[1] Guidon was a rank peculiar to the Life Guards. It enjoyed a seniority equivalent to that of Captain in other cavalry regiments.
[2] Ilchester: Accounts, Personal (box 220): account-book of Fox's private expenses 1684–97, 22 Feb. and 3 Mar. 1696; ibid.: Family (box 238, bundle 8): various documents relating to George Compton. See also sources cited in the following note.

his estates which the Earl had found it necessary to raise a few years earlier, and made him a gift of a further £3,000. At about the same time he lent him £2,000 more on which for many years he did not press for any interest to be paid, and eleven years later when George was commissioned into the Life Guards he also advanced the Earl's share of the price. In 1705 he lent Jane £1,000, a loan on which interest was forgiven in return for her agreement to pay her daughters the twenty-four guineas' worth of New Year's gifts which their grandfather had customarily given them. On top of all this, in 1709 Sir Stephen contributed over £1,000 towards repairs of one of the Earl's houses, probably Castle Ashby, and in 1713 he paid the costs of enlarging his park, an undertaking which involved rebuilding the almshouses and doubtless a substantial amount of new walling, and altogether cost a further £2,121. At some time in the early months of 1714 Sir Stephen added up everything he had given to the Compton family since 1686, including minor items like birthday presents, and found that, over and above his daughter's marriage portion and the interest he had paid out on it, the total came to £22,369. 10s. 0d., which he added 'is entirely forgiven and neither principal or interest ever to be demanded'. In addition he reckoned that the Earl owed him £4,507 of principal and accumulated arrears of interest for moneys lent, which he agreed to write down to £3,000, thus effectively making Northampton the gift of a further £1,507. In the final version of his will, made shortly before his death in 1716, Fox bequeathed the Comptons £1,600 worth of legacies, which nearly balanced the £2,260 which the Earl then still owed him.[1]

At no time in this period was the financial situation of the Compton family anything like as precarious as that of the Cornwallises. There was no question of the Earl of Northampton needing Fox's support to stave off bankruptcy, yet he and his dependants received a fairly massive transfusion of capital, in all more than twice as large as the marriage portion agreed in 1686. Clearly the help given by Sir Stephen was important in enabling the Earl to maintain the position in society to which his rank entitled him, but which the

[1] B.L., Add. MS. 51325: note-book summarizing financial help given by Fox to his sons-in-law, ff. 1–4, 9ᵛ–11; Ilchester: Family (box 237): small volume with purple cover, ff. 23–8, 31–3, and (box 235, bundle 3): 'An Acct of ye bountys etc given to the Earle of Northampton and his Lady', and document on the financial relations between Fox and Northampton, 31 Oct. 1715. Also Fox's will of 25 May 1716, doc. cit.

reduced size of the family estate after the property sales of the Civil War period, and his numerous children, would otherwise have made it difficult for him to support. Whatever Northampton may have done with the large sums he received from Fox as portion, gift, and loan, it is apparent enough that Sir Stephen contributed in an important way to the maintenance of his son-in-law's social role in two very sensitive areas: provision for his children and support of his country mansion. Sir Stephen launched one Compton into the world in a fashion befitting the younger son of an Earl, and helped to secure an appropriate marriage for one of the daughters, while Charles Fox did as much for one of the others by leaving her £1,500 in his will.[1] In addition, Sir Stephen paid to keep Castle Ashby in repair and to improve its grounds. Without such a wealthy father-in-law both the fourth Earl of Northampton and his children would certainly have cut less of a dash in the early eighteenth century.

[1] B.L., Add. MS. 51336: volume containing abstract of Charles Fox's will and statement of his debts.

CHAPTER XII

The Worthy Sir Stephen Fox

A GOOD deal has emerged during the course of this book as to what sort of a person Sir Stephen Fox was, but before we leave him it seems worth making some attempt at a character sketch. The portraits of him painted by Lely and Baker show, beneath the wig fashionable at that period, a face with a rather dark colouring and strong but regular features. They suggest a man with ample self-confidence, considerable presence, and a dignified bearing, who had been physically attractive when young, and who was still impressively good-looking in late middle age. Evelyn, writing in 1680, describes him as handsome, and so we need not suspect that the artists had been unduly flattering to their subject. Fox was also endowed with a pleasing personality, and he seems to have been one of the most likeable parvenus of any age: indeed his great personal charm was almost certainly an important factor in his success. He seems to have had just the right blend of politeness and cordiality, of sincerity and discretion, and his manner was altogether that of a well-bred and well-spoken gentleman, as even those who had no particular cause to flatter him were prepared to admit. 'A very fine gentleman', noted Pepys at their first meeting, and on a later visit to Fox's lodgings in Whitehall the young Admiralty clerk recorded approvingly that he had been treated 'with a great deal of respect'. He clearly liked Sir Stephen, as did Evelyn who knew him better and refers to his 'sweete nature'. Evelyn also recorded that, despite his wealth and worldly success, 'he still continues as humble, and ready to do a courtesie, as ever he was'.[1] Certainly, even at the height of his career, he did not forget his origins, and he always retained a deep sense of attachment to the place where he had been brought up, and a great loyalty to the other members of his family.

Three factors in Fox's early life combined to give him the polish and courtly bearing for which he was renowned. Despite the relative poverty of his own parents we have seen that he had received

---

[1] *Evelyn*, iv. 217–19; *Pepys*, i. 157, 299.

the schooling of a gentleman, which had not only introduced him
to classical learning but had also taught him the essential graces
of the polite world of the seventeenth century.[1] Secondly, he had
been introduced to the royal Court while still at a highly impres-
sionable age, and his early training in the Prince of Wales's Household, and as a page with a series of aristocratic families, must have
done much to shape his personality: certainly he always regarded
himself as a royal servant in a more literal sense than was usual in
one who held such high offices. Particularly important in this
respect, perhaps, was the severe discipline which, according to
Clarendon, Lord Percy imposed on those whom he employed.[2]
Thirdly, Sir Stephen had spent a long period abroad in the later
1640s and 1650s, obtaining a proficiency in languages and an
experience of the world outside England which a man of higher
social origins might have picked up on a Grand Tour, but which
someone of Fox's background would not normally have had a
chance to acquire.

Thus, although he had been born into a village society of small
farmers and cottagers, he betrayed few traces of this in later life.
The lessons he had to learn in his youth may have been hard, but
once mastered they stood him in good stead thereafter, and provided him with a passport for his journey up through the class
system of the later seventeenth century. His personal acceptability,
his close connection with the royal Court, and his friendship with
Charles II, meant that he found a ready entrée into the highest
levels of society. Unlike other *nouveaux riches*, whose wealth alone
brought them into contact with the established élite, he did not
find himself cold-shouldered, laughed at behind his back, and his
acquaintance sought only by those who needed his financial help.
Sir Stephen made an immense fortune as a financier, but he was
a courtier who had learnt the ways of finance, not a business man
who was trying to pick up the rudiments of gentility. It was also
important that he had no past of 'trade' or petty moneylending to
live down. He had entered finance straight away at the highest and
most respectable level, that of raising large loans for the government, and when he did diversify into private lending his clients
were principally courtiers and aristocrats. Fox indeed was always
a courtier first and foremost, as is demonstrated by the great store

[1] See above, pp. 2–3.
[2] Clarendon, *History of the Rebellion*, v. 337–8.

he set on his employment as Clerk of the Green Cloth and his chagrin at the loss of the Cofferership in 1689. Consequently other courtiers were prepared to accept him on terms of equality. Lady Sunderland was certainly interested in Fox's money when she proposed that her son should marry his youngest daughter, but there is no reason to doubt her sincerity when she told Evelyn, 'I had rather marry my son to Sr Steven Foxes daughter wth twelve thousand pound if our own circumstances would admitt of it, then to any other I can thinke of wth twice ye sum, so great a value have I for thos two good people he and his Lady.'[1] Some of the greatest aristocrats in the land were glad to number Fox amongst their friends. The Duke of Ormonde, Lord Steward of the Household and Lord-Lieutenant of Ireland, who had shared the exile of the 1650s, was such a one. For instance, in November 1681, after a short hiatus in their correspondence, he told an acquaintance that his friendship with Sir Stephen was 'of longer date and upon better grounds than to be shaken for want of a letter', whilst in 1684 the Duke signed his letters to the latter 'Yr most affectionate servant'.[2] The Duchess of Buccleuch was another great personage with whom Fox had had an even closer friendship, and one which extended over more than thirty years. In a letter to him written from Brome in 1688 she told him that 'I will say nothing in commendation of this place now, for it will never be quit [sic] to my mind till you are here, and my Lady Fox'. She went on to call him 'the best friend that ever was born', and concluded by signing herself 'most graitfully, most affectionatly, and most faithfully, your servant'.[3] The Duchess quarrelled with him in the end, but the eventual collapse of their relationship seems to have been mainly the result of her own instability of character. Fox was thus equally at home in two essentially distinct worlds of late Stuart London, that of Whitehall and the Court, and that of Lombard Street and City magnates such as Backwell and Duncombe. Indeed, after his long service on the Treasury, he was also part of a third: the world of professional administrators and career civil servants like Pepys, Blathwayt, Southwell, Ellis, and Lowndes.

[1] B.L., Add. MS. 15889, f. 61.

[2] H.M.C., *Ormonde*, N.S., vi. 224; B.L., Add. MS. 51326, ff. 45–6: Ormonde to Fox, 1684.

[3] Ilchester: Family (box 238, bundle 15): Duchess of Buccleuch to Fox, 10 June 1688. See also above, pp. 279–84.

The strength of his position in each of the three owed much to the fact that he was so well entrenched in the others.

There is ample evidence of Fox's fondness for children, and as a parent and grandparent he was affectionate, indulgent, and considerate, and after his offspring and adopted offspring had grown up, extremely generous. He was also very much aware of his responsibilities to his wider family, which was large. He had himself been one of ten children, and four of his brothers and two sisters survived into adult, married life. Of their children, at least sixteen lived long enough to marry, and in turn to beget more than twice as many great-nephews and nieces for Sir Stephen. Indeed, since he lived to so great an age, a fourth generation of his father's descendants was already reaching maturity before he died. Sir Stephen seems to have had hardly any cousins on his father's side, although the rather disreputable, or perhaps unfortunate, Peter Fox, for whom a place was eventually found as Caretaker of the Galleries at Chelsea Hospital at 1s. 6d. per day, was probably one.[1] However, he had a large number on his mother's, and so by the later years of his life he stood at the centre of an extended family circle which could be numbered literally in scores, all of whose members looked for advancement or assistance to the one of their number who had achieved wealth and influence. Nor did he disappoint them, for his willingness to do what he could for his family was of longer standing than his success. Back in the dark days of 1649 he had lent his elder brother John all his savings, in order to save his sister-in-law and her child from destitution:[2] and as his power to help steadily increased with the passage of every decade after 1660, so his relatives benefited on a growing scale. He employed them in the Pay Office, as nominees in the various financial offices which he acquired, in the discharge of his private business affairs, and in the management of his landed estates; and although not all his agents were related to him, a remarkably high proportion were. He used his influence as Clerk of the Green Cloth to secure posts in the King's Household for some, and his share of Treasury patronage to obtain posts in the revenue for others. He is also found repeatedly promoting the marriages of the younger ones; exerting his influence to secure for them employment or ecclesiastical benefices which were in the gift of other great men of his acquaintance; providing the funds for the purchase of army com-

---

[1] P.R.O., A.O. 1/1466/1.   [2] See above, pp. 6, 8.

missions; and, in appropriate cases, providing cash pensions to supplement the incomes of those whom he could not aid in any other way. But the form of help he was most ready to give was to pay for an education which would ensure its recipient the same good start in life which the kindness of his great-uncle had given him. Thus in the mid-1670s we find him supporting his nephew Stephen Baber, whom he sent to the same boarding-school which his own sons had attended a few years earlier; and at the same time financing the stay of another nephew, Henry Fox, at Christ Church, Oxford. Henry incidentally took his M.A. degree in 1681 and two years later became one of the royal chaplains, an appointment which he must also have owed to Sir Stephen, who even paid the fees incurred when he was sworn in.[1] In the early eighteenth century Sir Stephen saw his great-nephew, Stephen Fox, Thomas's son, through both Balliol and the Inner Temple; paid for another great-nephew to attend school in Wiltshire, almost certainly at the Salisbury Cathedral school; and paid £25 a year for the education of a grandson of his mother's aunt until the boy was able to obtain an exhibition at Queen's College, Oxford.[2] In yet other cases he tried to get scholarships for his protégés by exerting influence in the right quarters. In 1691 he unsuccessfully attempted to secure a New College award for Thomas Ridge, a grandson of his brother John, and subsequently an M.P. who achieved notoriety when he was expelled from the Commons in 1713 on grounds of fraud in the matter of supplying beer to the navy. Fox failed to get Ridge a scholarship because the contact he approached at Winchester, where his great-nephew was at school, had insufficient influence to ensure his nominee's election, so when in 1698 yet another great-nephew, Nicholas Fenn junior, was ready for the university he applied pressure at a higher level, and wrote to the Secretary of State's office for a royal nomination.[3] So, thanks to their relationship with Sir Stephen, several generations of Foxes and Fox

---

[1] Ilchester: Accounts, Household (boxes 210 and 213): Sir S. Fox's household account for 1673–6, and summary of household accounts for 1682–8; ibid.: Official, Sir S. Fox, Army: ledger for 1672–9, ff. 103, 302; J. Foster, *Alumni Oxoniensis* (Early Series, 4 vols., Oxford, 1891–2).

[2] Ilchester: Accounts, Personal (box 220): 'The Accot of the late Brigr Row's children as also of Mr. Stephen Fox'; ibid.: Accounts, Wiltshire Estate (box 209): Wilts. estate account, 1707–9; B.L., Add. MS. 51324, ff. 21–2: notes by Sir Stephen on the Johnson family.

[3] Ilchester: Family (box 235, bundle 2): Jos. Nicholas to Fox, 24 July, 11 Aug., and 29 Sept. 1691; B.L., Add. MS. 28883, f. 111.

connections found their prospects marvellously improved. As Sir Stephen himself climbed the social and economic ladder so he pulled up behind him a whole host of relatives, and a number of his servants as well.

Fox was proud of the fact that his worldly success had enabled him to be, as he put it, 'a Joseph' to all his relations,[1] but concern to help those less fortunate than himself was not confined only to members of his own family and household. We have seen that he played the leading role in the establishment of Chelsea Hospital in the early 1680s, and he also made a substantial number of private charitable benefactions. The most important of these were bestowed on his birthplace and childhood home, Farley near Salisbury. He succeeded in purchasing the lease of the manor in September 1678,[2] and at once began to implement plans, which he had probably long had in mind, to provide this small and remote village with the facilities it lacked. His first undertaking was an almshouse, or hospital as he usually called it, to provide free accommodation and a small pension for six elderly men and six elderly women, either from Farley itself, or from the immediately neighbouring villages of Pitton and Maddington. The building was completed by the middle of 1682 at a total cost of £1,835. 8s. 8d., including £34. 12s. 8d. for landscaping the gardens and planting trees. It still stands, a dignified and pleasing structure of warm pink brick surrounded by fields and woods.[3] At first, Fox intended that the warden of the new hospital should also be a schoolmaster, a man in full holy orders 'fit as well to preach as to teach', for he envisaged the establishment of a free school on the same premises. Twelve boys from Farley, Pitton, and Maddington, who had already been taught to write and do accounts, were to receive a more advanced education which was to include the study of Greek and Latin 'if their parents will permit them to learn so much'. Most of them were expected eventually to become apprentices to 'masters of good working trades', and Fox set aside £20 a year out of the fund established to support the new institution to pay their apprenticeship premiums. But he also intended that the education provided

---

[1] B.L., Add. MS. 51324, f. 105: autobiographical fragment without date, heading, or endorsement.

[2] See above, p. 172.

[3] Farley Hospital MSS.: Great Book of Farley: summary of building accounts. The local tradition that the architect was Sir Christopher Wren seems to be unjustified.

would equally well fit them to be 'academical scholars', which seems to suggest that he envisaged that they might go on to one of the universities. Fox knew very well how important a good education had been to his own success, and there seems little doubt that he was trying to make the same advantage available to future generations of village boys by providing them with a local grammar school. In fact these educational plans proved to be unduly ambitious, and after a few years the school was discontinued. The hospital accounts contain occasional references to it in the early years, but there is no indication that any pupil ever reached a place of higher learning, and only one even seems to have been bound out as an apprentice, to a carpenter. Perhaps there were not enough able boys in Farley and the surrounding villages; perhaps the parental opposition to teaching them classics, which Fox seems to have anticipated, proved insurmountable; and certainly there were better established schools not far away. As the hospital warden put it: 'by experience it was found that a school could not with advantage take effect in that lonely retired village, it being neare Salisbury where there are two eminent schools, and not far from Winton, famously endowed for the education of youth . . .'[1]

At any rate by January 1689, when Fox formally endowed his foundation by settling an income of £188 per year upon it, the school had ceased to function, for the deed of settlement contained no reference to it or to any teaching duties expected of the warden.[2] Not until over twenty years later was a second attempt made to provide Farley with a charity school, and on this occasion the intention was much more modest, for it attempted to give only a basic education. Twenty children 'of the poorest sort' were to be taught, the boys to read and write and to do accounts, the girls just to read and write. A master was engaged at Michaelmas 1711 at the salary of £10 a year, and a house built to accommodate the school, which, unlike its predecessor, long outlived its founder.[3]

The other amenity which Farley lacked, when Fox bought it,

[1] Ilchester: Parish and Charity, Wiltshire (box 259): draft regulations for the hospital and school, 27 Mar. 1682; Farley Hospital MSS.: Great Book of Farley: preface, and accounts for 1682-9.

[2] Ilchester: Deeds, Wiltshire, Alderbury (box 122): release, 23 Jan. 1689.

[3] Ilchester: Parish and Charity, Wiltshire (box 259): account-book of Farley Hospital 1703-20, pp. 63, 94; ibid.: Deeds, Wiltshire, Alderbury (box 122): release, 22 June 1711. B.L., Add. MS. 51330: expenditure account for the Wiltshire estate, 1713-14.

was an adequate place of worship. It was too small a village to be a parish on its own, and the parish church was a couple of miles away at Pitton. There was, it is true, a chapel, but it was 'auncient and ruinous', and inconvenient of access for most people who lived there. So in April 1688 Sir Stephen had it taken down, and began construction of a new one on a fresh site opposite his hospital. Sir Christopher Wren was probably the architect, and he designed a more generously proportioned church than many much larger villages could boast of. Built in the same now-mellowed brick and tile as the hospital across the road, it is rather austerely simple from without and relieved from plainness only by the contrasting angles of the roofs, and the restrained ornamentation of the tower. Within, it seems long, high, and spacious, with large windows which flood it with light. The total cost was some £2,054, which included £5. 10s. 0d. for a modest 'entertainment' at its dedication by the Bishop of Salisbury in the spring of 1690.[1] Fox thus provided the small village of his birth and childhood with a hospital for the old and lonely; a school for the young and hopeful; and a place of worship for all. There is no doubt of the strength of the feelings he always retained for the place from which he had once set forth as an almost penniless boy to seek his fortune, and it was his choice to be buried there, in Wren's lovely chapel, rather than in Westminster or Chiswick where he had lived for the last fifty-six years of his life. Nowhere else attracted his benevolence on a comparable scale, although, as we shall see, a number of other places with which he had personal connections benefited from it to a lesser degree.

Sir Stephen was described by Evelyn as 'very religious', and he himself recalled that he had been brought up in a home where religion had been a powerful influence.[2] Religion was clearly significant to him on a personal level, as is suggested by the care with which he prescribed the prayers to be used by the almsfolk at Farley, and the importance which he attached to their regular attendance to take the sacrament, which he recommended they

[1] N. Pevsner, The Buildings of England: Wiltshire (Harmondsworth, 1963), p. 216; Ilchester: Parish and Charity, Wiltshire (box 259): account of the charge of building a chapel at Farley, and declaration by the Bishop of Salisbury, 17 Apr. 1690; B.L., Add. MS. 51319, f. 93: Bishop of Salisbury to Fox, 21 Apr. 1690.
[2] Evelyn, iv. 219; B.L., Add. MS. 51324, f. 30: autobiographical account of Fox's early life.

should do 'monthly, or at least quarterly', as an example to the rest of the parish.[1] There are some hints of a Calvinist theology in the wording of the prayers, and though there is no doubt whatsoever of Sir Stephen's firm adherence to the Anglican church throughout his career, there are other pieces of evidence which suggest he was mildly puritanical in his code of ethics and behaviour. His own way of life was remarkably unostentatious, considering his immense wealth and his close involvement in the Restoration Court, and he intensely disapproved of drunkenness, gambling, and womanizing. His nephew John Fox felt that he was never really forgiven for his youthful transgressions in these respects,[2] and both at Chelsea Hospital and at the Farley almshouse Sir Stephen demanded a very high level of conduct from inmates. When he asked Evelyn to frame the regulations for the Hospital he told him that they were to be as strict as those prevailing in a religious institution; and at the almshouse swearing, cursing, and intemperate drinking were strictly forbidden, and the warden was instructed to ensure that those under his care 'do lodge within their own apartments in the hospital and [do] not gad abroad in the day time'.[3]

Fox's concern with matters of religion also found expression in the additions he made to the incomes of two poorly endowed church livings. The minister of Maddington, near Farley, received an additional £60 a year from at least as early as the mid-1680s, and in the last years of his life Fox made this a permanent charge on the estates he left to his successor. The minister of Shepton Montague, near Redlynch in Somerset, also received a perpetual augmentation of half as much at the same time. Redlynch was the centre of Fox's other main block of estates, and he also established a charity school there in 1713, although this was even less ambitious than the one begun at Farley two years before. It was to provide accommodation, diet, and some instruction, for nine girls who were to be admitted at the age of ten, 'unless objects of very great compassion', when they might be taken in at eight or nine. The inmates were to be trained for domestic service 'as well as to other

---

[1] Ilchester: Parish and Charity, Wiltshire (box 259): draft regulations for the hospital and school; ibid.: Deeds, Wiltshire, Alderbury (box 122): release, 22 Jan. 1689, which recites the final version of the regulations.

[2] B.L., Add. MS. 51324, f. 10 et seq.: narrative of the life of John Fox junior.

[3] *Evelyn*, iv. 270. Ilchester: draft regulations for the hospital and school, doc. cit.

work', and were expected to devote a large part of their time to doing their own domestic chores, and to contribute to their keep by spinning. In spare moments they were 'to be carefully kept to reading their catechism'. Sir Stephen, it seems, had no advanced notions about education for women.[1] It is also probable, although unfortunately it cannot be established for certain, that the rebuilding of the choir school in the close at Salisbury, which was completed in 1714, was partly, if not wholly, paid for by Fox. We find him involved in a project to promote a charity school at Chiswick which was to be supported by public subscriptions, and he was one of the subscribers to a similar school near his son-in-law's seat of Castle Ashby. On the estate of his other son-in-law, Lord Cornwallis, he spent something over £1,300 on an almshouse at Brome and on the repair or rebuilding of Culford church, and a list of his minor benefactions would surely be a long one.[2]

Unlike most men of his age Sir Stephen made his gifts to charity when he was alive, rather than by bequests in his will, and this does seem to be evidence of a real desire to give help to those at the bottom of the social scale. That he was not merely obeying the dictates of convention in his philanthropy is confirmed by the close personal interest he took in his foundations, not just during the period of their establishment, but subsequently. He remained one of the three Commissioners responsible for Chelsea Hospital until 1703. As for the others, the time that he could devote to their affairs during his busy years as Lord of the Treasury must have been extremely limited, but he managed to visit Farley twice during the building of the almshouse, and when at last he retired he could do more. In 1702, 1703, and again in 1706, for instance, he came to Farley and himself conducted the annual 'visitation' which had normally been carried out on his behalf by one of his agents. On the second of these occasions the warden recorded how Sir Stephen gave orders for the admission of a new inmate in place of one who had died, and for the payment of allowances of a shilling a week to two other old people for whom there was apparently no room in

[1] Ilchester: Parish and Charity, Somerset (box 258): account-book of the Redlynch charity; ibid.: Estate, General (box 175, bundle 2): document endorsed 'Chas. Lee abt the tythes . . .'
[2] Robertson, *Sarum Close*, pp. 222–3; B.L., Add. MS. 51324, f. 126: proposals for a Charity School at Chiswick; Marquess of Northampton, *History of the Comptons*, p. 159; Ilchester: Family (box 237): purple and gold booklet, p. 21; Eyre, *Sermon*, pp. 12–13.

the hospital. As late as September 1711, when he was eighty-four years of age, Fox again came on a visit timed to coincide with the opening of the new school.[1] It was not everyone of his eminence who would have taken the trouble.

A strong religious faith on the one hand, and his code of gentlemanly behaviour on the other, provided Fox with the foundation for his honesty and incorruptibility; and these virtues probably owed something to two other personality traits which emerge strongly from his writings. He took a great pride in the efficient discharge of the tasks allotted to him, and was always anxious to please his various employers. Huge sums of government money passed through his hands, and yet in an age when corruption was common, and when justified or unjustified accusations of malpractice were equally common, Sir Stephen's name remained unsullied. Evelyn commented in 1680 that his fortune was 'honestly gotten and unenvied, which is next to a miracle'; and after Sir Stephen's death thirty-six years later the same distinction was remarked upon by Canon Eyre who claimed for him 'a mind above all corruption; so that he was allow'd to get a great estate in places at Court, without ever having his integrity once call'd in question: a rare felicity with our great men!' A biographer of 1717 echoed the same refrain with his references to the 'vast integrity . . . justice and uncorrupted sincerity' with which Fox discharged his official responsibilities.[2] Sir Stephen, then, had a most unusual reputation for probity, and no evidence has emerged to suggest that it was anything but deserved. Had there been any grounds for suspicion, critics in plenty would have sprung up, but as it was, the only dissentient voices were unashamedly and scandalously partisan.[3] At different times Fox also handled the financial affairs of numerous private individuals, from the Duke of Monmouth downwards, and only one of them ever seems to have found cause for complaint. This was Sir Stephen's own great-nephew, Nicholas Johnson's son Charles, who, more than a quarter of a century after

[1] Ilchester: Accounts, Personal (box 220): account of Sir S. Fox's private expenses, 1680–1; ibid.: Parish and Charity, Wiltshire (box 259): account-book of Farley Hospital 1703–20.

[2] *Evelyn*, iv. 219; Eyre, *Sermon*, pp. 9–10; Anon., *Memoirs of Sir Stephen Fox*, p. 71.

[3] For instance: Library of Wilts. Arch. Soc., Devizes, Hungerford Family Collections: Personal History, iii. 59a; B.L., Add. MS. 28937, f. 161; *Ailesbury Memoirs*, i. 241.

his father's death, got it into his head that Fox, as Nicholas's executor, had misappropriated part of his estate. Charles had seen some old ledgers, and detected what he thought were items for which Sir Stephen had failed to render an account. But Charles did not realize that much of the business transacted in his father's name had in reality been Sir Stephen's, or if he did realize it, decided nevertheless to start legal proceedings in the hope of being bought off. Fox's early answers to his charges were admittedly unsatisfactory, but he was over eighty at the time and it is not surprising that he was confused about the details of his financial relationship with a man who had died twenty-seven years earlier. The case dragged on long after his own death in 1716, but in the end one is left in no doubt that he had discharged his executorship with perfect propriety.[1]

Good-looking, likeable, polished in his manners, kind-hearted, pious, honest, and of course immensely capable and hard working —was Sir Stephen Fox a man without flaws? Obviously not, but there is much less evidence about his vices than about his virtues. However, there is no question that he liked to get his own way and that he was sometimes overbearing to his dependants, and beneath his charm there may have lurked a sharp temper, for several of those who knew him refer to his anger. For instance he became 'very angry' with Pepys on one occasion, but the diarist added lightly that he 'valued it not', which seems to imply that Fox's anger came and went easily and was not to be taken too much to heart.[2] In old age he became increasingly touchy and irritable, and in 1704 even quarrelled briefly with his much-loved daughter Jane, apparently taking offence at the tone of the letters she had recently written him, and because she had forgotten to thank him for a birthday present. But Jane had meant no harm and after a few months good relations were restored.[3] Not a great many of Sir Stephen's own letters survive, but his various autobiographical and other writings betray a good deal about his inner self. They show that he was extremely conscious of his own merits, and resentful

---

[1] B.L., Add. MS. 36148, ff. 137–8; Ilchester: Family (box 235, bundle 3): paper by Charles Johnson enclosed in a letter to William Gore, 27 May 1719; ibid.: Legal (box 247): printed version of the respondent's case in the suit of Ward and Fenn v. Margaret Johnson and others, 1725.

[2] *Pepys*, viii. 586.

[3] Ilchester: Family (box 238, bundle 16): letters from Jane, Countess of Northampton, to Fox written in 1705.

if they did not receive the recognition and reward he thought they deserved. They confirm that he was easily offended, and show that if he felt he had been wronged he was slow to forgive and would nurse his grievance for years. There were a number of people, notably Danby, Lord Newport, and, after they had quarrelled, the Duchess of Buccleuch, against whom he seems to have borne an almost everlasting grudge. This, together with an insistent need for the approval of all with whom he came into contact, which his writings also reveal, suggests a deep-seated sense of insecurity, despite the superficial assurance with which he faced the world. A chance remark recorded by the younger John Fox points in the same direction. 'As I am an honest man,' Sir Stephen is alleged to have said in order to head off a request for a small loan, 'I don't know but I may want bread before I dye.' Whether such insecurity was psychological in origin, or based on a realistic appreciation that a fortune made in government finance might be lost a great deal more easily than it had been made, it is perhaps not to be wondered at in a man who had risen so far above the social milieu in which he had been brought up. Sir Stephen was sympathetic to the unfortunate, but he did not tolerate weakness or failure in others, as his nephew John Fox discovered, and although he was usually normally very generous to his family and friends, on occasion he would drive an unnecessarily hard bargain with them. John Fox again had cause to complain of this, for when Sir Stephen resigned his place on the Board of Green Cloth to him in 1689 he did so on such 'gripeing conditions' that John felt that he had been better off in his old post as Clerk of the Spicery.[1] Sir Stephen thus had his share of personality defects, but few of them were apparent to contemporaries, and most onlookers, if not quite all, were as favourably struck by his personality as they were impressed by his rise to power and wealth. Canon Eyre did not greatly exaggerate when he said in his funeral address that 'it was indeed the singular happiness of Sir Stephen Fox to have the universal good will, and good word of all sides'.[2]

[1] B.L., Add. MS. 51324, f. 10 et seq.: narrative of the life of John Fox junior.
[2] Eyre, *Sermon*, p. 10.

CHAPTER XIII

An Interval Betwixt Business and Death

SIR STEPHEN was still in harness at the Treasury when Queen Anne came to the throne, although he was seventy-five years old and finding the remorseless pressure of the work increasingly hard to sustain; but the change of sovereign at last provided him with the opportunity to resign without giving undue offence. However, before his final retirement into private life one last honour was bestowed on him and one last service required. The position of Master of the Horse, titular head of the royal Stables and one of the most prestigious offices of state, was vacant. Its holder was usually a great noble, frequently of royal blood, but for the Queen to make an appointment necessarily meant offending the disappointed aspirants and so it was decided that she should not do so, and instead commissioners were nominated to discharge the duties involved. Most of these duties were concerned with routine business, but there were also certain ceremonial functions, of particular importance in a coronation year, and these Sir Stephen, as First Commissioner of the Stables, had to perform.[1] So on the day of the coronation itself Fox had a leading role to play. It was he who took the Queen by the hand and led her down from the throne after the crown had been placed on her head, a duty which at his advanced age he found extremely nerve-racking. He wrote later that 'he thanked God [it] was happily perform'd, tho' the stairs were steep and not well cover'd ...' Then it was Fox's coach, a new one specially ordered by him for the occasion at a cost of £500, which led the procession of splendid equipages belonging to other Great Officers and peers of the realm, as it threaded its way through the streets of the capital. It was a fitting public finale to Sir Stephen's sixty-three years in the royal service.[2]

Behind the scenes, however, his career came to a less gratifying

[1] Sir Stephen had actually been First Commissioner of the Stables once before (1679–82), but that had not been a time when the ceremonial aspects of the position had been so much to the fore. *C.T.B.* vii (1681–5), p. 674.

[2] B.L., Add. MS. 51324, ff. 52–3: document endorsed 'Proceedings at the Greencloth agst Sr Stephen Fox'.

conclusion. Also at the beginning of Anne's reign he had been asked, as an experienced ex-member of the Board of Green Cloth, to frame a new establishment for the Queen's Household, and in doing so he suggested economies which aroused the antagonism of certain powerful officials, whom Sir Stephen does not name but who doubtless included the Earl of Bradford (the former Lord Newport). Having made his proposals he seems to have hoped that he would be offered the much desired Cofferership, in which capacity he would have been able to supervise their implementation. But the offer was not forthcoming, and indeed he found that he was unable to prevent his enemies on the Board revenging themselves upon him by dismissing three of the relatives for whom he had found posts in the Household: Nicholas Fenn, Serjeant of the Woodyard, William Yardley, Clerk of the Kitchen, and Thomas Pavey, 'a working chandlery man'. They also succeeded in stopping a Green Cloth pension of £350 a year which Fox himself had received since Charles II's reign, and the title to which he had originally purchased.[1] Sir Stephen may have been wrong in his interpretation of these events, which may have been an extension of the economy drive rather than deliberate revenge, but either way it was a hurtful reminder to him that his influence at Court was already dead. He was much affronted, and any satisfaction he may have gained from the prominent part he had played in the coronation seems to have been overlaid by this new grievance.[2]

When retirement at last came to Sir Stephen in 1702, it was the more complete because he lost his seat in Parliament at much the same time as he resigned from the Treasury. Since 1698 he had sat for Cricklade, and in the general election at the beginning of Anne's reign he had contested the borough again, only to be beaten at the polls by a Tory squire, Samuel Barker of Fairford. Sir Stephen's defeat was in part caused by the general swing to extreme Toryism, but in addition, for some reason, the Fox interest at Cricklade seems to have been in decline: some years later indeed, in 1710, Charles Fox stood there and secured only four out of 254 votes, where he had once dominated elections.[3] Whether this was

[1] See above, p. 184 and note 1 to it.
[2] B.L., Add. MS. 51324, ff. 52–3: document endorsed 'Proceedings at the Greencloth agst Sr Stephen Fox'.
[3] R. Walcott, *English Politics in the Early Eighteenth Century* (Oxford, 1956), 217; *Members of Parliament*, i. 584, 591, 598, 605; B.L., Add. MS. 51319, ff. 197–8: note of the votes cast at the Cricklade poll, 7 Oct. 1710.

because the Foxes, though local landowners, had no great house locally, and rarely if ever visited Cricklade, is uncertain, but whatever the explanation the 1702 result effectively ended Sir Stephen's parliamentary career. It is true that he briefly represented Salisbury in 1714, but by then he was too old to take any active part in the proceedings, although it was reported that he was often to be seen in the House.[1]

He may have regretted his exclusion from Parliament, but he was certainly glad to be free of the continual pressure of Treasury business, and he celebrated his freedom with a long holiday in the summer of 1702, during the course of which he called on a number of friends, including Lord Fitzharding, William Blathwayt, Sir Robert Southwell, and Lord Sunderland, at their country seats, besides spending a month in Bath and another month at Castle Ashby.[2] Rest, however, does not seem to have brought contentment. That he was not a happy man at this time is indicated by the strident and complaining tone of the numerous autobiographical fragments he composed in the early years of his retirement, and in which he went over his grievances again and again, especially the loss of the Cofferership and his treatment at the hands of the Duchess of Buccleuch.[3] Unhappiness, moreover, is confirmed by a revealing comment he made in an answer to a letter from an old acquaintance, Thomas Povey, written a few months before he left office. After acknowledging some compliments that Povey had paid him he went on to tell him: 'Yr example is much beyond mine for you enjoy a comparative narrowness with a better grace than I can my seeming plenty.' Whether Sir Stephen had always been unhappy and discontented, despite his worldly success, it is impossible to say, but it is more likely that he had become increasingly lonely in old age.[4] Lady Fox had died in 1696, and after George Compton went off to Eton in 1698, for the first time he found himself living in a house without children.[5] Charles Fox and his wife Elizabeth seem still to have been living with the old man at this stage, but they were a childless and now ageing couple and perhaps Sir Stephen found them dull. However, Elizabeth had a friend

---

[1] Kensington Central Library: Local History Collection, extract from the *Salisbury Journal, c.* 1768.

[2] Ilchester: Family (box 238, bundle 7): account of Sir S. Fox's journey.

[3] See above, note 1, p. 247, and notes 3 to p. 282, 1 and 2 to p. 284.

[4] Gloucestershire R. O., D.1799/C.9: Fox to Thomas Povey, 11 Sept. 1701.

[5] See above, p. 300.

from her home county of Lincolnshire, a young spinster lady in her twenties by the name of Christian Hope, who had also been living in the household for a number of years, and Fox found some solace in talking to her and in getting her to read books on religion and history to him. So much so, indeed, that eventually he proposed to her, was accepted, and in July 1703 married her. Sir Stephen recorded that Christian 'always guided herselfe by a strict rule of piety, and was very helpfull to mee by reading and thereby entertaining my spare hours in my retirement wth such advantage that I thought her conversation would bee usefull to my olde age by having so good a companion for the remainder of my liffe, being advanced in my 77 yeares'. Yet even in his late seventies Fox did not treat marriage purely as a matter of reading aloud and conversation, and he was still, as an anonymous biographer commented shortly after his death, 'of a vegete and hale constitution'. So fifteen months after the wedding Christian, who was then twenty-seven, bore him a son who was named after his father. Sir Stephen admitted that this was a great surprise to himself 'as well as . . . ye wonder of ye world', but a year later an even greater wonder happened—twins! In all Christian produced four children, the youngest, a girl named Charlotte, born in 1707 when her father was eighty. Only three of them survived, unfortunately, since one of the twins died after falling from an open window at Chiswick.[1]

We have seen that Fox had lost interest in building up his country properties back in the 1680s, when it had begun to seem that his then only surviving son Charles would not be able to give him an heir, but that since then he had acquired several large estates, Little Bradley, the two Norfolk manors, the Isles of Aran, and Wilton in Cleveland, as a result of his dealings with the third and fourth Lords Cornwallis.[2] He had bought another, Lambeth Wick, at least partly to enable its former owner, who had owed him money, to discharge his debt,[3] and come by several miscellaneous pieces of property, mostly of small value, wholly because of similar reasons. Meanwhile, the West Country estates he had built up in the 1670s and 1680s seem to have been left largely to their own devices. Only Farley, his birthplace, received much attention, and

---

[1] B.L., Add. MS. 51324, ff. 25, 152–4: booklet marked 'children'. Anon., *Memoir of Sir Stephen Fox*, p. 92; Lord Ilchester, *Henry Fox, First Lord Holland* (2 vols., London, 1920), i. 14–15.

[2] See above, pp. 280–1, 289–93.   [3] See above, p. 212.

there he not only built the almshouse, church, and school, but he even made a few additional purchases of land to consolidate his possessions.[1] Little has survived to tell us how the Wiltshire and Somerset lands were managed in the period 1690 to about 1712, but what evidence there is speaks of neglect and indifference. Even at Farley, according to a report of 1709, the woodlands had been ruined by thefts of timber and failure to keep out grazing livestock, which had destroyed most of the young growth, while squatters had established themselves on unoccupied land without let or hindrance.[2] Nor is there any sign of the substantial investment, mainly in new buildings, and amounting to nearly £4,000 between 1685 and about 1705, which Fox made on the Chiswick estate where he actually lived.[3] Some years before he died, however, his attitude to his Somerset and Wiltshire lands changed. As his young family began to grow up it is clear that Fox became more and more taken with the prospect of the eldest of them, Stephen, one day taking his place in society as a great landed proprietor. He abandoned earlier intentions to divide the western estate at his death and determined that Stephen should have the whole of it.[4] He also decided that he should have a respectable country house, perhaps to encourage him to live in Somerset rather than at Chiswick. Thus at some time, probably between 1709 and 1712, he ordered the demolition of the old mansion at Redlynch, which had probably deteriorated beyond redemption in the twenty years since a member of the family had last lived in it, and had a new one built on an adjacent site. He spent £3,000 or more, and for the price had erected a neat and compact gentleman's residence, rather in the style which had been at the height of fashion a generation earlier, and without either pretensions to grandeur, or to any of the new architectural influences which were beginning to influence design by the second decade of the eighteenth century.[5] Fox also began

---

[1] See above, pp. 308–10. For the land purchases, see Appendix II.

[2] Ilchester: Family (box 236, bundle 2): document entitled '4th May 1709, about my woods at Farley etc.'; ibid.: Estate, Wiltshire (box 178, bundle 1): J. Pavey to Mr. Fenn, 6 Sept. 1716.

[3] B.L., Add. MS. 51324, f. 149: account of expenditure on improvements at Chiswick. [4] See below, pp. 327–9.

[5] For the cost of the new house at Redlynch, see the reference in a memorandum of 1712, Ilchester: Family (box 237): booklet containing the 1700 version of Sir S. Fox's will. Also ibid.: General Estate (box 170): particular of Somerset estate, 1712. The house still stands, though possibly enlarged later in the eighteenth century: there appears to be virtually nothing in print about it.

once again to buy land in Somerset in order to extend and consolidate the estate surrounding the new house. In 1713 he made his first purchase in the county since 1678, in the form of a holding in South Brewham for £900, and then in 1714 he paid £1,050 for the rectory of Shepton Montague.[1] Certainly he would have bought more had he lived, but as it was he had not left himself enough time to make any really large acquisitions in the district, and the further expansion of the estate had to wait until the next generation.

By the beginning of the eighteenth century Fox had greatly reduced the scale of his dealings in government paper, although for a year or two longer he still made a few large loans: between August and December 1701, for instance, he lent £11,420 'on the credit of the £3,700 per week'. However, during the whole of 1702 his new advances came to only £4,000, during 1703 to £4,300, and by the latter part of 1705 his entire holding of stock had been reduced to the £5,000 in the Bank which he had purchased back in 1694 and some Exchequer annuities of various types yielding £254. 16s. 0d. a year. In the following years he frequently put a few hundred pounds of spare cash into lottery tickets, and occasionally one or two thousands into Bank or South Sea securities, but he was no longer a major investor.[2] When he died in 1716, £6,325 of Bank stock, which was worth considerably better than par, and fetched £8,647. 10s. 0d. when sold by his executors the following year, and the same three annuities he had held eleven years before, and which were probably worth about £4,500, were the full extent of his portfolio.[3]

Fox's private lending, on the other hand, continued on a large scale for rather longer, although in this sphere too his activities contracted in the sense that his advances came to be largely confined to people with whom he had a well-established personal and

---

[1] Ilchester: Deeds, Somerset (box 296): conveyance, 28 Feb. 1713; ibid.: Family (box 223, bundle 1): conveyance, 30 Nov. 1714.

[2] Ilchester: Official, Sir S. Fox, Treasury (box 273): cash books for 1697–1702, 1702–10, and 1710–15, marked 'No. 2', 'No. 3', and 'No. 4' respectively; ibid.: Family (box 235, bundle 4): documents entitled 'An accompt of severall funds in the Bank . . .' and 'A collection of fee farm rents . . .' (sic); B.L., Add. MS. 51324, f. 100 et seq.: booklet marked 'Estate and a general acct thereof to Lady Day 1706'.

[3] Ilchester: Accounts, General Estate (box 191): booklet marked 'A computation of ye yearly value of ye lt Sr Ste Fox's estates', and small volume marked 'Receipts from the severall estates'.

social relationship. There were, for instance, the substantial loans he made to his grandson, Lord Cornwallis, and his son-in-law, the Earl of Northampton, although these should perhaps not be regarded as matters of business at all, even though Fox charged them interest on some parts of what he lent.[1] More of a business transaction, but combined with a desire to oblige and help, was the credit he extended to the Duke of Northumberland, one of Charles II's bastards, whose affairs he had long supervised, and who by 1708 owed him £5,000, of which part bore interest at 6 per cent and part at 5 per cent.[2] The loan of £3,000 at 6 per cent (1707), subsequently increased to £5,000, to the Dowager Countess of Sunderland, who more than twenty-five years before had tried to persuade Sir Stephen to betroth his daughter Jane to her son, undoubtedly involved the same mixture of motives, as did his dealings with the Earl of Clarendon.[3] Fox had originally lent the latter £3,000 on bond at 6 per cent in 1685, but Clarendon, apparently taking advantage of the personal relationship existing between them, had proved neglectful of his obligations as a debtor and allowed unpaid interest to accumulate until by 1700 the total debt had risen to £6,155. He then discharged the original principal but allowed the accumulated interest to remain outstanding until, after ten years more, interest upon the interest had once again increased the amount due to almost £6,000. Fox apparently got everything that was owed to him in the end, but the difficulty he experienced in getting it illustrates that the pitfalls of lending money to friends were as deep then as they still are.[4]

Another of Sir Stephen's aristocratic connections who borrowed from him in this last phase of his career, and indeed the one to whom he lent the largest sums, was the second Duke of Ormonde, grandson and heir of his old friend and colleague on the Board of Green Cloth, the first Duke. By the opening years of the new century Ormonde's affairs had reached a state of labyrinthine complexity, and he was relying very heavily on Fox's financial support: at one time (1707) the latter's advances to him totalled no less than £47,000! However, Ormonde's solvency was never seriously in

[1] See above, Chapter XI.

[2] B.L., Add. MS. 51321, ff. 145-9: documents concerning Fox's financial relationship with the Duke of Northumberland.

[3] Ilchester: Family (box 224): declaration of trust, 24 Dec. 1707, and enclosure.

[4] B.L., Add. MS. 51323: booklet concerning Fox's relationship with the second Earl of Clarendon.

doubt, for his assets, a vast landed estate in Ireland and several lucrative offices there and in England, were far greater than what he owed. He thus gradually succeeded in paying off this enormous debt, and by the end of Sir Stephen's life no more than £2,850 remained outstanding.[1] The latter seems to have used the money he received back from the Duke in the years after 1707, partly to reduce his own outstanding liabilities to those from whom he had taken up money in the past, and partly to finance the heavy capital spending which arose out of his support for Lord Cornwallis and the Comptons. The purchase money for the manor of Wilton, for instance, which he bought from the former in 1709 for £20,000, was covered in large part by the £18,974 remitted on Ormonde's account from Ireland during the course of the same year.[2] But there was little or no fresh lending outside the immediate family circle, and although in the last year of Fox's life (1716) the total of his outstanding advances was still about £30,250, some £4,590 of this was reckoned to be irrecoverable, and some three-fifths of the remainder (£15,897. 6s. od.) had either been lent to, or on behalf of, Cornwallis and the Earl of Northampton. The only substantial sums owed by people who were not close relations were the Duke of Ormonde's £2,850, and £4,356 due from his brother the Earl of Aran. When money due from tenants on the estates, and from others who had incurred debts to Fox without having formally borrowed from him, are added to the outstanding advances whose repayment was considered probable, the total of good debts owed to Sir Stephen in May 1716 came to £27,536. 15s. 11d., which was just about sufficient to cover the £28,228 which he owed to others.[3] An exact accountant to the last, after fifty-five

[1] B.L., Add. MS. 51326, *passim*, but esp. ff. 58, 63–5, 73–8, 100–1, 106, 127–30, 147; Ilchester: Deeds, Ireland (box 134): deeds, 30 Sept. 1704 (and 'Copy of the Duke of Ormonde's proposall' enclosed in it) and 26 Mar. 1725; ibid.: Deeds, Norfolk (box 71): 'An abstract of ye Duke of Ormonde's security . . . 1703'; ibid.: Accounts, Personal (box 221): account-book relating to Fox's advances to Ormonde, 1687–1708, and volume of accounts recording the receipts and payments of Mr. Watson for Sir S. Fox; ibid.: Family (box 237, loose): booklets marked 'Copys of papers relating to ye Duke of Ormonde's affairs' and 'Cop: of the state of account to 23d March 1712 . . .'

[2] For the purchase of Wilton, see above, pp. 291–3. For the Irish receipts, Ilchester: Accounts, Personal (box 221): volume of accounts recording the receipts and payments of Mr. Watson for Sir S. Fox.

[3] Ilchester: Family (box 227, bundle 2): schedules of Sir S. Fox's credits and debts at 25 Mar. 1716, attached to deed, 2 June 1726; ibid.: Family (box 237, loose): particular of debts owing to and by Sir S. Fox at the time of his death.

years as a financier, Fox left his books in almost perfect balance.

The good order in which Fox left his affairs enables us to disregard money owed and owing when assessing the size of the fortune he had to bequeath to his heirs, and this is consequently omitted from Table XII which summarizes the remaining assets

TABLE XII

Sir Stephen Fox's Assets, 1716

(£. s. d.)

		Capital value	Gross income[1]
Country Property			
Somerset	Estate	18,402[2]	691 6. 0½.
	House	3,000	—
Wiltshire	Water Eaton	21,908[3]	1,075 6. 8.
	S. Wilts manors	27,644	1,100 16. 4½.
Chiswick	Estate	6,000[4]	455 2. 4.
	House	6,000	—
Suffolk (Little Bradley)		9,200[5]	450 0. 0.
Yorkshire (Wilton)		20,000	1,133 15. 8.
Surrey (W. Horsley)		800	27 0. 0.
Urban and Suburban Property			
Whitehall apartments		600[6]	—
Hungerford Market, three-quarter share		10,875	1,050 3. 3.
Lambeth Wick		7,500[7]	419 10. 0.
Fee Farm Rents		21,286[8]	1,064 5. 4.
Offices and Pensions			
South Wales Receivership		2,150[9]	220 0. 0.
Annuity out of First Fruits and Tenths		5,520[10]	1,000 0. 0.
Government Securities			
Bank stock, £6,325 nominal		8,647[11]	506 0. 0.
Exchequer annuities		4,492[12]	254 16. 0.
	TOTALS	174,024	9,448 1. 8.

[1] The figures for gross income are mostly derived from Ilchester: Accounts, General Estate (box 191): booklet marked 'A computation of ye yearly value of ye lt Sr Ste Fox's estates'. In some cases these figures are either net of certain outgoings or incomplete, and they have therefore been supplemented by ibid.: Accounts, Estate, Somerset (box 207): account for the Redlynch estate, 1713–15; Estate, Middlesex (box 162): accounts of Hungerford Market and associated property, 1708–16; and Family (box 237, bundle 4): accounts of the South Wales Receivership, 1696–1716. For the annuities see note 2, p. 321. The dividend

on the Bank stock is assumed to have been 8 per cent p.a., which, according to Clapham, it was in the years 1712–14 and 1716–18. Clapham, *Bank of England*, i. 292. The houses at Chiswick, Whitehall, and Redlynch, of course, produced no income.

[2] The Somerset lands were valued at £15,951. 19*s*. 2*d*. in 1712, but this excluded the advowson of Kilmington which had cost £500 to buy. Since then Fox had purchased property costing £1,950, so that the total value was about £18,402. Ilchester: Estate, General (box 170): particular of Redlynch estate, 1712. See also above, p. 321, and Appendix II. The cost of the new mansion at Redlynch is stated to have been 'upwards of £3000' in Ilchester: Family (box 237, loose): booklet containing copy of Fox's will, 6 July 1700, at end.

[3] The figure given for Water Eaton is the cost of the estate when Fox bought it in the 1670s, but twenty years' purchase of the current rent-roll (a fair valuation for freehold land in the mid-1710s) yields a very similar one. The figure for the S. Wilts. manors represents their purchase price, less that of the holdings sold in 1682 and 1689–90, plus the price of properties acquired since then and the value (at seven years' purchase) of two annuities of £25 and £97. 10*s*. 0*d*. respectively, each on one life, with which the West Grimstead farms had been charged when they were bought and which had by this time expired. See above, pp. 207–8, and Appendix II.

[4] The Chiswick estate was roughly valued at £12,000 in 1709, and a price of £6,000 for the house and gardens alone was agreed on with a potential buyer when Fox's executors tried to sell them in 1719. Ilchester: Family (box 237, loose): booklet containing cancelled will, 5 Aug. 1709; ibid.: Deeds, Yorkshire (box 311): unexecuted deed, 18 Aug. 1719.

[5] The value given for Little Bradley is the 1690 purchase price plus the value of two small holdings acquired in 1705 and 1709 respectively. See above, p. 281; and for the two holdings, B.L., Add. MS. 51334: volume marked 'Orders of the executrix and trustees', f. 12ᵛ. The values given for Wilton and West Horsley are the prices at which they were purchased in 1709. See pp. 292, 326 n. 4.

[6] The values given for the apartments and Hungerford Market are the prices at which they were sold by Sir Stephen's trustees in 1718–19. B.L., Add. MS. 51334: volume marked 'Orders of the executrix and trustees', ff. 9 and 13.

[7] The value given for Lambeth Wick is the price at which it was purchased in 1694. See above, p. 212.

[8] The value given for the fee farm rents is twenty years' purchase of their gross yield.

[9] The value given for the S. Wales Receivership is the second (improved) offer made by a potential purchaser in 1716. Ilchester: Family (box 237, bundle 4): Sir H. Howarth to Sir S. Fox, 1 and 11 May 1716.

[10] The annuity had six and a half years (twenty-six quarterly payments) to run before the expiry of Fox's grant at Lady Day 1721/2. On the basis of the 5 per cent legal maximum rate of interest prevailing in 1714, £1,000 p.a. for six and a half years would have been worth £5,520 down.

[11] Sir Stephen's trustees sold his Bank stock early in 1717 at rates varying between 135 and 137½, thereby raising £8,647 10*s*. 0*d*. Ilchester: Accounts, General Estate (box 191): small volume marked 'Receipts from the severall estates'.

[12] Fox's Exchequer annuities were £70. 16*s*. 0*d*. p.a. in perpetuity, redeemable on payment of £1,180; £100 p.a. for ninety-nine years from 1704; and £84 p.a. for ninety-six years from 1696: see references cited in note 2, p. 321. No valuation for the last two is forthcoming from Fox's papers and I have reckoned them at eighteen years' purchase: this may be unduly conservative.

in his possession at the time of his death. The landed estate in Somerset was, we have just seen, only slightly enlarged since Sir Stephen had discontinued making purchases there in 1678, although it now had a brand-new mansion house upon it. The Wiltshire estate, too, remained in extent more or less as the sales of 1689–90 had left it, save for some very small acquisitions, mostly in Farley, in all costing a mere £1,441, although it should be noted that the death of his son Charles without issue in 1713 meant that Water Eton, which had been settled on the latter at the time of his marriage, had returned into his possession. Chiswick was also apparently unenlarged, except perhaps by the odd slip of land, since Fox had acquired the prebend manor in 1685; and although there had been some changes in the composition of the Hungerford Market estate since 1691, these had not greatly affected its value, which had, incidentally, been seriously depressed by the Whitehall fire of twenty years earlier.[1] However, the death of the Queen Dowager, Catharine of Bragança, in 1705, meant that the fee farm rents of which Fox had purchased the reversion thirty and more years before[2] were at last yielding their return, and his gross income from that source was now some £1,064 per annum. Of the landed properties he had bought in the last twenty-six years of his life, Waborne and Hemblingham had already been put into Lord Cornwallis's hands, and the Isles of Aran had been resold in 1713,[3] but the others—Little Bradley, Lambeth Wick, Wilton, and a small estate at West Horsley in Surrey which had been conveyed to him by a creditor in order to discharge a debt[4]—had been retained. Also retained had been the £1,000 annuity out of the First Fruits and Tenths, which Fox had originally purchased from the Earl of Sunderland, and of which he had received a fresh grant for twenty-one years in 1701;[5] and the Receivership of Crown revenues in South Wales, worth £220 a year or more, which had also come to him (in 1700) as a by-product of his financial dealings with the Sunderlands.[6] Altogether the value of the country estates was some

---

[1] For the Wiltshire purchases, see Appendix II. For Hungerford Market, note 1, p. 192.

[2] See above, pp. 167–8.   [3] See above, pp. 287–90.

[4] Ilchester: Deeds, Surrey (box 121): copy of court roll, 27 Oct. 1712; ibid.: Estate, Surrey (box 176): document endorsed 'Mr. Nicholas Fenn his accompt . . .'

[5] See above, pp. 185–6, 244.

[6] Ilchester: Family (box 237, bundle 4): accounts of the South Wales Receivership; B.L., Add. MS. 51332: schedule of deeds, f. 40; C.T.B. xi (1696–7), p. 147.

£112,954, from which should be deducted £5,980 for a capitalization at twenty years' purchase of the £299 per annum of rent charges which Fox had imposed on them for the support of Farley Hospital and other charities, thus leaving them worth £106,974 clear. Urban and suburban property added a further £18,975, fee farm rents £21,286, and the total value of all Fox's assets (other than money owed to him on mortgage or bond) was thus about £174,000, yielding a gross income of some £9,448 per annum. He thus died a very rich man, but there is no mistaking the fact that the size of his fortune was significantly smaller than it had been thirty years earlier.[1] He had experienced some capital losses through defaulting debtors and the drop in the value of both the Somerset estate and Hungerford Market,[2] but the main cause of this shrinkage was undoubtedly his own generosity. The endowments he had established for charitable purposes had reduced the value of his Wiltshire estate in particular, but far overshadowing these was the financial help he had given to the Cornwallises and Northamptons. His gifts and interest-free loans had cost him many tens of thousands of pounds, and had indeed been one of the principal uses to which he had put his capital in his last years.[3]

Ever since the 1670s Charles Fox had, of course, been Sir Stephen's heir apparent, but long before the death of his wife, late in 1703, it had appeared probable that he would have no children. Sir Stephen had therefore determined to divide the bulk of his property between his Cornwallis and Compton grandchildren, but in order that part of it might pass to someone bearing his own name he also intended that the Somerset estate should go to a young great-nephew, Stephen Fox, grandson of his brother Thomas. His second marriage did not at first necessitate any major change in these dispositions beyond making rather modest financial provision for Christian in case she survived him, but the arrival of children made their complete revision essential.[4] First, great-

---

[1] See above, pp. 188–97, and Tables X and XI.

[2] For the losses through bad debts, see the references quoted in note 3, p. 323; for the fall in the value of the Somerset estate, above, pp. 199–203, 209–11; and for Hungerford Market, note 1, p. 192.

[3] See above, Chapter XI.

[4] Ilchester: Family (box 237): cancelled will of Sir S. Fox, 6 July 1700, and papers relating to Stephen Fox junior; B.L., Add. MS. 51324, f. 167 et seq.: cancelled will, 27 Nov. 1703.

nephew Stephen lost his place in the calculations, although he was compensated with a gift of £2,000 when he grew up. Further, now that Christian was a mother as well as a companion, she merited much more generous treatment. Originally Fox had settled only £300 a year on her, but by the time he died he had increased this to nearly £1,200 yearly, together with a lump sum of £2,000 and tenancy of the Chiswick mansion for her life. More difficult than his second wife's jointure was the question of how he should treat his daughters' children now that he had every prospect of leaving descendants in the male line. Fox's solution to the problem was to continue to provide considerable financial help both to Lord Cornwallis and to the Comptons until the end of his life, but to scale down drastically the bequests they were to receive after his death.[1] To the former he confirmed the settlements he had already made on him of the Norfolk and Suffolk estates which he had bought from the third Lord. However, he made him no further gifts of real estate and none at all to the Comptons, though he did forgive both them and Cornwallis certain debts, and left them all modest cash legacies in his will. Virtually everything Sir Stephen owned at the time of his death was thus retained for division between his own sons, Stephen and Henry. The way he divided his estate between them was, however, far from equal, and the latter, as a younger son, had to make do with the South Wales Receivership, the leasehold property at Lambeth, and an annuity of £70, which together yielded only about £660 a year. All the rest of Fox's estates and investments, except for some £9,962 of the latter which were settled on Charlotte to provide her with a marriage portion when she grew up, were to go to Stephen. Stephen was thus due to inherit not only the country estates in Somerset and Wiltshire, with the newly built mansion at Redlynch, but also the estate at Wilton in Yorkshire which Sir Stephen had recently bought from Lord Cornwallis, the three-quarters share of Hungerford Market, and the £1,000 annuity payable out of the First Fruits and Tenths until the year 1721. After his mother's death the expiry of the annuity would be more than counter-balanced by Chiswick and the fee farm rents, both of which were included in her jointure. He had also to assume responsibility for Sir Stephen's debts which, after the bequest to Charlotte had been paid, would no longer be fully matched by money owed to him, but even so he could look

[1] See above, pp. 293–4, 301.

forward to eventually inheriting about £6,500 a year over and above all encumbrances.[1]

Stephen and Henry were sent away to school at Eton in 1715, when they were aged eleven and ten respectively, where their old father urged them to be assiduous in their study and their religious observance, whilst their mother kept them supplied with pigeon pie, sweet cake, chocolate, and advice on the clothing appropriate to the time of year. Then came Christ Church, Oxford, and later still, the Grand Tour. On his return to England Stephen duly commenced living at Redlynch as his father had intended and, though he entered Parliament in 1726, was a member for fifteen years, and even briefly held ministerial office, he devoted most of his life to country pursuits and the care of his estates. He made considerable additions to those in the West Country by piecemeal purchases over the years, and it was principally on the strength of his landed wealth that he was created Lord Ilchester in 1741. He added enormously to that wealth by a somewhat sensational marriage to the thirteen-year-old heiress, Elizabeth Strangways, who eventually brought him the huge estates of her family in Somerset, Dorset, and elsewhere, which included the great mansion at Melbury where their descendants subsequently resided. By the end of his life Lord Ilchester, who was created Earl in 1756, was one of the largest landowners in the West. Meanwhile, his younger brother Henry, having inherited no more than a competency, had also entered active politics but with the intention of making a career, and emerged as one of the leading figures in national affairs in the middle decades of the century. His greatest prize was the office of Paymaster-General of the Forces, which he held during the Seven Years War, almost a century after his father had first been appointed to pay the Guards. As is well known, Henry Fox also made a fortune out of the Paymastership, though by his day the opportunities for profit which the place offered were very different from those of which his father had taken advantage. Sir Stephen had grown rich by lending money to the government; Henry Fox did so by investing to his own profit the balances of government money which he was able to retain in his own hands. Henry too acquired a great estate, principally by purchase but

---

[1] Ilchester: Family (box 223, bundle 1): settlement, 6 Jan. 1713; ibid.: Family (box 236): cancelled will, 22 Jan. 1713; Ilchester: Deeds, Somerset and Wiltshire (box 306): final version of Sir S. Fox's will, 25 May 1716.

partly by marriage, and like his brother was promoted to the peerage, as Lord Holland. In the next generation his son, Charles James Fox, made an even greater name for himself than either his father or his grandfather, and in a very different way from either.[1]

None of these things would ever be known to old Sir Stephen. For him Stephen, Henry, and their sister Charlotte were important because their arrival meant that his house was once again full of children, the fourth generation for whose upbringing he had been responsible. Without doubt they made a great difference to his last years, and as the very old and the very young often seem to get on so well together, he may have been closer to these offspring of his old age than ever he had been to those whom he had seen born and die half a century earlier. At any rate Stephen and Henry seem to have retained a respectful affection for him into later life. Sir Stephen eventually died in his ninetieth year in 1716, long after most contemporaries of the early and even the middle part of his career. The age of lavish public funerals was over by the early eighteenth century, and Fox had directed that no more than £400 should be spent on his obsequies. He was buried on 7 November in the church he had himself built in the fields just beyond the last houses of the village of Farley,[2] which he loved so well but which he had visited all too rarely since those far-off days in 1651 when, prospects apparently shattered by the battle of Worcester, he and his brother John had contemplated trying to make a living as farmers. And there, in that quiet and seldom visited church, his memorial tablet, inscribed in a curiously archaic French, is still to be seen, recalling for the few who read it the story of the village boy who gained the reputation of being the richest commoner in three kingdoms and was seventeen times a Lord of the Treasury. A wonderful child of providence indeed!

---

[1] *Complete Peerage*, under 'Ilchester' and 'Holland'; Lord Ilchester, *Henry Fox*, esp. i. 18–21; Romney Sedgwick, *The House of Commons, 1715–1754*, ii. 48–50; L. S. Sutherland and J. D. Binney, 'Henry Fox as Paymaster of the Forces', *Eng. Hist. Rev.*, 1955.

[2] Eyre, *Sermon*.

APPENDIX I

Genealogical Tables

Fig. 1
Descendants of William Fox, father of Sir Stephen (simplified)

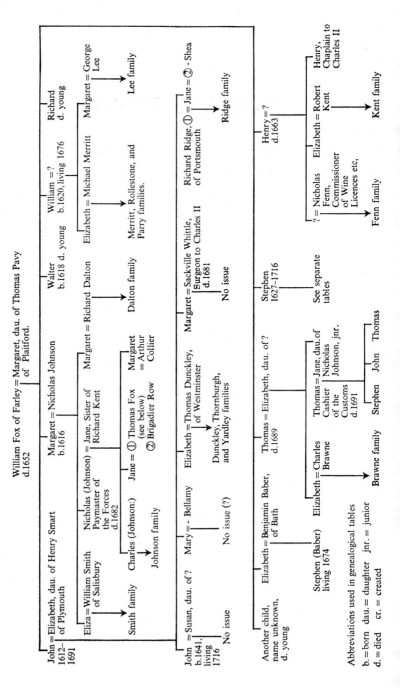

William Fox of Farley = Margaret, dau. of Thomas Pavy
d.1652   of Plaitford.

Abbreviations used in genealogical tables

b. = born   dau. = daughter   jnr. = junior
d. = died   cr. = created

Fig. 2
Descendants of Sir Stephen Fox by his first marriage

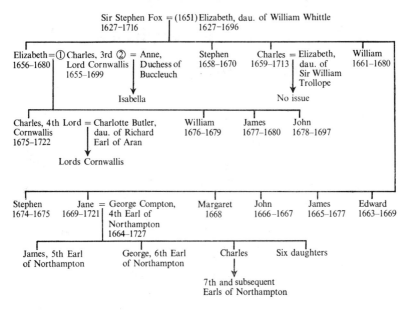

Sir Stephen Fox = (1651) Elizabeth, dau. of William Whittle
1627–1716   1627–1696

Elizabeth = ① Charles, 3rd ② = Anne,   Stephen   Charles = Elizabeth,   William
1656–1680   Lord Cornwallis | Duchess of   1658–1670   1659–1713 | dau. of   1661–1680
             1655–1699 | Buccleuch | Sir William
                                                                      | Trollope
                        Isabella   No issue

Charles, 4th Lord = Charlotte Butler,   William   James   John
Cornwallis | dau. of Richard   1676–1679   1677–1680 1678–1697
1675–1722 | Earl of Aran

          Lords Cornwallis

Stephen   Jane = George Compton,   Margaret   John   James   Edward
1674–1675   1669–1721 | 4th Earl of   1668   1666–1667   1665–1677   1663–1669
                        | Northampton
                        | 1664–1727

James, 5th Earl   George, 6th Earl   Charles   Six daughters
of Northampton   of Northampton

                                        7th and subsequent
                                        Earls of Northampton

Fig. 3
Descendants of Sir Stephen Fox by his second marriage

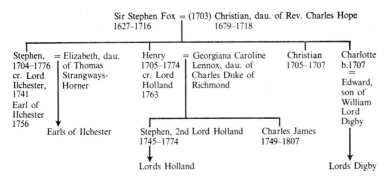

Sir Stephen Fox = (1703) Christian, dau. of Rev. Charles Hope
1627–1716   1679–1718

Stephen,   = Elizabeth, dau.   Henry   = Georgiana Caroline   Christian   Charlotte
1704–1776 | of Thomas   1705–1774 | Lennox, dau. of   1705–1707   b. 1707
cr. Lord | Strangways-   cr. Lord | Charles Duke of   =
Ilchester, | Horner   Holland | Richmond   Edward,
1741   1763   son of
Earl of   William
Ilchester   Lord
1756   Digby
          Earls of Ilchester   Stephen, 2nd Lord Holland   Charles James
                                 1745–1774   1749–1807

              Lords Holland   Lords Digby

Sir Stephen Fox's Purchases in the West Country, 1670–1716[1]

Date	Property	County	Price ($£. s. d.$)
31 May 1670	Farm at Charlton	Wilts.	1,102 13. 4.
29 Aug. 1671	Fee farm rent out of Water Eaton	Wilts.	207 15. 9.
24 Mar. 1672	Manor of Water Eaton	Wilts.	20,000 0. 0.
4 June 1672	Manor and capital messuage of Redlynch	Somerset	8,700 0. 0.
23 June 1673	Pigott's farm and other lands in S. Brewham and Redlynch	Somerset	2,065 0. 0.
27 Feb. 1675	Jones's Leaze in Water Eaton	Wilts.	1,700 0. 0.
27 Feb. 1675	Manor of Maddington	Wilts.	5,400 0. 0.
20 Mar. 1675	Two cottages in S. Brewham	Somerset	8 0. 0.
17 Apr. 1675	Willmott's Mead and other closes in S. Brewham	Somerset	450 0. 0.
4 May 1675	Close in S. Brewham	Somerset	91 0. 0.
14 May 1675	House and land in Redlynch	Somerset	40 0. 0.
18 Nov. 1675	Capital messuage and lands in Kilmington	Somerset	3,600 0. 0.
2 Mar. 1677	Manor of Norton Ferris and lands in Kilmington	Somerset	3,600 0. 0.
20 Apr. 1677	Advowson of Kilmington	Somerset	500 0. 0.
9 July 1677	Fee farm rent out of Kilmington	Somerset	285 0. 0.
21 July 1677	Manor of Erlestoke[2]	Wilts.	3,900 0. 0.

[1] The information in this table is principally derived from the following sources: Ilchester: Deeds, Wiltshire, *passim*; ibid.: Deeds, Somerset, *passim*; ibid.: Accounts, Estate General: ledger marked 'Sir S.F.'; ibid.: Official, Sir S. Fox, Army: ledger for 1672–9; ibid.: Family (box 235, bundle 4): lists of Sir S. Fox's purchases; B.L., Add. MS. 51332.

[2] See also Library of the Wilts. Arch. Soc., Devizes, Brouncker Family MSS., vol. for 1641–1780: copy of conveyance, 21 July 1677.

Date	Property	County	Price ($£. s. d.$)
14 Mar. 1678	Manor of Allington	Wilts.	2,940 0. 0.
18 Sept. 1678	Lease of the manor of Pitton and Farley; and freehold land there	Wilts.	5,200 0. 0.
18 Feb. 1679	Land in Kilmington	Somerset	80 0. 0.
19 Mar. 1679	Lands in W. Grimstead, Laverstock, and Winterborne Ford; with Milford Farm	Wilts.	5,502 0. 0.
7 June 1679	Manor of Plaitford	Wilts.	7,000 0. 0.
– Dec. 1681	Tenement in Farley	Wilts.	52 0. 0.
22 May 1682	Manor of W. Grimstead; and advowsons of Grimstead and Plaitford	Wilts.	450 0. 0.
8 July 1682	Manor of Little Somerford	Wilts.	7,000 0. 0.
4 Mar. 1684	Manors of Codford St. Peter, Sutton Magna, Warminster Scudamore, Upton Scudamore and Dilton	Wilts.	11,600 0. 0.
26 June 1684	Norridge Woods[1]	Wilts.	1,500 0. 0.
2 Feb. 1695	Four messuages in Farley	Wilts.	90 0. 0.
2 Oct. 1700	Lands in Whaddon	Wilts.	600 0. 0.
13 Nov. 1700	Messuages in Farley	Wilts.	550 0. 0.
26 Mar. 1703	Cottage and land in Pitton	Wilts.	21 10. 0.
13 July 1703	Tenement and land in Pitton	Wilts.	100 0. 0.
6 Oct. 1704	Land in Pitton	Wilts.	80 0. 0.
28 Feb. 1713	Messuage and land in S. Brewham	Somerset	900 0. 0.
30 Nov. 1714	Rectory and advowson of Shepton Montague	Somerset	1,050 0. 0.

[1] See also Ilchester: Estate, Middlesex (box 162): volume of Hungerford Market estate accounts, at end.

Bibliography

MANUSCRIPT SOURCES

British Library
Additional Manuscripts
i. Holland House Papers, Add. MSS. 51318–51336. These
   volumes comprise that part of the vast collection purchased
   from the trustees of the late Earl of Ilchester which relates to
   Sir Stephen Fox.
   Hyde Papers, Add. MSS. 15892–15898. These volumes include
   many of the official papers of Lord Treasurer Rochester:
   Add. MSS. 15896 and 15897 were the most useful.
   Leeds Papers, Add. MSS. 28040–28095. These volumes include
   many of the official papers of Lord Treasurer Danby: Add.
   MSS. 28078 and 28082 were particularly useful.
   Sir Robert Southwell's letter-book, Add. MS. 38146.
   The Sunderland–Evelyn correspondence, Add. MS. 15889.
ii. Also consulted, but of very limited value for the purposes of
    this study, were the Blathwayt Papers, Add. MS. 38694–
    38713; and the Ellis Papers, Add. MS. 28875–28894.
iii. Miscellaneous items
    Account of moneys received and disbursed during the Second
    Dutch War, Add. MS. 30999, ff. 1–3.
    Debts incurred by Charles II whilst in exile, Add. MS. 38854,
    ff. 31–6.
    Grant of Arms to Stephen Fox, Esq. (1658) (copy), Add. MS.
    15856, ff. 89ᵛ–90.
    List of office holders in the Royal Household and other depart-
    ments of state (1661), Add. MS. 36781.
    Satirical proclamation concerning Fox as Paymaster (1672),
    Add. MS. 28937, f. 161.
    Schemes of retrenchment of government expenditure, Add.
    MS. 40781, ff. 177–8, 181.
    'The Appellant's Case' in Ward v. Johnson, Add. MS. 36148,
    ff. 137–8.
    Warrants for army pay, Add. MSS. 5752, 5755.
Egerton Manuscripts
    Nicholas Papers, especially Egerton MSS. 2542 and 2543.

Harleian Manuscripts
  Establishment of the Guards and Garrisons for 1679–80, Harleian
    MS. 6425.
  Establishment of the Prince of Wales's Household for 1639–40,
    Harleian MS. 7623.
  Establishment of the Royal Household for 1689, Harleian MS.
    5010, ff. 20 et seq.
  Financial Memoranda of Lord Treasurer Southampton, and
    associated papers, Harleian MS. 1223.
  Papers relating to army agents, Harleian MS. 7018, ff. 107 et
    seq.
Stowe Manuscripts
  Grant of augmentation to the arms of Stephen Fox, Esq. (1658)
    (copy), and list of monthly payments to courtiers and attendants
    (1657), Stowe MS. 677, ff. 78, 80.
  Ordinances for the Conduct of the Royal Household (1660), Stowe
    MS. 562.
Castle Ashby, Northamptonshire
  Correspondence between Fox and the fourth Earl of Northampton,
    MS. 1093.
Dorset Record Office, Dorchester
  Ilchester Papers, MS. D.124. This huge collection, deposited piece-
    meal over a number of years by the late Earl of Ilchester and his
    trustees, is still largely unlisted. Only a relatively small proportion
    of it relates to Sir Stephen Fox, but the part that does represents
    the bulk of those of his personal, official, business, and estate
    papers which survive. The remainder are in the Holland House
    MS. in the British Library. The division between the two collec-
    tions is clearly arbitrary.
Farley Hospital, Farley, Wiltshire
  The 'Great Book' of Farley.
Gloucestershire Record Office, Gloucester
  Blathwayt Papers, D. 1799.
Kensington Central Library
  Local History Collection: extract from *Salisbury Journal* of *c.*
    1768.
Library of Christ Church, Oxford
  Evelyn Letter-book, Evelyn MS. 39b.
Library of the Wiltshire Archaeological Society, Devizes
  Hungerford, Brouncker, and Everett Papers.
National Register of Archives
  Calendar of the Dering–Southwell correspondence (N.R.A. 16180).

Public Record Office
  Declared Accounts. Audit Office
    Accounts of Paymasters General of the Forces, 1661–85: A.O.
      1/48/9 to A.O. 1/53/39.
    Accounts of Paymasters and Treasurers of the Forces, various:
      A.O. 1/308/1207; 309/1214, 1215.
    Accounts of the Royal Hospital, Chelsea, 1680–92: A.O. 1/1466/
      1–6.
  Declared Accounts. Pipe Office
    Accounts of Paymasters General of the Forces, 1661–85: E. 351/
      59–80.
    Accounts of Paymasters and Treasurers of the Forces, various: E.
      351/353, 364, 366.
    (These make good a few gaps in the Audit Office series of accounts.)
  Lord Steward's Department. Miscellaneous Books: L.S. 13/31–39.
  Patent Books. Auditors', 1660–83: E. 403/2462–2467, 2507–2511.
  Privy Seal Books. Auditors', 1662–84: E. 403/2571B–2576, 2593.
  Privy Seal Books. Pells, 1661–84: E. 403/2609–2614.
  State Papers. Domestic Series.
  War Office Papers. Establishments: W.O. 24/1–7.
  Wills proved in the Prerogative Court of Canterbury.
Somerset Record Office, Taunton
  Abstract will of Benjamin Baber, DD/X/SR, p. 55.
Williams and Glyns' Bank
  The Ledgers of Edward Backwell.
Wiltshire Record Office, Trowbridge
  Various collections, W.R.O. 84, 132, 212B, 445.

PRINTED SOURCES

ANON., Memoirs of the Life of Sir Stephen Fox Kt. (London, 1717).
BLENCOWE, R. W., Diary of the Times of Charles the Second by the
  Honourable Henry Sidney (2 vols., London, 1843).
BOND, M. F., The Diaries and Papers of Sir Edward Dering (London,
  1976).
Calendar of the Clarendon State Papers (5 Vols., Oxford, 1872–1970).
Calendar of State Papers. Domestic Series.
Calendar of Treasury Books.
CHAMBERLAYNE, E., Angliae Notitia (1682 edn.).
COBBETT, W., Parliamentary History of England (36 vols., London,
  1806–20), iv–vi.
COKE, SIR EDWARD, The Institutes of the Laws of England (London,
  1669 edn.).
A Complete Collection of State Trials (London, 1730 edn.).

DALRYMPLE, SIR JOHN, *Memoirs of Great Britain and Ireland* (3 vols., London, 1790 edn.).

DEFOE, D., *A Tour Through the Whole Island of Great Britain* (ed. G. D. H. Cole, 2 vols., London, 1928).

The Diary of John Evelyn (ed. E. S. De Beer, 6 vols., Oxford, 1955).

The Diary of John Hervey, First Earl of Bristol (Wells, 1894).

The Diary of Samuel Pepys (ed. R. Latham and W. Mathews, 10 vols., London, 1970 continuing).

ELLIS, HON. G. A., *The Ellis Correspondence* (2 vols., London, 1829).

EYRE, R., *A Sermon Preach'd at the Funeral of ... Sir Stephen Fox* (London, 1716).

FIRTH, C. H., 'The Memoirs of the First Lord Lonsdale', *English Historical Review*, 1915.

GREY, A., *Debates in the House of Commons 1667–1694* (10 vols., London, 1763).

HAMILTON, A., *Memoirs of the Count de Grammont* (London, 1906).

HENNING, D. B., *The Parliamentary Diary of Sir Edward Dering* (New Haven, 1940).

Historical Manuscripts Commission:
Buccleuch and Queensbury MSS.
Downshire MSS.
Finch MSS.
Hodgkin MSS.
Lindsey MSS.
Ormonde MSS., New Series
Portland MSS.
Reports, Seventh and Ninth, and Appendices.

HORWITZ, H., *The Parliamentary Diary of Narcissus Luttrell 1691–1693* (Oxford, 1972).

HUTT, G., *Papers Illustrative of the Origin and Early History of the Royal Hospital at Chelsea* (London, 1872).

JAMES, G. P. R., *Letters Illustrative of the Reign of William III* (3 vols., London, 1841).

JAPIKSE, N., *Correspondentie van Willem III*, Tweede Gedeelte (Rijks Geschiedkundige Publicatien. Kleine Serie, 24, 27. 's Gravenhage, 1928, 1935).

Journals of the House of Commons.

The Letter Books of John Hervey, First Earl of Bristol (3 vols., Wells, 1894).

The Life of Edward, Earl of Clarendon (2 vols., Oxford, 1857).

LUTTRELL, N., *A Brief Historical Relation of State Affairs* (6 vols., London, 1857).

MACRAY, W. D., *The History of the Rebellion ... by Edward Earl of Clarendon* (6 vols., Oxford, 1888).

Memoirs of the Earl of Ailesbury (2 vols., Roxburghe Club, 1890).
ROBERTS, C., *The Diary of John Milward, Esq.* (Cambridge, 1938).
SINGER, S. W., *The Correspondence of the Earls of Clarendon and Rochester* (2 vols., London, 1828).
SNYDER, H. L., *The Marlborough–Godolphin Correspondence* (3 vols., Oxford, 1975).
THOMPSON, E. M., *Correspondence of the Family of Hatton* (2 vols., Camden Society, 1878).
WARNER, G. F., *The Nicholas Papers* (2 vols., Camden Society, 1886–1892).

SECONDARY AUTHORITIES

ASHTON, R., 'The Disbursing Official under the Early Stuarts', *Bulletin of the Institute of Historical Research*, 1957.
—— *The Crown and the Money Market 1603–1640* (Oxford, 1960).
AYLMER, G. E., *The King's Servants* (London, 1961).
BAXTER, S. B., *The Development of the Treasury 1660–1702* (London, 1957).
BOUCHER, R., 'Kent of Boscombe', *Wiltshire Notes and Queries*, 1912.
BROWNING, A., 'The Stop of the Exchequer', *History*, 1930.
—— *Thomas Osborne, Earl of Danby* (3 vols., Glasgow, 1951).
BURTON, I. F. et al., *Political Parties in the Reigns of William III and Anne* (Special Supplement to the *Bulletin of the Institute of Historical Research*, 1968).
CARTE, T., *The Life of James, Duke of Ormond* (6 vols., Oxford, 1851).
CHANDAMAN, C. D., *The English Public Revenue 1660–1688* (Oxford, 1975).
CLAPHAM, SIR JOHN, *The Bank of England* (2 vols., Cambridge, 1944).
CLARK, D. K., 'Edward Backwell as Royal Agent', *Economic History Review*, 1938.
—— 'A Restoration Goldsmith-Banking House: The Vine on Lombard Street', in *Essays in Modern English History in Honour of W. C. Abbott* (Harvard, 1941).
CLAY, C., 'The Price of Freehold Land in the Later Seventeenth and Eighteenth Centuries', *Economic History Review*, 1974.
CLAY, C. G. A., 'Two Families and their Estates', Cambridge University Ph.D. thesis, 1966.
CLODE, C. M., *The Military Forces of the Crown* (2 vols., London, 1869).
COLEMAN, D. C., 'London Scriveners and the Estate Market in the Later Seventeenth Century', *Economic History Review*, 1951.
—— *Sir John Banks* (Oxford, 1963).
COLLINS, A., *The Peerage of England* (6 vols., London, 1741–50, 2nd edn. and supplement).

DAVIS, O. R. F., 'The Wealth and Influence of John Holles, Duke of Newcastle', *Rennaissance and Modern Studies*, 1965.

DEAN, C. G. T., *The Royal Hospital Chelsea* (London, 1950).

DE BEER, E. S., 'Chelsea Hospital, Charles II, Nell Gwyn, and Sir Stephen Fox', *Notes and Queries*, 1938.

DICKSON, P. G. M., *The Financial Revolution in England* (London, 1967).

Dictionary of National Biography.

DUCKETT, SIR GEORGE, 'Proposed Repeal of the Test and Penal Statutes ... in 1688', *Wiltshire Archaeological and Natural History Magazine*, 1879.

FAULKNER, T., *An Historical and Topographical Description of Chelsea* (2 vols., Chelsea, 1829).

—— *The History and Antiquities of Brentford, Ealing and Chiswick* (London, 1845).

FEILING, K. G., *A History of the Tory Party* (Oxford, 1924).

FORTESCUE, J. W., *A History of the British Army* (13 vols., London, 1910–30).

FOSTER, J., *Alumni Oxonienses* (Early Series, 4 vols., Oxford, 1891–1892).

FOXCROFT, H. C., *Supplement to Burnet's 'History of My Own Time'* (Oxford, 1902).

FRASER, W., *The Scotts of Buccleuch* (2 vols., Edinburgh, 1878).

GARDINER, S. R., *History of the Great Civil War, 1642–1649* (4 vols., London, 1893).

G. E. C. (ed.), *The Complete Peerage* (13 vols., London, 1910–40, revised edn.).

GILL, D. M., 'The Relationship between the Treasury and the Excise and Customs Commissioners (1660–1714)', *Cambridge Historical Journal*, 1932.

GRASSBY, R., 'The Personal Wealth of the Business Community in Seventeenth Century England', *Economic History Review*, 1970.

HABAKKUK, H. J., 'The Landowners in the Civil War', *Economic History Review*, 1965.

HOARE, SIR RICHARD COLT, *The History of Modern Wiltshire* (14 parts, London, 1822–44).

HOLMES, G. S., *British Politics in the Reign of Anne* (London, 1967).

HORWITZ, H., *Revolution Politicks. The Career of Daniel Finch, Second Earl of Nottingham* (Cambridge, 1968).

—— *Parliament, Policy and Politics in the Reign of William III* (Manchester, 1977).

HUGHES, E., *Studies in Administration and Finance 1558–1825* (Manchester, 1934).

ILCHESTER, LORD, *Henry Fox, First Lord Holland* (2 vols., London, 1920).

JONES, W. H., *Fasti Ecclesiae Sarisberiensis* (Salisbury, 1879).

JUDGES, A. V., 'Philip Burlamachi: a Financier of the Thirty Years War', *Economica*, 1926.

KENYON, J. P., *Robert Spencer, Earl of Sunderland* (London, 1958).

LYSONS, D., *The Environs of London* (4 vols., London, 1792–6).

MACAULAY, LORD, *The History of England* (8 vols., London, 1858–62 edn.).

MACKINNON, D., *The Origin and Services of the Coldstream Guards* (2 vols., London, 1833).

MARTIN, J. B., *The 'Grasshopper' in Lombard Street* (London, 1892).

NICHOLAS, D., *Mr. Secretary Nicholas* (London, 1955).

NICHOLS, G. O., 'English Government Borrowing, 1660–1688', *Journal of British Studies*, 1971.

NORTHAMPTON, MARQUESS OF, *History of the Comptons* (London, 1930).

OGG, D., *England in the Reigns of James II and William III* (Oxford, 1955).

—— *England in the Reign of Charles II* (2 vols., Oxford, 1956 edn.).

PEVSNER, N., *The Buildings of England: Wiltshire* (London, Harmondsworth, 1963).

PHILLIMORE, W. P. W., and WHITEAR, W. H., *Historical Collections Relating to Chiswick* (London, 1897).

Return of the Names of Every Member Returned to Serve in Each Parliament . . . (2 parts, House of Commons Papers, No. 69, 1878).

RICHARDS, R. D., *The Early History of Banking in England* (London, 1929).

—— 'Mr. Pepys and the Goldsmith Bankers', Economic History Supplement to the *Economic Journal*, 1933.

ROBERTSON, D. H., *Sarum Close* (London, 1938).

ROSEVEARE, H. G., 'The Advancement of the King's Credit, 1660–1673', Cambridge University Ph.D. thesis, 1962.

—— *The Treasury* (London, 1969).

SCOTT, E., *The King in Exile* (London, 1905).

—— *The Travels of the King* (London, 1907).

SCOTT, W. R., *The Constitution and Finance of the English* . . . *Joint Stock Companies to 1720* (3 vols., Cambridge, 1912).

SCOULLER, R. E., *The Armies of Queen Anne* (Oxford, 1966).

SEDGWICK, R., *The House of Commons 1715–1754* (2 vols., London, 1970).

SIMPSON, A., *The Wealth of the Gentry* (Cambridge, 1961).

SPECK, W., *Tory and Whig* (London, 1970).

STONE, L., *The Crisis of the Aristocracy* (Oxford, 1965).

STRYPE, J., *Stow's Survey of London and Westminster* (2 vols., London, 1720).

Survey of London (30 vols., London, 1900 continuing), xi (the parish of Chelsea, part iv) and xvi (Charing Cross).

SUTHERLAND, L. S., and BINNEY, J., 'Henry Fox as Paymaster of the Forces', *English Historical Review*, 1955.

THIRSK, J. (ed.), *The Agrarian History of England and Wales, 1500–1640* (Cambridge, 1967).

Victoria History of the Counties of England—Wiltshire (London, 1957 continuing).

WALCOTT, R., *English Politics in the Early Eighteenth Century* (Oxford, 1956).

WALKER, J., 'The Secret Service under Charles II and James II', *Transactions of the Royal Historical Society*, 1932.

WALTON, C., *History of the British Standing Army 1660–1700* (London, 1894).

WILSON, C., *England's Apprenticeship 1603–1763* (London, 1965).

WOODHEAD, J. R., *The Rulers of London* (London, 1965).

Index